THE PASSION TRANSLATION

THE BOOKS OF

THE MINOR PROPHETS

The Twelve

BroadStreet
PUBLISHING

The Passion Translation®
The Minor Prophets: The Twelve

Published by BroadStreet Publishing® Group, LLC
BroadStreetPublishing.com
ThePassionTranslation.com

The publisher and TPT team have worked diligently and prayerfully to present this version of The Passion Translation Bible with excellence and accuracy. If you find a mistake in the Bible text or footnotes, please contact the publisher at tpt@broadstreetpublishing.com.

9781424569915 (paperback)
9781424569922 (ebook)

Printed in China

24 25 26 27 28 5 4 3 2 1

CONTENTS

A NOTE TO READERS

It would be impossible to calculate how many lives have been changed forever by the power of the Bible, the living Word of God! My own life was transformed because I believed the message contained in Scripture about Jesus, the Savior.

To hold the Bible dear to your heart is the sacred obsession of every true follower of Jesus. Yet to go even further and truly understand the Bible is how we gain light and truth to live by. Did you catch the word *understand*? People everywhere say the same thing: "I want to understand God's Word, not just read it."

Thankfully, as English speakers, we have a plethora of Bible translations, commentaries, study guides, devotionals, churches, and Bible teachers to assist us. Our hearts crave to know God—not just to know about him, but to know him as intimately as we possibly can in this life. This is what makes Bible translations so valuable, because each one will hopefully lead us into new discoveries of God's character. I believe God is committed to giving us truth in a package we can understand and apply, so I thank God for every translation of God's Word that we have.

God's Word does not change, but over time languages definitely do, thus the need for updated and revised translations of the Bible. Translations give us the words God spoke through his servants, but words can be poor containers for revelation because they leak! Meaning is influenced by culture, background, and many other details. Just imagine how differently the Hebrew authors of the Old Testament saw the world three thousand years ago from the way we see it today!

Even within one language and culture, meanings of words change from one generation to the next. For example, many contemporary Bible readers would be quite surprised to find that unicorns are mentioned nine times in the King James Version (KJV). Here's one instance in Isaiah 34:7: "And the unicorns shall come down with them, and the bullocks with the bulls; and their land shall be soaked with blood, and their dust made fat with fatness." This isn't a result of poor translation, but rather an example of how our culture, language, and understanding of the world has shifted over the past few centuries. So, it is important that we have a modern English text of the Bible that releases revelation and truth into our hearts. The Passion Translation (TPT) is committed to bringing forth the potency of God's Word in relevant, contemporary vocabulary that doesn't distract from its meaning or distort it in any way. So many people have told us that they are falling in love with the Bible again as they read TPT.

We often hear the statement "I just want a word-for-word translation that doesn't mess it up or insert a bias." That's a noble desire. But a word-for-word translation would be nearly unreadable. It is simply impossible to translate one Hebrew word into one English word. Hebrew is built from triliteral consonant roots. Biblical Hebrew had no vowels or punctuation. And Koine Greek, although wonderfully articulate, cannot always be conveyed in English by a word-for-word translation. For example, a literal word-for-word translation of the Greek in Matthew 1:18 would be something like this: "Of the but Jesus Christ the birth thus was. Being betrothed the mother of him, Mary, to Joseph, before or to come together them she was found in belly having from Spirit Holy."

Even the KJV, which many believe to be a very literal translation, renders this verse: "Now the birth of Jesus Christ was on this wise: When as his mother Mary was espoused to Joseph, before they came together, she was found with child of the Holy Ghost."

This comparison makes the KJV look like a paraphrase next to a strictly literal translation! To some degree, every Bible translator is forced to move words around in a sentence to convey with meaning the thought of the verse. There is no such thing as a truly literal translation of the Bible, for there is not an equivalent language that perfectly conveys the meaning of the biblical text. Is it really possible to have a highly accurate and highly readable English Bible? We certainly hope so! It is so important that God's Word is living in our hearts, ringing in our ears, and burning in our souls. Transferring God's revelation from Hebrew and Greek into English is an art, not merely a linguistic science. Thus, we need all the accurate translations we can find. If a verse or passage in one translation seems confusing, it is good to do a side-by-side comparison with another version.

It is difficult to say which translation is the "best." "Best" is often in the eyes of the reader and is determined by how important differing factors are to different people. However, the "best" translation, in my thinking, is the one that makes the Word of God clear and accurate, no matter how many words it takes to express it.

That's the aim of The Passion Translation: to bring God's eternal truth into a highly readable heart-level expression that causes truth and love to jump out of the text and lodge inside our hearts. A desire to remain accurate to the text and a desire to communicate God's heart of passion for his people are the two driving forces behind TPT. So for those new to Bible reading, we hope TPT will excite and illuminate. For scholars and Bible students, we hope TPT will bring the joys of new discoveries from the text and prompt deeper consideration of what God has spoken to his people. We all have so much more to learn and discover about God in his Holy Word!

You will notice at times we've italicized certain words or phrases. These portions are not in the original Hebrew, Greek, or Aramaic manuscripts but are implied from the context. We've made these implications explicit for the sake of narrative clarity and to better convey the meaning of God's Word. This is a common practice by mainstream translations.

We've also chosen to translate certain names in their original Hebrew or Greek forms to better convey their cultural meaning and significance. For instance, some translations of the Bible have substituted James for Jacob and Jude for Judah. Both Greek and Aramaic manuscripts leave these Hebrew names in their original forms. Therefore, this translation uses those cultural names.

The purpose of The Passion Translation is to reintroduce the passion and fire of the Bible to the English reader. It doesn't merely convey the literal meaning of words. It expresses God's passion for people and his world by translating the original life-changing message of God's Word for modern readers.

We pray this version of God's Word will kindle in you a burning desire to know the heart of God, while impacting the church for years to come.

Please visit **ThePassionTranslation.com** for more information.

Brian Simmons and the translation team

THE BOOKS OF

THE MINOR PROPHETS

The Twelve

BroadStreet
PUBLISHING

EXCURSUS ON THE MINOR PROPHETS

HISTORICAL DATING, CONTEXT, AND ORIGIN

The prophetic books that follow were originally contained in one book, which the Jewish people call "the Twelve." According to the Talmud, the "men of the great assembly," who lived during the Persian period, compiled the scroll of the Twelve.[a] In antiquity, scroll capacity was limited by practicality and size. Thus, each of the three Major Prophets (Isaiah, Jeremiah, and Ezekiel) fills up one unique scroll. The other twelve prophets were combined into one scroll. A more contemporary analogy is the music CD, which was designed to hold the totality of Beethoven's Ninth Symphony but can also be filled with many shorter musical numbers.

Broadly, the books cover the following themes:

- Three books of the Twelve cluster around the fall of the Northern Kingdom of Israel (722 BC): Hosea, Amos, Micah (as does the book of Isaiah).
- One book focuses on the fall of the Southern Kingdom of Judah (586 BC[b]): Zephaniah (as do the books of Jeremiah, Lamentations, and Ezekiel).

---

a Lawrence H. Schiffman, *Texts and Traditions: A Source Reader for the Study of Second Temple and Rabbinic Judaism* (Hoboken, NJ: KTAV Publishing House, 1998), 118–19.

b Note that there is much debate surrounding many of the dates mentioned here and throughout the books of the Minor Prophets.

- Two books focus on the rebuilding of the temple: the prophecies of Haggai and Zechariah (520 BC).
- Six books have a less precise historical focus, and their dates are disputed in some cases: Joel (800s or 500s BC, among many other possibilities); Obadiah (800s or early 500s BC); Jonah (events occurred in the mid-700s but writing date is unknown; perhaps post-612 BC or later); Nahum (sometime in the second half of the 600s BC); Habakkuk (sometime between 612 and 586 BC); Malachi (sometime between 515 and 430 BC).

The prophets themselves demonstrated their genuine humanity in their respective books. And although we do not know everything about them—or, indeed, anything, in some cases—we know enough to be able to understand the main thrust of their messages. Precise dating and comprehensive biographical details may be helpful and interesting, but these are not essential for appreciating the primary emphases of their prophetic oracles and visions.

A great deal of emphasis was placed on the geographical centrality of Israel and Judah. None of the Twelve was born in captivity except, perhaps, Zechariah, who was most likely born in Babylon and then returned to Judah from captivity with the exiles around 538 BC.

In the Persian period (about 539 to 332 BC), Jerusalem had a population of fifteen hundred to four thousand, down from the prosperity of the late monarchy with twenty-five thousand inhabitants, complete with a king, his royal complex, and Solomon's Temple.

After the great catastrophe of 586 BC, when the Babylonians laid waste to Jerusalem and the people were exiled, Judah had become a backwater client kingdom of a superpower. The people asked the question, *What do we do about our powerlessness?* The Twelve used memories of the past and visions of the future to put things into perspective and give people hope. Their message: "This is not the end of the road for Israel but rather a step in the journey toward a brighter future that will also bless the nations." Such a message revealed their recognition of the central importance of the divine covenant in the history of the nations of Israel and Judah.

THE CENTRALITY OF THE DIVINE COVENANT

As we read through the prophecies in the Twelve, there is no doubt that the covenant undergirded their entire worldview. This covenant was one that encapsulated both the blessings and curses of that intimate divine-human relationship between God and his people, and that divine grace and compassion were extended to the nations as well. This was the case even though in Obadiah and Nahum, the primary focus is on God's judgment against wicked nations, and in Jonah, the focus is God's compassion for a penitent gentile city. Nonetheless, in these three books, the covenant foundation is still there, even though it's implicit rather than explicit. The following list notes covenant emphases in the Twelve:

Hosea. Israel was indicted for her "spiritual adultery" against YAHWEH—that is, her idolatrous worship of pagan deities—and subsequently condemned to exile at the hands of the Assyrians: the curse of the covenant. But God then promised to restore his people to their homeland and renew them spiritually and materially: the blessing of the covenant.

Joel. Israel was condemned for her self-indulgent lifestyle and suffered a catastrophic locust plague: the curse of the covenant, expressed here as a manifestation of the day of YAHWEH. And again, God promised to heal the land and cleanse his people from their sin: the blessing of the covenant.

Amos. For her economic corruption and social injustices, Israel was condemned to exile at the hands of the Assyrians: the curse of the covenant. And then the Lord promised her restoration and spiritual renewal after her punishment: the blessing of the covenant.

Obadiah. The focus here is slightly different in that God cursed Edom for her brutal treatment of his people: an example of God applying the covenant curse to an enemy of his people. The curse declared that Edom would be destroyed but the kingdom of Israel would be blessed and prosper by the implicit covenant faithfulness of YAHWEH.

Jonah. Unlike the other books among the Twelve, Jonah's work is "a narrative account of a single prophetic mission"[a] and does not contain an oracle as such. However, it certainly demonstrates the compassionate love of God toward those who confess their sin and put their trust in him. This includes not only the people of YAHWEH but also repentant gentiles, like this penitent generation of Ninevites. And, again, the *NIV Study Bible* notes, "This book depicts the larger scope of God's purpose for Israel: that she might rediscover the truth of his concern for the whole creation and that she might better understand her own role in carrying out that concern."[b] Readers can also note that such a concern has a distinctive covenantal foundation.

Micah. This book contains a series of alternating oracles of covenant curses and blessings. The prophet indicted Israel for her constant violations of the divine covenant statutes: injustice, corruption, cruelty, godless leadership, and the like. However, such judgment

---

a "Introduction to Jonah," *NIV Study Bible*, New International Version (Grand Rapids, MI: Zondervan, 1985), 1364.

b "Introduction to Jonah."

was accompanied by promises of forgiveness and renewal, including freedom from the oppression of her enemies.

Nahum. Similar to Obadiah, the book of Nahum focuses on the impending destruction of a wicked gentile nation, in this case, Assyria, via its capital city, Nineveh. It is again an example of the application of the covenant curse to a pagan nation. However, the blessings of the covenant were not forgotten here either, as God promised that the land of his people would never again be invaded by its enemies, for its enemies would be completely destroyed.

Habakkuk. This book is also unusual in the prophetic writings. It is an extended dialogue between the prophet Habakkuk and YAHWEH, starting with the prophet feeling overwhelmed by the *impression* that God did not care about the rampant wickedness of the people of Judah. However, this conversation ultimately provoked a prayer of confession and praise from the prophet in which he recognized YAHWEH's faithfulness in delivering his people down through the ages and concluded with a determination to wait patiently for God's redemptive purposes to be fulfilled. Again, the underlying framework for this interaction is clearly a covenantal one.

Zephaniah. The main theme of Zephaniah is the approaching day of YAHWEH, signaling an outpouring of divine judgment (i.e., covenant curse) on both the pagan nations and Judah for their respective godlessness. And again, there is the concluding promise of YAHWEH to bless his people and restore the fortunes of the Judean nation.

Haggai. In this postexilic prophetic book, Haggai proclaimed to his people that they were under the judgment of God because they had neglected the rebuilding of the temple in Jerusalem—a judgment with clear covenant undertones. As a result of the movement of the Spirit of God, the people responded in obedience, and God's blessing was again poured out upon them when they resumed the rebuilding of the temple. That blessing was expressed both as a contemporary material prosperity and as a promise that anticipated a blessed Messianic future, when YAHWEH declared that "the glory of this new temple will surpass the glory of the original" (Hag. 2:9).

Zechariah. This book contains a profound blend of prophetic visions along with judgment and salvation oracles, all undergirded by the foundation of covenant blessing and curse. In the end, the encouragement to the people of YAHWEH is the dominant theme, expressed via these oracles declaring the future arrival of the long-awaited Messiah and his kingdom.

Malachi. After the people of Judah had returned to their homeland, the quality of their worship of YAHWEH deteriorated to the point of rank corruption. The people further displayed their contempt for the covenant by widespread divorce in violation of their marriage vows, made worse by the practice of intermarriage with pagan women. All these abhorrent practices were understood as covenant violations deserving of divine punishment. However, YAHWEH promised to send "the prophet Elijah" (Mal. 4:5) as a messenger to prepare his people for the coming day of YAHWEH and to bring them to repentance—a promised blessing of the covenant.

To summarize, the causes of the slow spiritual decline of Israel, according to the prophets, may be expressed as twin failures of covenant obligation: corruption and disintegration.

- **Corruption.** Historian Lord Acton once said: "Power tends to corrupt, and absolute power corrupts absolutely."[a] There is a constant call to more uprightness and justice throughout the Minor Prophets (and especially in the book of Amos). All the canonical prophets, both major and minor, commonly called out covenant violations involving injustices such as economic malpractice, corrupt business ethics, and oppression of the poor and vulnerable in Israelite society.
- **Disintegration.** This is the opposite of integrity. Israel had lost track of its primary focus: the covenant in the Torah. This was the organizing principle of society. When the people went after other gods, their loyalties became divergent, and society disintegrated. The primary cause of this disintegration, and, arguably, the Israelites' most heinous sin according to the prophets, was indeed the worship of pagan deities. Idols totally distracted the people of God from their covenant fidelity and rotted their culture from within. This is as true for us today as it was for Israel in the times of the Twelve. Our obligation to love the Lord our God with all our hearts and minds has not disappeared, but our obligation has been refocused to serve and obey our risen Savior and Redeemer, the Lord Jesus Christ.

If we carry over the metaphor used in the preceding paragraph, we can see that the prophets point out "internal dry rot," not external forces, as the primary cause of Israel's downfall. There is a robust capacity for

---

a Cited in his letter to Archbishop Mandell Creighton, April 5, 1887. Retrieved on August 23, 2023, from history.hanover.edu.

self-critique in the prophetic culture of ancient Israel, which brings conviction and the realization of guilt but also the opportunity for repentance and restoration. The message of the prophets: "The Assyrians, Babylonians, and Persians did not do this to us, and outside alliances would not have saved us from them. We rotted, over time, from the inside, and this made us vulnerable. The essence of our problem has centered on the abandonment of our covenant with YAHWEH."

NONLINEAR LANGUAGE

Before proceeding any further, it will be helpful to offer some comments on a distinctive linguistic feature of biblical Hebrew, along with its concept of time and history, and how that linguistic approach informed the understanding of the covenant for the minor prophets and their original audiences.

A characteristic of the Hebrew language of the Old Testament is that it does not employ past, present, and future tenses in the same linear sense as English does. Semitic languages are not time oriented, but rather space oriented. A small rowboat can illustrate this spatial orientation well. The Hebrews saw the "future" as behind us as we row the boat of our lives "forward" with our backs to this future (which we cannot see or visualize). We row, facing the stern, by faith and not by sight. The "present" is right in front of our face: that with which we are dealing right now. The "past" is farther away from us but in front of us and receding into the distant past. The farther we row, the harder it is to see the past, and eventually it falls off the horizon and is forgotten. Thus, the prophets bring us out of our "nearsightedness" (just us and the boat) and vastly expand our worldview to explain how we got here and that which awaits us, "behind" us, as we row our boat into a promised future.

Another result of such a nonlinear approach is that a Hebrew understanding does not see cause and effect throughout history in the straightforward domino-effect understanding that English nudges its speakers toward. This has a bearing on the way ancient Hebrew prophets thought about the divine covenant: they were *not* locked into a rigid linear view of the past with consequences for the future that could never change or be changed. For example, in a linear view of history, whenever the Israelites disobeyed the statutes of the covenant, the consequences of that disobedience (i.e., God's judgment) would be irrevocable and unchangeable. But this is not the view of the biblical prophets and writers. For them, the covenant, though originating in the past, was a dynamic nonlinear phenomenon that was and always would be ever-present and continually demanding of the people of God—past, present, and future. In other words, for the Twelve, the Israelite nation's choices in relation to the covenant—choices made in the past and the present—have consequences for both the present and the future. Everything—whether blessing or judgment—depended on how they responded to the demands of the covenant at any given point in time.

The eminent Old Testament scholar Brevard Childs makes the following claim in relation to the progressively unfolding revelation of the divine plan of redemption in Scripture: "The Old Testament makes no sharp theological distinction between God's intervention in human affairs within history or at the end of history. The issue at stake is the qualitatively new elements of the divine will at work."[a] What he is referring to here is the manner in which God reveals and applies the divine covenant to his

---

a Brevard S. Childs, *Old Testament Theology in a Canonical Context* (London: SCM Press, 1985), 237.

people at every stage of their history, past, present, and future. From Childs' comments here, we may argue that there is a timeless quality to the prophetic portrayal of the promises of God to his people throughout their history. This is *not* to deny the reality or importance of a historical past for the Israelite nation. But rather, it beautifully emphasizes that the covenant promises of redemption throughout Scripture have relevance for both the contemporary audience of the prophet as well as future generations of readers and believers.

Let us take, for example, all the references in the Twelve—as well as those in the Major Prophets—to the prophetic anticipation of Israel's coming King, who will defeat all of Israel's enemies and establish the universal kingdom of God that will endure forever. God revealed to his people progressively over many centuries the various elements that make up the prophetic picture of this victorious divine royal figure. All these elements then coalesced into a profound prophetic portrait of the Messianic King and came to fulfillment in the person of Jesus Christ, as revealed in the New Testament. But the process of this prophetic phenomenon is not a static one rooted in a single instance in the past, which is then projected forward to a single instance in the present and then to a single instance in the future with nothing in between.

Rather, the truth is that such a phenomenon is an ongoing dynamic process of covenant fulfillment that has its origin in early Israelite history and then moves on through the various stages of prophetic revelation, increasing in detail and complexity. It then finds its ultimate fulfillment in the emergence of Christ the King in the pages of the New Testament. Parallel to these promises and blessings are the progressive revelations of the covenant curse, again, recorded throughout the history of Israel in Holy Scripture and coming to a catastrophic conclusion in the final, eternal destruction of the enemies of God at the end of time.

When the reader bears the preceding comments in mind, the treatment of the divine covenant across the Twelve provides the following key takeaways:

- Yahweh alone rules the heavenly realm and all the kingdoms and empires of earth throughout the past, present, and future generations of the people of God. He sees all of time from his vantage point.
- These prophets opened a window in heaven, speaking forth Yahweh's message and perspective. They showed how he is constant in his covenant love and justice from beginning to end (Mal. 3:6; see also Heb. 13:8) and yet has unique ways of dealing with his wayward children, depending on what is going on. Yahweh is not just the composer of the world but also the living conductor, dynamically engaged with us.
- These prophets thus spatially expanded the perspective of the original audience, who was hearing these messages during a low point in Israel's history. The prophets gave the people an explanation for their predicament, putting their pain and disappointments and concerns into place within a larger plan—Yahweh's plan. Knowing our place in God's story, and that the story is not yet finished, has been a rock of hope for people in all places and all times. At the same time, the prophets showed the original audience—and us—a best-case scenario for the future, a vision worth striving for. They show us how to act in accordance with Yahweh's vision and requirements for us.
- These prophets also vastly expand the worldview of their hearers or readers to better anticipate what awaits them in the future. The Lord's words from the heavenly realm redirect his people's eyes from what

they can see to an eternal yet well-grounded hope that comes directly from him. From our vantage point in the New Testament era, we can see that many of the promises of the Minor Prophets (and the Old Testament as a whole) have been partially fulfilled with the birth, death, and resurrection of Jesus Christ. But we still, along with the original audiences of the prophets, await the final climactic fulfillment of God's promised plan of redemption: the return of Christ the King and the ushering in of his eternal kingdom, the new heavens and the new earth. We eagerly long for the perfect justice and perfect peace of his reign and the perfect relationship we will have with him and each other.

- This is what makes reading these books as valuable for us as it was for those during the nadir of Israel's history, the Persian period. We all need our perspective expanded. These prophets expand our perspective of Yahweh's sovereignty, his faithfulness, and his engagement with us and the world. They put our current situations, including whatever pain or complexity they encompass, into the perspective of the larger plan of God's redemption, refocusing us on our ultimate hope in Christ and his past, future, and currently unfolding ultimate victory. These books were collected to affect, not just inform, the readers.

THE DAY OF YAHWEH: A DIVINE MERGING OF JUDGMENT AND BLESSING

The "day of Yahweh" (or "day of the Lord" in many translations) motif is, in fact, a subtheme of the covenant phenomenon, and anywhere it is mentioned in the Twelve there is an indisputable association with the covenant. This motif is characterized by the twin phenomena of blessing and judgment. While it is explicitly present in all the Minor Prophets—except for Jonah, Nahum, and Habakkuk, where its presence is implied—it occurs as a dominant theme in the books of Joel, Obadiah, Zephaniah, Zechariah, and Malachi. In every instance, the complexity of the day of YAHWEH is evident, for the manifestations of divine blessings and judgments are applied to both the people of God and the nations. It is a day to be feared since God will pour out eternal judgments on those who scorned and rejected YAHWEH and his covenant. It is also a day we should eagerly long for since we will fully realize all the promises of redemption and restoration from the totality of Scripture: YAHWEH will pour out blessing on his people who heeded his covenant and establish his reign of perfect justice once and for all on the new heavens and the new earth.[a]

> May the bones of the Twelve Prophets send forth new life from where they lie, for they comforted the people of Jacob and delivered them with confident hope.
>
> —Sirach 49:10 (NRSVCE,[b] from the Apocrypha)

---

a Some of the points for this Excursus were gathered from the *Jewish Study Bible*, 2nd Ed., (New York: Oxford University Press, 2014), 1125–30, which is a great source for further study on this topic.

b This verse marked NRSVCE is taken from New Revised Standard Version Bible: Catholic Edition. Copyright 1989, 1993, Division of Christian Education of the National Council of the Churches of Christ in the United States of America. Used by permission. All rights reserved.

THE BOOK OF

HOSEA

Amazing Love

BroadStreet
PUBLISHING

HOSEA

Introduction

AT A GLANCE

Author: Hosea the prophet

Audience: Originally, the Northern Kingdom of Israel; later the Southern Kingdom; today, people of God everywhere

Date: The era preceding the fall of Samaria (capital of the Northern Kingdom) in 722 BC

Type of Literature: Prophecy

Major Themes: The covenant: violation and renewal; love; corruption; disintegration through spiritual adultery; hope; Jesus as the faithful husband

Outline:

- I. Superscription: author and setting — 1:1
- II. Hosea's marriage and its symbolism: unfaithful wife, faithful husband — 1:2–3:5
  - a. Hosea's marriage; birth of children (unknown fathers); readoption into the family of God — 1:2–2:1
  - b. Allegory of Gomer, the unfaithful wife — 2:2–23
    - i. Inevitable divine judgment on Israel — 2:2–13
    - ii. Promised divine renewal and restoration of Israel — 2:14–23
  - c. Hosea's reconciliation with his wife — 3:1–5
- III. Faithless nation and faithful God — 4:1–14:9
  - a. Summary of charges (the *rib*): YAHWEH's legal indictment of Israel's covenant violations — 4:1–3
  - b. Charges laid and sentencing brought down — 4:4–10:15

- i. Punishment of priests and people for their idolatry — 4:4–19
- ii. Punishment of priests, Israelites, and royal leaders for their violence, injustice, and corruption — 5:1–15
- iii. A counterfeit repentance — 6:1–3
- iv. Indictments of Israel for their covenant-breaking — 6:4–7:16
- v. Punishment of Israel for their covenant-breaking — 8:1–10:15

c. YAHWEH's faithful love — 11:1–14:9

- i. YAHWEH's fatherly love — 11:1–11
- ii. Punishment for the people's covenantal unfaithfulness — 11:12–13:16
- iii. Israel's promised restoration and renewal following their genuine repentance — 14:1–9

ABOUT THE BOOK OF HOSEA

For more information on the twelve books of the Minor Prophets in general, please see the excursus on the Twelve preceding this book.

Hosea is a very personal account of the life and ministry of the titular prophet. God told Hosea to marry a woman who would be unfaithful to him. They had three children (and Hosea may not have been their father) who were named by God and represented prophetic messages not only for Hosea but also for Israel and for us today.

Hosea's ministry was contemporary with the reigns of the following kings (note that some of these reigns overlapped, incorporating coregencies): in Israel, Jeroboam II, 793–753 BC; in Judah, Uzziah (Azariah), 792–740 BC; Jotham, 742–735 BC; Ahaz, 735–715 BC; Hezekiah, 715–687 BC.

One of the older books in the Bible, Hosea perhaps reached its final form even before many of the scrolls of the Hebrew Bible were compiled and put in order, certainly before many of the other prophets even lived. Many of the verses may reflect older Hebrew usage and are hard to translate. There's a similar situation in the New Testament: the letter of Paul to the Galatians was likely in its final form before the Gospels were compiled and put in order even though the Gospels narrate earlier activity.

Hosea frequently called out Israel using the metonymy *Ephraim*. Ephraim was one of the tribes of Joseph and the most powerful of the Northern Tribes. This is parallel to calling the Southern Kingdom "Judah." Over the centuries, Ephraim (with its capital, Samaria) and Judah (with its capital, Jerusalem) had emerged as the primary tribes from among the twelve, and the Northern and Southern Kingdoms, as a whole, were often called by the names of these two tribes.

PURPOSE

Over history, the book of Hosea has functioned with at least three purposes.

Initial purpose: The Northern Kingdom of Israel, although very prosperous, had big spiritual and ethical cracks in its foundation, brought about fundamentally by her violation of the terms of the divine covenant (Hos. 4:1–19; 6:7; 8:1). The book is dominated by the threats of inevitable divine judgments against the people of Yahweh for their covenant rebellion against him. However, notwithstanding the predominance of these threats, Yahweh, out of love for them, issued through the prophet promises along with warnings: If they repented of their faithlessness and returned to their God, he would renew and restore them in their intimate covenant relationship with him. On the other hand, if they continued in their rebellious ways, destruction at the hands of the Assyrians would be inevitable.

Second purpose: By the time this book was put in its final form and added to the scroll of the Twelve, there were few survivors, if any, from the Northern Kingdom to read it; we have never heard of the "ten lost tribes" again. The action in Hosea is set in the season of decline before the fall of the Northern Kingdom (722 BC) but was added to the scroll of the Twelve to benefit the survivors of the fall of the Southern Kingdom (much later, in 586 BC) by helping them avoid the same mistakes the Northern Kingdom had made. One can picture a parent saying, "Don't make the same mistakes your big brother made!" (see 4:15).

In much the same way, this book served as essential, practical wisdom during the years of restoring and rebuilding Jerusalem allowed under the Persians.

Third purpose: As readers today, we all, individually and collectively, as communities and nations, face the same kinds of challenges that the Northern Kingdom of Israel faced. As we grow in prosperity, the temptations of corruption and arrogant selfishness can begin to look more attractive, and we start to believe we have the power to pull it off. Also, when we look to human leaders ("kings" in the book of Hosea; 5:13; 7:7; 8:4; 10:3–4, 7; 13:10–11) rather than the Lord for solutions, we start to go astray. When an individual or a society loses focus of the Creator who brought us into the world and who has a plan for our lives, things start to unravel. Hosea warns, and it is still true, that these tendencies can lead to a point of no return. However, the book ends with a call to return from these false paths to the promises of God and his love for us. This message is still vitally relevant for us today: we need to continue to do this on a regular basis, being eternally grateful for the enactment of the new covenant age via the person of Jesus Christ, our Lord and Savior. Never again need we fear the curses of the old covenant—as

Hosea's audience did—because Jesus has borne them on our behalf.

AUTHOR AND AUDIENCE

Hosea of Beeri wrote the book bearing his name. Hosea's name means "He [Yahweh] has saved"; it is a variant of the name Joshua, which is the English name for Jesus (Num. 13:16).

Hosea was most likely from the Northern Kingdom of Israel. He was a contemporary of the prophet Isaiah in the Southern Kingdom of Judah. Amos also lived during this generation.

Like Jeremiah, Hosea was a man of deep feelings, including anguish over the sins of his people. He had a fearless spirit and demonstrated selflessness in his dealings with others. The message burned inside his heart, and he knew he must be faithful to bring that message to his nation. He was intensely human, filled with emotion.

Jewish tradition has his burial site in Tsfat, Israel (Galilee). Unlike some of the other prophets, he is not mentioned elsewhere in Scripture.

The original audience of Hosea's message was the people of the Northern Kingdom in the times before the fall of Samaria. Hosea called them Israel, Jacob, Ephraim, and Samaria in this book. Destruction by the Assyrians loomed over them, and Hosea warned the people, hoping that they might avoid this catastrophe.

The secondary audience was the people of Judah (the Southern Kingdom) much later on, who were in captivity in Babylon and Persia (like Daniel and Esther) or rebuilding Jerusalem (like Ezra and Nehemiah). Eventually, as one of the parts of the scroll of the Twelve, Hosea's words were repurposed during the Persian Era as a calling out to the faithful remnant of the Southern Kingdom (Judah) that they might live into God's preferred future for them and avoid the mistakes of the Northern Kingdom, which had, by that time, disappeared as a nation.

The third audience is the contemporary reader. We face the same truths, challenges, promises from God, and options that the Northern Kingdom did.

MAJOR THEMES

The Covenant: Violation and Renewal. This theme pervades the entire book. The opening three chapters describe the living metaphor of Hosea's marriage, by YAHWEH's command, to Gomer, an "adulterous woman" (1:2), who would be guilty of infidelity on a number of occasions. She bore him three children—whom the prophet may or may not have fathered—and they were all given names that symbolized the judgment of God against his people: Jezreel, No-Tender-Mercy, and Not-My-People (1:2–2:1). It is abundantly clear that Gomer symbolized the faithless people of Israel (and Judah), with YAHWEH as the "betrayed husband." Israel's underlying infidelity was a spiritual one, namely, her abandonment of YAHWEH as her unique covenant God—worshiping pagan idols in his stead.

Like Gomer, Israel would bear the painful consequences of rebellion and faithlessness: Gomer would suffer for her marital infidelity, violating her marriage covenant (2:2–13), and Israel likewise, for violating the divinely revealed covenant—in particular, the first commandment to worship YAHWEH exclusively (beginning with ch. 4). However, God commanded Hosea to take his adulterous wife back—to rebetroth her, if you like (3:1–5), just as YAHWEH promised to rebetroth his people, renewing his covenant relationship with them (2:14–23; 11:8–11; 14:1–9). The application of this living metaphor to YAHWEH's relationship with Israel occupies the remainder of the book (chs. 4–14). And this promise of covenant renewal finds its ultimate fulfillment in the person and work of Jesus Christ. All the topics listed and discussed below are submotifs of this principal theme.

Love. The theme of love is a significant one in the book of Hosea. However, the issue is complex, for the term *love* is used in polar opposite contexts—from YAHWEH's amazing covenant love (Hb. *chesed*; see below) to the idolatrous, immoral, and illegitimate love of self, as demonstrated by the wayward Israelites. There are three different words (including two couplets—a verb and a noun) for "love" employed by the prophet, and together they amount to nearly thirty occurrences. Each term reflects varying semantic elements.

The most theologically profound of these terms is the Hebrew word *chesed*. The word occurs four times in this book. It denotes the pure, selfless love of YAHWEH, expressed in the administration of the covenant, and is often translated "loving-kindness" throughout the Old Testament. As an attribute of YAHWEH, *chesed* is used once, in 2:19, where God promised to betroth himself anew to Israel in his everlasting "love." The other three uses of the term are found in varying contexts: In 6:4, God indicted Israel for her shallow "faithfulness" for him that dissipates like the morning mist. In 4:1, God similarly indicted his people for their total absence of "love" toward him. And finally, in 12:6, God demanded that his people return to him (i.e., in repentance), maintaining "love" and justice in all their dealings with one another.

Secondly, the words *racham/ruchamah* denote the action of "loving tenderly" and the quality of "tender love." They are found eight times in the book, and the prophet used them both positively and negatively. The most significant negative usage occurs in the opening two chapters, where God named one of Gomer's children—a daughter—No-Tender-Mercy (1:6; 2:23). But then the term is used positively, when God promised to rename the child Shown-Tender-Mercy at the time of Israel's promised renewal and restoration (2:1, 23).

The third set of words, *'ahab/'ahabah*, denotes love that is both human and divine. These words occur seventeen times in the book, describing the action and quality of love of both God and the people of Israel. Some contexts are positive, where the love of God is affirmed (e.g., 11:1, 4), and others are negative, where the love demonstrated by the Israelites is corrupted, idolatrous, or self-centered (e.g., 4:18; 9:1).

Corruption. The Northern Kingdom (Israel) had grown prosperous. Human beings tend to form hierarchies, and those at the top of the ladder are often tempted to feather their nests and protect their positions, hanging on to power. A poor person can be dishonest but does not always have the power to exercise corruption, which is an abuse of power (much like the fact that a stranger cannot betray you; only a friend can do that). English historian and philosopher Lord Acton famously said: "Power tends to corrupt, and absolute power corrupts absolutely."[a] In asking for a hierarchical system—demanding a king in 1 Samuel 8:1–11—Israel had paved the path to potential corruption, which started with Solomon and seemed to get worse over time. The prophets, like Hosea, decried the absence of the traditional Hebrew virtues of justice and uprightness in the face of this corruption (Hos. 5:1, 3, 10–11; 6:10; 7:1; 9:9; 10:4; 12:6, 8). Corruption, like disintegration (see below), is not sustainable, and a society filled with corruption will crumble from the inside.

Disintegration through Spiritual Adultery. Hosea emphasized the sin of idolatry and illustrated Israel's

---

a Cited in his letter to Archbishop Mandell Creighton, April 5, 1887. Retrieved on August 23, 2023, from history.hanover.edu.

spiritual adultery in her relationship with God by his own marriage to an unfaithful woman. Hosea's own reconciliation also illustrates Israel's ultimate promised restoration (1:1–3:5).

Disintegration is the opposite of integrity. When one is integrated, he or she is not double-minded or conflicted on the inside. The first commandment, to have no other gods before God, is a call to individuals and communities to live an integrated life and to avoid those things (symbolized and illustrated by idols in the Bible) that create disintegration within us. Disintegration is spiritually fatal. We can be forgiven for it, but unless we address it seriously, it can rip our lives to shreds (13:5–8), and collectively, it can bring down an entire civilization. For Israel, an integrated existence consisted of keeping the first commandment, avoiding idols, and living in accordance with the covenant—an existence that Israel failed to maintain (3:1; 4:7, 10–19; 6:10; 8:4–6; 9:1, 10; 10:5–6; 11:2; 13:2).

Other sins that Hosea mentioned include injustice (12:7), violence (4:2; 6:9; 12:1), hypocrisy (6:6), rebellion (7:3–7), forming alliances with foreign nations (7:11; 8:9), arrogance (13:6), and ingratitude (7:15). Again, we can note that all these sins constitute a subset of the primary transgression of violating the covenant.

Hope. While the theme of hope is scattered throughout the book (1:10–2:1, 14–23; 3:5; 5:15; 11:8–11), Hosea ends on a particularly expanded note of hope (14:2–9). God's promises to his people in the Northern Kingdom were laid out in front of them (14:2–9)—free for the taking. Alas, they rejected these promises at the time, and the dry rot of corruption and disintegration became full-blown. The capital, Samaria, fell in 722 BC, never to be restored. Nonetheless, it must be acknowledged that this hope of restoration and renewal turned out to be a historical certainty. Notwithstanding Israel's failure to live up to God's demands, Israel's deliverance from captivity and subsequent spiritual renewal, did, in fact, take place with the people's return to their homeland in 538 BC. And this hope continues to call out to anyone who will listen, down through the ages unto this very moment—a hope that is grounded in the fulfillment of God's plan of redemption, fully realized in the coming of Jesus Christ, the Son of God, the Messiah and Lord, to this earth. Eternal renewal and restoration are found only by trusting in his atoning sacrifice for our sins.

Jesus as the Faithful Husband. This theme has been anticipated in the previous discussions on the violation and renewal of the covenant and the preceding thematic summary of hope. The prophet Hosea, who loved the unfaithful woman, showed a foretaste of the faithful love of Jesus. Through the eyes of faith, we see Hosea's marriage to Gomer as a parallel to Jesus and the church (Eph. 5:25–32). He still loves her despite her sin (Rom. 5:8) and sacrificially bought her back.

Jesus is visible in the book of Hosea in the following additional ways:

The name *Hosea*, which means "He has saved" (Matt. 1:21)

The "one head" (or leader) who reunites his people (Hos. 1:11; Eph. 2:11–22; Col. 1:18–20)

The son called from Egypt (Hos. 11:1; Matt. 2:14–15)

The "David-like king" (Hos. 3:5; Matt. 1:1; Rom. 1:3; Rev. 19:16)

HOSEA

Amazing Love

1 Here is YAHWEH's message that came through *the prophet* Hosea son of Beeri.[a] At that time, Uzziah, Jotham, Ahaz, and Hezekiah ruled as kings of Judah, and Jeroboam the son of Joash was king in Israel. 2This is the beginning of what YAHWEH spoke through Hosea.

Hosea's Marriage

YAHWEH said to me, "Go and marry an adulterous woman[b] and have children of adultery[c] because the people of the land are adulterers. They have forsaken me." 3So I married a woman named Gomer,[d] Diblaim's daughter. She became pregnant and bore a son.

---

a 1:1 *Beeri* means "my wellspring." Jewish tradition states that Beeri was a prophet who was a wellspring of revelation and greatly influenced Isaiah.

b 1:2 Or "Go marry a woman of harlotries." It is possible that Hosea was told to marry a temple prostitute from the fertility cult of Baal. However, some view this description as a prediction—that is, that she was not necessarily a prostitute when Hosea married her but would prove to be unfaithful to him in the future. Gomer is nowhere called by the Hebrew word *zonah* ("prostitute"). Commentators and translators are varied in their explanations and translations of the Hebrew.

c 1:2 Or "she will have children born through unfaithfulness [adultery]." Throughout the Old Testament, prostitution is a symbol of Israel's unfaithfulness to God and of pursuing false gods (idolatry). See Jer. 2–3; Ezek. 16; 23.

d 1:3 *Gomer* means "all finish with her" or "ending."

4 Yahweh said to me, "Name him Jezreel[a] because it will not be long before I punish the dynasty of Jehu for the massacre at Jezreel and then destroy the kingdom of Israel. 5 At that time, I will smash Israel's military power[b] in the Valley of Jezreel."[c]

6 Later, Gomer became pregnant again and gave birth to a daughter.[d] Yahweh said to me: "Name her No-Tender-Mercy[e] because I will no longer have tender mercy on the nation of Israel. I will certainly not forgive them. 7 I will, however, have compassion on the nation of Judah.

"I will rescue them! I will not give them victory through their weapons and military might.[f] It will not be their horsemen and chariots that deliver them. I, Yahweh their God, will save them!"

8 After Gomer weaned her daughter, No-Tender-Mercy, she became pregnant again and gave birth to a son.[g]

---

a 1:4 *Jezreel* means "God sows" or "may God sow." However, Jezreel was best known as a place, the location where Jehu assassinated Israel's King Ahab and his family (see 2 Kings 9–10).

b 1:5 Or "bow," a metonymy for military power.

c 1:5 The Valley of Jezreel runs eastward from the capital city of Jezreel near Mount Gilboa toward the Jordan River. The Valley of Jezreel was the location where invaders from the north entered the land (see Judg. 6:33) and a frequent site of large battles in history. The valley was flat and navigable for chariots (as opposed to the Judean highlands). Many such clashes took place here, generally initiated by the superpowers Egypt and Mesopotamia trying to extend their reach into the lands between them (such as Israel). The prophecy of this verse was fulfilled when the Assyrians invaded and defeated Israel.

d 1:6 It is entirely possible that Hosea was not the father of this child.

e 1:6 The Hebrew root word is *racham*, a word of tender love, like motherly love for a child. It has a homonym that means "womb." Perhaps "womb-love" could be a possible translation for the word translated here as "tender mercy."

f 1:7 Or "through their warrior's bow, sword, and warfare."

g 1:8 It is entirely possible that Hosea was not the father of this child.

9Then YAHWEH said to me, "Name him Not-My-People[a] because you, Israel, are not mine anymore, and I am not yours."[b]

Israel's Restoration

10Yet someday,[c] the number of the people of Israel will become as innumerable as the sand of the sea, which cannot be counted.[d] Although[e] *God* named them Not-My-People, he will *restore* them and call them Children of the Living God.[f]

11The divided people of Judah and Israel will reunite. They will appoint themselves one head[g] and will once again cover the land like grass that sprouts from the ground. How great will be the day when *the meaning of* Jezreel's name is fulfilled: *God sows*!

---

a 1:9 To paraphrase this in language that shows the emotional power of the prophet's mandate, we could describe Hosea's family as follows: "He is married to a harlot, has one kid named after a disaster [Jezreel] and two others called, essentially, 'Unloved' and 'Unwanted' " (Joel Hoffman, *And God Said: How Translations Conceal the Bible's Original Meaning* [New York: St. Martin's Press, 2010], 226).

b 1:9 Or literally "I [am] not I AM for you" (cf. Ex. 3:14) or "I do not exist for you." A solemn statement indeed! This serves as a decree of divorce. God canceled the covenant relationship between himself and Israel.

c 1:10 In the Hebrew Bible, this paragraph is the first part of ch. 2. Most English translations keep this paragraph as part of ch. 1.

d 1:10 Even when God sends judgment, mercy will prevail. He will restore and renew and reveal his love again. See Hab. 3:2.

e 1:10 Or "In the place where," which could be a reference to Jezreel.

f 1:10 We must always remember that mercy triumphs over judgment. God always remembers to show mercy (see Isa. 54:8).

g 1:11 Jesus is the "one head" over all his scattered people. He has reunited Jew and gentile into one new person (see Eph. 2:15). We are the seeds he has sown into the earth (see Matt. 13:1–23, 38), and he is the Head of the church (see Col. 1:18).

Yahweh's Unfaithful Wife

2 "Call your brothers My-People and your sisters
Shown-Tender-Mercy.
2 Go to court. Take legal action against your mother[a]
and put her on trial.
For she is no longer my wife,
and I am no longer her husband.[b]
She must remove *the symbols*[c] of prostitution from her
face
and the *seductive charms* of her adulteries from
between her breasts.
3 If not, I will strip her naked and humiliate her
and expose her nakedness as on the day she was
born.[d]
I will make her as bare as the desert,
turn her into a barren land,
and let her die of thirst.[e]
4 I will feel no pity for her children,

---

a 2:2 Or "Plead with your mother" or "Accuse [indict] your mother." The Hebrew word for "plead" is *rib* or *riyb* and is frequently used for filing a legal complaint and is associated with taking someone to court. Implied in the text is that Yahweh was taking Israel to court but her children (the remnant of Israel) must file a complaint for the court case.

b 2:2 This statement is usually seen as a formal divorce decree. The covenant between Yahweh and Israel had been broken by Israel's unfaithfulness.

c 2:2 This is likely a reference to cosmetics, jewelry, or symbols on her forehead that would identify her as a prostitute.

d 2:3 See Ezek. 16:39.

e 2:3 A thriving nation is rich in children. But in this prophecy, Israel would become depopulated and less fruitful. The commandment to be fruitful and multiply (God's first command and one he repeated many times) involves both productivity and procreation. Hosea was evoking both here.

since they are the children of her shameless
prostitution.
5 Yes, their mother has prostituted herself,
the one who conceived them has disgraced herself.
For she said, 'I will chase after my lovers;[a]
they will provide all I need:
my robe, my clothing,[b] my oil, and my wine.'
6 Behold! I will block her way with thorns
and build up a wall against her to stop her in her
tracks.
7 Then when she tries to chase her lovers,
she will not be able to catch them.
When she looks for them, she will not find them.
Eventually, she'll say, 'I must go back to my own
husband.[c]
I was much better off then than I am now!'[d]
8 Yet, she never understood
that I was the one who was giving her
the grain, sweet wine, and olive oil.[e]
I lavished upon her an abundance of silver and gold,

---

a 2:5 In this allegory, Israel's lovers would be the pagan gods she worshiped and alliances with Egypt, Syria, or Mesopotamia (whoever happened to be in charge there, the Assyrians, Babylonians, Persians, or Greeks).

b 2:5 Or "my wool, my flax." Robes were often made of wool, and flax is used to make linen clothing.

c 2:7 Or "to my man, the first."

d 2:7 Israel may have chased other gods, but there is only One who loved her: YAHWEH. Gomer may have had many lovers, but Hosea was the first who genuinely loved her. Jesus first loved us, and that's why we love him. For the believer, it is futile to chase after anyone other than Jesus. For you will discover in the end that you were better off with Jesus alone.

e 2:8 The irony is clear. The "fertility" gods she chased after couldn't provide her with what she needed. God was providing for her even as she wandered from him.

which she[a] took and made into idols of Baal.
9 So I will take back my grain at harvest time
and my new wine when the grapes are ripe.
I will snatch away my wool and my flax
used *for clothing* to cover her naked body.
10 Then very soon I will publicly expose her disgrace
before her lovers' gawking eyes[b]—
so that no man will steal her from me.
11 I will put an end to all her joyful festivities,
her feasts, her new moons and her Sabbaths,
and her celebrations will all cease.
12 I will ruin her vines and fig trees
of which she used to say,
'These are the fees that my lovers pay to me.'
I will turn vines and fig trees into a jungle
and make their fruit nothing but food for wild beasts.
13 I will make her pay for the feast days,
feasts for her to burn incense to the Baals.
She got all dressed up and chased after her lovers,
adorned with earrings and necklaces for them.
And me? She has forgotten about me.
This is YAHWEH speaking *to you*!"

God's Amazing Love for His People

14 "Behold, I am going to romance[c] her
and draw her into the wilderness;[d]

---

a 2:8 Or "they."

b 2:10 People try to hide sexual immorality because conscience tells us it is shameful. The proper punishment is to expose it.

c 2:14 Or "allure" or "seduce." The Hebrew word *patah* most definitely carries the connotation of romance.

d 2:14 The wilderness, the desert of Mount Sinai, was where God "married" Israel in the covenant he made with them. Symbolically, God was drawing his people back to the place where they first trusted him to care and provide for them.

I will speak[a] tenderly to her there with words of love
and win her heart back to me.
15 There I will give her back her vineyards,[b]
and make the Valley of Trouble[c] an open door to
hope.[d]
There she will *respond to me* and sing[e] as when she
was young,
as on the day when she came up from Egypt.

16 "And I, Yahweh, declare that when that day comes,
you will call me 'My Husband'

---

a 2:14 There is a wonderful wordplay that is lost in English. The word for "wilderness" (Hb. *midbar*) is taken from the root word for "to speak." The wilderness is the place where God speaks. He draws his people there and speaks to them in their wilderness. It is often in our difficult wilderness, a place we would never choose, that we hear most clearly the words of God's tender love that pierce our hearts.

b 2:15 The vineyard can represent abundance, new wine, overflowing joy, and supernatural life. We can find restoration even in the wilderness.

c 2:15 Or "the Valley of Achor." Achor is a variant form of the name Achan. *Achan* means "trouble" or "misery." See Josh. 7:24–26.

d 2:15 In every troublesome valley of your life (see previous footnote), God will open a door to hope. The poetic nature of the Hebrew text can be easily lost in translation. God promises to transform the place of deepest trouble into a doorway of hope. It would be akin to saying a "weeping willow tree laughs." There is an opportunity of hope hidden in our trouble. God will open a door to hope so that we can see his glory where we once were devastated. Like the rainbow that filled the sky after the flood (see Gen. 9:12–17), God's promise of hope and restoration remains forever. Look up and find your door to hope today.

e 2:15 Or "answer." Both "sing" and "respond" are possible meanings of the Hebrew word *ʿanah*. To sing praises to God in your "Valley of Trouble" is proof that you trust him. Nothing is more pleasing to God than a human heart that still worships him while surrounded by disappointment.

and no longer call me 'My Master.'[a]
17 I will banish the names of the Baals from her lips,
and she will never mention their names again.
18 When that day comes, I will make a covenant for you,
my people,
with all the birds and wild animals
and creatures that creep upon the ground.[b]
I will break the bow and the sword
and remove the weapons of war from the land,
and I will let you live in peace and safety.
19 I will take you to myself as my wife forever.
I will make you mine in righteousness and justice,
with unfailing love and tender affection.
20 Yes, I will commit myself to you in faithfulness.[c]
Then you will know me intimately as YAHWEH.
21 When that day comes, I will *be the God who*
responds,"[d]
declares YAHWEH.
"I will respond to the heavens,

---

a 2:16 Or "my Baal [master]." "To know God as our loving Master is good. But to know him as our Beloved Bridegroom is better. One is a relationship of boss/servant. The other is a relationship of love/union. . . . The wilderness forces us to be intimate with Jesus. It's in the wilderness that our Bridegroom transforms us into the bride, for our difficulties were designed to bring us into his heart. In the desert our garden becomes his garden, and he takes possession of our soul" (Brian and Candice Simmons, *The Wilderness—Where Miracles Are Born* [Savage, MN: BroadStreet Publishing, 2016], 15).

b 2:18 That is, God promised a time when the wild animals will lose their ferocity and will no longer be harmful to humanity. See Job 5:22; Isa. 11:6.

c 2:20 YAHWEH promised to take his people as his bride, and as the bride-price, he promised five things in vv. 19–20: righteousness, justice, unfailing love, tender affection, and faithfulness.

d 2:21 The word for "respond(s)" in vv. 21–22 can also be translated "answer."

and the heavens will respond to the earth,
22 and the earth will respond to the grain, the wine, and the olive oil,
and they will respond to Israel.[a]
23 I will sow her in the land as my very own.
I will show my tender mercy to No-Tender-Mercy.
I will declare to Not-My-People my words of endearment:
'You are my people,'
and they will say to me, 'You are my *One-and-Only* God.' "

An Illustration of God's Amazing Love

3 YAHWEH said to me, "Go again to her. Love her and demonstrate love to your wife[b] again even though she has another lover.[c] Love the adulteress with the same love

---

a 2:22 Or "Jezreel," a poetic and complicated metaphor. *Jezreel* means "God sows [seed]." It also sounds like the word *Israel*, and in this context, *Jezreel* becomes a poetic term for the people of Israel.

b 3:1 Or "a woman," likely a reference to Hosea's wife, Gomer. There are two different ways to interpret YAHWEH's instruction. Some believe this refers to a second woman who is a metaphor for the Southern Kingdom, Judah. Gomer (the Northern Kingdom of Israel) was in Assyrian captivity and would not return—that divorce was final. Therefore, YAHWEH told Hosea to go find another adulterous woman to take as his wife. However, it is more likely that God was telling Hosea to go back to Gomer. It is good to remember that prophecies often have more than one interpretation and sometimes more than one fulfillment. Prophecies usually contain many layers of meaning and application.

c 3:1 Or "who is loved by another man." The Syriac reads "who loves another man." The Septuagint reads "who loves evil." The vowel markings in this passage make interpretation of the Hebrew text difficult. No doubt, Hosea was still in love with Gomer even though she loved another man. This illustrates God's unfailing love for a people who are wayward and prone to wander from his heart.

that I, Yahweh, have for the adulterous Israelites who turn to other gods and love to give offerings to their idols."[a]

[2]So I negotiated to buy her for the bride-price of fifteen shekels of silver[b] and nine bushels of barley.[c] [3]And I said to her, "*Your sinful life is now over*, and you must stay with me *in my home* for many days. You will no longer commit adultery by giving yourself to another man, and I will remain faithful to you in the same way."[d]

The Explanation: Israel's Period of Discipline

[4]For the Israelites will have to spend many days deprived of political leaders, outward forms of religion, and the

---

a 3:1 Or "they love raisin cakes [which they offer to idols]."

b 3:2 Fifteen shekels would be approximately 6 ounces (170 grams) of silver.

c 3:2 Or "a homer and a lethech of barley." It is difficult to say precisely how much grain this would be, but assuming a "homer" is approximately what a donkey can carry (about 50 gallons or 220 liters), the Nueva Biblia Viva translates it as "one and a half donkey loads." It has been estimated that this amount of barley would likewise cost about fifteen shekels. Hosea paid in all the equivalent of thirty shekels of silver, the price of a slave in the law of Moses (see Ex. 21:32). In place of "a lethech of barley," the Septuagint adds "and a skin of wine." Since Hosea split his payment between silver and barley (and possibly wine), he seems to have had to scrape together enough to buy Gomer back. He was giving everything he had to take home his bride.

d 3:3 That is, Hosea committed to not sleep with Gomer for that length of time, possibly for reasons of purification. He did not lay a burden on her that he did not also put upon himself. A combination of syntax, multiple idioms, and the arrangement of phrases makes this verse difficult to interpret.

means of foretelling the future.[a] [5]But afterward, the Israelites will return and again long for YAHWEH their *covenant* God and for a David-like king.[b] They will turn trembling in awe to YAHWEH and *rediscover* his goodness and gifts in the future.

God's Indictment of Israel

4 Israelites, hear the words of YAHWEH, for he has charges to bring against the citizens of the country!

"There is no faithfulness in the land,
no tenderness and love—
no knowledge and understanding of God.
[2]Your crimes are these:
cursing others, lying, breaking your promises,
murdering, stealing, and committing adultery.
You have no moral decency,[c]
and bloodshed is the order of the day.[d]

---

a 3:4 Or "without king or prince, without sacrifice or pillar [places for sacrifices], and without ephod or teraphim [household idols]." This time of deprivation refers to the captivity of Israel. Yet God would not choose another nation; after their captivity, he resumed his place of loving and leading Israel. The Northern Kingdom would return to the dynasty of David (Southern Kingdom). The scattered remnants of the ten lost tribes would be included in the rebuilding of the nation, which led to the Second Temple period, into which was born Jesus of Nazareth.

b 3:5 Like most prophecies, this has multiple layers of meaning. The literal text is "they will seek . . . David their king." But David was dead. It means a ruler from the lineage of David. However, many Jewish interpreters see this as a Messianic prophecy of the King, whom we know as Jesus Christ. The Jewish Targum refers to him as "the king Messiah."

c 4:2 Or "break all bounds [boundaries]." This is a metaphor for breaking down the figurative walls of a moral society.

d 4:2 Or "blood touches blood."

3 This is why the land withers away,
and all who live in it waste away—
the wild animals, the birds, even the fish disappear."

God's Indictment of the Priests and Prophets

4 "But let no one accuse or blame others,
for my contention is with you, the priests.[a]
5 So, you *priests* will stumble *on the road to ruin* in broad daylight,
and the prophet will stumble with you in the dark.
I will destroy *Israel*, who gave you birth.[b]
6 My people are destroyed because they do not know who I am.[c]
Since you have refused to let them know who I am,
I will refuse you as my priests.
Since you have ignored the teaching of your God,[d]
I will ignore your children."

Yahweh's Warning

7 "The more you *priests* increase in number,
the more of your sins against me I have counted.
You have exchanged me, your glorious God,

---

a 4:4 The meaning of the Hebrew text is uncertain.

b 4:5 Or "You have destroyed your own people." The Hebrew is literally "I will destroy your mother." *Mother*, in this context, is figurative and refers to the nation of Israel.

c 4:6 Or "My people are destroyed for worn-out [old] ways of knowing me." That is, the priests had failed to teach the people to acknowledge God and give them fresh understanding of who Yahweh truly is.

d 4:6 See Mal. 2:7–9.

for something shameful.[a]
8 The *priests* lead my people into sin
so they can eat more of their sin offerings.[b]
They want the people to sin more and more.
9 The people get the priests they deserve![c]
I will punish them both for their conduct;
their evil deeds will cling to them.
10 They will eat but never be satisfied;
they will have sex but will remain infertile[d]
since they are unfaithful to me, YAHWEH,
and are devoted to other gods instead.
11 Here is what robs their ability to understand:[e]
giving themselves to prostitution
and to old and new wine."

---

a 4:7 As translated from the Syriac and the Targum. That is, the priests and people had exchanged the God of glory for a vile idol. God is the glory of his people. The shameful things are the idols and false gods they worshiped. The Hebrew is "I will change their glory into shame." There is a powerful pun in the text that is lost in translation. The word for "glory" can also mean "weighty," and the word for "shame" can also be translated "lightness [something lightly esteemed or disregarded]."

b 4:8 The priest often charged fees to offer a sacrifice for the penitent worshiper and was then allowed to eat the meat offered in sacrifices (see Lev. 6:24–29; 7:7). The priests benefited from the sins of the people. A hungry and greedy priesthood took advantage of the people's sins (see 1 Sam. 2:12–17). Clericalism cultivates a constant sense of guilt and shame among its followers in order for clerics to benefit from the insecurity of the people.

c 4:9 This verse is likely a proverb of that day quoted by Hosea. It can be translated "Like people, like priest"—that is, one is as bad as the other.

d 4:10 That is, they will worship the fertility gods and have sex with the temple prostitutes but will remain infertile.

e 4:11 Or "what takes away the heart."

The Core Issue: Israel's Idolatry

12 "My people seek revelation from a block of wood
and ask a stick what they should do.[a]
They have left me and are led astray by their spiritual adultery.[b]
They have deserted their God
13 to offer sacrifice on the mountains.
They burn incense on the hills,
under oaks, and every tall sacred tree,[c]
worshiping false gods in their pleasant shade.
This is why your daughters became cultic prostitutes
and your daughters-in-law commit adultery.
14 I will not punish your daughters for their prostitution
nor your daughters-in-law for their adultery
because it is you men[d] who are wandering off with whores
and offering sacrifice with cultic prostitutes.[e]
So *the saying is true*:
'A people without understanding will come to ruin.' "

God Warns Judah and Israel

15 "Although you, Israel, are unfaithful to me,
there is no need for Judah to sin by following your example.

---

a 4:12 Or "their staff gives them oracles." This is known as rhabdomancy. See Ezek. 21:21.

b 4:12 Or "a spirit of adultery has led them astray" or "the wind of harlotry has blown them astray."

c 4:13 Or "poplar and terebinth." See Deut. 12:1–9.

d 4:14 In the context, the "men" seems to refer to the priests. Pagan shrines were built in Israel's high places where it was believed that sex with cultic prostitutes (lit. "holy women") would ensure the fertility of their fields, of their herds, and of the women.

e 4:14 Due to the wicked example of their fathers and husbands, the women's guilt is viewed as less severe.

Do not go for worship at Gilgal[a]
or go up to the wicked Bethel.[b]
Do not swear oaths any longer, saying, 'As surely as Yahweh lives,'[c]
16 for Israel is as stubborn as a mule.[d]
So do they really think that I, Yahweh, am going to pasture them
like an *obedient* lamb in a broad meadow?[e]
17 Ephraim is under the spell of idols—leave him alone![f]
18 Their drunken orgy over,
the people delight in their prostitution,

---

a 4:15 Gilgal was the first base for Israel after crossing the Jordan (see Josh. 4:19). They had erected a stone pillar there to honor God, but that "worship" was now defiled by their mixing of pagan practices with the worship of Yahweh.

b 4:15 Or "Beth Aven," which means "house of evil." This is likely a term of derision for Bethel (*Bethel* means "house of God"), where the dwelling place of God (or tabernacle) once rested (see Judg. 20:26–27). Hosea was telling the people that the house of God had been perverted and defiled by pagan worship. Gilgal and Bethel became centers of idolatrous worship during the days of Jeroboam (see Amos 4:4).

c 4:15 See Amos 8:14.

d 4:16 Or "a cow with calf," which, for most English speakers, does not convey the intended meaning of the idiom. As a stubborn mule is tied up to keep it from wandering away, so Israel will be brought into captivity.

e 4:16 The difficult syntax of this verse can be understood as a declaration: "Yahweh cannot feed them like lambs in a meadow." However, the simile in this verse is more likely a rhetorical question that implies that God is not going to protect and provide for his straying people.

f 4:17 Or "Ephraim is wedded to idols. Let him do as he wishes!" *Ephraim* is a metonymy for the Northern Kingdom of Israel.

preferring shame to honor.[a]
19 They will be swept away on the wings of the wind,[b]
and their pagan sacrifices will bring them
nothing but disgrace."

Judgment Coming for Israel and Judah

5 "Hear this, you priests!
Pay attention, you leaders of Israel!
Listen, all of you among the royal household!
You are responsible for administering justice,[c]
but you have led the people into idolatry
by setting a trap at Mizpah
and spreading a net over Mount Tabor.[d]
2 You have dug a deep ditch of sexual immorality,[e]
and so, I will punish you all.

3 "Israel, you cannot hide from me;
for I know Ephraim[f] through and through.

---

a 4:18 The Hebrew of this verse is uncertain. The second half reads literally "they have loved they love the shame of her shields [gifts]." Another possible translation is "You have barely recovered from your hangover, yet you rush to the harlots. You are fond of the disgrace of their gifts."

b 4:19 Or "The wind has wrapped her in its wings."

c 5:1 Or "For judgment applies to you." Hebrew prophetic poetry often has a double meaning. If this is the case, one could translate this verse: "Since you are the ones who are supposed to bring justice, judgment will fall on you." See Mic. 3:9–12.

d 5:1 Mizpah and Mount Tabor were two places where the leaders entrapped their people in the cultic worship seen among the neighboring nations.

e 5:2 Or "They are entrenched in their deceitfulness" or "They have made a deep pit of [at] [the city of] Acacia." The Hebrew of this line is uncertain and possibly has some emendations.

f 5:3 *Ephraim* is used poetically as a metonymy for the Northern Kingdom of Israel.

Yet you have been unfaithful to me.
Israel's worship of me is *grossly* defiled.
4 They no longer even know me, YAHWEH.
Their evil deeds block the way for them to return to me, their God,
because they are possessed by a spirit of prostitution.
5 Israel's own arrogance speaks for itself.
Israel and Ephraim *have no one else to blame*,
for their own guilt makes them stumble.
Judah will be dragged down with them.
6 No matter how many animals they bring
to offer as sacrifices to YAHWEH,[a]
they will not find him,
for he has withdrawn himself from them.
7 They have been proven unfaithful to YAHWEH,
having fathered illegitimate children.
Now, before the new moon festival,
they and their fields will be devoured."[b]

Sounding the Alarm in Benjamin

8 "Sound the shofar in Gibeah, blow the trumpet in Ramah,
and raise the war cry at Bethel:[c]
'On your guard, men of Benjamin!'[d]
9 When the day of reckoning comes, Ephraim will be overthrown.
For I have pronounced certain *doom* on the tribes of Israel."

---

a 5:6 Or "With their flocks and herds they go to seek YAHWEH."

b 5:7 The meaning of the Hebrew of this sentence is uncertain and has a number of interpretations.

c 5:8 Or "at the house of evil [Beth Aven]," a derisive term for Bethel. Once the house of God, Bethel had become a center of idolatry.

d 5:8 Or "Tremble, O Benjamin" or "We are behind you, Benjamin." The Hebrew is uncertain.

The Crimes of God's People

10 "I am angry with the leaders of Judah,
for they came into *the Northern Kingdom* and stole their land.[a]
I will pour my wrath out on them like a flood.
11 Ephraim is oppressed, crushed by the verdict,
for having deliberately chased a lie.[b]
12 Because of this, I will be like a maggot[c] in the wound of Ephraim
and like gangrene[d] for the people of Judah.
13 Once Ephraim realized that he was sick
and that Judah had an ulcer,
Ephraim then turned to Assyria *for help*
and sent messengers to the great king,[e]
but he has no power to cure you
or to heal your wound.
14 For I will attack Ephraim like a lion
and the land of Judah like a young lion.
I will maul my prey and drag them away,
and no one will be able to snatch them from my hands.
15 I will return to my place
until they confess their guilt and seek my face.
Then, in their distress,
they will eagerly seek me *and my grace*."

---

a 5:10 Or "for the princes of Judah are the ones who have removed the ancient boundary stones."

b 5:11 Or "human reasoning," "vanity," or "dung"; that is, idolatry.

c 5:12 Or "moth," "larvae," or "pus," the discharge from a festering wound. The Septuagint reads "I will be like a terror to Ephraim."

d 5:12 Or "dry rot."

e 5:13 Or literally "a king who will contend," likely an Aramaic idiom for "a great king." Assyria eventually laid waste to Ephraim in 722 BC.

A Song of Repentance

6 *And they will say to one another:*
"Come, everyone! Come back to YAHWEH.[a]
Although he hit us hard,[b] now he will heal us.
Although he wounded us, now he will bandage our wounds.
2 After two days, he will revive us,
and on the third day he will raise us up.[c]
Then we will live in his presence[d]
3 and truly know him.
Let us come to know YAHWEH intimately
and eagerly press in to know him fully.
He will come to us
as surely as the sun rises *to greet us* each day.[e]
He will come to us like *refreshing* rain,
like a spring rain that *showers* the earth."

YAHWEH Responds

4 "Ephraim, what am I going to do with you?
How should I deal with you, Judah?[f]

---

a 6:1 Verses 1–3 are in the form of a poetic song of repentance, called a penitential song, like Ps. 6 and Ps. 51. It is possible that these verses were used liturgically by the priests who led the people in worship. These verses in Hebrew truly reflect the beauty of Hebrew poetry.

b 6:1 Or "has torn us."

c 6:2 From the writings of the New Testament onward, this text has been applied to the resurrection of Christ on the third day and our resurrection with him. See Matt. 27:63; Luke 24:46; 1 Cor. 15:4; Eph. 2:6.

d 6:2 Or "so that we may live before his face."

e 6:3 Or "His going forth is as sure as the dawn" or "As sure as the morning, we will find him" (LXX).

f 6:4 *Ephraim* is a poetic term of reference for the Northern Kingdom of Israel, *Judah* for the Southern Kingdom.

For your faithfulness is *as fleeting* as the morning
mist,
like the dew that quickly disappears.
5 This is why I have used my prophets to slice you
open[a]
and the words of my mouth to slay you.
For my judgments *wake you up*[b]
like the blazing light of dawn.
6 What I want from you is steadfast love[c] not simply
dead sacrifices;[d]
I want you to know me intimately not simply give
burnt offerings.
7 But, like Adam, you have broken my covenant.[e]
How unfaithful you are to me!

8 "Gilead is a city with streets stained with bloody
footprints,
a city known for its evildoers.

9 "The priests are like a gang of robbers waiting in
ambush,

---

a 6:5 The word of YAHWEH spoken by the prophets was like a sword in their mouths. Their message was a message of judgment and impending destruction.

b 6:5 Or "my judgment goes forth."

c 6:6 Or "to show mercy" (LXX).

d 6:6 What pleases God is not outward rituals but the expressions of love that we demonstrate through our lives. Love and mercy are always supreme over every other virtue or deed. See Matt. 9:13; 12:7; 1 Cor. 13.

e 6:7 Or "at [in] Adam they have broken my covenant." "Adam" may be a reference to a town (see Josh. 3:16). There are obviously a number of possible meanings hidden in this poetic sentence. The essence of this verse is that God's people have walked over God's love-covenant and treated it like dirt. There is a play on words with the name Adam (Hb. *'adam*) and the word for "dirt" (Hb. *'adama*).

a gang of priests who commit murder on the road to
Shechem.
What heinous crimes they have committed![a]

10 "I have witnessed a horrible thing in Israel's temple;[b]
there Ephraim practices temple prostitution,
grossly defiling Israel.
11a Listen to me, Judah!
A harvest of judgment is in store for you too."[c]

God's Righteous Judgment of Israel

7 6:11b "Whenever I long to make my people prosperous
again,[d]
1 whenever I desire to heal Israel,
I am confronted by Ephraim's guilt,
and all I can see is Samaria's sin.
For they all practice deceit.
No place is secure. They break into homes and steal.
Gangs raid in the open.
2 But it never occurs to them[e]

---

a 6:9 By opening a door of darkness into the land, the priests with their pagan compromises were guilty of causing the deaths of many people. God held them responsible for the judgment he poured out on the people because of their sins. Therefore, they were described as murderers by Hosea.

b 6:10 Or "the house [temple] of Israel."

c 6:11a This was a bitter warning of the impending captivity of the people of the Southern Kingdom. The Hebrew text adds a line to this verse: "when I restore the fortunes of my people." However, based on the *Biblia Hebraica Stuttgartensia* and Hebrew parallelism, this line actually belongs with the first verse of ch. 7 and begins a new section of the book of Hosea. It is important to remember that verse and chapter numbers and headings have all been added to Scripture and are not part of the inspired text.

d 6:11b See the footnote for 6:11a.

e 7:2 Or literally "They do not speak to their hearts."

that I, *Yahweh*, remember all their evil deeds.
They are all prisoners of their own wickedness,
and their sin stares me in the face."

Conspiracy in the King's Court

3 *Yahweh says*, "They deceive the king with their wickedness[a]
and the rulers with their lies.[b]
4 They are all unfaithful to the king.
Their *anger* is like an overheated oven.[c]
Their oven burns so hot that the baker could knead his bread *at night*
until it rises *in the morning*
and he still wouldn't need to stoke the fire.
5 On the king's day *of celebration*,
his officials are drunk with wine,[d]
and the king trusted the traitors.
6 Their hearts are like an oven that burns with treachery.
All night long, their anger[e] smolders;
then in the morning, it bursts into flame.
7 Yes, they are all as hot as an oven,
ready to consume their rulers.

---

a 7:3 The Hebrew is ambiguous. It could also be translated "People make the king happy with the wickedness."

b 7:3 This section speaks of the assassination plots against the kings of Israel. Four kings from the Northern Kingdom of Israel were assassinated between 743 and 732 BC (Zechariah, Shallum, Pekahiah, and Pekah).

c 7:4 Mutiny was common in the Northern Kingdom during this era, and many of its kings were assassinated.

d 7:5 Or "his officials became sick from the poison in the wine."

e 7:6 Or "all night long their baker smolders." The Hebrew words for "anger" and "baker" are homonyms. It is possible that the palace baker was the central figure in the plot.

All their kings have fallen in this way,
yet not one of them has ever called on me."

Israel Fails to Ask Yahweh for Help

8 Yahweh says, "Ephraim mixes with the nations.[a]
My people are like half-done flatbread,
burnt on one side and raw dough on the other.
9 Ephraim does not realize alliances with foreigners
devoured his strength;
even his hair has turned gray,
but he has no clue.
10 Israel's arrogance has become his own accuser.
Yet in spite of all these troubles,
they do not seek me, Yahweh their God,
nor come back to me.

11 "Ephraim is like a dove, silly and senseless,[b]
first calling on Egypt *for help*
then turning to Assyria.[c]

---

a 7:8 In vv. 8–16, Yahweh condemned Israel for three reasons: (1) seeking help from other nations (Egypt, Assyria) instead of turning to God, (2) worshiping pagan gods, and (3) turning away from Yahweh to adopt a powerless pagan god. Verses 8–10 show Israel as feeble, like an old man. Verses 11–12 show Israel as nervous and flighty, like a foolish dove. And in vv. 13–16, Yahweh pronounced doom on those who rebel against him.

b 7:11 Or "without wisdom and without a heart."

c 7:11 The two superpowers then continued to clash in chariot battles back and forth across Israel and the Fertile Crescent. Assyria, Babylon, and Persia took turns ruling Mesopotamia (modern Iraq), which had great wealth because of irrigation from the Tigris and Euphrates Rivers. The same was true of Egypt and the Nile. Israel had no such river system to ensure harvests and was often a political football between the two super-regions, having done time as slaves in Egypt and exiles in Babylon/Persia.

12 Wherever they turn,
I will spread out my net and catch them.
I will bring them down like the birds from the air.
I will punish them for the evil they have done."[a]

Debauchery and Drunkenness

13 "They are doomed for having fled from me.
Destruction will seize them for having rebelled
against me.
I longed to pay their ransom time and time again,
but they have *believed and* spoken lies about me.
14 Their cries to me are not with a sincere heart,
and they wail like heathens on their beds.[b]
When they ritually mutilate themselves
to cause their grain and grapes to grow,
they know they are rebelling against me.
15 Though I held them up, giving strength to their arms,
they plotted evil against me.
16 They turned in the wrong direction
to a god who is no god at all.
They are like a warped bow *that can't shoot straight.*
Their leaders will be killed in war
because of all their arrogant, defiant words.
Oh, how the Egyptians will mock them!"

The Coming Judgment

8 "Blow the shofar! *Sound the alarm!*
Like a scavenging vulture,[c]
disaster is swooping down on YAHWEH's land[d]
because they have violated my covenant

---

a 7:12 Or "according to the report to their congregation."
b 7:14 "Their beds" may be a reference to cultic prostitution.
c 8:1 Or "Like an eagle."
d 8:1 Or "the house of YAHWEH."

and rebelled against my instruction.
2 Of course, they cry out to me, 'Our God!'
My people, Israel, you claim that you know me,
3 but you have rejected what is good.
Therefore, your enemies will pursue you."

Rebellion and Idolatry

4 "They have selected kings but without my consent,[a]
and appointed leaders but without seeking my advice.
They have made idols out of their silver and gold—
what an excellent way to lose their money!
5 Samaria,[b] I reject your calf-idol![c]
My anger blazes against your people.
How long before they reclaim their purity?
6 Surely, this *calf-idol* originated with Israel.
A craftsman made it; it's not even a god at all.
Yes, this calf of Samaria will be shattered to pieces."

Israel's Forbidden Alliances

7 "Since they sow the wind, they will reap the whirlwind.[d]

---

a 8:4 The Northern Kingdom of Israel had a total of ten dynasties. Each ended with the assassination of the king for reasons of political ambition and without consulting Yahweh.

b 8:5 Samaria is another name for the Northern Kingdom.

c 8:5 Several ancient Near Eastern gods (e.g., Baal) were worshiped by means of idols covered with silver and gold and fashioned into images of young bulls. The Israelites had fallen into pagan idolatry with idols at Bethel and Dan (see 1 Kings 12:28–30; 2 Kings 10:29).

d 8:7 This is a Hebrew idiom. The wind they sow is the many sins of Israel; the whirlwind they reap is the trouble and judgment that are sure to come.

They will reap headless stalks of grain that produce
no flour,[a]
and even if they did produce grain, foreigners would
swallow it.
8 Israel has already been swallowed up[b]
and is now powerless among the nations.
Israel, you are like a useless piece of broken pottery.[c]
9 For indeed, you have sought assistance from Assyria,
like a wild donkey wandering alone.[d]
Ephraim[e] has sold herself to other lovers.
10 Although they have hired allies from among the
nations,
I will round them up *for judgment.*
They are already wasting away
under the oppression of the king of princes."[f]

Israel Has Forgotten His Maker

11 "The more altars Ephraim builds,
the more places the people have to sin—
altars for sinning *and not for sin offerings.*
12 Although many times I have written many rules for
my people,

---

a 8:7 The Baal fertility cult reaps infertility.

b 8:8 Israel was "swallowed up" in 733 BC by the Assyrian invasion of King Tiglath-Pileser III, who seized many of Israel's inhabitants and scattered many more among the nations (see 2 Kings 15:29; 1 Chron. 5:26).

c 8:8 Or "like a vessel in which there is no pleasure."

d 8:9 The "wild donkey" is the onager, a species of donkey known for staying away from other animals and people.

e 8:9 Ephraim is another name for Israel. There is a Hebrew play on words that is lost in translation. The word for "wild donkey" is a rearrangement of the consonants of the name Ephraim.

f 8:10 Or "They will soon cease anointing kings and princes" (LXX). The term *king of princes* may be a reference to the emperor of Assyria.

Ephraim regards them as something strange and foreign.
13 They love to offer sacrifices to me
so that they can eat the meat.
But I, YAHWEH, take no pleasure in them.
I will not forget their guilt,
and I will punish them for their sins.
They will have to go back to Egypt.
14 Israel has built palaces[a]
but has forgotten his Maker.
Judah keeps on building fortified towns,
but I will rain fire down on his cities
to devour the strongholds with flames."

Israel's Sorrow While in Exile

9 Stop rejoicing, people of Israel!
Stop rejoicing as you celebrate your festivals like pagans,
for you have deserted your God
and committed fornication *with other gods.*
You have loved the prostitute's pay on every threshing floor
as if Baal were the one who could give you good harvests.
2 You will not be able to enjoy the bounty of your harvest—
for others will consume your wheat, oil, and wine.
3 Ephraim will not remain in YAHWEH's land;
they will have to go back to Egypt
or eat Assyria's polluted food.[b]
4 Their sacrifices will not be pleasing to YAHWEH.

---

a 8:14 Or "temples" (Targum).

b 9:3 In exile, the Israelites had to eat the polluted (ceremonially unclean) food of Assyria. See Ezek. 4:13.

They will not be able to offer their firstfruits
nor pour out drink offerings of wine to him,
for their food will be like funeral fare—
food given to those in mourning.
Whoever eats it will become unclean.
They will only have sufficient food to satisfy their hunger
and not enough to offer to YAHWEH in his house.

5 What will you do on the appointed feast days,
on the day you gather for YAHWEH's festivals?[a]
6 Look! Even if you flee from destruction,
Egypt will round you up.
Your gathering together
will be for your burial in Memphis.[b]
Your silver treasures will be lost among the weeds,[c]
and thornbushes will overgrow your homes.
7 Your day of punishment has come,
and the time for recompense has arrived,
and Israel will know it.[d]
You say, "The prophet is a fool.

---

a 9:5 That is, the three annual feasts (Passover, Pentecost, and Tabernacles), which could not be observed properly in exile, for they required going to the temple. It seems like the Northern Kingdom did not coalesce in Assyrian exile as Judah did in Babylonian/Persian exile. In fact, we never hear from the ten lost tribes again after 722 BC. Apparently, they were victims of total or almost total ethnic genocide, or at least culturally extinguishing cleansing. Many in the North were worshiping the golden calves at Bethel and not even going to Jerusalem. Some of the remnant were left behind to mix with others, producing the Samaritans of the New Testament era.

b 9:6 Or "Moph," also called "Noph."

c 9:6 The meaning of the Hebrew is uncertain.

d 9:7 As translated from the Aleppo Codex, Leningrad Codex, and the Masoretic Text.

This man of the Spirit is crazy!"[a]
But your guilt is great,
even greater than all your deep-seated hatred.
8 This prophet of my God is a watchman for Israel.
Yet, everywhere he goes, the people set traps for him.
He is considered an enemy in the house of his God.[b]

Israel's Sins at Gibeah

9 Israel has sunk so deeply into depravity—
just as you did at Gibeah.[c]
God will not overlook the guilt of your actions;
he will punish you for your sins.

Israel's Sins at Baal Peor

10 *Yahweh says*, "When I found you, Israel,
it was *as pleasing* as finding ripe grapes in the desert.
When I saw your ancestors,
it was *as delightful* as seeing the early ripe figs[d]

---

a 9:7 This appears to be a derisive description regarding God's Spirit coming upon the prophet, who would go into a trance or ecstatic state and prophesy.

b 9:8 Or literally "A watchman Ephraim with my God, a prophet, a snare of a fowler on all his paths, hatred in the house of his God." Verses 7–8 are the most difficult verses in Hosea to translate, as the Hebrew text is uncertain. There is a lack of certainty whether these words (or some of them) were spoken by Hosea or by the people of Israel. It seems more fitting in the context to view them as spoken by Hosea.

c 9:9 Perhaps one of the lowest points of Israel's history took place at Gibeah. The men of the city raped and killed a Levite's concubine (see Judg. 19:22–30), which led to a civil war that nearly wiped out the tribe of Benjamin. Gibeah would also be recognized by the people of that day as the place where Israel asked God for a king (see 1 Sam. 8). Instead of Yahweh being their king, the Israelites ended up with Saul.

d 9:10 See Mic. 7:1.

on a new fig tree in its first productive season.
But when they reached Baal Peor[a]
they devoted themselves to the shameful *god*, Baal,[b]
and became as shameful as the things they loved.[c]
11 The glory of Israel[d] will fly away from you like a bird,[e]
leaving you infertile—no pregnancy, no conception.
12 Even if they raise their children, I will remove them,
and not one will be left alive.
Even worse than that will be when I desert you.

---

a 9:10 *Baal Peor* means "lord of the [mountain] gap." See Deut. 4:3–4.

b 9:10 Or "they devoted themselves to Shame [i.e., Baal]." Hebrew speakers of that day were accustomed to substituting *Shame* for *Baal*. This is specifically Baal of Peor, a local Moabite Baal, not the Baal introduced to Israel by Jezebel. See Num. 25:1–15; Ps. 106:28; 1 Cor. 10:8; Rev. 2:14.

c 9:10 This could be a reference to the Moabite women the Israelite men slept with in Acacia who led them astray into pagan idolatry.

d 9:11 Although the shining presence of God could be in view here, the next line indicates that Ephraim's (Israel's) glory is their children, the generation to come. Moral corruption of a nation often results in a decline of the birthrate, as God's punishment of evil. Also note the sharp contrast between the shame in v. 10 and the "glory" departing in v. 11.

e 9:11 The Hebrew word for "glory" is *kabod*. It is a very loaded word in the Old Testament. God's glory is heavy, weighty. The glory that left the temple (see Ezek. 11:23) will come crashing back in (see Ezek. 43:1–5) with the restoration. This glorious heaviness is beautifully and poetically contrasted with the lightness of a bird flying away. Later rabbis also described this, equivalently, as the Shekinah, a cloud of YAHWEH's presence. This imagery goes back to the cloud of the dwelling place and Solomon's Temple that was also present at the Mount of Transforming Glory (see Ex. 33:18; 2 Chron. 7:1; Matt. 17:5).

13 Ephraim, I once saw you like the city of Tyre[a]
planted in a pleasant setting,
but now you must send out your sons
to be slaughtered *in battle*."

14 YAHWEH, give them . . .
Yes, what punishment should I ask you to give?
Give them wombs that miscarry and breasts with no milk.[b]

Israel's Sins at Gilgal

15 *YAHWEH says*, "All of Ephraim's evil began at Gilgal.
It was there that I started to become their enemy.
I will drive them out of my house
because of the evil they have done.
I will no longer love them
because all their leaders are rebels.
16 Ephraim, you're finished!

---

a 9:13 Tyre was a beautiful port city and the mother of the Carthaginian (Semitic; "Punic" is the Latin pronunciation of *Phoenician*) culture which, with Hannibal's leadership, rivaled Rome. Many empires tried to conquer Tyre but were only partially able to do so. Tyre had plenty of money to pay tribute if she had to. Only Alexander, in the most extensive siege warfare ever seen up to that date, was able to fully take the city (332 BC). This could be translated "like a palm tree" instead of "Tyre." The first line of this verse is uncertain in the Hebrew. Many translations defer to the Septuagint for clarity.

b 9:14 The broken sentence in the first line of this verse seems to be the most accurate translation, even though it is ambiguous in English. It appears that Hosea was deeply struggling in his heart over God punishing his unfaithful people. Perhaps because Hosea's wife was unfaithful, he saw his own feelings as a mirror of YAHWEH's feelings for his wife, Israel. Hosea began to pray for his people, but his feelings rose up abruptly, so he asked instead what God would do. Should he demonstrate his love or condemn her? Hosea submitted to God's choice.

Your root has dried up,
and you will bear no more fruit.[a]
Even if the women do give birth,
I will put their beloved children to death."

17 My God will disown you
because you have not listened to him.
You will become wanderers among the nations.

Hosea Prophesies against Israel's Pagan Altars

10 Israel was once like a lush vine
that produced plenty of grapes.
Yet the more his fruit increased,
the more pagan altars he built.
The more abundantly his land increased,
the more abundant were his sacred fertility pillars.
2 Israel's devotion is false[b] and divided;
soon the people must pay the penalty for their guilt.
Yahweh will demolish their altars
and shatter their sacred pillars.
3 Then they will say,
"We have lost our king
because we have not feared Yahweh,
but what could a *human* king do for us anyway?"
4 All they do is make empty speeches,
phony promises, and useless treaties.
Their so-called justice spreads like poisonous weeds
among the furrows of the fields.[c]

---

a 9:16 This verse is loaded with significant irony, for the name *Ephraim* means "doubly fruitful."

b 10:2 Or "slippery."

c 10:4 See Amos 6:12.

Israel's Sins at Bethel

5 Samaria's citizens will tremble and mourn
over the loss of their sacred calves of Bethel.[a]
Everyone will wail over its loss
along with their idolatrous priests
because their "glory" has gone into exile.
6 *They* will carry the calf-idol to Assyria
as tribute to the great king.
Ephraim will reap the shame.
What a disgrace for Israel!
7 Samaria—your king has had his day.
Your king will disappear
like a twig on the surface of the waters.[b]
8 The hilltop shrines,[c] the vanity and sin of Israel,
will be demolished.
Thorns and thistles will overgrow and cover their altars.
Then they will say to the mountains, "Bury us!"
and to the hills, "Fall on us!"

9 "Israel, since the days of Gibeah,[d]
you have not stopped sinning.
From then until now, you have persisted in your ways.
Were not the evildoers overtaken by war in Gibeah?
10 When I am ready, I will discipline these wayward people,
and armies will be gathered against them

---

a 10:5 Or "Beth Aven," a derisive term for Bethel. *Bethel* means the "house of God." *Beth Aven* means "the house of evil."

b 10:7 Or "like a [wood] chip on the surface of the waters" (LXX).

c 10:8 Or "Beth Aven [house of evil]." See the footnote on 10:5.

d 10:9 That is, when Israel's monarchy got started. See 1 Sam. 8.

to put them in bonds for their double sins."[a]

11 YAHWEH says, "Ephraim was once obedient like a well-trained cow
that loved to thresh the grain.
Seeing her fair neck,
I thought I would put Ephraim in the yoke.
Judah will have to plow;
Jacob must level the soil.[b]

12 Sow *seeds* of righteousness for yourselves,
and you will reap a harvest of *God's* unending love.[c]
Break up the hard, fallow ground of your heart.[d]
For it is time to seek YAHWEH's favor
until he comes to pour out
righteousness on you like falling rain.[e]

---

a 10:10 Or "It was my desire to tame/break them in, binding together the peoples for double furrows [i.e., an extra-wide, double-blade plow]."

b 10:11 Ephraim represents the Northern Kingdom, Judah the Southern Kingdom, and Jacob the entire nation.

c 10:12 The harvest of the Spirit is love (see Gal. 5:22–23). There is so much grace in the Old Testament, and grace is still broadcasting from God's heart every day. He is the God of love, mercy, and grace. He has always been the same from the beginning. See Mal. 3:6; Heb. 13:8; James (Jacob) 1:17.

d 10:12 This sentence seems to be out of order, for breaking up the fallow ground should precede sowing and reaping. However, the text implies that it is *new* ground that must be taken. In other words, the process of sowing, reaping, and harvesting must continue while still looking to find new ground that needs the righteousness of God planted within it. The ground is an obvious metaphor for the human heart, for we are made from the soil. The heart must pursue righteousness and reap unending love as well as break up new ground that may be hidden in our lives.

e 10:12 Righteousness is a gift that God pours out from heaven; it is not a result of our striving. The key to biblical spirituality is receptivity. And this is the reason we need to plow up the hard places in our hearts.

[13]But instead, you have cultivated lawlessness
and reaped a harvest of injustice.
You have eaten the fruit of your lies.
Because you have trusted in your own strength[a]
and in your vast, mighty army,
[14]war cries will break out against your people,
and all your fortified cities will be destroyed.
Just as Shalman destroyed Beth Arbel on the day of battle,[b]
when children and their mothers were dashed to death on the ground,
[15]so it will be done to you, Bethel,[c]
because of your evil stacked upon evil.
At dawn, *as the battle begins*, your kingship will be no more."[d]

Israel, God's Wayward Son

11 "I have deeply loved Israel from his very beginning.
From Egypt, I called my son.[e]

---

a 10:13 Or "in your own way" or, if the text is emended, "your [many] chariots" (also LXX). However, Israel was not known for many chariots, compared to Egypt and Assyria.

b 10:14 This may be a reference to the Moabite king, Salamanu, and his destruction of Beth Arbel (Irbid) in Gilead. See 2 Kings 15:10.

c 10:15 Or "house of Israel" (LXX).

d 10:15 The last king of Israel was Hoshea, and he was taken captive by the Assyrians even before they began their siege against Samaria (see 2 Kings 17:4–6).

e 11:1 It was the love of a tender Father that called Israel out of Egyptian bondage (see Ex. 4:22–23). God set his love upon the people of Israel and chose them to demonstrate his love for them. He loved them when they were weak and helpless. He raised up Joseph to meet their needs during a famine. He loved them when they were outcasts and in slavery. However, these words find their fulfillment in Jesus, who also was brought out of Egypt. See Matt. 2:14–15.

2 The more the people of Israel were invited to come *to me*,
the more they turned away from me.
They sacrificed to the Baal-idols
and burned incense to pagan images
3 even though I was the one who taught Israel to walk.
I took them up in my arms and carried them,
yet they did not acknowledge that I was their healer.[a]
4 I *gently* pulled them to my heart
with the cords of affectionate love.[b]
I stooped down to care for them and gently fed them.
I showed them the same kind of tender love
as one who picks up an infant and holds it to his cheek."[c]

---

a 11:3 The Hebrew word *rapa'* can also mean "prosper," "restore [favor]," "comfort," "impart wholeness," and "care for," as well as "heal."

b 11:4 Or literally "I led them with human cords." God was showing Israel how tenderly he had dealt with them. What a beautiful picture of God's care as he gently taught Israel, his "son," to take his first steps. He would pick his people up and carry them when they were weak, and he repeatedly healed and restored them. He pulled them into his heart and lovingly fed them throughout their existence. He held them to his cheek in tender embrace to affirm them and comfort them. Hasn't God done all these same things for you?

c 11:4 Or literally "I was to them like one who lifts a yoke from their jaws and gently fed them." The imagery of this verse is not easily understood in Western culture. God compared himself to a farmer who will take the yoke from the shoulders of an ox so that it can freely eat. There is a clear wordplay in Hebrew that is lost in translation: the root word for "yoke" is the same as the root word for "infant." The original readers of this would have understood the play on words; God was comparing himself to a caring Father and Israel to the child he loved.

Israel Returned to Slavery in Egypt and Assyria

5 "Israel will return to the land of Egypt,
and Assyria will rule over them
because they refused to return to me.
6 The whirlwind of war will break down the bars of their gates[a]
and ravage their cities[b]
in return for all their schemes.
7 My people are bent on turning away from me,
and together they call upon Baal,
who will not help them at all."[c]

Judgment or Mercy?

8 "Ephraim, how could I ever give up on you?
Israel, how could I ever let you go?
How can I treat you like Admah
or deal with you like Zeboiim—*cities I destroyed*?[d]
My heart beats for you,[e]

---

a 11:6 There is a play on words in the Hebrew that is lost in translation. The words for "bars of their gates" can also be translated "their oracle priests." In other words, both their city gates and their false prophet-priests would be destroyed.

b 11:6 The history of Israel is filled with warfare. It took many battles to secure the land. Afterward, the Israelites were besieged by the Assyrians and taken into captivity.

c 11:7 There are a number of difficulties to understanding the text of this verse, which is literally "And my people are hanging to turning away from me, and to a height they call to him. Altogether he will not exalt them." The "height" (Hb. *'el ʿal*) may be a reference to either God or to Baal or to a yoke.

d 11:8 Admah and Zeboiim were two cities near Sodom and Gomorrah that were once rescued by Abraham (see Gen. 14) but later destroyed for their blatant wickedness (see Gen. 19; Deut. 29:23).

e 11:8 Or "My heart is overturned within me" or possibly "I have had a change of heart."

and my compassion rekindles a deep love for you
within me.[a]
9 I will certainly not punish you in my burning anger,
nor will I turn around and destroy Israel again,
for I am God and not a *mere* human being.
I am the Holy One in the midst of you;
I will not come to you in my wrath."

God Summons the Exiles to Return to Him

10 "When I, YAHWEH, roar like a lion,
my people will march behind me.
Yes, I will roar like a lion *to gather my own around me*![b]
Indeed, when I roar,
my children will come trembling from the west.
11 They will return trembling like a bird from Egypt,
like a dove from Assyria,
and I will settle them in their homes.
I, YAHWEH, have spoken."[c]

---

a 11:8 Or "all my tenderness is stirred within me."

b 11:10 The image of a male lion roaring to gather his pride around him points to God giving a summons (roar) to the exiles to gather around him and follow him once more.

c 11:11 The Hebrew Bible renders the verse most English Bibles set as 11:12 as v. 1 of ch. 12. See the first footnote on 11:12.

Israel, a Deceitful Son

12 11:12 *Yahweh says:*[a] "All around me are the lies of Ephraim,[b]
and nothing Israel says can be trusted.
Judah, *on the other hand*, still walks with God;
he remains faithful to the Holy One.
1 Ephraim *follows fantasies*, like feeding on the wind.
They chase the desert wind all day long;[c]
they multiply their lies and violence.
They make a treaty with Assyria,
and at the same time, they send a gift of olive oil to Egypt."

2 Yahweh is bringing charges against Judah.
He will punish Jacob[d] as his conduct deserves;
he will repay the people for what they have done.
3 In his mother's womb, Jacob grabbed his twin brother's heel;
when he grew to be a man, he struggled with God.[e]

---

a 11:12 In the English Bible, v. 1 is included in ch. 11 as v. 12. However, the Hebrew text labels the verse as 12:1, and indeed, the content of the verse fits better in this context. Therefore, the translation team has placed this verse in ch. 12 for smoother reading while retaining the English notation. The team reminds the reader that verse and chapter numbers have been added to Scripture by translators and are not part of the inspired text.

b 11:12 Or "I am besieged [as with a surrounding army] with Ephraim's lies."

c 12:1 Or "the east wind [off the desert]," which is a metaphor for Assyria. See Jer. 18:17; Ezek. 17:10; Hos. 13:15.

d 12:2 Jacob was the ancestor of both the Northern and Southern Kingdoms, and his name is used here as a metonymy for the people of Israel.

e 12:3 See Gen. 32:24–30.

4 He wrestled with the angel and won;
he wept and sought his blessing.[a]
God met him at Bethel,
and there he spoke to us.
5 *Yes*, YAHWEH is the God of Angel Armies.
YAHWEH—remember his name!

Return to God

6 And you, to your God you must return.
Stand guard over divine love and justice
and always put your trust in him
as you wait patiently for your God.[b]
7 *Israel*, you are like merchants[c] using fraudulent scales.
How you love to cheat your customers!
8 Ephraim boasts, "Look how rich I have become!
I've made a fortune all by myself.
There's nothing wrong with the profits I have made.
Is there anything sinful about that?"[d]

---

a 12:4 Or "favor." The implication is that if God gave strength and endurance to Jacob to prevail in his wrestling match, wouldn't God also give the Israelites strength to prevail without their having to turn to Egypt and Assyria for help?

b 12:6 The Hebrew can be translated as both "put your trust in your God" and "wait patiently for your God." This translation includes both forms.

c 12:7 There is a play on words that is lost in translation. The word for "merchants" is also the word for "Canaanites." Hosea was comparing the dishonesty of the Israelites to that of their pagan neighbors, the Canaanites. The implication is that the Israelites were acting as dishonestly as their cheating neighbors.

d 12:8 Or "In all that I have gained, I did not incur guilt." There is a play on words with the word for "guilt" (Hb. *'on*), which has a homonym meaning "wealth."

9 "I, Yahweh, have been your true God
ever since your days in Egypt.
Yet, I will make you live in tents again[a]
as you did when we first met in the Tent of Meeting."[b]

10 "I am the One who speaks through the prophets,
and reveals to them vision after vision.
Through the ministry of prophets,
I reveal my message in parables."[c]

11 "Gilead is full of nothing but iniquity![d]
Therefore, its people will be wiped out.
Do they sacrifice bulls in Gilgal?
That is why I will make their altars
nothing but heaps of stones
on the furrows of the plowed fields."

12 Jacob fled to the land of Aram,[e]
where Israel became a servant to win a wife.
He took care of *another man's sheep* to pay the
bride-price.[f]
13 By a prophet, Yahweh brought Israel out of Egypt;

---

a 12:9 That is, as punishment for their apostasy, Israel would be dislodged from their homes and live a nomadic life again in tents, as they did in their wilderness wandering.

b 12:9 See Ex. 33:7.

c 12:10 Or "oracles of doom." Some Jewish commentators translate this as "I appeared under many guises." Jesus' preferred method of teaching was allegory (parables; see Matt. 13:34; Mark 4:34).

d 12:11 The meaning of the Hebrew is uncertain.

e 12:12 This is the land of Haran, where Abraham came from. See Gen. 27:41–45.

f 12:12 See Gen. 29:15–30.

By a prophet *named Moses*, he cared for his people,
Israel.[a]
14 But the people of Israel have provoked him to bitter
anger.
YAHWEH will hold the Israelites responsible
for the crimes of bloodshed they have committed.[b]
Their master will make them pay
for all the disgraceful things they have done.

Summary of YAHWEH's Case against Israel

13 When Ephraim used to speak,
his words commanded great respect.
He once had great authority in Israel,[c]
but he became guilty of Baal worship
and signed his own death warrant.
2 And now they sin more and more
by making silver idols for themselves,
cleverly crafted idols of their own invention—
each skillfully made by human hands.
"Sacrifice to them," they say.
Why would men kiss idols of calves?[d]
3 Therefore, *the entire tribe of Ephraim* will vanish
like the morning mist,
like the dew that quickly disappears,
like the chaff blown by the wind from the threshing
floor,
like smoke rising from a chimney.

---

a 12:13 God was reminding Israel of the many blessings that came to them through his prophets and urging them not to despise the prophets' ministries. See 1 Thess. 5:20.

b 12:14 Or literally "and his bloods upon him he will leave."

c 13:1 Early in Israel's history in the land, the people of Ephraim were powerful. See Josh. 24:29–30; Judg. 8:1–3; 12:1–6.

d 13:2 Or "Those who offer human sacrifice kiss [images of] calves."

Yahweh Is Still the God of Israel

4 "I, Yahweh, have been your true God
ever since your days in Egypt.[a]
You must know no other god but me.
There is no other god who can save you.
5 I tenderly cared for you[b] in the desert,
in the land of dreadful drought.[c]
6 When I pastured you, you were full,
but when you were satisfied, your hearts grew proud,
and you completely forgot about me.
7 So now I will be[d] like a male lion to you,
like a leopard lurking beside the path.
8 I will attack you like a charging bear robbed of her cubs,
and will rip open your chest.[e]
Like a lioness, I will devour you on the spot;
like a wild beast[f] I will tear you to shreds!
9 Israel, you have destroyed yourself,
because you are against me, your only help."[g]

---

a 13:4 The Septuagint adds a sentence before this verse: "I am the Lord your God who set the heavens firm and keeps the earth steady; my hands have created the whole array of heaven, but I have not shown these to you for you to follow them. It was I who brought you up out of Egypt."

b 13:5 The Syriac and the Septuagint read "I shepherded [fed] you." God was reminding his people that he had always provided for them, even in a difficult season of their lives.

c 13:5 Or "burning heat."

d 13:7 There is a possible play on words, for "I will be" in the Hebrew is very close to the name for Yahweh, "I AM that I AM" or "I AM who I will be."

e 13:8 The irony is stinging. They would not open their hearts (chest) to the things of God, so now, God would rip their hearts open in judgment.

f 13:8 Some Jewish scholars view the "wild beast" as the Assyrians.

g 13:9 Literally "He/It has destroyed you, Israel, because with/in me [is] with/in your help." The meaning of the Hebrew is uncertain.

Israel's Ruin

10 "Where is your king now,
who could save you in all your cities?
Where are your rulers, of whom you said,
'Give us a king and leaders'?
11 In my anger, I gave you kings,
and in my wrath, I have taken them away.[a]

12 "Ephraim's sin is recorded;
his guilt is on record and kept in store.

13 "You are like a senseless baby
at the point of childbirth;
labor pains have begun, and his time is due,
but he refuses to leave the womb.[b]
14 Shall I save my people from the clutches of Sheol?[c]
Shall I ransom them from Death's firm grip?
Hey, Death! Tell me, where is your punishment?
Hey, Grave![d] Tell me, where is your sting?
Revenge will be hidden from my eyes."

---

a 13:11 In the greater context of Hosea and his unhappy marriage, the Hebrew verbs translated "gave" and "taken" are frequently used to describe a women "given" in marriage and a man having "taken" a wife.

b 13:13 The metaphor of childbirth demonstrates that Ephraim had experienced catastrophes (labor pains) that were designed by God to produce a change of heart (the birthing of new life). But since Ephraim refused to learn from his disasters (leave the womb) and refused to repent (be born anew), he was doomed.

c 13:14 The Hebrew concept of Sheol is the dark underworld, the world of the dead, and at times a reference to the grave.

d 13:14 "Grave" is the Hebrew word *Sheol*.

Final Warning

[15]Though *Ephraim* bears more fruit[a] than his brothers,
YAHWEH's breath will blow from the desert.
The scorching wind will come from the east;[b]
it will dry up his springs,
and his wells will run dry.
The wind will come to plunder his treasury,
robbing it of every precious thing.
[16]Samaria will be punished
because she has rebelled against her God.
Her people will fall by the sword;
even her little ones will be dashed to pieces
and her pregnant women split open.[c]

Return to YAHWEH

14 Israel, return to YAHWEH!
Come back to your true God,
for your sins have become your downfall.
[2]*Repent!* Choose the words of your confession
and come back to YAHWEH.
Say to him, "Take all my guilt away;
be gracious to us and receive us.[d]
Instead of animal sacrifices,
we offer to you *the praises of* our lips.[e]
[3]Assyria will not be our savior; *you will.*

---

a 13:15 This is an obvious play on the word *Ephraim*, which means "doubly fruitful." See Gen. 41:52.

b 13:15 The wind of the east is a reference to Assyria, the nation that God would bring against his people in judgment.

c 13:16 Although this verse is noted as 14:1 in the Hebrew Bible, most modern English versions follow the Septuagint in numbering it as 13:16. The subject matter of this verse fits better with ch. 13.

d 14:2 Or "accept us, O Good One."

e 14:2 Or literally "we will offer bulls, our lips."

No longer will we trust in our military might.[a]
We will not call our handmade *idols* 'our god.'
For in you, the orphan finds tender mercy."

Yahweh's Promise of Forgiveness

4 "I will heal[b] you of your unfaithfulness.[c]
I will love you with all my heart,[d]
for my anger has turned away from you.
5 My presence will fall like *refreshing* dew[e] on Israel.
My people will blossom as the fair lily
and become firmly rooted as *the cedars of* Lebanon.
6 My people will spread out
like the beautiful branches of olive trees[f]

---

a 14:3 Or "war horses," which is a synecdoche for military might. See Ps. 20:7–8; Isa. 30:1–5; 31:1–3.

b 14:4 This entire segment (vv. 4–8) is written in the Hebrew imperfect tense. This means that any promise discussed in this passage is something that God has initiated and was/is coming into being, incomplete, and not yet certain. It depended on whether the people of the Northern Kingdom (and we for that matter) chose to receive this free-gift promise and take part in making this potentiality a reality. These are not "predictions" of a certain future, but they are available to Israel and to us should we receive them and live into them. Classical Hebrew has no future tense in the sense that we have a future perfect in English. These promises are incomplete possibilities that can be made finished and perfect should we receive them. They are ours for the taking. They also can be ignored and discarded. The Northern Kingdom chose the latter and, after 722 BC, was heard from no more.

c 14:4 Hosea used wordplay throughout his book. Here, the word for "unfaithfulness" comes from the same root word as the word translated "return" and "come back" in vv. 1–2.

d 14:4 Or "I will love you freely [without restraint]." The Hebrew word for "freely" also means "freewill offering." God's love for you is extravagant, generous, and without limit.

e 14:5 The dew is a metaphor for God's anointing, favor, and presence that causes all things to be fresh and new.

f 14:6 Or "have splendor [majesty] like the olive tree." The olive tree is where the oil of anointing originated. See Ps. 52:8; Jer. 11:16.

and carry the *desirable* scent of Lebanon's cedars.
7 They will come back to live beneath the shadow of
my *blessing*.[a]
They will flourish like a *sunlit* field of wheat
and thrive as a blossoming vine.
Their wine will be as famous as the wine of Lebanon.
8 Ephraim will say,
'Why would I ever want to worship idols anymore?'
I, *Yahweh*, am the one who hears, responds, and
watches over him.
For I will *shelter* him *under my branches* like an
evergreen cypress.
Ephraim, you owe your fruitfulness to me."[b]

An Epilogue

9 Do you consider yourself wise?[c]
Then you will understand these words.
Are you discerning?
Then you will discover their meaning.
For Yahweh's paths are smooth for walking,
and the righteous will walk in them,
but the rebellious sinners will stumble in them.

---

a 14:7 Or "Those who live in my shade will come back." Shadow or shade is a common Hebrew metaphor to indicate God's favor, blessings, comfort, presence, and protection.

b 14:8 This is another play on words with the name Ephraim (*Ephraim* means "doubly fruitful") and God as Israel's source of "fruitfulness." The Hebrew is "from me your fruit is found."

c 14:9 A reallocation of the verse sequence is evident here: the Hebrew text of Hos. 14 ends with v. 10. However, the English translation of the prophecy concludes with v. 9. No content has been excluded in this translation; this simply reflects a difference in verse numbering. Verse and chapter numbers were not original parts of the inspired texts but instead were later additions.

THE BOOK OF

JOEL

The Outpouring

BroadStreet
PUBLISHING

JOEL

Introduction

AT A GLANCE

Author: Joel the prophet

Audience: The survivors of a locust plague

Date: Unknown; estimates span centuries of possible dates

Type of Literature: Prophecy

Major Themes: The day of YAHWEH; repentance; Spirit-filling; *chesed*; hope; seeing Jesus in the book

Outline: The focal point of the book of Joel is the dual manifestation of the day of YAHWEH. The structure of the book may be described as a chiasmus, comprised of two reinforcing, contrasting, and parallel emphases on that day—one negative and one positive. These two cycles hinge on the central call to repentance in 2:12–17. This pivotal central section serves as a transitional movement from presenting the day of YAHWEH as a dreadful judgment on his people for their disobedience to displaying that day as a manifestation of God's supreme grace.

A: 1:1–2:11 The day of YAHWEH in judgment

- i. Locust invasion (a): literal economic devastation of the land (1:1–12)
- ii. Initial call to repentance (1:13–14)
- iii. Locust invasion (b): economic devastation continued (1:15–20)
- iv. Locust invasion (c): likened to a military destruction of the land (2:1–11)

B: 2:12–17 Central call to repentance
   i. Exhortation to return to the Lord God (2:12–14)
   ii. Instructions to declare a fast and summon a sacred assembly before Yahweh (2:15–17)

A[1]: 2:18–3:21 The day of Yahweh in blessing
   i. Yahweh promises blessing: compassion, renewal, economic prosperity, detailed future prosperity, and a restored covenant relationship with his people (2:18–27)
   ii. The spiritual consummation of the day of Yahweh: God's Spirit poured out, celestial signs, and salvation for all who call on Yahweh (2:28–32)
   iii. The day of Yahweh: judgment on the enemies of God's people and deliverance, restoration, spiritual renewal, and pardon for God's people (3:1–21)

ABOUT THE BOOK OF JOEL

This book is one of the most difficult in the Bible for determining the *Sitz im Leben* (who was writing to whom at what specific time for what specific reason). Serious attempts to answer this question have Joel writing anytime from just after Samuel's work until deep into the Hellenistic occupation some one thousand years later. The book provides some vague clues but nothing conclusive. This gives Joel a universal appeal, even to us today. It fits anytime and anywhere when people of faith, either as individuals, groups, or nations, go through a devastating season and seek to find meaning and redemption in the wake of it.

That being said, there are several traditional Jewish dating theories for the book of Joel:

1. The days of Samuel (according to Rashi, one of the great rabbis). This seems to make little sense as there was no temple in the time of Samuel.

2. The days of King Jehoram, the son of King Ahab and Queen Jezebel. Another J(eh)oram of Judah was king in the south at about the same time (850–841 BC).
3. The days of King Manasseh (687–643 BC) of Judah (Seder Olam Rabbah, second century AD), son of King Hezekiah and Hephzibah. According to this chronology, Joel received Torah instruction from the prophet Micah.

There are many more theories, including the times of King J(eh)oash (836–797 BC) or King Josiah of Judah (640–609 BC).

While we cannot unequivocally rule out an early date such as those mentioned, there does appear to be a consensus that a later date may be a better fit for several reasons.

First, there seems to be a Jerusalem and a temple but no king, thus indicating Second Temple Judaism and not the exilic time between the temples. Kings are virtually always mentioned by name in the prophetic books.

Second, the fact that Joel quoted from so many other prophets shows that he was, like Luke, summarizing and curating from previous works. (See Luke's explanations of his work in Luke 1:1–4 and Acts 1:1.) Many see Joel's work as an anthology of Bible wisdom. His message draws on brilliant insights of many other biblical prophets, as the following examples (there are many more) show:

Joel 1:15—Isa. 13:6; Ezek. 30:2–3; Zeph. 1:7
Joel 2:2—Zeph. 1:14–15
Joel 2:3—Isa. 51:3; Ezek. 36:35
Joel 2:6—Nah. 2:10
Joel 2:17—Ps. 79:10
Joel 2:27—Isa. 45:5–6, 18; Ezek. 36:11
Joel 2:28—Ezek. 39:29
Joel 2:31—Mal. 4:5

Joel 2:32—Obad. 17
Joel 3:4—Obad. 15
Joel 3:10—Isa. 2:4; Mic. 4:3
Joel 3:16—Isa. 13:13; Amos 1:2
Joel 3:17—Ezek. 36:11
Joel 3:18—Amos 9:13

Joel thus reads a bit like an anthology and perhaps was intended to be a capstone to the prophetic tradition. It is more likely that he was quoting from many Old Testament sources than that all of them were quoting from him. But again, this cannot be dogmatically asserted.

Third, the prophet mentioned Israel's sin (a major theme) but didn't tell readers what the sins were. Perhaps Joel assumed that readers were familiar with the sins mentioned by the other prophets and/or wanted the book to apply to any of them or to anything any reader is going through in his or her current time.

Finally, in 3:6 Joel mentioned Greeks, who would most likely have come in contact with Israel at a later date. However, evidence also indicates that Sidon (one of the most important ancient Phoenician city-states, along with Tyre) was actively trading with the ancient Greeks (i.e., Ionians) by the late 800s BC. And this could well have included trading in slaves—as mentioned here in 3:6.

Part of the message of Joel is that cascading malfunctions occur around us from time to time. Our actions cannot ever be entirely separated from the causes of these disasters. Thus, these difficult times are an opportunity for us to change our path and learn from what has happened. The concept of repentance (*shuwb*, in Hebrew, "to change direction") is a major key to the book of Joel. In fact, if we don't alter course, an even bigger tidal wave of troubles awaits us. It is a hard truth, but the fact is that we learn more from hard times than from easy times, if and only if we take advantage of the opportunity to change direction.

A burst of light shines through in 2:12–17: if we make this course correction, YAHWEH is patient, full of unconditional love for us, and will restore us.

In the end, Joel is a prophet of hope. Repentance leads to restoration, abundance, and human flourishing. It is not just a nostalgic return to the better times of the past but rather an upgrade to a Spirit-filled future (2:28–32) in direct communication with the living God, with a renewed creation coming alive all around us.

May your reading of Joel plant just such a seed of hope in your soul as it has for so many people of every generation.

PURPOSE

The book of Joel seems to gather the best of the prophetic tradition into three power-packed chapters. Despite the mysteries surrounding the time and place of the book's writing, Joel's reasons for writing seem clear:

1. Find meaning in a recent locust plague.
2. Show listeners that human behavior and large disasters cannot be totally separated.
3. Challenge and invite people to take responsibility for their part when things go wrong around them and express sorrow for those actions.
4. Challenge and invite people to change their behavior, for true repentance involves much more than mere verbal expression of regret.
5. Give them a reason to engage in that repentance: to receive a full pardon for sin and an eternally renewed relationship with the living God (2:12–17).
6. Give them a hope for which to live: God's Spirit filling them and his presence among them bringing abundance.

So, what is God's purpose through Joel's book for us today? What it meant is important. What it means is perhaps always more important.

Our souls are sealed off from one another, in terms of direct experience. But we are not sealed off from the living God. This "opening" is that through which prophets like Joel experience a *dabar* ("word"; Joel 1:1) from God, and they share it with us through language . . . words.

Words are all we have to *tell* others the story about what is going on in our souls. We cannot *show* anyone our inner life. Human consciousness is one of the most mysterious phenomena in the universe since it, by its very nature, is impervious to outside observation and thus unreachable through any scientific probing.

Therefore, it is so important to freshen and present again the words of Joel, from his soul to ours. Joel has long passed from this life, but his words echo on, especially in the Jewish liturgy of confession and repentance on the Sabbath before Yom Kippur, the Day of Atonement. The word *catechesis* contains the root word *echo*; the communal recitation of God's Word, back and forth, received and passed on by Joel, has long sustained the Jewish people through countless calamities, not unlike the ones described so vividly in Joel's book. Faith is not about the denial of the catastrophic, which falls upon us from time to time, but rather about overcoming the plagues of life, whether they be swarms of locusts, the scourge of war, persecution, injustice, or pandemics.

Even though we are indeed cut off from direct experience of each other's lives other than through testimony and storytelling, Joel promised us a wide-open portal to personal connection with the Creator, through the Holy Spirit, through whom we have the only true path to unity and fellowship with one another. Joel gave a foreshadowing of Pentecost to come (Acts 2:1–41). Why? Because he experienced this opening to heaven in a personal way. It's hard to know if the writers of the Bible realized they were writing Scripture in the sense that we understand it. But with Joel, we get a sense that he knew that his words would be used, in all times and places, to give expression to pain and voice to faith and hope, for young and old, male and female, wealthy and poor. All flesh.

AUTHOR AND AUDIENCE

We know only one thing about the author, Joel: that the name of his father was Pethuel. It's as though Joel wanted his book to be about God's kingdom and not about himself.

Jo-el is perhaps an inversion of the name Eli-jah, both meaning, roughly, "YAHWEH (Jah-) is (my) God (El)." Some Jewish scholars have surmised that Joel was a Levite priest and was once connected to temple worship since he included many references to temple practices and procedures.

Joel's audience is universal: people of faith everywhere and in every season. If he had wanted it to reach a specific group, he would have added clear historical frames of reference, but he did not. It's as if he wanted to share the best of the entire prophetic tradition with everyone.

In times of calamity, God has an answer. In the age of the canonical prophets, it fell to their divinely appointed lot to herald a new day and awaken the people to return to YAHWEH. They became, in that sense, "awakeners," of whom Joel was a prime example. This does not refer primarily to a better methodology but to a better messenger. In the era of the new covenant, in the absence of divinely inspired fresh revelation (that age has passed), "awakeners" may be those who, via the gifting of the Spirit of God, apply and teach the meaning of God's Word to God's people today.

Now Joel's original writing may indeed have been a spiritually motivated response in the aftermath of a specific locust plague since the original audience would be those who were left to ponder the meaning of the devastation. Joel provided for them an interpretation and a call to action based on his insights, but it seems that he, also, consciously and intentionally used a broad funnel to collect, curate, and present the best wisdom of the ancient prophetic tradition and a trumpet on the other end with which to call out and reach as many people as possible with that treasure that he synthesized. The locust plague was perhaps just an opportunity for him to do so, the grain of sand around which he produced a pearl for all time.

MAJOR THEMES

The Day of Yahweh. This motif is the dominant theme of the book of Joel. It incorporates both positive and negative elements. First of all, considering the negative fulfillment of this phenomenon, it denotes how all of creation, led by the Creator, turns on people when they are out of sync with the Source of all things. We "sow the wind [and] reap the whirlwind" (Hos. 8:7). If we live unhealthy lives, devastating medical diagnoses can be the result. If we cultivate deceptive relationships and dishonor others, an entire culture starts to come unglued. Corruption by leaders keeps many nations poor for generations. We need to "come back to Yahweh [our] God" (Joel 2:13), for it is only in harmony with him that true, lasting *shalom* can spread among us. *The day of Yahweh* is a poetic and spiritual term for the very tangible catastrophic results of behavior that is disconnected from God and the high ideals he requires us to live by.

Second, regarding the positive fulfillment of this day, it not only signifies the ultimate destruction of all the enemies of God—both corporate and individual—but also, and wonderfully, the Spirit-filled renewal of the people of God, past, present, and future. This is an accomplishment grounded in the finished redemptive work of Jesus Christ on the cross. Such a renewal will last for eternity—a never-ending day of salvation, renewal, and joy.

Repentance. We English speakers tend to see repentance as a state of mind rather than a positive action to take. We see it primarily as being sorry or apologetic. To the Hebrews, however, repentance (*shuwb*) had a lot more to do with action, with changing direction, literally, "turning" to take a new and better path. Repentance is not just feeling bad about what we've done but actually doing something about it. In both passages in Joel where repentance is front and center (1:13–14; 2:12–17), the mandatory *actions* of God's people repenting dominate these sections more than just words and cries of mourning and regret—although these are also required.

Spirit-filling. Joel took other Old Testament promises of the Spirit coming in a special way (Isaiah, Jeremiah, Ezekiel) and brought them into full blossom with a prophecy of the Spirit of God coming in a universal and powerful way, a hope not unlike the hope for a coming Messiah that was developing during the time of the prophets. Jesus was aware of this hope for the Spirit's fullness and called it the promise of the Father (Luke 24:49). Peter saw the fulfillment of Joel's hope in the day of Pentecost, when many were filled with the Holy Spirit, giving birth to the church (see Acts 2:14–41, especially vv. 17–21).

Chesed. *Chesed* (pronounced with a guttural "h") is arguably one of the most important words in the Old Testament and a key thematic component of the book of Joel—although the word itself is found only in Joel 2:13 and is translated "extravagant love" (often "kindness" or "love" in other translations). It is the divine love that flows from God's very nature. It is unearned and available always. The key is our receptivity to this *chesed*, not our trying to produce it on our own. David's psalms can be called a pursuit of *chesed* in the midst of troubles. The word is loosely translated as something like *agape* ("love") and *charis* ("grace") in the New Testament. The heart of biblical spirituality is the ability to be receptive to *chesed* and to live out of the transforming power it brings us.

Hope. The Israelis call their national anthem *Hatikvah* ("The Hope"). It echoes the bold aspirations of the final segment of Joel, where Zion is restored and God's power and healing emanate from his dwelling among his people in new and powerful ways. Joel starts with a plague and ends with a promise.

Seeing Jesus in the Book. The crucial passage in Joel that reveals an undeniable allusion to the person of Jesus and the gospel is 2:28–32: the spiritual consummation of the day of Yahweh, with God's promise to "pour out my Spirit on everyone." The reason we can be so sure of this claim lies in the recorded words of the apostle Peter's sermon on the day of Pentecost in Acts 2:14–41, in which he explicitly quoted this passage (Acts 2:17–21) and some three thousand people were converted and baptized (Acts 2:41)—a phenomenon that signaled the birth of the new covenant church community and the beginning of the new covenant age of the Spirit of God. Immediately prior to this sermon, the Holy Spirit was visibly poured out on Peter and the other apostles in the form of "tongues of fire."

The focus of Peter's message was on the reality and centrality of Jesus' physical resurrection from the dead after his atoning sacrificial death on the cross that led to his body lying in the grave for three days. Following his resurrection, Jesus ascended to heaven and took his seat at the right hand of his Father. He then actioned the pouring out of the Spirit of God, initially on his apostolic followers and then on all of his followers from that point on. After Peter concluded his sermon, he immediately exhorted his listeners to repent in the name of Jesus Christ for the forgiveness of their sins (Acts 2:38). And if they did so, they would receive the same gift of the Spirit of God as the apostles had a short time before. None of this could have happened if Jesus Christ had not been crucified, had not perished and lain in the grave for three days, and had not risen from the dead and ascended to heaven to reign with his heavenly Father. The prophet Joel foresaw all of this in the climactic prophetic passage of Joel 2:28–32.

JOEL

The Outpouring

The Plague of Locusts

1 These are the words of Yahweh that came[a] to Joel[b] son of Pethuel.[c]

[2]Listen to this, you leaders[d] in the land;
everybody everywhere, pay attention!
Has anything like this ever happened in your lifetime
or in the days of your ancestors?
[3]Tell your children about it!
And tell them to tell their children
and to tell their children to tell the next generation.

---

a 1:1 Or literally "that was or came to be." The prophet Joel received these "words [message]" by supernatural means (a vision, dream, trance, audible voice, divine visitation). Joel's prophecies come to us with the authority of God himself.

b 1:1 The name *Joel* means "Yahweh is God."

c 1:1 Or "Bethuel" (LXX, Syriac), which was a common name in Hebrew (see Gen. 22:20–23; Josh. 19:2–6; 1 Chron. 4:30). *Pethuel* may possibly mean "enlarged by God," "the vision of God," or "the youth of God." See Ludwig Koehler and Walter Baumgartner, *Lexicon in Veteris Testamenti Libros* (Leiden: E. J. Brill, 1958), 786.

d 1:2 Or "elders."

4 What the cutting-locust[a] has left,
the swarming-locust[b] has eaten;
what the swarming-locust has left,
the hopping-locust[c] has eaten;

---

a 1:4 Is this locust plague to be interpreted literally or figuratively? Possibly both. Historians recorded many plagues of locusts that destroyed the land. However, as with all prophetic writings, there can be a metaphorical interpretation as well as a literal one. Joel used four distinct Hebrew words for the locust plague. These four names likely refer to the four stages of the locust as it develops. The first is the Hebrew word *gazam*, which refers to the larva of a locust that, after hatching, begins to cut and feed or gnaw on the sprout or first part of a plant that emerges. It is similar to a palmerworm or cutworm. Metaphorically, it speaks of doctrines or teachings that "cut" off significant portions of the Bible or "cut" out passages that contradict espoused theological positions. We must not cut or leave out anything from the Bible, even though portions may be confusing, difficult to understand, or beyond our experience. We are not to nibble on the pieces of the Word of God that we prefer but to consume it in its entirety. Locusts are a biblical symbol of intimidation that will keep believers from taking their inheritance by faith. John the Baptizer arrived on the scene and made locusts his food, eating up that symbol of intimidation—devouring the devourer (see Matt. 3:4). All end-time awakeners will likewise swallow up all that comes against them.

b 1:4 This is the Hebrew word *'arbeh*, which addresses the mature locust that comes in swarms over the land. It can represent the religious spirit that intimidates and makes others feel inferior. The Bible mentions locusts over thirty times.

c 1:4 This is the Hebrew word *yeleq*, which is likely related to the Akkadian word *ilqitu* (Ovid R. Sellers, "Stages of Locust in Joel," *The American Journal of Semitic Languages and Literatures* 52, no. 2 [1936]: 82), meaning "jumping" or "swift." This is the juvenile locust that has wings but does not yet fly. It can represent the believer who "hops" about, having not yet learned to soar in the ways of the Holy Spirit (see Nah. 3:16; Rom. 8:2).

what the hopping-locust has left,
the destroying-locust[a] has eaten.[b]

Wake Up!

5 Wake up, you drunkards, and weep!
Wail, all you wine-drinkers!
For the new wine has been snatched from your lips.
6 For a nation has invaded my land,
powerful and innumerable,
with teeth like a lion's teeth,
and with the fangs of a lioness.
7 They have completely destroyed my vineyards
and reduced my fig trees[c] to splinters;
they have stripped off the bark and thrown it away,
leaving their branches white.

---

a 1:4 This is the Hebrew word *chasil*, which describes a locust known as the "finisher" or "devourer." This is the full-blown religious spirit that crucified the One who was sent from heaven. This "devourer" will always seek to destroy the harvest and will be rebuked by the Lord (Mal. 3:11).

b 1:4 The destroying-locust (or "consuming-locust") is the locust horde that completely devastated the land and darkened the sky. This was the eighth plague that God sent upon Egypt in the days of Moses (see Ex. 10:1–20). These locusts are symbolic of the enemies of the gospel of the kingdom—man's traditions and lies that attempt to consume the harvest. See Matt. 15:9; Mark 7:13; Col. 2:20–23. It was a "grasshopper [locust] mentality" that kept Israel from going into the promised land (see Num. 13:25–33). Revelation 9:1–12 describes smoke rising from a pit, and from the smoke come locusts, who have the devil as their king. Like a smoke screen, the lies of the Evil One keep people from seeing the truth.

c 1:7 Vineyards and fig trees are important symbols in the Hebrew and Christian traditions. Vineyards are used metaphorically to refer to all of God's people—both Israel and the universal church (Jew and gentile)—while the fig tree is often used as a symbol for Israel.

8 Lament like a young bride-to-be dressed in sackcloth
for the bridegroom of her youth.[a]
9 YAHWEH's ministers, the priests, are in mourning
because there is no more grain and wine[b]
to offer in YAHWEH's temple.
10 The fields are stripped bare,
and the ground is plunged into sadness[c]
over the ruined harvest.
The grapes have dried up, and there is no new wine;[d]
only a trickle of olive oil remains.[e]
11 Be ashamed, you farmers,
for there is no harvest of wheat and barley.
You vinedressers, cry out in despair,
for the harvest of the fields has been lost.
12 The vine has withered,
and the fig tree wilts away.
In fact, every tree of the field has withered—
pomegranate, date palm, and apple tree.[f]
And in the same way, the people's joy and gladness
has withered[g] too.

---

a 1:8 Sadly, many in the church today have left their first love of the heavenly Bridegroom, Jesus Christ.

b 1:9 That is, "grain offerings and wine offerings." See Lev. 2.

c 1:10 The ground is personified and pictured as mourning over its loss of crops.

d 1:10 Or "the new wine is ashamed."

e 1:10 God's blessing of the land was traditionally found in the abundance of grain, wine, and oil. These three blessings had been removed from the land.

f 1:12 See Song. 2:3.

g 1:12 The Hebrew word for "withered" can also be translated "ashamed," "confused," "disappointed." As believers, our joy withers when we allow our own ideas and circumstances to replace the joy of the Lord.

A Call to Repentance

13 You priests, put on *sackcloth* and weep.
You ministers who serve at the altar, mourn and wail!
Go, spend the night in the temple,
you servants of my God,
because there is no more grain or wine offerings
to bring to the house of your God.
14 *Declare* a holy fast.[a]
Call a solemn assembly.
Gather the leaders and all the people of the land
to the house of YAHWEH your God.
Cry out *with all your hearts* to YAHWEH!

The Day of YAHWEH

15 How awful that time will be!
Look! The day of YAHWEH[b] is certainly coming—
the day when the Divine Destroyer brings
destruction.[c]
16 Has not the food supply[d] been cut off
before our very eyes?
Have not the joyful celebrations been silenced

---

a 1:14 Or "Sanctify [set apart as holy] a fast."

b 1:15 The Hebrew concept of "the day of YAHWEH" is not a twenty-four-hour day but a period of time when YAHWEH rises to judge. The phrase "the day of YAHWEH" is found five times in Joel (1:15; 2:1, 11, 31; 3:14) and another eighteen times in the Old Testament.

c 1:15 Or "destruction from Shaddai." There is a play on words in the Hebrew text that is diminished in an English translation. The word for "destruction" (Hb. *shod*) resembles the word *Shaddai*. One of the many possible translations for *Shaddai* is "the Divine Destroyer." For additional translations that show more of the depth of meaning in this incredible name of our God, see Gen. 17:1 and second footnote; 28:3.

d 1:16 That is, the food brought to the temple as grain offerings and sacrifices.

in the temple of our God?[a]
17 The seeds shrivel under the *dry* clods.[b]
The storehouses are empty;
the barns are *bare and* broken down
because the harvest has disappeared.
18 How *loudly* the cattle groan
because they have no pasture!
The herds wander bewildered.
Not even the flocks of sheep are able to graze.
19 YAHWEH, I cry out to you *with all my heart*,
for fire[c] has devoured the open pastures,
and flame has scorched all the trees of the field.
20 The sources of water have run dry
and fire has devoured the pasturelands,
leaving the wild animals panting loudly for you.

---

a 1:16 These are the fellowship offerings or peace offerings that were associated with the joy and gladness of worship in the temple (see Deut. 12:7). These offerings were eaten by the worshipers.

b 1:17 Or "beneath their shovels." The meaning of the Hebrew is uncertain since three of the four words of this line are used nowhere else in the Hebrew text. The word for "clods" may also mean "shovels." The Qumran manuscript 4QXXII[c] reads "the heifers decay in [their] stalls," while the Septuagint reads "the heifers stomp in their stalls." The seed under the dry clods can also be seen in believers today who have the "seed" of God's Word within them (1 Peter 1:23), but it may remain beneath the dirt (clod) of our flesh. God's Word must penetrate our hearts and pierce the flesh with its truth.

c 1:19 It is possible that the "fire" is a metaphor for the severe drought that covered the land.

The Day of Yahweh Is Coming

2 [a] Blow the shofar in Zion,[b]
sound the alarm on my mountain of holiness!
Shake the people awake,
for the day of Yahweh is coming.
Yes, it is almost here.

---

a 2:1 Chapter 2 was written as an ambiguously poetical description of a coming army. Is it meant to be taken literally as locusts or figuratively with application to believers today? Possibly both, for all the prophets of the Old Testament have mysteries and depths to their prophecies that take us beyond the literal meaning. The traditional understanding of this chapter is that it discusses a literal advancing army of locusts, perhaps as a metaphor to describe an army coming to invade the land. However, this army is coming from the north (see v. 20), while the locusts swarmed over the land coming from the south, so this may hint that the subject is not a literal army of locusts. There were enemies to Israel's north that could be part of the meaning of this chapter. Either way, it appears that an allegory is embedded within this chapter that the Holy Spirit wants to reveal to us. Joel's army is the army of Yahweh (see v. 11), coming in the last days as holy awakeners. They will be those who bring the dawn of a new day. Both literal and allegorical interpretive models should be recognized as valid when considering this chapter.

b 2:1 Although Zion has become synonymous with Israel, Zion is more than a location; it is a realm where God is enthroned (see Pss. 2:4–6; 87:5). Zion is a synonym for the people of God, the dwelling place of his Spirit (see Pss. 9:11; 74:2; 76:2; Heb. 12:22–24). The perfection of beauty is in Mount Zion, where the light of God shines (see Ps. 50:2). Perfected praise rises to the Lord in this place of perfect rest (see Ps. 65:1–2). The Mountain of Zion is where the Lord is known in his greatness (see Ps. 99:2; Isa. 12:4–6). It is the hope of all the afflicted (see Ps. 102:16–22; Isa. 14:32; 51:11). Although the precise etymology of the Hebrew word *Zion* is uncertain, it may be related to a verb meaning "to surround" or "to protect." In its noun form, *Zion* would mean "a refuge," a fitting description for the place where God dwells. The New Testament concept is that Zion is a designation of the church of Jesus Christ that is seated in the heavenly realm (see Eph. 2:6) and is "a city that stands on a hilltop" (Matt. 5:14).

[2]It will be a day of darkness and gloom,
a black and cloudy day.[a]
As the dawning *light* spreads across the mountains,[b]
so will a great[c] and powerful people advance,[d]
an army such as has never been seen before
and such as will never be seen again,
not even in all the ages to come.[e]
[3]Fire blazes before them,
and behind them the flame consumes.[f]

---

a 2:2 God comes down from heaven with thick clouds of darkness, which brings dread to the hearts of people. See Ex. 19:16–20; Ps. 18:9–10; Isa. 60:1–2.

b 2:2 The simplest and most literal meaning is that an army is destroying whatever is in its path and leaving a wake of devastation behind. Yet Joel said that the day of Yahweh will be both a day of blackness and a day of dawning light. Joel compared a coming army to the dawn. How is their coming like the dawn? The dawn comes slowly. First the purple hues are seen in the eastern sky. Then purple gives way to red, to orange, then the full light of day breaks forth. And so it will be in the last days as God's awakeners walk in his paths. They will emerge in a time of darkness shining like the dawn (see Prov. 4:18; Song. 6:10). The dawning light hits the top of the mountains first; then it spreads down the slope, bringing the light of a new day. So are the people of God shining in the high places and spreading out to touch the world in its darkness. The Hebrew word for "dawn" has a homonym that means "blackness." The blackness of night is broken by the dawning of a people who arise and shine (see Isa. 60:1–3). Dawnmakers are coming. They will not wait for a new day; they will bring it (see Isa. 58:8).

c 2:2 Or "abundant."

d 2:2 Note that this coming army is made up of a great number of mighty *people*, not locusts.

e 2:2 Or literally "until the years of generation and generation." The coming "army" of awakeners will be unlike anything seen in history.

f 2:3 The fire of God surrounds these holy awakeners. They have come out of the fire and go into the fire. Our God is the God who answers the cries for awakening with his holy fire (see 1 Kings 18:24).

Before their eyes, the earth is like the garden of
Eden,[a]
and behind them they leave a devastated[b]
wilderness.[c]
Nothing escapes them *unscathed*.
4 Their appearance is like horses *prepared for battle*;
like war horses, they charge ahead.[d]
5 They rumble like war chariots;
they leap over the mountaintops.[e]
They devour the land,
with the sound of a wildfire devouring stubble.[f]

---

a 2:3 Or "The garden of Eden, the land before their face." Compared to the devastation the army is leaving behind them, the unspoiled land in front of them is like the garden of Eden, a virtual paradise. But viewed allegorically, there is a people with paradise before their face. They view a restoration of all things (see Acts 3:21) ahead of them—the garden of Bliss (*Eden* means "bliss," "pleasure," "delight"). They live for the pleasure of God and have a vision of bringing heaven on earth.

b 2:3 Or "astonished."

c 2:3 The soldiers leave devastation behind them in their wake. Like Jeremiah, they will be called to "to uproot and demolish, to destroy and dismantle" (Jer. 1:10).

d 2:4 They are not horses nor people on horses; rather, these warriors are like horses in some way. A horse can be a metaphor or picture of the overcomer, the victorious believer who has been "harnessed" by the Lord. The faithful lover of God (Shulamite) was likewise compared to a horse (see Song. 1:9). Jesus will return with an army of his saints riding on horses (see Rev. 19:14). See Job 39:19–25; Rev. 9:7.

e 2:5 These awakeners become like their Lord: they leap over mountaintops (see Song. 2:8). Mountains can symbolize the barriers that separate a believer from intimacy with Christ (e.g., fear, doubt, compromise). They will leap over what many stumble over. The Hebrew word for "leap" is the same word used to describe David's dancing before the ark (see 1 Chron. 15:29).

f 2:5 The traditions of men and the works of the flesh are like stubble (see 1 Cor. 3:11–15).

They are a mighty people
who are prepared for the battle.
6 At the sight of this army, nations panic,
all their faces grow pale.[a]
7 They press forward like mighty warriors,
and scale walls like *elite* soldiers,[b]
each marching straight ahead,
not swerving from his path.[c]
8 They never jostle each other,[d]
for each one stays on his own path.
They *storm the city* and burst through its defenses.[e]
Together they are unstoppable.[f]
9 They rush against the city
and scale its walls.
They climb up into the houses
and enter through the windows like thieves.

A Vision of the Day of Yahweh

10 As that army advances, the earth shakes,
and the heavens tremble.[g]
The sun and moon grow dark,[h]
and the stars no longer shine.

---

a 2:6 Or "all their faces gather beauty."

b 2:7 Or "like men of war." Nothing is insurmountable to them. Man-made walls will not keep them back. See Josh. 6:5; 2 Sam. 22:30; Ezek. 8:7–9; Eph. 2:14.

c 2:7 Or "not abandoning his path." The picture presented is that of a mighty, cohesive army with each soldier fulfilling his assigned task.

d 2:8 That is, they do not get in each other's way. They do not compete with others.

e 2:8 Or literally "They fall upon spears," which is interpreted as a synecdoche for bursting through the city's defenses.

f 2:8 Or "They do not break ranks."

g 2:10 See Hag. 2:6–7; Heb. 12:26–27.

h 2:10 See Mic. 3:6.

[11]YAHWEH's voice thunders[a]
as he leads his valiant troops.
Numberless are the mighty ones
who obey his commands.[b]
Yes, the day of YAHWEH is great and astonishing![c]
Who can withstand it?

A Call to Repentance

[12]"But it's not too late," declares YAHWEH.
"Come back to me now with all your heart,
with fasting, weeping, and mourning.[d]
[13]Tearing your clothes in sorrow is not enough—
tear open your hearts!"[e]
Come back to YAHWEH your God,
for he is gracious[f] *to welcome you home*

---

a 2:11 See Ex. 19:16; Job 37:4–5; Pss. 18:13; 29:3–9; Amos 1:2.

b 2:11 Or "because the operation of his words is irresistible."

c 2:11 Or "fearful."

d 2:12 This section (2:12–17) is the most significant and pivotal portion of Joel's passionate plea for the people to return to YAHWEH. They must (1) know that God will receive and restore them (see v. 13); (2) come back to God's paths "with all your heart" (v. 12); (3) come with fasting (see v. 12); (4) come with weeping (see v. 12); (5) come with mourning over their sins (see v. 12); (6) tear open their hearts (see v. 13); (7) trust in the goodness, mercy, and forgiveness of YAHWEH (see vv. 13–14); and (8) consecrate their hearts afresh to God (see vv. 15–17).

e 2:13 Coming to God with a tender, teachable heart is the only way to advance in God's kingdom. It is not a matter of external duties and works but of turning from sin in the innermost part of a person's life to embrace the goodness and kindness of God that brings us to repentance. We experience repentance as God's gracious work of kindness to welcome us back to his heart. Turning to God in repentance is by no means only an Old Testament truth. At least nine times, the New Testament teaches repentance as the way of restoring the heart of a penitent one.

f 2:13 Or "kindhearted."

and compassionate[a] *to embrace you.*
Yahweh is slow to anger
and so rich in extravagant love *for you.*[b]
He is always ready to forgive and cancel judgment.
14 Who knows if he will not turn around and show pity,
leaving behind a blessing.[c]
Then you can bring offerings of grain and wine
to be presented to Yahweh your God.

15 Blow the shofar in Zion!
Call for a fast
and proclaim a solemn assembly.
16 Gather the people together,
and prepare them for a sacred meeting.[d]
From the oldest to the youngest,
assemble the community,
even the nursing infants.
Let the newly wedded bride and bridegroom
come from their chamber.
17 *With everyone gathered in the courtyard,*
the priests, the ministers of Yahweh,
must stand weeping between the portico
and the altar *of burnt offering.*

---

a 2:13 Or "full of mercy." This is the Hebrew word *racham*, which has a homonym meaning "womb." God has "womb-love" for us, as though he carries us within his innermost being.

b 2:13 Or "abounding in loyal love." The list of divine attributes found in this verse reveals the heart of Yahweh, displaying the God of the Old Testament as the same gracious, loving, merciful God we find in the New Testament revealed by Jesus Christ. See Ex. 34:6; Neh. 9:17; Pss. 86:15; 103:8; 145:8; Jonah 4:2. Both Judaism and Christianity set forth these divine attributes as the ideal pattern for humanity.

c 2:14 This blessing has many components, but in the context, it is the blessing of abundant harvests.

d 2:16 Or "sanctify the community."

Let them *face the sanctuary and intercede*,
saying, "Spare your people! Have pity, YAHWEH!
Do not expose your very own people
to the contempt and sarcasm of the nations.
Why give the nations cause to say,
'Where is their God now?' "

YAHWEH's Answer

18 Then YAHWEH showed his great love for the land
and *showered* compassion upon his people.[a]
19 YAHWEH answered their cry and said,
"Behold, now *your fast is over.*
I am providing you with
plenty of wheat, wine, and olive oil[b]
until you are satisfied.
Never again will I make you
an object of scorn among the nations.
20 I will remove your northern *enemy* far from you
and drive him into a dry, desolate land,
with his front ranks to the Dead Sea[c]
and his rear guard to the Mediterranean Sea.[d]
I will destroy them for their boastful deeds,
and people will smell the stench of their dead bodies."
Truly, he has done great things!

---

a 2:18 God would bring about a complete reversal of the trauma that his people had experienced. What he promised to do for Israel, he will do for you. When you turn to him, he will restore his blessings over your life and shower you with his mercy.

b 2:19 The Qumran manuscript 4QXXII[c] inserts here the words "and you will eat."

c 2:20 Or "eastern sea."

d 2:20 Or "western sea."

Joel's Vision of Plenty

21 My land, do not fear, for *your restoration has come*!
Be glad and rejoice, *you people*,
for YAHWEH has done marvelous things *for you.*
22 Animals of the field, do not be afraid,
for the pastures of the wilderness are green again,
the trees bear their fruit,
and the vine and fig tree yield their richness.[a]
23 Children of Zion, be glad!
Celebrate *the mighty acts of* YAHWEH your God,
for he has given you a teacher of righteousness
whose teaching is like the refreshing spring rains.[b]
And he will pour down the rains for you,
the spring and autumn rains[c] as before.

---

a 2:22 Or "give their strength."

b 2:23 Or "he has given you the early [spring] rain for your vindication." Examining the homonyms of the Hebrew words used here is fascinating. The Hebrew word *mowreh* can be used for "early rain" or for "teacher." Hebraic thought often refers to teaching using the symbol of rain that falls from heaven and refreshes the heart (see 1 Kings 8:36). Jerome's Latin Vulgate, which may have incorporated readings from even earlier manuscripts of Joel, reads *doctorem iustitiae*, "teacher of righteousness." Qumran manuscripts, the Targumic paraphrase, and the Masoretic Text likewise follow in translating *'et-hammowreh lisdaqah* as "teacher of righteousness," a Messianic designation. Jewish scholars often note that "a teacher in the end time would come and answer all questions"; this "was a quite familiar conception in Rabbinic Judaism." See Gert Jeremias, *Der Lehrer der Gerechtigkeit*, Studien zur Umwelt des Neuen Testaments 2 (Göttingen: Vandenhoeck & Ruprecht, 1963), 287.

c 2:23 Or "early and latter rains." God promises to teach us righteousness, which was the theme of Paul's treatise to the Romans. Our teacher of righteousness is Jesus Christ, who transfers his righteousness to those who believe.

Yahweh's Promise of Blessing

24"The threshing floors will be full of grain,
the pits beside the presses[a]
will overflow with new wine and fresh oil.
25I will make up for the years
the swarms of locusts ruined your harvest—
the hopping-locusts, the destroying-locusts,
and the cutting-locusts—
my great army that I sent against you.
26You will eat to your heart's content[b] and be satisfied.
You will gloriously praise the name of Yahweh your God,
who has treated you so wonderfully.
And never will my people be despised again.
27Then, Israel, you will know without question
that I am dwelling among you.
I am Yahweh your God, and no one else.
I say again: no more will I surrender my people to shame."

The Outpouring of God's Spirit

28[c]"Then afterward, I will pour out my Spirit[d] on everyone.[e]
Your sons and your daughters will *boldly* prophesy, your
elderly will have *supernatural* dreams, and your youth will

---

a 2:24 Although most translations use the word *vats*, these storage units were actually holes or pits dug into rocks with their sides plastered so that wine and olive oil could be collected. These pits were always located near the wine/olive presses.

b 2:26 Or literally "eating you will eat."

c 2:28 Verses 28–32 comprise Joel ch. 3 in the Hebrew Bible. Virtually every English Bible includes these verses with ch. 2.

d 2:28 The Hebrew verb for "pour out" implies an abundant pouring, an entire, complete, total pouring out until everyone experiences the Spirit of God. "My Spirit" could also be translated "my breath."

e 2:28 Or "all flesh."

experience *ecstatic* visions. 29And I will even pour out my
Spirit in those days upon every servant, both male and
female.[a]

30"And I will display *amazing* wonders[b] in the heavens
and on the earth, blood and fire and columns of smoke.
31The sun will be darkened, and the moon will appear as
red as blood. *These events will occur* before the great and
awesome day of YAHWEH comes. 32And everyone who sin-
cerely worships YAHWEH will be saved.[c] For in Mount Zion
and in Jerusalem there will be a remnant who are spared,
as I, YAHWEH, have promised.[d] They will be the chosen
survivors whom I, YAHWEH, will call."

God Will Judge the Nations

3[e] "Behold! In those days,
when I restore the fortunes[f] of Judah and Jerusalem,
2 I will gather all the nations together.
I will bring them to the Valley of YAHWEH's Judgment.[g]
I will take them to court there
for all they have done against Israel—

---

a 2:29 See Ezek. 36:26–27; 39:29; Acts 2:16–21. Peter quoted this passage from Joel and applied it to the blessings of God's Spirit poured out on the day of Pentecost. The entirety of Joel's prophecy remains to be fulfilled, but the Spirit is now being poured out around the world.

b 2:30 Or "signs" or "miracles."

c 2:32 Or "all who call upon the name of YAHWEH will be delivered." To call upon God's name is an act of prayer and worship.

d 2:32 See Isa. 4:2–6; Obad. 17.

e 3:1 Starting with v. 1, this begins ch. 4 of Joel in the Hebrew Bible.

f 3:1 Or "when I turn the turning" or "bring back the captives."

g 3:2 Or "the Valley of Jehoshaphat." *Jehoshaphat* means "YAHWEH judges." This is the symbolic name for the valley where YAHWEH judges the nations. It is also called the "Valley of Decision." Tradition locates the Valley of Jehoshaphat near Jerusalem, between the temple and the Mount of Olives. It's known today as the Kidron Valley.

my people and my inheritance.
I will execute judgment upon them
because they have scattered my people among the nations[a]
and divided my land among themselves.
3 They cast lots for my people
and sold them into slavery.
They traded a boy to pay for a prostitute
and trafficked a girl for a drink of wine.[b]
4 And what have you done to me, Tyre and Sidon
and all you regions of Philistia?[c]
Are you trying to take revenge on me?
If you are, I will swiftly and speedily pay you back
and return your revenge so that it lands squarely on your own heads.
5 For you have stolen my silver and gold
and carried off my valuable treasures into your temples.[d]
6 You have sold the people of Judah and Jerusalem to the Greeks[e]
to be taken *as slaves* far from their homeland.
7 Behold! I will rouse them to return
and come back from the places
to which you have sold them.
I will do to you
the very thing that you have done to them.
8 Your sons and daughters will be sold *as slaves*

---

a 3:2 This is likely a reference to the deportations of 597 and 586 BC. See Ezek. 21:23–27; Obad. 11–14; Nah. 3:10.

b 3:3 This pathetic situation reveals the cheapening of human life.

c 3:4 Tyre, Sidon, and Philistia were neighboring coastal lands of Israel and Judah.

d 3:5 Or "for your palaces." See 1 Sam. 5:2; 31:10.

e 3:6 Or "the Ionians," the ancient name of the Greeks, descendants of Javan (see Gen. 10:2 and the fourth footnote). See also Amos 1:9.

to the sons of Judah,
who in turn will sell them to the Sabaeans,[a]
who live in a distant land.
I, YAHWEH, have spoken!"

A Time for War

[9] Proclaim this message among the nations:
"Prepare for war!"[b]
Awaken the champions!
Let all you soldiers gather, advance, and march.
[10] Hammer your plowshares into swords
and your pruning hooks into spears.[c]
Let the weakling say, "I am a champion!"[d]
[11] Hurry[e] and *join the battle*,
all you surrounding nations.
Come and assemble there.

YAHWEH, send down your champions, your warring *angels*!

YAHWEH's Valley of Judgment

[12] "Let the nations stir themselves up
and march to the Valley of YAHWEH's Judgment.[f]

---

a 3:8 The Sabaeans were Arab traders from Sheba in southwest Arabia. See 1 Kings 10:1; Job 6:19; Jer. 6:20; Luke 11:31.

b 3:9 Or "Sanctify war!" There is a time for war (see Eccl. 3:8). God was summoning the nations to their destruction as his judgment for how they had treated his people, Israel.

c 3:10 This is the reversal of the commands in Isa. 2:4 and Mic. 4:3.

d 3:10 Or "I am a mighty warrior!" See Zech. 12:8.

e 3:11 The Hebrew word is a hapax legomenon, which some have translated as "Gather" or "Rally [to help]."

f 3:12 Or "the Valley of Jehoshaphat." See v. 2 and the first note there.

There I will sit in judgment
on all the surrounding nations.[a]

13 "Swing the sickle,
for the harvest is ripe *for judgment.*
Come and tread *the grapes of wrath.*
The winepress is full
and the vats are overflowing[b]
for their wickedness is so great!"

14 Multitudes! *So many* multitudes
in the Valley of Decision!
For the day of YAHWEH is near
in the Valley of the Verdict.

The Day of YAHWEH

15 The sun and moon grow dark,
and the stars no longer shine.[c]
16 YAHWEH roars from Zion,
and his voice thunders from Jerusalem;
heaven and earth tremble.
But YAHWEH will be a shelter for his people,
a *faithful* fortress for Israel.

The Glorious Future of Israel

17 "Then you will know that I am YAHWEH your God,
who dwells in Zion, my holy mountain.
Jerusalem will be a sanctuary,

---

a 3:12 Although the nations gather to attack Judah, God's purpose is to bring them to judgment and destruction.

b 3:13 Or "Go in, tread [the grapes], for the winepress is full. Cause the vats to overflow" (LXX). Both the winepress and the sickle are biblical metaphors for God's judgment (punishment) of the nations. See Isa. 17:5; 63:1–3; Matt. 13:39; Rev. 14:14–20.

c 3:15 See Joel 2:10.

and foreigners will never conquer it again.
18 A time is coming when the mountains
will drip with new wine
and the hills will flow with milk,[a]
and all the *arid* streambeds of Judah
will run with water *year-round.*
A fountain will spring from Yahweh's temple
and descend to the valley of acacia trees.[b]

19 "Egypt will become a desert
and Edom a desolate wilderness
because of the *atrocious* acts of violence
they committed against the people of Judah,
whose innocent blood they shed in their land.
20–21 I will avenge their blood and not spare the guilty,
but Judah will be inhabited forever,
Jerusalem from generation to generation,
and Yahweh will dwell in Zion."

---

a 3:18 That is, the mountains will be covered with freshly planted vineyards, which will produce grapes for new wine, and the hills will graze many flocks and cattle, which will supply the people with an abundance of milk. See Amos 9:13.

b 3:18 The valley mentioned here is Acacia or Shittim (*shittim* means "acacia bushes"). This was the location of the last camp Israel made before crossing the Jordan River and entering the promised land (see Josh. 2:1 and second footnote; 3:1). Joel was prophesying an outpouring of water from the Temple Mount that will flow into the Jordan Valley and beyond, watering even the desert (see Ezek. 47:1–12).

THE BOOK OF

AMOS

The Prophet of Justice

BroadStreet
PUBLISHING

AMOS

Introduction

AT A GLANCE

Author: Amos the prophet

Audience: The Northern Kingdom of Israel

Date: Mid-700s BC, during the reigns of Kings Jeroboam II of Israel and Uzziah of Judah

Type of Literature: Prophecy

Major Themes: Righteousness; justice; economic oppression of the poor; true and false prophecy; religious blending (syncretism); the responsibility of leaders; the day of YAHWEH; Bethel; Samaria; seeing Jesus in the book

Outline:

- I. Superscription: author and setting — 1:1–2
- II. Judgment on the nations, including Israel — 1:3–2:16
  - a. Judgment on three gentile nations — 1:3–10
  - b. Judgment on three nations related to Israel — 1:11–2:3
  - c. Judgment on Judah — 2:4–5
  - d. Judgment on Israel — 2:6–16
    - i. Israel's injustice, profane worship, and covenant breaking — 2:6–12
    - ii. Crushing of a rebellious culture — 2:13–16
- III. Oracles against Israel — 3:1–5:17
  - a. Divine legal indictment against the chosen covenant people — 3:1–15
  - b. Judgment on an arrogant, unrepentant people — 4:1–13

i. Condemnation of oppressive, upper-class Israelite women — 4:1–3
ii. No repentance after punishments — 4:4–13
c. Judgment on an unjust, oppressive people — 5:1–17
i. Funeral lament — 5:1–3
ii. Exhortation to seek life in God (i) — 5:4–6
iii. Indictment of social, legal, and economic injustices — 5:7–13
iv. Exhortation to seek life in God (ii) — 5:14–15
v. Mourning for the loss of prosperity — 5:16–17
IV. The day of Yahweh: visions of divine judgment and an ultimate blessing — 5:18–9:15
a. A woe-oracle: misplaced hope in the coming day of Yahweh — 5:18–27
b. A woe-oracle: indictment of Israel's complacent pride — 6:1–14
c. Visions of divine retribution — 7:1–9:10
i. Judgments averted: a swarm of locusts and a devastating fire — 7:1–6
ii. Inevitable judgments: the plumb line, the basket of fruit, Yahweh by the altar — 7:7–9:10
d. The blessing of the day of Yahweh: the restoration of the dynasty of David and the return of Israel to the promised land — 9:11–15

ABOUT THE BOOK OF AMOS

Amos is arguably the most strident and outspoken of the prophetic books. It is classified as a "minor" prophet but only because of the book's brevity, not as a reflection of the power and timelessness of its message.

This book has eternal significance because every civilization that achieves prosperity runs the risk of losing touch with its foundational principles, ensuring its eventual downfall. As it turns out, Amos was correct in his warnings. A generation after his prophecies, the "ten lost tribes of Israel" were wiped out by the Assyrians, never to be heard from again.

A nation can only endure if it continues to cultivate the values of justice and righteousness, without which its religious activity is a sham.

> Spare me the monotonous melodies of your
> "worship."
> I don't want to hear your strumming guitars
> anymore.
> It's just noise to me.
> However, I delight in
> a land where justice flows like a river
> and where true righteousness rolls like a steady
> flowing stream. (Amos 5:23–24)

Amos would have no respect for those of us religious insiders who perhaps insist that our faith has no place in the public square or the marketplace. It was his very faith that drove him to confront the corrupt leaders of both.

PURPOSE

Amos saw his vocation as agricultural, not religious, but he felt compelled by God to call the leaders of the Northern Kingdom of Israel to account even though he was from the Southern Kingdom of Judah. What emerged is powerful preaching of righteousness and justice in the face of corruption and decadence—both political and spiritual. Peering over the border to the north at Israel, Amos observed a wealthy nation that was overripe and slipping into decadence, losing touch with its own covenant identity, and he intended to do something about it. He left his hometown of Tekoa and embarked on a scorching speaking tour of his neighbor to the north, sending leaders running for cover and asking him to go back home and prophesy there instead.

The initial oracles given to Amos by God concern the surrounding pagan nations as well as Israel and Judah (1:3–2:16), and they effectively enhance the impact of Amos' central purpose: calling the rebellious nation of Israel to account. This opening passage contains eight powerful indictments and accompanying catastrophic judgments against a succession of godless nations, the final two of which are Judah and Israel. What is significant here is the ethnic, religious, and cultural identity of these nations, considered sequentially, along with the consistently repeated and ominous refrain throughout: "For the three terrible crimes of . . . no, make that four" (1:3, 6, 9, 11, 13; 2:1, 4, 6).

The first three indictments are leveled against Aram (and her city Damascus), Philistia (and her city Gaza), and Phoenicia (and her city Tyre). These nations were all culturally, ethnically, and religiously pagan, three of the many gentile territories in the geographic vicinity of the covenant people of Israel.

However, the next three nations Amos condemned were Edom, Ammon, and Moab, which may be designated as "family nations" related to Israel. These all originated from the wider family of the patriarchs who received the covenant of promise from Yahweh himself: Edom was founded by the descendants of Esau, the twin brother of Jacob, father of the twelve sons who formed the tribal nucleus of the nation of Israel (Gen. 25:19–34; 27; 32–33). The nations of Ammon and Moab were founded, respectively, by the descendants of the two sons of Lot, the nephew of the patriarch Abraham. Ammon (also known as Ben-Ammi) and Moab were born to the two daughters of Lot as the result of an incestuous union with their father (Gen. 19:30–38). The final two nations to be indicted were

Judah and Israel. And the most detailed condemnation by far was reserved for Israel (Amos 2:6–16).

The ordering of the successive condemnation of all these nations is significant. Amos' original audience would have been well aware that the condemnation began with rank "outsiders," the pagan gentile nations of Aram, Philistia, and Phoenicia. Then, as the indictments of Edom, Ammon, and Moab followed, the Israelite audience would have begun to feel uncomfortable since these nations had "blood connections" with the covenant people of God. Then the final manifestation of divine judgment fell upon them—first of all Judah, then Israel. It is hard to see how this approach could have been the result of anything other than deliberate intent or purpose.

What follows in the prophecy, right up until almost the very end, is a devastating series of judgment oracles designed to expose the very core of Israel's rebellion against their covenant God, Yahweh, resulting in a terrifying sequence of punishments that functioned essentially as covenant curses. It is, in fact, only right at the end of Amos' prophecy (9:11–15) that God reveals his ultimate promise of forgiveness, renewal, and restoration for his wayward people.

Amos highlights Yahweh's goodness as a God of righteousness and justice alongside his resultant judgment—judgment that has no favorites. He does not pass over those who think they are safe as religious "insiders" and yet persist in practicing oppression and injustice.

The Lion still roars from Zion (1:2), but that "roar" will ultimately be replaced by a gentle yet powerful expression of divine compassion, mercy, and forgiveness directed toward the people of God. Eventually, the undying, eternal fulfillment of God's covenant promises will be realized.

AUTHOR AND AUDIENCE

Amos called himself a sheep breeder and fig dresser from the town of Tekoa, near the border between Judah (south) and Israel (north). Obviously not a peasant farmer, Amos spoke with great confidence, potency, and authority, as someone used to giving, not receiving, orders. He clearly saw himself as a peer with the leadership of Israel and had no fear of them (7:12–17).

It is important for the modern reader to understand the geography and history of the time of Amos. The united kingdom of Israel of Saul, David, and Solomon had split in two some two hundred years earlier. The Northern Kingdom (ruled from Samaria) retained the name Israel, and the Southern Kingdom (ruled from Jerusalem) went by the name of its most powerful tribe, Judah. Sometimes the prophets referred to both nations together, collectively, as Israel/Jacob, and sometimes the same label meant only the Northern Kingdom. Amos was from the south and prophesied in the north.

The apocryphal (not considered Scripture by Jews or Christians) book *Lives of the Prophets* suggests that Amos may have been murdered by Northern Kingdom priests and buried in Tekoa. But we are unable to know this with any certainty.

Amos' command of language is on par with any biblical author, as he expressed himself with exceptionally bold clarity. This suggests not only a high level of education but also the pragmatic wisdom of someone accustomed to leadership and public speaking. No one who heard him could have any doubt about what he was trying to say. Amos wastes no time going for the throat. It is unclear whether Amos spoke these things and others wrote them down or if he both wrote and spoke these words.

The original audience was without a doubt the people and leaders of the Northern Kingdom of Israel. Later, during the Babylonian captivity, the rabbis saw the eternal value of the book and included it with other prophetic books, which became known as the Twelve.

Amos is one of the most chillingly relevant books in the Bible. Just because the stock market may be doing well does not mean that our civilization is safe from collapse from within. May your reading of Amos spur you to speak out boldly against injustice and corruption wherever you find them, even if you find them within yourself.

MAJOR THEMES

Righteousness. The Hebrew root for "righteousness" is *tsaddiq*. It is all about uprightness and integrity, living one's life above reproach both privately and publicly, literally "walking tall." It is an especially important quality for those who lead a society, whether in religion, politics, or the marketplace. When people lose trust in the leadership of a nation, destruction is around the corner. The lust for power without righteousness leads to the disintegration of the very foundation on which a nation is built.

Justice. *Shapat*, the Hebrew root for "justice," is all about judging and discerning with an unusually stubborn pursuit of pure truth, totally free of bias and spin. Amos had an innate gift for sensing when this essential insight was missing. He came down hard on those who perverted justice (5:9–12).

Economic Oppression of the Poor. One powerful expression of the lack of righteousness and justice in Israel in the mid-700s BC was that of economic oppression and exploitation of the poor in the land. The book shows several instances of this throughout: 2:6–7; 3:9; 4:1; 5:11–12; 8:4–6. One specific illustration of this abuse was the practice of making debt-slaves of the poor (2:6). When corruption follows prosperity, the poor are the ones who suffer most. Usury, the practice of charging high interest on financial loans, has been a demon lurking under banking and lending tables since the dawn of time. Our word *mortgage* (think *mortality*) comes from the French for "death pledge" or "a pledge until you die."

Corruption is also a powerful subset of the practice of economic oppression. The marketplace was rigged (8:4–6). The currency was manipulated. Diminishing the buying power of the public through dishonest weights and measures or debasing/inflating the currency is a trick that has been played by those "regulating" the exchange of goods and services since the first marketplaces were established deep in our human past. It has become more sophisticated in our day, but clearly, it is still going on.

True and False Prophecy. "YAHWEH says this" is a common phrase in Amos (and much of prophetic literature). The prophets saw themselves as a pipe through which the living water of YAHWEH's word would flow out to the people. In modern usage, the word *prophet* has deteriorated into "fortune teller." The original Hebrew word *nabi'*, in contrast, suggests a fountain through which the word of YAHWEH springs forth. The prophet spoke a message for his own present time, often with eternal and future implications. Biblical prophets saw themselves, literally, as mouthpieces for the Almighty, speaking to the issues of the day.

However, Amos' prophecy has clear instances where God condemned the Israelites for the emergence of false prophets—impostors—who claimed to be the mouthpieces of YAHWEH but, in fact, were not. They were only concerned with their fabricated messages that reflected their own selfish agendas (2:11–12). A particularly powerful divine indictment and subsequent punishment were leveled against the false prophet and priest Amaziah, who challenged and then dismissed Amos as a voice that could not be taken seriously (7:10–17). In the end, God promised to withdraw his word entirely from his people via a famine of the word of God; that is, there would be no more genuine prophets of Yahweh available to convey divine revelation to his people (8:11–12).

Biblical Hebrew does not have the same past-present-future verbal system used in English. Rather, the two main tenses are complete (perfect) and incomplete (imperfect). The people of ancient Israel did not think of things in terms of a timeline progression, as English speakers do, but rather in terms of being either finished or in process. The beautiful linguistic dance between complete and incomplete was the playing field of the prophets, brought to its highest apex in the book of Isaiah, and sheds light on the words of Jesus, who on the cross spoke forth, “It is finished” (John 19:30).

Religious Blending (Syncretism). Israel had recently conquered neighboring peoples and had tolerated or even incorporated the worship of their gods. The technical term for such religious duplicity is *syncretism*, and Amos contains several references to such idolatrous worship by both Judah and Israel (Amos 2:4; 5:25–26; 8:13–14). There is only one creation and thus one Creator (4:13; 9:5–6), and any diffusion or fragmentation of worship among many gods and their images (idols) leads to cultural confusion, incoherence, decline, and eventual erosion of any society’s foundational principles. These principles were embodied in Israel’s unifying covenant relationship and its high standards, with the one Creator-God, Yahweh, who cannot be represented by any graven image.

The Responsibility of Leaders. With great authority comes great responsibility to care for all people, including the poor. Israel also had a special calling from Yahweh, who brought her out of slavery in Egypt (2:10). With this empowering calling, responsibility increased even more.

Neglect of such responsibility, thus, had crushing consequences. It was about these gathering storm clouds of consequence that Amos was warning the people, much as his words warn us today. Examples of flawed and corrupt leadership in Amos include 3:9–10; 4:4–5; 5:7–10, 15; 6:1–8; 7:10–17.

The Day of Yahweh. Most of us who believe in God think, to this day, that the day of Yahweh (5:18) will be a good day for us and perhaps a bad day for people we don't like. This is what the people of Amos' day believed, but the prophet issued an alarming woe-oracle against those Israelites who longed for such a day. The Israelites were not as blameless as they thought; the day of Yahweh might not be as good for them as they self-righteously assumed.

However, notwithstanding these observations, this final major section of the book (5:18–9:15) makes it very clear that the day of Yahweh has two distinctive and contrasting sides: it will be a day of judgment and a day of blessing. To be sure, the negative element of judgment—textually speaking—predominates from 5:18 right through 9:10. Then the final verses of the prophecy (9:11–15) constitute the glorious climactic manifestation of that day, where the positive element shines through—namely, the realization and fulfillment of God's covenant blessing to pardon, renew, and restore the wayward people of Israel to their land. It is a promise that will never fail because such a restoration, initially fulfilled in a literal return to the promised land after exile, will find its ultimate consummation in the eternal kingdom of God. See the final section of the introduction, Seeing Jesus in the Book, for further comments on this theme.

Reading Amos forces us to be watchful for corruption and dishonesty in our own lives and to ask ourselves if we are perpetuating or benefitting from rigged systems of economic or political injustice. If you hire people, are you taking good care of your employees or just getting the most you can out of them while paying them the least you can get away with? Do you market your goods or services to people who can't afford them, forcing them into a cycle of debt? Do your votes saddle future generations with government debt? Amos was very clear that Yahweh will be balancing the books, and "that day" of reckoning is always just around the corner.

Bethel. Amos focused on Bethel, the symbol of everything that was wrong with the Northern Kingdom spiritually, throughout the book. Bethel was the location of a temple that was a rival counterpart to the one in Jerusalem (Southern Kingdom) and where King Jeroboam II worshiped (7:13). References to the religious blight associated with Bethel are found in 3:14; 4:4; 5:5–6; 7:10–13.

Samaria. Likewise, Amos focused on Samaria, the political capital of the Northern Kingdom, when lambasting the leaders for neglecting righteousness and justice. Relevant references are found in 3:9, 12; 4:1; 6:1.

Seeing Jesus in the Book. The majority of the book of Amos focuses on the indictment of the faithless nation of Israel and her inevitable downfall that will follow as a manifestation of the judgment of the day of Yahweh. However, there is also the inescapable and glorious climax of the coming blessing of the day of Yahweh (9:11–15). It is here that the Christological focus of the prophecy may be found. The climactic blessing of the day of Yahweh is bound up with the consummation of redemption, expressed in the ultimate pardon, renewal, restoration, and manifestation of the everlasting kingdom of God. Such a kingdom embodies both an initial earthly fulfillment and then a heavenly one, expressed via the metaphor of the new heavens and the new earth.

After the hard-hitting and very specific indictment of Israel throughout Amos for her sins and the description of her resulting downfall, why this shockingly sudden turn to blessing and renewal? How can Israel, who has oppressed the poor and harbored injustice, experience the blessing side of the day of YAHWEH? For that matter, how can any of us? The key to this final manifestation of the blessing of the day of YAHWEH lies in the coming of the Messianic King, Jesus Christ, the Son of God and Redeemer of the world. In other words, Jesus Christ unlocks the doorway to the climactic and eternal fulfillment of the day of YAHWEH—if we understand the good news of Jesus, we will understand why and how the day of YAHWEH will be fulfilled.

At the heart of the gospel is the redemptive, atoning sacrifice of Jesus on the cross: a personal substitutionary offering that covered and atoned for the sins of the world, for all those who believe in him, confess their sins, and trust in his redemptive self-sacrifice to obtain that forgiveness, once and for all. No matter how great and iniquitous our sins—both individual and corporate—the blood of Christ cleanses us, and we remain ever pure. Only through Jesus' redemption of his people can the good promises tied to the day of YAHWEH be given to the Israelites in spite of their sins.

The final verses of Amos 9 express this hope in its earthly fulfillment for the people of God—namely, in the promise that God will repair the damage done to the house and lineage of David and restore that kingdom to the people of Israel (v. 11), including those nations over whom David had formerly ruled (v. 12). The promised prosperity, in line with the language of the old covenant associated with literal, economic, and material blessing, guarantees the future of Israel as one of unparalleled affluence (vv. 13–14). The final verse (v. 15) makes explicit the promise that the Israelites will never again be uprooted from the land that God had given to them. Now, the ultimate fulfillment of this promised kingdom renewal is not literal and physical but spiritual and otherworldly. The conclusive expression of the kingdom of God will not be found on this earth but in the glorious environment of the new heavens and the new earth.

AMOS

The Prophet of Justice

Amos Prophesies Yahweh's Message

1 There was a prophet named Amos,[a] a herdsman[b] from the town of Tekoa.[c] Two years before the great earthquake,[d] when Uzziah was king of Judah, and Jeroboam son of Jehoash[a] was king of Israel, God

---

a 1:1 The name *Amos* likely means "burden-bearer." It can be compared to the name Amasiah (see 2 Chron. 17:16), which in Hebrew sounds like "Yahweh bears [the burden]." Amos may even be a shorter form of the same name. See M. Noth, *Die israelitischen Personennamen* (1928), 178.

b 1:1 The word here translated "herdsman," *noqed*, is not the usual Hebrew word for "shepherd." Jewish scholars view this as referring to one who oversees and breeds a special kind of dwarf sheep famous for their wool, known by Arabs today as *nakad*. Hence, an alternative translation of this word may be "sheep breeder."

c 1:1 *Tekoa* has a homonym that is translated "a stockade" or "a trumpet blast." The village of Tekoa is about five miles (eight kilometers) southeast of Bethlehem on the edge of the Judean wilderness. See 2 Sam. 14:2.

d 1:1 It is believed this great earthquake shook the entire ancient Near East during the mid-700s BC. This mention therefore helps us to date the book of Amos very accurately. Geologist Steven A. Austin has written extensively about this earthquake in the days of Amos; he dates this magnitude 8 earthquake around 750 BC and places the epicenter just north of Israel. See Steven A. Austin, Gordon W. Franz, and Eric G. Frost, "Amos's Earthquake: An Extraordinary Middle East Seismic Event of 750 B.C.," *International Geology Review* 42, no. 7 (2000), 657–71. See also Ps. 75:3; Amos 9:5; Mic. 1:4; Zech. 14:5.

revealed these prophetic visions to Amos about Israel.
[2]Amos said:

> "Yahweh comes roaring out of Zion;
> from Jerusalem he comes with his *thunderous* voice.
> The shepherds' lush pastures are dried up,[b]
> and the trees on top of Mount Carmel[c] wither."

Damascus

[3]Here is the message of Yahweh:

> "For the three terrible crimes of the people of Damascus—
> no, make that four[d]—
> I will not turn back *my wrath*.[e]
> For they have treated the people of Gilead *with savage cruelty*,

---

a 1:1 Or "Joash," a variant form of Jehoash. Amos prophesied during the reigns of Uzziah of Judah in the south (792–740 BC) and Jeroboam II of Israel in the north (793–753 BC).

b 1:2 The Hebrew word *'abal* is the root of two homonyms that mean "mourn" and "dried up."

c 1:2 There was no place in Israel that was more fertile than Mount Carmel, which overlooks modern Haifa. *Carmel* means "fruitful land." God's judgment on Israel was powerful and significant.

d 1:3 Amos used the literary tool of a Hebrew idiom ("three . . . make that four") to emphasize the cumulative effect of their sin. See Prov. 30:15. These numbers are symbolic, indicating that there is no limit to the wickedness of Damascus (i.e., Syria) here, plus all the other nations that follow—including, eventually, Israel herself (see Amos 2:6–16). There is also the possibility that the combined total of seven sins, in each case, may itself constitute a perfect symbolic (i.e., spiritual) storm of offenses that knows no bounds.

e 1:3 Or "I will not bring it"; that is, God's decree of punishment or the city of Damascus itself. See vv. 6, 9, 11, 13; 2:1, 4, 6.

running over them with a threshing sledge equipped
with iron teeth.[a]
4 So I will send fire down on the dynasty of Hazael[b]
to devour the royal palaces *defended* by Ben-Hadad.[c]
5 I will smash the city gates of Damascus,
I will cut down the *ruler* who sits in the Valley of
Wickedness,[d]
the one who holds the royal scepter
in the Paradise of Pleasure.[e]
And the people of Syria[f] will go back
to where they came from—to Kir,"[g]
declares YAHWEH.

---

a 1:3 This denotes the practice of laying people on the ground and running over them with large threshing carts equipped with toothed iron wheels used at harvest time to thresh the harvested grain. Such a cruel torture was also indicated in 2 Kings 13:7, where the king of Aram (i.e., Syria) similarly reduced the army of Jehoahaz to dust. Gilead was a territory populated with Israelite people east of the Jordan. Iron was a big deal back then. Whoever had the most access to iron had the military (and agricultural) upper hand. The rest had to settle for bronze. That's why the Philistines (who used iron) kept beating up on the Israelites (equipped with bronze) in David's era.

b 1:4 That is, the kingdom of Syria, or Aram-Damascus.

c 1:4 *Ben-Hadad* means the "son of [the false god of] power."

d 1:5 This is more than a literal valley (the location of the literal valley is disputable); it is more likely a metaphor for Damascus and the kingdom of Aram.

e 1:5 Or "the House of Beth Eden [Pleasure]," a derogatory term for Damascus.

f 1:5 Or "Aram," another name for Syria.

g 1:5 See 2 Kings 16:9. The exact location of this land of Kir is uncertain.

Gaza and Philistia

6Here is the message of YAHWEH:

"For the three terrible crimes of the people of Gaza—
no, make that four—
I will not turn back my wrath.
They have deported an entire community of exiles
as slaves to Edom.
7I will send fire down on the walls of Gaza
to consume its fortresses.
8I will cut off the ruler of Ashdod
and the one who holds the scepter in Ashkelon.
I will strike my blows against the city of Ekron,[a]
and what's left of the Philistines will perish,"
says the Lord YAHWEH.

Tyre

9YAHWEH says this:

"For the three terrible crimes of the people of Tyre—
no, make that four—
I will not turn back my wrath.
For they deported entire people groups
into exile in the land of Edom.
In so doing, they broke[b] the covenant of brotherhood.[c]
10So I will send fire down on the city walls of Tyre
to devour her fortresses."

---

a 1:8 The five notable cities of the Philistines were Ashdod, Ashkelon, Ekron, Gaza (see vv. 6–7), and Gath. Gath was not mentioned here, for it had already been leveled by Hazael (see 2 Kings 12:17) and again by Judah under King Uzziah (see 2 Chron. 26:6).

b 1:9 Or "did not remember."

c 1:9 This may be a reference to the friendship between Solomon and Hiram. See 1 Kings 5.

Edom

11YAHWEH says this:

“For the three terrible crimes of the Edomites—
no, make that four—
I will not turn back my wrath.
For Edom hunted down his relatives,[a]
the Israelites, with the sword,
and he refused to show mercy.
His anger never died down,
and his rage continued to the end.
12I will set *the city of* Teman[b] on fire
to burn up the fortresses of Bozrah.”

Ammon

13YAHWEH says this:

“For the three terrible crimes of the Ammonites—
no, make that four—
I will not turn back my wrath.
In order to seize more land for themselves,
they ripped open the pregnant women of Gilead.
14Therefore I will burn down the city walls of Rabbah[c]
to consume its fortresses.
War cries will be heard on the day of battle;
like a whirlwind, war will ravage the land.[d]
15*Ammon's* king will be taken into captivity,
he and his officials with him,”
says YAHWEH.

---

a 1:11 Or “his brother [Jacob].” See Gen. 25:21–24; 36:1–19.

b 1:12 Teman was an important city of Edom.

c 1:14 Rabbah was once the capital of Ammon.

d 1:14 In ancient Near Eastern literature, a windstorm (whirlwind) is used as a metaphor for judgment and destruction. See Isa. 29:6; Jer. 23:19; Hos. 8:7.

Moab

2 YAHWEH says this:

"For the three terrible crimes of the Moabites—
no, make that four—
I will not turn back my wrath.
They burned the bones of the king of Edom to lime.[a]
2 So I will send fire down into Moab
to devour the fortresses of Kerioth.[b]
Moab will perish in the heat of battle
amid war cries and the blaring of shofars.
3 I will destroy Moab's ruler[c]
and slaughter all officials there with him,"
says YAHWEH.

Judah

4 YAHWEH says this:

"For the three terrible crimes of Judah—
no, make that four—
I will not turn back my wrath
because they have despised YAHWEH's instructions[d]
and not kept his commandments.
Their lies,[e] which their ancestors followed,
have led them astray.

---

a 2:1 This historical event of burning the king's bones did not take place immediately after the death of the unknown king but apparently sometime later, when his tomb was opened and desecrated. The ancient Semites considered this offensive act to be odious.

b 2:2 The Septuagint translates *Kerioth* not as a proper name but as "towns."

c 2:3 Or "judge."

d 2:4 Or "torah [law]."

e 2:4 That is, their idolatry.

5 I will send fire down on Judah
to devour the fortresses of Jerusalem."

Israel

6 YAHWEH says this:

"For the three terrible crimes of Israel—
no, make that four—
I will not turn back my wrath.
For *a few pieces of* silver,
they sold honest people into slavery.
They even sold
the poor,
who couldn't pay their debts,
for a pair of sandals.
7 They trample the poor and helpless into the dirt[a]
and shove aside the rights of the destitute.[b]

---

a 2:7 The Hebrew for the word translated "trample" has a homonym meaning "to be eager," "to pant for," or "to long for." That is, the oppressors "long for the dust of the earth on the head of the poor." It would then imply that the rich are satisfied only when they see the poor with dust on their heads in a miserable condition. The ever-present (to this day) temptation for those at the top of the economic pyramid, especially during times of prosperity, is to protect their position (with force if necessary) and turn a blind eye to those at the bottom. Hierarchies will always naturally form as the able, intelligent, and powerful take on more responsibility. The question always remains: How are you going to behave when you get to the top? Amos deals with such wise insights that are so very applicable to this prosperous age in which we now live. The sin is not being "at the top." Someone has to run things. The sin is allowing corruption to pervert our time at the top.

b 2:7 Or "[they] bend the way of the afflicted" (i.e., they put stumbling blocks in their way or traps to impede the anticipated enjoyment of their lives).

A son and his father have sex with the same
woman,[a]
and by doing so, they profane my holy name.
8 They lay themselves down beside every altar
on garments taken as security for debts,
and in the house of God they drink the wine
they got from those who have been fined.

9 "Yet it was I who destroyed the Amorites[b]
before your very eyes.
They stood as tall as cedar trees
and as strong as oaks.
I destroyed them root and branch.[c]
10 It was I who brought you up from Egypt
and led you for forty years through the desert
to possess the land of the Amorites.
11 I raised up prophets from your sons
and Nazirites[d] from your young men.
People of Israel, is this not true?
I, YAHWEH, have spoken!

12 "But you made the Nazirites drink wine *and break their vow.*

---

a 2:7 Expositors are evenly divided over the identity of this young woman or girl. Some view her as a cultic prostitute, and others see her as a domestic servant violated by a son and his father.

b 2:9 The Amorites were the original pre-Joshua inhabitants of what became Israel.

c 2:9 Or "their fruit above and root below." This is a Hebraic figure of speech (i.e., "from crown to kingdom") to say that they were completely destroyed. See Job 18:16.

d 2:11 Nazirites were those completely set apart for the service of God. A Nazirite was not allowed to cut his hair, touch any dead thing (person), or drink wine. He had to take several vows that are described in the law of the Nazirite found in Num. 6:1–21.

You ordered the prophets,
'You'd better not prophesy.'
13 Very well! I will press you down[a]
like a cart overloaded with grain.
14 Even the swiftest runner will not escape,
physical strength will not be enough to protect the strong,
nor will the mighty warrior be able to save himself.
15 The archer will not stand his ground,
the fastest runners will not escape,
nor will the one who flees on horseback save his life.
16 In that day, even the bravest of warriors
will throw down his arms and run away.[b]
I, YAHWEH, have spoken."

Israel's Punishment

3 Israelites, listen to this prophecy that YAHWEH pronounces against you, against all the people I rescued from Egypt. 2 "Of all the nations of the earth, you are the only one I have intimately known *and have always*

---

a 2:13 The meaning of the Hebrew verb is uncertain. There are at least seven possible ways to translate *ʿuq* with variant nuances: (1) "to press down [crush]"; (2) "to groan"; (3) "to split [hollow out]"; (4) "to bring to a halt [hinder]"; (5) "to shake [earthquake]"; (6) "to collapse"; (7) "to cut in pieces." For a detailed study of each possible translation and their criticism, see Hartmut Gese, "Kleine Beiträge zum Verständnis des Amosbuches," *Vetus Testamentum* 12.4 (1962), 417–24; Hans-Peter Müller, "Die Wurzeln *ʿyq, yʿq,* und *ʿwq,*" *Vetus Testamentum* 21.5 (1971), 556–64.

b 2:16 Or "will flee stripped [ill-clad]."

cared for.[a] That is why I will punish you for all your wrongdoings."

Prophetic Riddles

3 Do two walk together[b]
unless they have agreed to do so?[c]
4 Does the lion roar in the bush
if it has no prey?[d]
Does the lion growl in his lair
if it has seized nothing?
5 Does a bird alight on a trap on the ground
if there is no bait inside?
Does the net spring up from the ground
if it has caught nothing?
6 Does the war trumpet sound in the city

---

a 3:2 Within the universe of meaning encompassed by the Hebrew word for "known" (*yada'*) is found several important components. It includes the meanings of choice, favor, affection, personal knowledge, sexual intimacy, intimate knowledge, and care, all of which can be wrapped into the context of God's love for his people. This accounts for the expanded rendering of this single verb form in this verse. This is held in tension with "I think as much of the Ethiopians as I do of you; you're all the same to me" (9:7). There are many tensions and paradoxes in Scripture, which is another proof of the Bible's authenticity. Real life is full of tension and paradox.

b 3:3 For two to walk together means they share a common purpose and goal. This Hebrew phrase is nearly identical to Abraham and Isaac walking together up Mount Moriah (see Gen. 22:6, 8). For believers today to walk with God, we must walk in the light and agree with the exposure that light brings (see 1 John 1:6–7).

c 3:3 Or "agreed to meet" or "without knowing each other" (LXX). These seven riddles of vv. 3–8 are linked together like the links of a chain.

d 3:4 See Ps. 104:21. Scripture frequently presents Yahweh as a lion roaring (see Hos. 5:14; Amos 1:2). In this riddle, the lion's prey are those he has captured in their sins, and he is ready to judge them for their evil.

without the people being frightened?[a]
Does calamity come to a city
if it has not passed through YAHWEH's hands?[b]
7 Indeed, Lord YAHWEH does nothing
without revealing his secrets to his servants the prophets.[c]
8 The lion has roared![d] Who is not afraid?
Lord YAHWEH has spoken! Who will not prophesy?

Samaria's Doom

9 Proclaim to the strongholds of Assyria[e] and Egypt,
and say to them,
"Gather on the hills around Samaria;

---

a 3:6 See Jer. 6:1; Ezek. 33:3. The shofar or trumpet is a biblical metaphor for the message or the messenger. This verse speaks of the prophetic word in the symbolism of the shofar blast. See Isa. 58:1; 1 Cor. 14:8; Rev. 1:10. When the war trumpets warn of impending conflict, the people must prepare. Yet Israel did nothing when God sounded his warnings through his prophets.

b 3:6 Or "has the Lord not acted?" Some of the many meanings of the Hebrew word *ʿasah* include "to manufacture," "to frame," "to make," "to touch," and "to caress."

c 3:7 In the context, the secret that God reveals is within the calamity that passes through his hands. When he is behind the calamity, he has a secret that he reveals to his prophets, and at times, that secret is a warning of impending disaster. The Hebrew verb meaning "reveal" is the word *gala*, which is a word used for "exile," "captivity," or "uncovering." When God sends people into exile, it is because their sins were uncovered, revealed. Thus, God will not allow calamity to come without first uncovering the reason for the calamity and revealing to his servants the prophets the sin that has broken his heart.

d 3:8 YAHWEH is the lion who has roared out his message of judgment on the wicked.

e 3:9 As translated from the Septuagint. The Masoretic Text has "Ashdod."

take a good, hard look at the rampant disorder[a]
within the city
and see how oppressed the people are."
10 "They don't even know how to do right,"
declares YAHWEH.
"They hoard in their palaces
the spoils of their violence and extortion.
11 Therefore, I, Lord YAHWEH, say:
an enemy[b] will soon overrun the land.
He will topple your strongholds
and plunder your palaces."

12 This is what YAHWEH says:
"As a shepherd can only rescue two leg bones or a
piece of an ear
out of the jaws of a lion,[c]
so the Israelites who live in Samaria
will only be able to salvage one leg of a bed
and a piece of a headboard *from their ravaged city*."[d]

Israel Will Likewise Be Punished

13 "I, Lord YAHWEH, the Mighty God of Angel Armies,
say:

---

a 3:9 The Hebrew word *mehumah* means "trouble," "chaos," "disorder," "turmoil," and "confusion." The opposite of this term would be *shalom*, which means "peace."

b 3:11 Thirty years after this prophecy, Assyria besieged Samaria and looted the city (see 2 Kings 17:5–6).

c 3:12 A shepherd was responsible for trying to rescue his sheep from a lion. If he presented bones or pieces of the lamb, the owner of the flock considered him an honest and brave shepherd (see Ex. 22:9–12; 1 Sam. 17:34–35; see also par. 266 of the Code of Hammurabi). In this instance, the shepherd is YAHWEH, with his prophet Amos.

d 3:12 The Hebrew of this verse is uncertain.

Listen! Warn Jacob's descendants.[a]
14 On the day when I punish Israel for her crimes,
I will also destroy the altars of Bethel.[b]
The horns of the altar will be hacked off[c]
and fall to the ground.
15 I will tear down the winter house *of the wealthy*
along with your summer house.[d]
Your luxury homes decorated with ivory[e]
and your *lovely* mansions will likewise be destroyed.
I, YAHWEH, have spoken."

Israel Must Return to God

4 Listen to this, you *women of Samaria*!
You're like the *fattened*, *well-fed* cows of Bashan[f]
grazing on the *fertile* mountain of Samaria.
You women who exploit the weak
and crush the poor and then command your husbands:
"Bring us some drinks!"

---

a 3:13 Or "Testify against the house of Jacob."

b 3:14 Bethel, once a place of true worship, had degenerated into a center of cultic worship.

c 3:14 Removing the blood-sprinkled horns of the altar was a powerful statement for the Hebrews. It meant there would no longer be a place where a fugitive could secure himself from arrest or violence by catching hold of altar-horns (see Ex. 21:14; 1 Kings 1:50; 2:28). The concept of a "horn" in Hebrew often carries the sense of strength and power, which is missing in English.

d 3:15 The wealthy would often have a home they lived in during the cooler winter months and a second home for the summer months.

e 3:15 See 1 Kings 22:39.

f 4:1 Bashan was famous for its pastureland and excellent cattle. Those who tormented Jesus during his crucifixion were described as strong bulls of Bashan (see Ps. 22:12 and footnote). The reference here to the "cows of Bashan" symbolizes the wealth and luxury of the women of Samaria. See Ezek. 39:18.

[2]Lord YAHWEH has sworn by his holiness:[a]
"Behold, the day is soon coming
when they will use hooks[b] to drag you away,
every last one of you with fishhooks.[c]
[3]They will force you *like cattle* in a chute
through the gaps of the broken walls
and herd you off toward Hermon.[d]
I, YAHWEH, have spoken."

Israel Refuses to Learn God's Lesson

[4]"Go to Bethel and sin!
Go to Gilgal and sin some more![e]
You sin when you bring your sacrifices each morning.
You sin when you bring your tithes every third day[f]
[5]and burn your thank offerings of bread made with
yeast.[g]

---

a 4:2 See Ps. 89:34–35.

b 4:2 Or "baskets." The Hebrew is uncertain.

c 4:2 Or "in fishermen's pots." The Hebrew is uncertain. The essential meaning of this verse is that nobody will escape deportation.

d 4:3 Or "Harmon" or "Haharmon." The Hebrew is uncertain. The essential meaning is that they will be taken captive to Assyria. Hermon is a mountain on the border of Israel and Syria. *Harmon* means "high fortress."

e 4:4 Verses 4–5 are very sarcastic. Bethel and Gilgal were once like "beachheads" for Israel in the promised land. Bethel and Gilgal were places where Israel worshiped God. YAHWEH was speaking scornfully of how the people polluted their worship of him. He was telling them that their pagan "worship" was sin.

f 4:4 The tribute offering of the tithe was a very ancient Hebrew custom dating back to Jacob's vow. See Gen. 28:22; Deut. 14:22–28.

g 4:5 In Lev. 2:11, Israel was commanded not to offer as a burnt offering to God anything containing yeast or honey. This is perfectly in line with the scathing sarcasm of the divine indictment here—namely, that God instructed his people to do explicitly what he had forbidden them to do in the law in relation to godly worship practices. This reinforces the brutal irony of the preceding verse. See Lev. 7:13.

Brag about your extra offerings, people of Israel,
for this is what makes you happy!
I, Lord YAHWEH, have spoken.

6 "In every town, I left you hungry[a]—
a food shortage in all your villages—
and still, you would not hunger for me.[b]
I, YAHWEH, have spoken.

7 "I even withheld the rain from you
three months short of harvest.
I sent rain to fall on one town
but not on another.
One field had plenty of rain,
and another became dry as dust.
8 People would stagger from city to city,
longing for a drink of water
yet never quenching their thirst.
And still you had no thirst for me.[c]
I, YAHWEH, have spoken.

9 "I struck your crops with blight and disease
and dried up your many gardens and vineyards.
Locusts kept devouring your fig trees and olive trees,
and still, you would not return to me.
I, YAHWEH, have spoken.

10 "I sent plagues against you
like I did against Egypt.

---

a 4:6 Or "I gave you clean teeth," a figure of speech for having nothing to eat.

b 4:6 Or "you would not come back to me." God expected his punishments of his people to bring them to repentance, but they refused.

c 4:8 Or "you would not come back to me."

I killed your young men with the sword
and stole away all your war horses.
I filled your nostrils with the stench
of your unburied corpses,[a]
and still, you would not return to me.
I, YAHWEH, have spoken.

11 "I destroyed some of you
like I destroyed Sodom and Gomorrah.
Your survivors were like burning sticks
plucked from a fire,
and still, you would not return to me.
I, YAHWEH, have spoken.

12 "So here is what I plan to do to you, Israel,
and because of what I am planning,
prepare to meet your God."

Doxology

13 Behold, the Mountain-Maker
and Wind-Creator,
who reveals his intimate thoughts to people,[b]
who changes the dawn into darkness[c]
and moves over the mountains of the earth.
His name is YAHWEH,
the God of Angel Armies.

---

a 4:10 Or "stench of your camps [armies]."

b 4:13 Or "who reveals the thoughts of people." The Septuagint is interesting here: "who reveals his *christos* to people." Literally "who reveals his Christ [Anointing] to people."

c 4:13 Or "who makes dawn and darkness" (LXX).

Amos' Song of Mourning over Israel

5 Listen to this funeral song
that I sing over you, people of Israel:
2 "Virgin Israel[a] has fallen, never to rise again.
There she lies, abandoned on her own soil,
with no one to lift her up."

3 Lord YAHWEH says this:
"The city that deployed a thousand soldiers
will only have a hundred come back,
and the city that deployed a hundred soldiers
will only have ten *survivors.*"[b]

No Salvation without Repentance

4 For YAHWEH says this to the people of Israel:

"*Come*, seek me, and you will live.
5 But don't go down to seek me at Beersheba.
Don't try to find me at Bethel's shrines
or at the altars at Gilgal.
For Gilgal will be taken into exile,[c]
and Bethel will be brought to nothing."

---

a 5:2 Israel is poetically portrayed as a virgin maiden who was carried off in death in her youth before she could marry and have a family.

b 5:3 Or "the house of Israel." This phrase is in v. 4 as well.

c 5:5 The Hebrew text (*haggilgal galoh yigleh*) employs a repeating sequence of *gl* four times, and each word begins or ends with *h*. Gilgal can be viewed as a poetic metaphor for the conquest of Israel under Joshua.

[6]Come back to YAHWEH and live,
or he will sweep down like fire upon the people of Israel.[a]
The fire will burn at Bethel
with no one there to put out the flames.

[7]They turn justice into a bitter *pill to swallow*[b]
and trample righteousness into the mud.

Creator and Destroyer

[8]Creator of Constellations—Maker of the Pleiades and Orion,[c]
you turn the deepest darkness into dawn
and daylight into the darkest night.
You draw up[d] drops of water *distilled* from the sea
to drench the earth with pouring rain.
YAHWEH is your name.
[9]You destroy the mighty with a blinding flash

---

a 5:6 Or "the house of Joseph." See v. 15 and footnote. Ephraim and Manasseh were the sons of Joseph and the two main tribes of the Northern Kingdom.

b 5:7 Or "They [Israelites] turn justice into wormwood [bitterness]." Instead of "turning" to God, they turned justice into something bitter.

c 5:8 See Gen. 1:14–15; Job 9:9; 38:31–33; Ps. 19:1. It is important to remember that God is the Creator of the stars and the one who set the constellations in the heavens. According to Josephus, the constellations were designated by Adam, Seth, and Enoch (see *Ant.* 1.2.12–13). God has set his glory in the heavens, which would include the zodiac. Although the modern meaning of the twelve signs of the zodiac (astrology) has no significance for today's believer (see Deut. 18:10), the word for "zodiac" (Hb. *mazzarot*), found in Job 38:32, makes it clear that God is the one who controls the movement of the stars.

d 5:8 Or "summon" or "gather."

and overwhelm their strongholds with certain
destruction.[a]

Amos' Warning

10 They[b] hate the one who challenges injustice
and despise the one who declares the whole truth in
court.[c]
11–12 For I know how outrageous are your many sins
and how many crimes you have committed.
You persecute the righteous,
trample[d] on *the rights of* the poor,
and seize their grain through extortion.[e]
By taking bribes, you prevent them
from getting justice in the courts.[f]
This is why you will not live
in the fine stone houses you build
or enjoy the fruits of your luxury.
You will not drink wine
from the lush vineyards you plant,
for your judgment is imminent.
13 Yes, the smartest thing for the prudent
is to remain silent in such an evil time as this.[g]

---

a 5:9 See Mic. 5:11. The precise meaning of the Hebrew text of v. 9 is uncertain.

b 5:10 Although the text is ambiguous, "They" may refer to corrupt judges/attorneys.

c 5:10 Or "at the city gate," the place where civic court was held and decisions were rendered.

d 5:11–12 Or "strike with the fist."

e 5:11–12 That is, taxation.

f 5:11–12 Or "in the [city] gates."

g 5:13 The implication is that those who understand God's ways will not criticize God's actions when he rises to judge wickedness.

Amos' Exhortation

14 Devote yourself to what is good, not evil,
so that you may live.
And YAHWEH, the God of Angel Armies,
will really be with you,
just as you claim he is.
15 Hate what is evil, love what is right,
and let justice prevail in the courts.
It may be that YAHWEH, God of Angel Armies,
will show mercy to the remnant of Israel.[a]

Israel's Impending Punishment

16 *Because of Israel's sins*,
Lord YAHWEH, God of Angel Armies, says this:
"Wailing and sorrow everywhere![b]
In every street they will mourn the dead.[c]
Those who work in the fields will be expected to mourn
along with the professional mourners.
17 There will be wailing in all the vineyards,
for I will pass through your midst *to punish you*,"[d]
declares YAHWEH.

False Sense of Security

18 Woe to you who long for the day of YAHWEH!
Why do you long for the day of YAHWEH?
Its arrival will mean darkness, not light.
19 You will be seized like someone who runs from a lion

---

a 5:15 Or "Joseph."

b 5:16 Or "in every public square."

c 5:16 Or "they will say, 'Ah! Ah!' " This is the Hebrew word *ho*, which is a variant form of *hoy*, a word used to express sorrow and mourning for the dead. See 1 Kings 13:30; Jer. 22:18; 34:5.

d 5:17 As God did to the Egyptians (see Ex. 12:12) in passing through their midst, so he will do to his rebellious people.

and a bear charges at him.
Then he hides indoors and leans his hand against the wall
only to have a venomous snake bite him.
20 Will not the day of YAHWEH bring darkness, not light—
a day of gloom without a ray of light?

YAHWEH's Rebuke of Religious Formalism

21 "I hate your religious festivals;[a]
I absolutely despise them!
Your pious gatherings make me sick![b]
22 Even though you offer me
your burnt offerings and grain offerings,
I will not accept them.[c]
And though you bring me choice peace offerings of fattened animals,
I won't even look at them.
23 Spare me[d] the monotonous melodies[e] of your 'worship.'
I don't want to hear your strumming guitars[f] anymore.
It's just noise to me.

---

a 5:21 The truth of this verse is repeated frequently by the prophets. Part of the role of prophetic ministry is to call the church away from dead formalism into a loving, obedient relationship with God. See 1 Sam. 15:22; Pss. 40:6–8; 50:5–15; 51:16–17; Isa. 1:10–16; 29:13–14; 58:1–8; Jer. 6:20; Hos. 6:6; Joel 2:13; Mic. 6:5–8; Zech. 7:4–6.

b 5:21 Or "I cannot smell your solemn assemblies." The implication is that God cannot tolerate pretentiousness and longs for us to meet with him heart-to-heart.

c 5:22 Or "I take no pleasure in them."

d 5:23 Or "Away with."

e 5:23 Or "noise." God finds the whole worship presentation intolerable.

f 5:23 Or "music of your harps [stringed instruments]."

[24] *However, I delight in*
a land where justice flows like a river
and where true righteousness rolls like a steady
flowing stream.
[25] Listen, people of Israel!
Didn't you worship me with your offerings and
sacrifices
during those forty years in the wilderness?
[26] Now you carry around[a] the pagan idols
that you made to worship your phony king, Sakkuth,[b]
and your very own star-god, Kaiwan.[c]
[27] Therefore, you can carry them all the way beyond
Damascus,[d]
where I am about to drive you into captivity,"
says Yahweh.
God of Angel Armies is his name!

The Party Is Over

6 Woe to you living so comfortably in Zion!
Woe to you who live with a false sense of security on
Mount Samaria,

---

a 5:26 Or "you used to carry around." There is some ambiguity here as to whether these idolatrous practices occurred in Israel's more distant past or closer to the time of Amos (mid-700s BC) or perhaps both.

b 5:26 An alternative reading here results from translating the Hebrew term *sikkut* as "shrine": "You have lifted up the shrine of your pagan king."

c 5:26 Sakkuth and Kaiwan are most likely Babylonian or Assyrian gods. Kaiwan (or Chiun) was another name for the Roman god Saturn. When God's people wander away from him, they quickly turn to false gods and vain idols (see 2 Kings 17:29–31; Jer. 2:13 and the footnotes). Additionally, there is a possible alternative reading, based on the translation of the Hebrew term *kiyyun* as "pedestal": ". . . and the pedestal of your idols—your star-god."

d 5:27 That is, to Assyria.

the elite of this foremost nation,
on whom Israel's people pin their hopes.
2 Travel to the city of Calneh[a]
and see for yourself *what happened.*
Then go on from there to Hamath,
the great *capital city of the Hittites.*
Make your way down to Gath in Philistia,
and ask yourself—
are you better than these kingdoms?
Is their territory larger than yours?[b]
3 You refuse to consider the day when disaster will come,
yet all your evil only brings that day closer.[c]
4 Lying on luxurious beds inlaid with ivory
and sprawled out on your couches,[d]
you feast on lambs from the flock
and stall-fattened veal.
5 You compose songs[e] like David
and strum away on your harps.
6 You guzzle wine by the bucketful,
and slather yourselves with the finest lotions.
Yet you do not grieve[f] over

---

a 6:2 Calneh was a city founded by Nimrod.

b 6:2 Or "Is your territory larger than theirs?"

c 6:3 Or "you bring near a seat [throne] of violence," which could mean something like "you are bringing nearer the time when violent men will reign."

d 6:4 The custom of eating while lying down on couches is mentioned here for the first time. By the time of the New Testament, it had become a more general custom. Jewish commentators view "sprawled out on your couches" as a euphemism for lewd behavior and revelry (see Rashi, Malbim).

e 6:5 Or "invent musical instruments." The Hebrew is ambiguous.

f 6:6 The Hebrew root word for "grieve" is *chalah*, which is "to be sick." They were not heartsick about or grieved over the collapse of their kingdom.

Israel's impending doom.[a]
7 That is why they will be the first
to go into captivity.
Their lying around while enjoying the good life
will come to an end.

God Hates Pride

8 Lord YAHWEH has sworn by his own being[b]—

YAHWEH, God of Angel Armies, declares:
"I hate the pride of *the people of* Jacob,
and I despise their strongholds,[c]
I will hand over their capital city[d] *to their enemies*
and everything in it."
9 Even if there are ten hiding in a house,
they will all die.
10 If a relative who is to light a memorial fire for the dead
comes to carry the bodies out of the house for burial
and asks, "Is anyone else inside the house with you?"
and that person answers, "No," then the one who asked will say, "Quiet!
We must not mention the name of YAHWEH."

---

a 6:6 Or "over the ruin of Joseph," a figure of speech for the kingdom of Israel. Despite the impending disaster, the self-centered, self-indulgent leaders remained unconcerned about the invasion soon to come upon their land.

b 6:8 See Gen. 22:16–17; Heb. 6:13.

c 6:8 Or "palaces."

d 6:8 That is, the city of Samaria.

Yahweh's Punishment

[11]Behold, Yahweh strikes with his command:
"Houses large and small will be smashed to pieces!"[a]

[12]Can horses gallop over rocky cliffs?
Can boulder-strewn hills be plowed with oxen?
Of course not!
Yet you have managed to pervert justice into poison
and the *sweet* fruits of righteousness into bitter
fruit.[b]
[13]You rejoice over *conquering the city of* Lo Debar,
saying, "Wasn't it by our own strength
that we captured Karnaim for ourselves?"[c]
[14]But look, house of Israel,
Yahweh, God of Angel Armies, declares to you:
"I will raise up a *mighty* nation to come against
you,[d]
and they will oppress you *and overrun your land*
from the northern to the southern borders of your
kingdom."[e]

---

a 6:11 Or "The great house shall be struck down into fragments, and the little house into bits." The Jewish Targum regards the "great house" as the kingdom of Israel and the "little house" as the kingdom of Judah.

b 6:12 Or "into wormwood."

c 6:13 The biting sarcasm of this verse is apparent in the Hebrew, which can be translated, "You rejoice over a no-thing [*lo' dabar*] and say, 'By our own strength we captured horns [Hb. *qarnayim*; horns are a symbol of strength].' "

d 6:14 That is, Assyria.

e 6:14 Or "from Lebo Hamath [Israel's northern border] to the brook of the Arabah [Israel's southern border near the Dead Sea]."

First Vision: Locusts

7 This is what Lord YAHWEH revealed to me *in a vision*:

Behold! Just after the hay had been cut for the king,[a]
when the new young grass started to grow again,
I saw YAHWEH forming a swarm of mature locusts.[b]
2 I watched as they began eating all the vegetation in
the land,
so I pleaded with God, saying,
"Lord YAHWEH, please forgive us, I beg you,[c]
or we will not survive![d]
Our nation is so helpless."[e]
3 My prayer moved God's heart to compassion.
YAHWEH said: "It will not happen."

Second Vision: The Drought

4 *In another vision*, YAHWEH revealed this to me:

Behold! He was calling for punishment by fire.[f]
The scorching heat dried up

---

a 7:1 Although this custom is not mentioned anywhere else in the Old Testament, it has generally been understood to mean that the king was to be given the first mowing of spring hay for his horses.

b 7:1 See Joel 1:4. Amos chs. 7–9 include a compilation of five supernatural visions God revealed to his prophet.

c 7:2 Amos the prophet began to intercede for God's forgiving grace. Intercession was and is one of the roles of a prophet. See Gen. 20:7; Jer. 15:1, 11; 18:20; Ezek. 9:8; Dan. 9:15–19. There are times that our intercession is meant to move God's heart to prevent judgment from falling on a nation.

d 7:2 Or "Jacob will not rise up." *Jacob* is a metonymy for Israel.

e 7:2 Or "small."

f 7:4 That is, a devastating drought that would cover the land (i.e., the burning heat of the sun). See Joel 1:19–20; 2:3.

the deep sources of water beneath the land[a]
and made the farmlands like dust.
5 So I pleaded with God, saying,
"Lord YAHWEH, please don't do this, I beg you,
or we will not survive!
Our nation is so helpless."
6 Because of my prayer,
God's heart was *stirred* with compassion.
"This also will not happen," said YAHWEH.

Third Vision: The Plumb Line

7 Lord YAHWEH revealed this to me *in another vision*:

I saw the Lord standing by a wall built true to plumb,
holding a plumb line in his hand.[b]
8 "Amos, what do you see?" YAHWEH asked me.
"A plumb line," I replied.
Then the Lord said, "Behold, I am about to set a plumb line
up against my people Israel *to test them.*
Never again will I look the other way *when they sin.*
9 I will destroy the high places

---

a 7:4 Or "It had devoured the great deep [abyss]." The people of the ancient Near East believed that a great ocean lay deep beneath the ground and occasionally sprang up to the surface. See Gen. 2:6; 7:11; 49:25; Ps. 36:6; Isa. 51:10.

b 7:7 A plumb line is a cord with a lead weight used by builders to be sure that walls are straight up and down. The Lord standing with a plumb line indicates he is coming to measure his people to make sure their standards are true and pure. See 2 Kings 21:13; Isa. 28:17; 34:11; Lam. 2:8.

where Isaac's descendants worship,[a]
and I will ruin the holy places of Israel.
With my sword in hand,
I will attack the dynasty of Jeroboam."

Amaziah Challenges Amos

10Then Amaziah the *chief* priest of Bethel sent the following message to Jeroboam king of Israel: "Amos has con-
spired against you in the very heart of Israel. We cannot
stand his speeches! 11For Amos says, 'Jeroboam is going
to die by the sword,[b] and Israel will go into captivity far
from its native land.' "

12Amaziah said to Amos, "Go away, you seer. Why don't
you escape to Judah while there is time? You can always
prophesy there and make your living. 13But don't stay
around here and prophesy at Bethel anymore. This is the
national temple, the place where the king worships."

14Amos replied, "I am not a prophet, nor am I one of the
sons of the prophets. I am merely a rancher, and I cultivate fig trees. 15But *one day*, YAHWEH called me as I was
managing my flocks and said to me, 'Go and prophesy to
my people Israel.'

---

a 7:9 The high places of Isaac may refer to the sanctuary of Beersheba. Perhaps Isaac is mentioned because he was offered to God on an altar on a mountain; in Amos' time, Israel was worshiping false gods on mountain altars. The high places were originally simply burial mounds where people would come with worship related to dead people, but later this developed into a fertility cult. See W. F. Albright, *The High Place in Ancient Palestine*, Volume du congrès Strasbourg 1956, *Supplements to Vetus Testamentum IV* (Leiden: 1957), 242–58.

b 7:11 Indeed, Jeroboam and his son Zechariah met with violent deaths (see 2 Kings 15:10).

16 "So now, Amaziah, listen to what YAHWEH says.
You say: 'Do not prophesy against Israel,
and do not prophesy doom on Isaac's descendants!'
17 Very well. This is what YAHWEH says:
'Your wife will become a prostitute in the streets,
and your sons and daughters will fall in battle.
Your land will be measured, divided up, *and given to others.*
And you yourself will die in a pagan land,
and Israel will go into captivity far from its own land!' "[a]

Fourth Vision: The Basket of Ripe Fruit

8 Lord YAHWEH revealed this to me *in another vision:*
a basket of ripe fruit.[b]
2 "Amos, what do you see?" he asked.
"A basket of ripe fruit," I replied.
Then YAHWEH said,
"The time is ripe[c] for my people Israel.
I will not continue to overlook their sins.
3 On that day, those singing songs in the temple[d] will wail instead,"
declares the Lord YAHWEH.

---

a 7:17 Amos had absolutely no fear of the leading figures of the Northern Kingdom.

b 8:1 The fruit was most likely figs.

c 8:2 Or "the end has come." The Hebrew contains a play on words that can easily be lost in translation. The word for "ripe [summer] fruit" is *qayits*, "ripe," and the word for "end" is *qets*. Some scholars believe these words may have been homonyms. See B. D. Rahtjen, "A Critical Note on Amos 8:1–2," *Journal of Biblical Literature* 83, no. 4 (1964), 416–17; Herbert Donner and Wolfgang Röllig, *Kanaanäische und Aramäische Inschriften* (Harrassowitz: 1942), 182.

d 8:3 Or "palace."

"There will be corpses piled up everywhere.
They will be cast out in silence."[a]

Prophecy against Those Who Exploit Others

4 Listen to this, all you who trample on the poor
and reduce the needy to nothing![b]
5 You say to yourselves, "We can't wait
for these holy days[c] to be over
so that we can sell our corn!"
And, "When will this Sabbath be over
so that we can open the storage and sell our wheat?
Then we can overcharge our customers, shortchange them,[d]
and deceive them by tampering with the scales.
6 We can even sell the worthless chaff we sweep up for silver.
We can buy the poor with silver *and make them our slaves*
because they cannot pay their debts,
even a debt so small as that of a pair of sandals."

---

a 8:3 Or "They will be cast out. Be silent!"

b 8:4 Any community can be judged by how it treats "the least important of these." Jesus highlighted this in Matt. 25:31–46.

c 8:5 Or "new moon [festivals]." See Lev. 23:24; 1 Sam. 20:5; Isa. 1:13; Hos. 2:11.

d 8:5 Or "that we may make the ephah small and the shekel great." The ephah was a unit of measurement (about eight gallons or thirty liters), and the shekel was their currency.

7 Yahweh, the Majesty of Jacob,[a] has sworn an oath:
"I will never forget all the evil they have done.
8 That is why the earth will tremble for this,
and all who live on it mourn.[b]
All of the land will rise up like the river Nile—
inundated and stirred up by floodwaters—
and then subside, just like the river of Egypt!"

Prophecy of Darkness and Mourning

9 "On that day," declares Lord Yahweh,
"I will make the sun set at noon
and darken the earth in the middle of the day.[c]
10 I will turn your festivals into funerals,
and all your lively singing into funeral dirges.
I will make you all wear sackcloth and shave your heads,
as if you were mourning the death of an only child.
That day will be bitter to the end."

---

a 8:7 Most modern translations make the text quite literal: "Yahweh has sworn by the pride of Jacob." Yet in most languages it makes no sense to swear by someone's pride, any more than it does in English. It is even questionable whether that is what the Hebrew really means. In the Old Testament, the Lord never "swears" by something or somebody else but always by himself. It makes more sense to read the text as Yahweh "swearing" an oath in his own name, "the Majesty [pride] of Jacob."

b 8:8 Or "be destroyed" (according to Jewish scholars such as Kimchi and those found in the Targums). This verse is a likely reference to the great historical earthquake mentioned in Amos 1:1 and in Zech. 14:5.

c 8:9 Or "in a day of light." This is likely a prophecy of a solar eclipse. It has been calculated that a complete eclipse of the sun happened on February 9, 784 BC and on June 15, 763 BC. The eclipse of 763 BC is mentioned in an Assyrian text. See R. W. Rogers, *Cuneiform Parallels to the Old Testament* (London: Henry Frowde/Oxford University Press, 1912), 233. God can turn the lights off on the old order whenever he chooses.

A Famine of the Word of God

11 “Behold, the days are coming,” declares Lord YAHWEH,
“when I will send a famine on the land.
People will not hunger for food nor thirst for water
but will starve for a word from YAHWEH.[a]
12 People will stagger from sea to sea
and wander from the north to the east
searching for a revelation from YAHWEH,
but they will not hear from me.
13 On that day, even your beautiful young women
and strong young men will collapse from thirst.
14 Those who swear by Ashimah,[b] *the idol of Samaria*,
who say, ‘Long live your golden calf-god of Dan!’[c]
and say, ‘As surely as the god[d] of Beersheba[e] lives!’—
they will all fall, never to rise again.”

Fifth Vision: The Sanctuary Crumbles

9 I saw the Lord standing over the altar,[f]
and he gave the command:[g]
“Smash the top of the pillars
so that the foundations shake!
Shatter the pillars and make them

---

a 8:11 That is, a famine of hearing God’s revelation. God will punish a rebellious people with silence. Tired of speaking without being listened to, God says nothing and sends no more prophets with a fresh word from heaven. God’s silence can be a form of his correction.

b 8:14 Amos again employed a play on words. The name of Samaria’s goddess Ashimah sounds similar to the Hebrew word for “sin,” *’ashmah*.

c 8:14 See 1 Kings 12:30.

d 8:14 Or “way,” a possible reference to the roads going to the shrines for pagan worship. See Amos 5:5.

e 8:14 “From Dan to Beersheba” is a common phrase for the totality of the promised land.

f 9:1 Or “on the altar” or “beside the altar.”

g 9:1 The Lord most likely gave this command to an angel.

crumble upon the heads of all *the worshipers.*[a]
And any survivors I will kill by the sword.
Whoever runs away will not go far.
Whoever tries to escape will not make it.
2 Even if they were to dig their way down to the underworld,[b]
my hand would haul them out.
Even if they were to climb up to heaven,
I would drag them down from there.
3 If they were to hide on top of Mount Carmel,[c]
I would hunt them down and snatch them.
If they were to try to hide from my eyes at the bottom of the sea,
I would order the serpent there to bite them.
4 If their enemies were to herd them into captivity,
even there I would order the sword to kill them.
Yes, I will fix my eyes on them
to destroy them and not to help them."[d]

Amos' Doxology

5 Lord YAHWEH, Commander of Angel Armies,
you touch the earth and it melts,
and everyone on earth mourns.
All of the land will rise up like the river Nile—
inundated and stirred up by floodwaters—
and then subside, just like the river of Egypt.
6 You build your lofty stairway in the heavens

---

a 9:1 This reference would remind the Jews of Samson pulling down the columns on the Philistines.

b 9:2 Or "Sheol," the place of the dead. In Jewish thought, Sheol is the gathering place for all the dead. It is often considered as a dark world, deep down under the earth, far deeper than the grave.

c 9:3 Mount Carmel was an ideal hiding place because of its thick forests and two thousand limestone caves.

d 9:4 Or "for evil and not for good."

and suspend your superdome over the earth.
You summon the waters of the sea
and pour them over the face of the earth:
YAHWEH is your name!

YAHWEH Declares: Sinners Will All Perish

7 "Israel, I think as much of the Ethiopians as I do of you;
you're all the same to me,"[a]
declares YAHWEH.
"*Yes*, I brought you out from Egypt.
But didn't I also bring out the Philistines from Crete[b]
and the Syrians[c] from Kir?
8 Behold, the eyes of Lord YAHWEH
are on the sinful kingdom of Israel.
I will wipe it off the face of the earth.
Yet I will not completely destroy the descendants of Jacob,"
declares YAHWEH.

9 "Behold, I will speak the command
to scatter the people of Israel among all the nations.
I will sift them the way sand is shaken in a sieve,
through which not a single pebble falls to the ground.
10 All the sinners of my people will die by the sword who say,
'Nothing bad could ever happen to us.' "

---

a 9:7 Israel's special position as God's people will not save her from punishment. She is no different from other nations.

b 9:7 Or "Caphtor." See Gen. 10:13–14.

c 9:7 Or "Arameans."

Restoration of David's Tabernacle

11 "One day I will restore
David's tabernacle that has fallen.
I will repair its broken places
and raise up its ruins *and fix it up like new.*
I will rebuild it and make it what it was long ago.[a]
12 As a result, David's people will conquer
the nations over which they once ruled for me,[b]
down to the last remnant of Edom.[c]
13 Behold, I, YAHWEH, make this decree:
The days of *acceleration* are coming,
when *the harvest will be so great*
that those plowing the field will overtake
those still reaping the harvest,
and the ones treading the grapes
will overtake those who are planting.
Blessings will stream forth
like new wine pouring from every mountain,
and every hill will flow *with favor.*
14 I will restore prosperity and good fortune
to the captives of Israel.

---

a 9:11 See Acts 15:16. The promise of the restoration of the tabernacle of David is considered a metaphor on at least two levels. First, it refers to the restoration of Israel and its people to the status they experienced under David's rule. Second, David's tabernacle was the place of worship during David's reign (see 1 Chron. 16:1–37). It was different from the dwelling place (or tabernacle) of Moses; essentially, David's tabernacle consisted of the unveiled ark of glory, with no other furniture, veil, or ritual surrounding it. God prophesied through Amos that this form of worship would be restored in the last days. Constant prayer and worship before God is the central feature of the restored tabernacle of David. It is in the spirit of David's fallen tabernacle that God, in these last days, has raised up houses of prayer with 24/7 worship as their central focus.

b 9:12 Or "all nations over whom my name is spoken [proclaimed]."

c 9:12 *Edom* shares the same root as *Adam.*

They will rebuild the ruined cities to live in.
They will plant vineyards to produce their wine.
And plant *lush* gardens and orchards
to eat their produce.
15 And I will plant them[a] in their own land,
never to be uprooted again
from the land that I have given them.
I, YAHWEH, your God, have spoken."

---

a 9:15 See Ps. 1:3.

THE BOOK OF

OBADIAH

The Servant of YAH

BroadStreet
PUBLISHING

OBADIAH

Introduction

AT A GLANCE

Author: Obadiah the prophet
Audience: Israel, Edom, and other surrounding nations
Date: Uncertain, but a plausible date is shortly following the Babylonian destruction of Jerusalem in 586 BC
Type of Literature: Prophecy
Major Themes: The complex relationship between Israel and Edom; *lex talionis*; inflated pride; the day of Yahweh; Edom and Adam; seeing Jesus in the book
Outline:

- I. Superscription: divine revelation given to Obadiah — 1a
- II. Divine judgment on Edom — 1b–14
  - a. The announcement of Edom's destruction — 1b–7
  - b. The consummation of Edom's destruction — 8–14
- III. The revelation of the day of Yahweh — 15–21
  - a. Certain divine judgment on the nations, including Edom — 15–16
  - b. Promised divine deliverance for Mount Zion and the people of God — 17–18
  - c. The expansion and establishment of the kingdom of God — 19–21

ABOUT THE BOOK OF OBADIAH

Obadiah is the shortest book in the Old Testament: just twenty-one verses. It starts out with a condemnation of Israel's neighbor to the east, Edom (also called Idumea by the Greeks and Romans, which had shifted location by New Testament times to the area around Hebron, in southern Judah). The people of Edom traced their ancestry back to Isaac and Rebekah through their son Esau, the brother of Jacob (also known as Israel). Jacob and Esau had a very complex relationship. The ongoing family feud between the two nations mirrored the stories of the two patriarchs who gave rise to these neighboring tribes.

When the superpower Babylon destroyed Jerusalem, the holy city of the descendants of Jacob, in 586 BC, some of the Edomites saw it as an opportunity to loot the city. Such behavior was more than simple destructive violence and theft; since it came from a brother nation, Obadiah saw it as raw betrayal.

PURPOSE

The book of Obadiah announces Yahweh's judgment against Edom and all humankind for those times when they descend into and operate out of the shadow side of human nature. God cannot tolerate evil. And yet, condemnation is never the last word in his covenant promises. Along with Joel and Amos, Obadiah shares a vision of the fulfillment of God's kingdom: a future where he blesses not only the tribe of Judah but also all the nations surrounding them and, by implication, eventually the entire world.

AUTHOR AND AUDIENCE

We know absolutely nothing about the prophet Obadiah except for his name (in Hebrew *Obadiah* means "servant of Yah[weh]"). There are other Obadiahs in the Bible (e.g., 2 Chron. 17:7), but no direct evidence is forthcoming to connect them to this prophet. And much like the name Theophilus in Luke's writing (Luke 1:1–4; Acts 1:1–3), the name Obadiah could be a description rather than a proper name. Theophilus could have been simply a "friend of God" (in Greek *theo* means "God" and *philos* means "friend"), or Luke could have been writing to a specific man named Theophilus. In the same way, we must also allow for the possibility that the book of Obadiah was written by an unnamed "servant" (Hb. *obed*) of YAHWEH, rather than someone with the proper name Obadiah. For the purposes of this discussion, the translation team will assume the proper name is the correct explanation.

We also do not know precisely when he wrote, although we do know that the incident that catalyzed the need for his prophecy was the Babylonian destruction of Jerusalem in 586 BC and the subsequent looting of the nation of Judah by the Edomites. Additionally, the content of Obadiah 1–9, Jeremiah 49:7–22, and Ezekiel 35:1–15 have distinct similarities regarding the divine judgment that was poured out on Edom, which has led many to suggest that Obadiah may well have been a contemporary of both Jeremiah (late 600s–early 500s BC) and Ezekiel (early 500s BC).

Of course, this prophecy was written to the people of Judah to help them interpret, from God's point of view, the horrific behavior of the Edomites toward them and to give the people of God hope. Additionally, one cannot rule out the possibility that Obadiah was also sending a direct message to Edom and, perhaps, to all the surrounding nations.

In a broader sense, Obadiah is also a warning letter to all humanity, alerting us to the consequences of striking out in unprovoked aggression toward others, especially when they are at their most vulnerable. Obadiah starts with a telephoto lens focusing on Judah and Edom, but the end of the book uses a wide-angle lens, applying the truths of the prophecy, both judgment and promise, to neighboring nations.

The message is timeless: YAHWEH will punish evil and bless the faithful remnant, as he has demonstrated so often in history. Eventual victory is assured via the triumph of his kingdom through his Son, Jesus Christ, the Messianic King. God will have his way with his creation.

MAJOR THEMES

The Complex Relationship between Israel and Edom. These nations saw their complex, troubled relationship originating from the stories of twin brothers, the sons of Isaac and Rebekah, Jacob and Esau in Genesis. Right at birth, Jacob emerged grabbing hold of his older twin's heel, and God prophetically announced that these sons would be the founders of two separate nations, and the older would serve the younger. The family was divided, with Isaac having a preferential love for Esau and Rebekah having a loving preference for Jacob (Gen. 25:19–28). Esau despised his birthright by swapping it for a plate of stew from Jacob, and later Jacob impersonated Esau and deceived their father into giving him the paternal blessing meant for Esau. Such blessings had legal force in the ancient Near East and included inheritances. At this treachery, Esau was furious and determined to murder his brother (Gen. 27:1–46). Jacob fled the family home and went to live with his uncle, Laban, the brother of Rebekah (Gen. 28–31).

After many years, Jacob finally reunited with Esau in the land of Edom, on his way back to Canaan (Gen. 32:1–21). Jacob arrived fearfully, with gifts and humility, and Esau responded with an embrace and kiss. There was no longer any grudge between them (Gen. 33:1–16).

However, while the relationship between the two brothers may have been reconciled, later years saw enmity reemerge between the two nations of Israel and Edom. Several other Old Testament texts refer to Edom's hostility toward the Israelites, also commonly known as "the sons of Jacob [Israel]." In particular, the Edomites refused to allow the Israelite tribes to pass through their territory en route to Canaan during their wilderness wanderings (Num. 20:14–21). Deuteronomy 2:1–6 records the Edomites' fear of the Israelites. Israel's hostility toward Edom in future successful military battles against the Edomites is recorded elsewhere (2 Sam. 8:13–14; 2 Kings 8:20–21).

Lex Talionis. This phrase is Latin for "the law of retribution." It calls for punishment that parallels the severity of the crime. Edom would be treated the same way she had treated others, including, of course, Israel. This is brought into sharp focus in Obadiah 15, which explicitly declares: "As you have done to others, so will it be done to you: you will be paid back for all that your deeds deserve." Just as Edom had treated Israel with contempt (Obad. 11–14), so would God similarly punish Edom (v. 15). Just as Edom had profaned the holy mountain of God in Jerusalem, so would she—along with the nations—keep on drinking the bitter cup of God's judgment (v. 16). The Hebrew phrase is *'ayin tachat 'ayin*, or "an eye for an eye" (Ex. 21:23–27).

Inflated Pride. The Edomites did not believe that the rules applied to them, as do many in our world today. They saw themselves, literally and figuratively, as "above" their neighbors (they lived at a high elevation; Obad. 3). Obadiah called them out on this and announced the consequences of such comparative thinking. God regards pride as one of the most heinous of sins, primarily because it displays an attitude of arrogant independence from God as both Creator and Lord. Those who are filled with arrogant pride—as the Edomites were—draw upon themselves the righteous anger of God, since they erroneously believe that they can live independently of God and have no need of him in their lives.

The Day of Yahweh. The concept of the day of Yahweh (the phrase is often translated as "the day of the Lord") is a common one throughout much of the prophetic literature and is likewise a major theme in the book of Obadiah. It has a twofold application, one profoundly negative and the other sublimely positive. Negatively speaking, Edom has a "day" in store for her judgment (v. 8), since she stood by on the "day" that her neighbor, Judah, was attacked—most likely at the hands of the invading Babylonian armies during the period 605–586 BC (vv. 11–14). Additionally, verse 15 records that all the nations have a bitter "day" of judgment coming to them.

However, the theme of deliverance brings us to the second application of this powerful motif, namely the wonderfully positive application of divine blessing and renewal. This is explicitly recorded in verses 17–21, where the day of Yahweh promises to usher in an era of restoration and renewal for the people of God. First, they will be restored to the land of promise, and Mount Zion, symbolizing the city of Jerusalem, will once again be renewed in holiness. Second, the nation of Edom will be totally eradicated at the hands of the house of Jacob, and God's people will have no more enemies from that source ever again. This manifestation of the day of Yahweh will also result in the reestablishing of the kingdom of God for all the people of God and, by implication and extension, the rest of the world. It will truly be a universal kingdom.

Edom and Adam. The Hebrews originally wrote without vowel markers. Thus, the words *Edom* and *Adam* would look exactly the same (*'dm*) to the original readers of the book of Obadiah. We don't want to read too much into this, but one can make the case that the first part of the book deals with the nation of Edom, while the second part deals with surrounding nations and, by extension, all humankind, the descendants of Adam. In other words, God speaks to all of us, all of the time, in his Word.

Seeing Jesus in the Book. The prophetic anticipation of the coming of Jesus Christ is found in the book of Obadiah, as it is throughout the entire Old Testament canon. The Christological focus here is embedded in the theme of the day of YAHWEH, where restoration and renewal are promised to the people of God. It is promised both that the covenant people of YAHWEH will themselves be rendered holy again and that the land of promise itself will be resanctified and returned to God's people. This will result eventually in the reestablishing and expansion of the kingdom of God for the entire world. The ultimate mechanism by which this divine transformation will be accomplished is the coming of the Messianic King, Jesus Christ, the Son of God, our Redeemer. The redeeming sacrifice of Christ on the cross will bring about ultimate renewal, resulting in the once-for-all eradication of sin and death for all who trust in him. And the renewal of the land of promise, the land of Canaan, is an earthly foretaste of the new heavens and the new earth, which will constitute the divine re-creation of the cosmos, where God the Father, the risen Christ, and his people from all over the world will one day live forever in the eternal kingdom of heaven.

OBADIAH

The Servant of YAH

Judgment Pronounced on Edom

1 This is the vision that Lord YAHWEH revealed
to Obadiah concerning Edom.

We have heard a report[a] from YAHWEH:
"I have sent a messenger throughout the nations,
saying,
'Rise up! Let us march against this people.
Prepare for war!'

2 "Behold, I have reduced you to the least among the
nations.
You are now utterly despised.
3 Your proud heart has deceived you;
you who are perched in the hidden places of the
rock,[b]

---

a 1 Or "message" or "directive."

b 3 Pride has the power to deceive and to destroy. The antidote to pride is hiding ourselves in the Rock, Jesus Christ, making his righteousness our own.

whose home is in the heights.[a]
You think to yourself,
'Who can ever topple me to the ground?'
4 Though you soar like an eagle,
and your nest is nestled among the stars,
I am more than able to bring you down from there.
I, YAHWEH, have spoken."[b]

Edom Annihilated

5 "When thieves come at night to rob *your home*,
wouldn't they only steal the things they wanted?
When people gather grapes,
wouldn't they miss a few and leave some gleanings behind?
But you, Edom—your enemies will totally destroy you![c]
6 How Esau's[d] *descendants* will be looted,
their hidden treasures sought out *and ransacked*![e]
7 Your allies will deceive you.
They will overpower you and chase you off your homeland.

---

a 3 That is, Edom's capital, Ha-Sela, which some believe is now Petra in Jordan. The Edomites were driven out of Petra by the Nabateans around 400 BC. The Edomites eventually settled south of Judea and were known by the Romans as Idumeans. Sela (*sela*ʿ is Hebrew for "rock") and Petra (a later Nabatean city; *petra* is Greek for "rock") are often confused with each other. The entire landscape of Edom is, indeed, rocky and elevated.

b 4 See the similarities between vv. 1–4 and Jer. 49:14–16.

c 5 Or "how [totally] you will be destroyed!"

d 6 *Esau* is used here as a synecdoche for the Edomites, of whom Esau was the progenitor. See Gen. 36:1, 8, 19.

e 6 Compare vv. 5–6 with Jer. 49:9–10. It is possible that Jeremiah quoted Obadiah. However, some scholars believe Obadiah was quoting Jeremiah.

Your 'trusted friends'[a] will lay a trap for you,[b]
and you'll have no clue it's coming.[c]
8 In that day, will I not destroy all the wise men of Edom
and erase all their *pseudo*-intelligence from the mountains of Esau?
I, YAHWEH, have spoken.
9 Teman,[d] all your brave warriors will be shattered
so that everyone will be destroyed from Esau's mountain."[e]

Edom's Guilt

10 "Shame will cover you
and you will be annihilated
because you violently slaughtered[f]
your relatives, the Israelites.[g]
11 *You deserted Israel at her time of need.*

---

a 7 Or "men of your peace your bread [those you sat and ate with]." There is the sense of "those from your close friendship circle," denoted by the Hebrew phrase *'aneshe shelomeka lechem*. This reading is legitimated by the term *shalom* within that phrase, which covers a broad semantic field, denoting the primary senses of "peace," "wholeness," "[sound] health," "prosperity," and "friendship."

b 7 See Ps. 41:9.

c 7 Or "he has no understanding."

d 9 Teman was a major city of northern Edom and is here used to designate the entire country.

e 9 That is, the kingdom of Edom.

f 10 This is the Hebrew word *chamas* (or *hamas* in an alternate transliteration style).

g 10 Or "your brother Jacob." *Jacob* is a synecdoche for the land of Judah. The Edomites violently mistreated their distant relatives and became Israel's perpetual enemies. See Gen. 25:22–28; 27:27–29; 32:4–33:16; Num. 20:14–21; Deut. 23:7–8; Ps. 137:7; Lam. 4:21–22; Ezek. 25:12–14; 35:5–12; 36:2, 5.

On that day *of infamy*, you stood aloof and did nothing
as foreigners broke through the city gates of Jerusalem[a]
and divided the city among themselves by casting lots.
Strangers carried off all her treasures,
and you were as one with the invaders.
12 Do not gloat over your relatives
on the day of their misfortune.
Do not rejoice over the people of Judah
on the day of their ruin.[b]
Do not boast[c]
that they suffered such anguish.
13 You should not have entered my people's city
on their day of calamity.[d]
You should not have feasted your eyes on their suffering
on their day of misery.
You should not have seized their wealth
on their day of sorrow.
14 You should not have waited at the crossroads

---

a 11 Verses 11–14 may also be seen as predictive prophecy of the events surrounding the destruction of the Second Temple and sacking of Jerusalem in AD 70 by the Romans. The Edomites were called the Idumeans by then. At that time, much as with these events that Obadiah narrated (the destruction of the First Temple and sacking of Jerusalem in 586 BC by the Babylonians), the Edomites failed to help their brothers.

b 12 All the verbs of v. 12 are imperatives. Literally "Gloat not . . . rejoice not . . . boast not." See Mic. 4:11.

c 12 Or "make your mouth big," which could mean derisive laughter.

d 13 There is a wordplay in the Hebrew that is lost in translation, as the word for "calamity" resembles the name *Edom*. See Ezek. 35:5.

to cut off[a] those who tried to escape.
Why did you hand over their survivors
on the day of their distress?"

God Will Judge the Nations

15 "The day of YAHWEH is drawing near
for all the nations.
As you have done to others, so will it be done to you:
you will be paid back for all that your deeds deserve.[b]

16 "Just as you have drunk *and caroused*
on my sacred hill,[c]
so all the surrounding nations
will drink continually from my bitter cup of
judgment.[d]
They will drink and drink and gulp it down,
but they will stagger and be destroyed."

Israel Will Defeat Her Enemies

17 "But on Mount Zion a remnant will escape,
for that place will be a reconsecrated sanctuary.
And Jacob's tribes will possess
what is rightfully theirs by inheritance.[e]

---

a 14 Or "kill."

b 15 This is *lex talionis*, Latin for "the law of retribution." This approach to justice is found in numerous verses of the Old Testament. See Ex. 21:23–26; Deut. 19:21; Jer. 50:15, 29; Lam. 3:64; Joel 3:4, 7.

c 16 That is, Mount Zion (Jerusalem). See Ezek. 35:12.

d 16 The metaphor of a cup of wine is frequently used for God's punishment (see Ps. 75:8; Jer. 25:15–29; 49:12; Hab. 2:16). The New Testament uses the metaphor of a cup pointing both to Christ's suffering (see Mark 14:36; John 18:11) and God's anger (see Rev. 14:10; 16:19).

e 17 Or "Jacob will dispossess those that dispossessed them."

[18]Then the people of Judah[a] will be a fire,
the people of Israel[b] a flame,
and the people of Esau[c] like stubble.
They will set them on fire and consume them,
and there will be no survivors from Esau's descendants.[d]
I, YAHWEH, have spoken."

The New Israel

[19]People from southern Judah will capture Edom;[e]
those from the western foothills will occupy Philistia;
Israelites will take back the territory of Ephraim and Samaria;
and the people of Benjamin will possess Gilead.
[20]The company of exiles from among the people of Israel
will possess the land of the Canaanites as far as Zarephath[f]

---

a 18 Or "house of Jacob."

b 18 Or "house of Joseph."

c 18 Or "house of Esau"—that is, the Edomites.

d 18 Esau's descendants, the Edomites, became known as the Idumeans, who eventually disappeared from history. The Herods of the New Testament were Idumeans. But after the wars between Rome and the Jews, the Idumeans were never heard from again.

e 19 Or "the mountains of Esau."

f 20 The town of Zarephath was where the prophet Elijah lived for a while (see 1 Kings 17:9–10; Luke 4:26). Zarephath was in modern-day Lebanon.

while the exiles from Jerusalem now in Sardis[a]
will occupy the cities of southern Judah.
21 Victorious deliverers[b] will go out from Mount Zion[c]
to rule[d] over the land of Edom,[e]
and the kingdom will be YAHWEH's.[f]

---

a 20 Or "Sepharad." *Sepharad* means "separated." The exact location of Sepharad is uncertain, and a number of possible locations have been suggested, including Spain, Media, and Libya. Modern scholarly opinion tends to agree that Sepharad is another name for the town of Sardis, the capital city of Lydia in Asia Minor. Archaeologists found in Sardis an inscription dated from the 400s BC that noted a significant Jewish community there at that time.

b 21 Or "saviors," "avengers," or "liberators."

c 21 Or "up to Mount Zion."

d 21 Or "to judge."

e 21 Or "the hill country of Esau."

f 21 Or "YAHWEH himself will be king."

THE BOOK OF

JONAH

The Reluctant Prophet

BroadStreet
PUBLISHING

JONAH

Introduction

AT A GLANCE

Author: Unknown; Jonah is named in the third person

Audience: Universal; Jonah speaks to all who see themselves as spiritual insiders and/or those who think they understand how God always acts

Date: The events of Jonah occurred mid-700s BC; date of writing is unknown

Type of Literature: Historical teaching narrative that carries profound philosophical and theological content

Major Themes: Outsiders and insiders; life from death; the balance of law and gospel; the complexity of repentance; God's radical independence; God sees and God is involved; rebellion and redemption; Jesus and Jonah

Outline:

- I. Yahweh's first call to Jonah — 1:1–2:10
  - a. Jonah disobeys and defects — 1:1–3
  - b. The storm — 1:4–16
    - i. The sailors worship Yahweh — 1:14–16
  - c. The great fish — 1:17–2:10
    - i. Jonah's prayer — 2:1–9
    - ii. God delivers Jonah — 2:10
- II. Yahweh's second call to Jonah — 3:1–4:11
  - a. Jonah obeys — 3:1–3
  - b. Jonah's prophecy — 3:4
  - c. Nineveh repents — 3:5–10
    - i. Jonah's second prayer — 4:1–4
  - d. Jonah and the shade tree — 4:5–11

ABOUT THE BOOK OF JONAH

Jonah is one of the best-known books of the Bible. The great fish is often called a whale in popular culture and gets expressed in the couplet "Jonah and the whale," much like "David and Goliath," "Noah and the flood," or "Samson and Delilah."

But far from being a fable best suited for children's books, Jonah carries an immense amount of philosophical and theological freight, all within the context of one of the most vivid and memorable stories in the Bible. Jonah is a "minor" prophet in name only. Along with the rest of the Twelve (the so-called Minor Prophets), this book shows that a huge helping of wisdom can be served up in a shorter format.

The story begins in Israel, moves to the Mediterranean seaport of Joppa, and concludes in Nineveh, the capital city of the Assyrian Empire along the Tigris River (modern-day Mosul in Iraq). At the time of the events of this book, Nineveh was still a powerful city.

The main character, Jonah, was an actual historical person living in the time when Nineveh was a great city, and Jesus affirmed this. Jonah, the prophet and son of Amittai, is also mentioned in 2 Kings 14:25. In Hebrew, *Jonah* means "dove." Is this an intentional reference to the (negative) connotations of doves as found in Hosea 7:11 and 11:11? Perhaps. Hebrew names are often more than simple labels.

Jonah is one of the few individuals revered by three world religions. Along with Christians and Jews, Muslims also honor him as the only prophet from among the Twelve mentioned by name in the Qur'an.

Tracing back to his father's hometown, we learn that Jonah was from the far north of the promised land, which was later called Galilee by the time of Jesus. Thus, the

Jewish leaders were mistaken when they claimed that prophets didn't come from there (John 7:52).

There are some fascinating parallels with Jonah in other parts of the Bible.

- The ships of Tarshish in Ezekiel 27:25–36 recall the ship Jonah attempted to flee on to Tarshish (Jonah 1:3).
- Elijah's manner while sitting under a tree praying that he might die (1 Kings 19:4) is evoked in Jonah's second prayer (Jonah 4:2–3).
- Jonah 2 echoes the literary style and the themes of the Psalms.

Eastern Orthodox and Jewish believers give this book a central place in their liturgies, the latter using it as the main text for Yom Kippur, the Day of Atonement. The book of Jonah both comforts and frightens readers or listeners as they travel on a wild ride with the prophet, who often acts like the kind of person we don't want to be.

The book of Jonah is not a typical "thus says the Lord" prophetic book, although Jonah is clearly a prophet. In fact, there is only one verse of Jonah's prophecy (3:4) in the entire book. Rather, this is the story of God turning a wayward city and a wayward prophet to repentance. It is the story of a huge fish and a small worm.

Much like the book of Job, the book of Jonah leaves readers without a Hollywood ending and with the ball in our court. How will we respond?

PURPOSE

The author intended to teach some of the more advanced, dynamic truths of our life with God through a vivid and fast-paced narrative. Stories often express depth better than lectures or philosophical descriptions, and we often retain, internalize, and implement the truths of these dramas better than colorless lists of facts. And we can mine incredible truth in these pages. The sublime density of the book of Jonah cannot be reduced to a single theme. The author masterfully wove multiple essential themes into a tight, powerful narrative.

It would be a mistake to focus too much on whether a person can survive being swallowed by a great fish. Lots of unexplained things happen every day. God, who brought the whole universe into existence, can certainly command storms and save people miraculously. God is not bound by our preconceived notions of what he can and cannot do. That was the mistake that Jonah continued to make, thinking he knew best about what God should or shouldn't do with the Ninevites. When we attempt to put our theological limits on God, we often misread what he is doing in our lives and all around us in the world. A personal relationship with God is a dynamic adventure with many unexpected turns, and we are not the ultimate authors of that story.

The book also challenges the reader not to make the same mistakes Jonah made. While we might laugh inside at his foolish responses to God's call and his ridiculous behavior in particular situations, we should also feel troubled and convicted. Why? Because we carry within us some of the same dysfunctional tendencies. Thus, the themes of Jonah are eternally relevant to every reader in every time and place.

AUTHOR AND AUDIENCE

There is no evidence pointing to a specific author whom we can name. Jonah appears in third person (*he*, not *I*). He is the flawed protagonist of the story; nothing indicates that he was the author. Similarly, the book gives no hint of when it was penned. No matter when it was written, it was intended to be read as a historical story taking place in the 700s BC. Regardless of whether the author who gave the book of Jonah its final form was from the same era as Jonah, a universal audience was intended, and it speaks well to people in every time and place. In this way, Jonah is one of the most timelessly valid works of antiquity. Small wonder that it is so well known by the public.

MAJOR THEMES

Outsiders and Insiders. Both the gentiles onboard the ship and the citizens of Nineveh were more responsive to God than the prophet Jonah himself. Jonah knew the Bible well (see his prayers) but totally misread God, over and over. Jesus capitalized on this theme in much of his life and teaching, praising the love and faith of Roman centurions (Matt. 8:5–13), Samaritans (Luke 10:25–37), tax collectors (Luke 18:9–14), and sinners (Luke 7:36–50) rather than that of those within the religious establishment. Even the magi (likely Zoroastrians from what is now modern-day Iran) found Jesus when Herod (king of the Jews) could not. Where would one hear or read the story of Jonah? Among Hebrew-speaking Bible people—insiders. The book is intended to unsettle those insiders who think they have it all figured out and to call them to repentance and some healthy intellectual humility.

In a related vein, this book contrasts nature with human nature. The great fish and even the ocean itself obeyed YAHWEH better than Jonah did. Nature is not a random and complex collision of material atoms. Wind and waves obey God. He gave the animals, fish, insects, and birds instincts that they always follow. Humans with free will, on the other hand, can disobey him. The book starts with Jonah in full-blown rebellion. Despite the many abilities God gave humans and the incalculable gift of his Word, we can still learn much from creation, which obeys God better than some of his ambassadors (Jer. 8:7).

Life from Death. When Jonah was thrown overboard, he expected to die. Many of us have survived a terrifying situation in deep water. When swallowed by a great fish, one expects to die. Perhaps, in a way, Jonah did die but was given a second chance when the fish spat him up on the beach. This clear foreshadowing of Jesus' death and resurrection on the third day compellingly shows readers God's power in hopeless situations and his grace to create beauty and life out of times when we can't even imagine a new start.

The Balance of Law and Gospel. It could be said that God has a left hand and a right hand. On the one hand, he convicts, calls out, and disciplines. On the other hand, he is gracious and merciful and brings us life to the full. This dance between law and gospel waltzes through the entire Bible, and the book of Jonah expresses it in full color, both at a personal (Jonah) and public (Nineveh) level. Our lives also run their course within this dynamic tension between gravity and grace, and no theological flow chart can describe it fully. The most dangerous thing, as Jonah found out, is to think we can outrun or control this paradox. It is better simply to respond in humility and worship, as the sailors and the Ninevites did.

The Complexity of Repentance. To what extent do we choose to repent, and to what extent does God force our hand, as he did with Jonah (and with the apostle Paul, for that matter)? Yes, we are made in the image of God, but we also, on our own, incurably tend toward sin. Can any human act, even repentance, be totally pure? After hearing the story of Jonah, we may well see the need to give God all the glory, even for our repentance. The blessing? Humble repentance releases revival.

God's Radical Independence. Jonah parallels the book of Job with its open ending, affirming God's royal rule over all creation. Even those touting a strict "sovereignty of God" theology often fall short of granting the Creator the potent independence that he reserves for himself. In our human flesh, we'd love just to have the Lord affirm all our limited human opinions instead and act as we expect. But God's tools, heart motives, and plans depart radically from our preconceived religious and theological notions of what he should say and do. He can use monstrous fish and tiny worms to accomplish his works. His mercy is greater, his holiness purer, and his love stronger than we can imagine. His thoughts and plans far exceed our smartest human efforts.

God Sees and God Is Involved. Imagine how differently we would behave if we took this to heart. We make our biggest mistakes in life when we assume that God is not watching. Those of us in the economically developed world often lose sight of the fact that he is also deeply involved in the physical universe. We ultimately relegate the Master of creation to an observer's seat. Jonah thought he could outrun God's field of vision and apparently preferred that Nineveh would just rot. God sees everything and is just as involved in the lives of outsiders as he is in ours. When we see unbelievers and outsiders as pre-Christians rather than as enemies, good things can start to happen. Mercy must always triumph over judgment.

Rebellion and Redemption. Many of us, like Jonah, go through a season of outright rebellion in our lives. God turned him around, and arguably, Jonah became the most successful of all prophets, getting an entire imperial capital city to repent. The Lord can bring forth new life out of any situation. He makes up for the years the locusts have ruined (Joel 2:25) and weaves every detail of our lives together for good (Rom. 8:28) for those who love him. Have you had—or are you in—a season of rebellion? Let the Lord make a beautiful turnaround testimony out of the rest of your life. The fact that you can't outrun God also means that you can't outrun his power to transform your life.

Jesus and Jonah. Jesus' life and ministry had many parallels with the messages of the book of Jonah. Much like YAHWEH in Jonah, Jesus often surprised people. In fact, he was killed for not meeting their expectations. When they asked him questions, he usually responded in a way no one expected. Do we dare enter into an authentic relationship with a powerful, living God, or are we tempted to choose a life with a self-constructed theological image of God that suits our sensibilities and carries with it no surprises? So often, we are more enamored with safe, artificial patterns of "God" than with that dangerous path where we take up our crosses and follow him. Additionally, Jonah's three days in the belly of the great fish foreshadowed Jesus' death and resurrection on the third day (Matt. 12:40).

Along with the fact that his ministry lived out many of these themes of the book of Jonah, Jesus referenced the prophet directly and emphatically (Matt. 12:39–41; 16:4; Luke 11:29–32). The message of Jesus drinks deeply from the challenging truths flowing in the oasis that is the book of Jonah.

JONAH

The Reluctant Prophet

Jonah Disobeys YAHWEH

1 One day YAHWEH revealed to Jonah,[a] Amittai's son,
this message: 2"Arise! Leave at once for the great city
of Nineveh[b] and proclaim judgment against her, for the
wickedness of her people is staring me in the face."[c]
3But Jonah bolted and ran in *the opposite direction*, determined to run away from the presence of YAHWEH. He went
down to the coastal city of Joppa and found a ship bound
for Tarshish. He paid his fare,[d] went down into the hold

---

a 1:1 Or "The word of YAHWEH came to Jonah." *Jonah* means "dove." Jonah is mentioned in 2 Kings 14:25 and by Jesus in Matt. 12:39–41 and in Luke 11:29–32. According to Jewish tradition, Jonah was the son of the widow of Zarephath, whom Elijah raised from the dead (see 1 Kings 17:8–24). Additionally, Jonah is credited with the anointing of Jehu (see 2 Kings 9:1–10). See Seder Olam Rabbah 18.

b 1:2 Nineveh (modern Mosul, Iraq) was the capital and most populous city of the Assyrian Empire. Although Jonah does not give us details of the wickedness of Nineveh, the book of Nahum does (see Nah. 2:12–13; 3:1–5, 19). Some scholars believe the name *Nineveh* means "city of Ninus," who was believed to be the mythical founder of Assyria. Others see its meaning as "house of fish" or think the city was named after a fish goddess. Nineveh was for decades the largest city in the known world. Genesis 10:11 states that Nimrod built the city of Nineveh. At least one ancient tradition is that Nineveh was Noah's hometown. God called Nineveh "great."

c 1:2 Or "its evil has ascended before me." See Ex. 2:23; 1 Sam. 5:12; 2 Kings 19:28; Ps. 74:23; Isa. 37:29; Jer. 14:2.

d 1:3 There is always a price to pay for disobedience to God.

of the ship, and set sail for Tarshish to flee from the presence of YAHWEH.[a] 4But YAHWEH unleashed a powerful, violent wind on the sea. The ship was caught in such a great tempest that it was in jeopardy of shattering. 5The sailors were terrified. Each of them began to call on his own god for help.[b] In order to lighten the ship they hurled the cargo and tackle overboard. Jonah, however, had gone down below and lain down[c] in the hold and was fast asleep.[d]

6The captain went *below* and asked Jonah, "How can you be sleeping so soundly at a time like this? Get up! Call on your god! Maybe he will feel sorry for us[e] and not leave us to die."

---

a 1:3 Or "from the face of YAHWEH." It is difficult to be certain of the exact location of Tarshish. Some have suggested the island of Crete, but more likely, Tarshish was the farthest western location known at that time, on the Iberian Peninsula in southern Spain. What stands out is not simply the location of Tarshish but also Jonah's desire to get as far away as he possibly could from God's presence. Perhaps Jonah thought that God had given him an impossible task of going alone to an enemy nation and proclaiming her doom. Jonah was filled with fear and unbelief. However, disobedience to God is never an option.

b 1:5 These seasoned sailors were all of different nationalities, and each with a god (idol) they worshiped. Sadly, there is no mention yet of Jonah crying out to the true God.

c 1:5 Notice how many times Jonah went "down." He went down to Joppa, down below deck, and lay down to sleep. Soon he will go down into the sea and down into the belly of the fish. The path of disobedience is a downward slope. But thankfully for Jonah (and for us), God heard his cry of despair and rescued him.

d 1:5 This is not the usual Hebrew word for "sleep" but a word used to denote a deep sleep, often a supernatural sleep. See Gen. 15:12; 1 Sam. 26:12. The Septuagint translates the verb as "snore." Nothing could be more exhausting than running from God. Jesus also slept during a storm but for a different reason: he was unafraid.

e 1:6 Or "he will take notice of us."

7Then the sailors said to each other, “Come on. Let’s
cast lots to find out who is to blame for bringing us this
calamity.”[a] They cast lots, and the lot pointed to Jonah.[b]
8So they interrogated him. “Tell us,”[c] they said, “what is
the purpose of your journey? Where do you come from?
What is your country, and who are your people?”
9“I’m a Hebrew,” he replied. “I worship the God of
heaven, the Creator of both sea and dry land. *His name is*
YAHWEH.” 10Jonah added, “*I am his prophet*, but I’m trying
to escape from him.”[d]

Hearing this, the sailors were gripped with fear[e] and said, “What terrible thing have you done?[f]
11What can we do
to you to make the sea calm down for us?” Even as they
spoke, the storm and waves were getting worse and worse.[g]
12Then Jonah said, “It’s all my fault that you are caught
in this violent storm. So just pick me up and throw me
into the sea, and it will calm down for you.”

---

a 1:7 In the ancient world, it was commonly believed that a ship could be endangered by having a guilty person on board.

b 1:7 God is radically involved in the world, this time even in the casting of lots. See the calling of Matthias in Acts 1:15–26.

c 1:8 Some Hebrew manuscripts insert here: “Who is to blame for this disaster?” A few Hebrew and Greek manuscripts leave this sentence out, perhaps because of its repetitive information since the casting of lots revealed that this was Jonah’s fault.

d 1:10 Or “The sailors knew that Jonah was running away from YAHWEH because he had already told them earlier.”

e 1:10 Or “the sailors feared a great fear.”

f 1:10 Or “What terrible thing did you do [to cause this]?”

g 1:11 Or “the sea was walking and storming.”

13*Reluctant to sacrifice Jonah*, the sailors rowed frantically trying to return to shore,[a] but they got nowhere. All the while, the sea was raging even wilder than before. 14*Losing hope*, they began to pray to YAHWEH and said, "Please, YAHWEH, *God of Jonah*, don't let us perish on account of Jonah. And don't hold it against us for throwing this man overboard. For you, YAHWEH, have acted in accordance with your will."

15So the sailors took hold of Jonah and tossed him into the *foaming* sea. *Then all at once*, the sea stopped raging. 16Awestruck, the men were gripped with the fear of YAHWEH, and they made vows and offered sacrifices to *Jonah's God*, YAHWEH.

A Huge Fish Swallows Jonah

17Meanwhile, YAHWEH directed[b] a huge fish *to be at that very spot* in order to swallow Jonah.[c] And Jonah was kept

---

a 1:13 On the surface, the Hebrew text reads simply "the men rowed to get back to dry land [the shore]." However, the verb used to denote "to row" is a colorful one (*chatar*), which carries the nuance of "digging into the water with oars." This implies strenuous effort, hence the appropriate use of the adverbial phrase "frantically trying to return to the shore." Their labor ended in failure given the turbulent sea they had to contend with.

b 1:17 Or "prepared," as translated from the Vulgate, Arabic, Syriac, and Targum. In the Hebrew Bible, this verse is the first verse of ch. 2. There are numerous serendipitous events in Jonah: the ship in Joppa going to Tarshish, the surprising storm at sea, and now the fish directed by God to swallow Jonah. Later, the plant, the worm, and the hot wind will also confirm that God was behind all that happened to his prophet.

c 1:17 It is apparent that God was in control of the sea and the storm, and this verse shows him in control of the huge fish. Whatever kind of fish this was, it was more obedient to God than Jonah was. One ancient Jewish tradition states that God created this unique fish on the fifth day of creation and preserved it in readiness for Jonah. See Pirqe Rabbi Eliezer 10.

alive in the stomach of the fish[a] for three days and three nights.[b]

Jonah's Prayer

2 This is Jonah's prayer to YAHWEH, his God, from out of the *darkness* inside the huge fish:

2 "I called out to YAHWEH from a place of total desperation
and he answered me.
From inside the belly of Sheol[c] I cried out,
and you heard my voice.
3 The waters closed in all around me;
all your mighty waves and currents
crashed over me.[d]
For you cast me into the deep,
and I sank down to the bottom of the sea.[e]

---

a 1:17 The story is replete with miracles. The fish was at the spot where Jonah was thrown overboard and sank into the ocean. The fish swallowed Jonah not to eat him but to shelter him. There are two miracles that may have happened. One, God kept Jonah alive, preserving him from being killed when swallowed and sustaining his life inside the fish. However, it is possible that Jonah died inside the fish and was miraculously resurrected by God (see 2:2). The word for "stomach" could be translated "womb," a possible reference not to the fish's belly but to the "womb of the grave." The God who raised Jesus from the dead after three days could raise Jonah from the dead as well. Regardless, even while running away from God, Jonah experienced the miracle-love of God.

b 1:17 See Matt. 12:40.

c 2:2 Sheol was known as the underworld, the realm of the dead (see Job 7:9–10; Ps. 141:7; Isa. 5:14; 38:17–18). This is possibly proof that Jonah, indeed, died inside the fish and was resurrected three days later.

d 2:3 See Ps. 42:7.

e 2:3 Or "heart of the sea."

4 I actually assumed[a] that you had banished me from
your sight.[b]
Yet, I know that I will one day gaze again upon your
holy temple.[c]
5 The waters rose to choke me to death.
The sea was closing in around me—
seaweed tightened around my head.
6 I sank down into the abyss,
to the roots of the mountains,
where the barred gates of that realm would lock me
in forever.[d]
But you, YAHWEH, are my God;
you raised my life from the pit.[e]
7 When my life was ebbing away,
my thoughts turned toward you.
My cries rose before you in your holy, heavenly
temple,[f]
and *my prayer entered your heart*, YAHWEH.
8 *It's true*—some abandon faithful love to you
by worshiping worthless idols.
9 But I will sing songs of praise and
offer my sacrifices to you.
I will keep every vow I've made to you, YAHWEH,
for salvation comes *only* from you."

---

a 2:4 Although the primary translation of the Hebrew verb *'amar* in the Qal form is "to say," it can also mean "to think to oneself," "to imagine," or even "it crossed my mind."

b 2:4 See Isa. 38:11.

c 2:4 Or, if a conjectural statement (as per Theodotion), "How will I ever see your holy temple again?"

d 2:6 See Rev. 1:18.

e 2:6 Or "grave." The term here literally refers to a "pit" (Hb. *shachat*), but in this context, it functions as a synonym for *Sheol* (see v. 2).

f 2:7 See Ps. 11:4.

[10]So YAHWEH spoke to the fish, and it vomited Jonah onto the dry land.[a]

Jonah Goes to Nineveh

3 YAHWEH spoke to *the prophet* Jonah for the second time.[b] [2]"Arise!" he said. "Leave at once for the great city of Nineveh and preach to the people the message I give you." [3]*This time*, Jonah set out for Nineveh in obedience to the word of YAHWEH. Now Nineveh was a very important city to God.[c]

It took three days to traverse the entire city.[d] [4]When Jonah entered the city, he walked a day's journey and began to preach: "*God* will destroy this city in forty[e] days!"

---

a 2:10 The Assyrians (of whose empire Nineveh was the capital) worshiped Dagon. Dagon was supposed to be their lord of lords, and in the coast cities, he was a fish. So, picture this: you're a Ninevite on the coast, and your god is a giant fish, and here comes a giant fish that vomits out a man with a message from God.

b 3:1 God was not finished with Jonah. He spoke to him a second time. Past failures cannot annul the grace of God in our lives. Our Father will discipline those he loves and will restore them to their calling and mission. Ministry is not an earned position; it is a grace-gift.

c 3:3 The Hebrew word *le'lohim* can mean "great [with many] gods" or, more likely, as an intense superlative, "great [in importance] before God." God is concerned not only for races and nations but also for cities.

d 3:3 Or "a visit [journey] of three days." Commentators vary in interpreting the meaning of the Hebrew phrase.

e 3:4 The number forty is the number of testing. Jesus was in the wilderness for forty days being tested by the devil. God was testing the people of the city and giving them time to repent. The Septuagint gives an even shorter time: "in three days." Jonah's short message was the only prophecy that Jonah gave in the entire book. And it didn't happen. But the city repented, which makes Jonah one of the only successful prophets (in terms of getting people to listen and act).

A City Turns to God

[5]The people of Nineveh believed *Jonah's message and turned* to God. *To show they had repented*, they called for a fast and put on sackcloth, from the greatest to the least of them. [6]When the news reached the king of Nineveh, he arose from his throne, took off his royal robe, put on sackcloth, and sat down in ashes.[a] [7]He then issued this proclamation:

> "People of Nineveh, by decree of the king and his nobles, no person or animal, herd or flock, may eat anything; they must not consume any food or water. [8]Each of you must cover yourself and your livestock with burlap and call on God with all your might. Everyone must turn away from his or her evil ways and violent behavior. [9]Who knows? Perhaps God may show us mercy and be willing to change his mind. Perhaps he will relent and turn from unleashing his fierce anger so that we will not die."

God Forgives

[10]When God saw their sincere efforts to turn from their wicked ways, he decided not to punish[b] the people of Nineveh and did not bring upon them the disaster he said would come.[c]

---

a 3:6 These actions undertaken by the king of Nineveh were classic expressions of mourning and repentance in the ancient Near East.

b 3:10 Or literally "he [God] sighed."

c 3:10 See Jer. 18:7–8. God had forgiven Jonah, and then he showed forgiveness to Nineveh.

Jonah's Response to God's Mercy toward Nineveh

4 Jonah was extremely upset[a] *that God would show mercy to Nineveh.* Indignant, he fell into a rage.[b] [2]He prayed to YAHWEH and said, "God, I knew this is what would happen even before I left home. For I know that you are a tender, compassionate God, who is extremely patient, rich in faithful love.[c] And I know you are always ready to relent from inflicting disaster. That was why I attempted to flee to Tarshish. [3]So now, YAHWEH, please take my life, for death seems better to me than life."

[4]YAHWEH replied, "What good reason do you have to be so angry?"[d]

---

a 4:1 Or "It was evil to Jonah, a great evil."

b 4:1 Or "it burned into him." The contrast is stark. God's burning anger over destroying Nineveh cooled off and dissipated while Jonah's anger burned intensely over God not destroying the city. Jonah wished for vengeance; God longed to show mercy. Perhaps Jonah was angry that he now appeared to be a liar to the Ninevites, for his prophecy of doom did not take place (see *Pirke de-Rabbi Eliezer*, trans. Gerald Friedlander [New York: Sepher-Hermon Press, 1981], 65–66). Sadly, today there are some who wish judgment upon the world. Yet God has sent us a Savior not to condemn the world but to save all those who believe in him (see John 3:16–17). Every day that judgment is delayed, more people are brought into the kingdom of God. Mercy must always take dominion over judgment in our hearts.

c 4:2 See Ex. 34:6; Neh. 9:17; Pss. 86:15; 145:8; Joel 2:13.

d 4:4 The Hebrew is "Does it burn to you rightly?" God was asking his wayward prophet, "Is it right that you are burning with anger?" We should rejoice when God shows mercy to sinners. Jonah rebelled and ran from God, yet the Lord gave Jonah another chance. Jonah had no right to be angry, for he himself had been forgiven by God.

Jonah Waits to See What Will Happen to Nineveh

5Then Jonah went out[a] east of Nineveh,[b] where he made
himself a makeshift shelter. He sat there under its shade
waiting to see what would happen to the city.[c] 6Now Lord
YAHWEH arranged for a *gourd* plant[d] to grow up over Jonah
to provide him shade to rest in and to soothe his sour
demeanor.[e] Jonah was thrilled with the plant. 7But at
dawn the next day, God sent a worm to chew through the
plant—and it withered. 8As the sun rose into the sky, God
sent a scorching[f] east wind. The wind and blazing sun
beat down so hard on Jonah's head that he was starting
to faint. So he begged God to end his life, saying, "I'm better off dead than alive."

9God said to Jonah, "Are you right to be so angry about
the plant that gave you shade?"

---

a 4:5 It is possible that vv. 5–11 are a flashback or a coda to the book. If so, the verbs need to be understood as pluperfect: "Jonah had gone out. . . . He had made a shelter." Regardless, vv. 5–11 serve to show that Jonah had no right to be angry when God had determined to show mercy to sinners.

b 4:5 Jonah's home was west of Nineveh; he went east instead.

c 4:5 It is possible that Jonah was hoping to see the people of Nineveh relapse into sin and bring God's punishment upon themselves.

d 4:6 The Hebrew *qiqayon* simply means "a plant." It was possibly a climbing gourd or the castor oil plant.

e 4:6 Or "his evil."

f 4:8 The adjectival term *charishit* here is derived from the verb *charash*, which carries the meaning "to be silent" or "to be quiet." But a reference to a "silent east wind" makes no sense in this context. In relation to the nature of a "wind," the rendering of a "very hot" or "scorching" wind makes much better sense, given the impact it had on Jonah.

He replied, "I have every right to be angry, angry enough to die!"[a]

[10]YAHWEH replied, "You are concerned for the vine, which you did not plant, nor did you do anything to make it grow. It sprang up one night and died the next. [11]Should I not have compassion for the great city of Nineveh, in which there are more than 120,000 people who cannot tell their right hand from their left,[b] to say nothing of all the animals?"

---

a 4:9 Jonah grieved over the loss of his shade but was seemingly unconcerned about the loss of many lives in Nineveh. Do you long for God to show mercy to those who do not believe in Jesus? God spared Jonah's life, the sailors' lives, and, mercifully, the lives of the people of Nineveh. God is our Savior.

b 4:11 That is, infants and toddlers who had not reached the age of understanding the difference between right and left. Indeed, there could have been millions of people living in the region of Nineveh at that time. The book ends not with information about what happened to Jonah but with the wonderful mercy of God that spared a wicked city that repented. How willing therefore is God to spare your city and your nation when they turn to God with sincere, repentant hearts!

THE BOOK OF

MICAH

Justice and Mercy

BroadStreet
PUBLISHING

MICAH

Introduction

AT A GLANCE

Author: Micah the prophet

Audience: Residents of Jerusalem and Judah and, by extension, all of Israel and Israel's enemies

Date: The book focuses on the late 700s BC

Type of Literature: Prophecy

Major Themes: Corruption and failures of leadership; Yahweh's legal indictment against Israel; the coming royal Messiah; *chesed*; visions of hope and renewal; the day of Yahweh; Yahweh's covenant faithfulness; seeing Jesus in the book

Outline:

I. Superscription: author and setting — 1:1

II. Oracles of divine judgment against Israel and Judah — 1:2–2:11

- a. Announcement of Yahweh's judicial witness against the nations — 1:2
- b. Vision of the destruction of Samaria and Jerusalem — 1:3–7
- c. Lamentation over the destruction — 1:8–16
- d. Indictment of corruption in Israelite society — 2:1–11
  - i. Economic exploitation — 2:1–2
  - ii. Yahweh's planned disaster for his people: Assyrian invasion and despoiling of Israel — 2:3–5
  - iii. Denunciation of false prophets — 2:6–11

III. Promise of divine deliverance — 2:12–13

IV. Indictment of corrupt leaders and prophets — 3:1–12
  a. Condemnation of national leaders for the corruption and exploitation of the people — 3:1–4
  b. Condemnation of false prophets for leading the people astray — 3:5–7
  c. Destruction decreed for the leaders of the nation, both spiritual and civil — 3:8–12

V. Vision of hope and renewal for the nation of God's people — 4:1–5:15
  a. Vision of universal peace on the mountain of Yahweh — 4:1–5
  b. Promised restoration of God's people to their land after the Babylonian exile — 4:6–13
  c. Promise of the coming royal Messiah — 5:1–5a
  d. Promise of deliverance from the Assyrians — 5:5b–15

VI. Yahweh's legal case against Israel and Judah: the *rib* — 6:1–16
  a. Yahweh's indictment of his people — 6:1–8
    i. Yahweh summons his people to hear his accusation (*rib*) and prepare their defense — 6:1–2
    ii. Yahweh's reminder of what he has done for his people — 6:3–5
    iii. True worship vs. false worship — 6:6–8
  b. Israel's guilt and imminent punishment — 6:9–16

VII. Despair turns to triumph — 7:1–20
  a. Lamentation for the corruption of Israelite society — 7:1–6
  b. Promise of hope, restoration, and victory — 7:7–17
  c. Celebrating Yahweh's covenant faithfulness — 7:18–20

ABOUT THE BOOK OF MICAH

The books of the twelve Minor Prophets some of the least studied by Christians today, but they contain some of the great themes of Scripture, such as God's mercy and judgment, his covenant with Israel, the day of YAHWEH, and the coming of the Messiah.

As with the book of Hosea, the original Hebrew text of Micah is in rough shape. Some parts are very challenging to translate. You will notice many divergent renderings when comparing different English translations of Micah. We are all searching for a faithful transmission of Micah's unique voice.

While Micah was living in the Southern Kingdom of Judah, the Northern Kingdom (Israel) was destroyed by the Assyrians (722 BC), and the "ten lost tribes" have never been restored in a reorganized manner. Judah, with its capital in Jerusalem, carried the covenant forward alone from this point on. We get the English word *Jew* from the Hebrew word for the people of Judah.

Micah was active between the mid-700s BC and the early 600s BC. Judah was coming off the prosperous reign of Uzziah (Azariah), who suffered from leprosy. Thus, Micah was prophesying during a period of relative decline from a national high point.

Micah's lifetime included the reigns of the following kings of Judah (the Southern Kingdom):

- Jotham (742–735 BC). He was coregent during the rule of Uzziah, who had leprosy, then king in his own right. Jotham maintained some degree of prosperity. There were some military victories. His reign was a season of much building and construction.
- Ahaz (735–715 BC). The great enemy Assyria emerged on the northeast horizon. Syria (732 BC) and then Samaria of the Northern Kingdom of Israel (722 BC)

fell to the Assyrians. Ahaz was a weak king; in some ways Judah became a vassal state of Assyria during his reign.

- Hezekiah (715–687 BC). Around the year 701 BC, the Assyrians invaded Judah and surrounded Jerusalem, but they were ultimately unsuccessful. Hezekiah attained more freedom from Assyria. He purified the worship culture in Jerusalem (see Jer. 26:17–19, which mentions how Hezekiah listened to Micah).

For more about historical events occurring as the backdrop to Micah's life and work, see 2 Kings 15:32–20:21, 2 Chronicles 27–32, and Isaiah 7, 20, and 36–39.

Micah is used in several Jewish liturgies, especially 7:18–20 with its emphasis on the hurling of our sins into the depths of the sea.

Some key verses in Micah are 5:2, which foretells the Messiah to be born in Bethlehem, and 6:8, which proclaims what God wants from us and is one of the most quoted verses in the Bible.

PURPOSE

Micah's period in history was a very uncertain time. The new superpower to the northeast, Assyria, was picking off smaller nations one by one and inching closer and closer to Jerusalem. Looking ahead, the book also mentions Babylon, which would, a century later, follow Assyria with a second wave of invasions into the Holy Land. Micah brought small-town bluntness and common-sense wisdom to address the perils, both internal and external, of his time.

The internal challenge manifested itself primarily in corruption and bad leadership. Also, worship had become a sham, and people had neglected the heart of their faith (Mic. 6:6–8).

Externally, the threat was from Assyria, a massive and expanding empire centered in Nineveh (see the book of Jonah). This threat increased markedly from the mid-700s onward. Like dominoes, Syria, the Northern Kingdom of Israel, and then even Jerusalem came under siege as the Assyrians marched southward.

Thus, Micah saw himself as promoting hope and God's unchanging and faithful love in a politically and militarily hopeless situation in which both internal and external threats demanded an urgent response. Unwilling to simplistically put all the blame on the people of Judah or on the Assyrians, Micah threaded the needle in a sophisticated and balanced way, showing that there was enough blame to go around and that something needed to be done—immediately. He called the people back to the foundation of what made them Israel in the first place: their divine call "to promote justice, to love kindness, and to walk humbly with your God" (6:8).

In the face of impossible odds confronting Judah, Micah crafted a great hope that would "stick" even if the Assyrians and/or Babylonians won the day and Jerusalem was eventually destroyed (something he never lived to see). A new royal leader, a Messiah (Hebrew for "Anointed One"), would be called forth from Bethlehem to gather, shepherd, and protect the people. The dynasty of David would be restored. And people of all the nations would flow toward Jerusalem's abundance.

AUTHOR AND AUDIENCE

Micah's name means "Who is like Yahweh [in question or statement form]" (see Ex. 15:11; Ps. 89:5–6; Mic. 7:18). Micah was a rough-edged country genius, not a sophisticated urbanite from Jerusalem. This folksy powerhouse emerged out of Moresheth, a small town in the southwest lowlands (Shephelah) on the edge of Judah's territory.

Since he was not classically educated, his potent, pithy, and colloquial language must have sounded almost vulgar to the elites in Jerusalem. He undoubtedly had a country accent. Yet the decadent rulers, prophets, and priests of the big city did not intimidate him in the least. Micah would stand his ground and speak his mind. However, his unvarnished style makes some passages in the book among the hardest in the Old Testament to translate.

Much like Amos, Micah is considered one of the rustic prophets who did not come out of the educated insider intelligentsia. He was a contemporary of Isaiah, whose soaring rhetoric (e.g., "The Wonderful One, the Extraordinary Strategist, the Mighty God, the Father of Eternity, the Prince of Peace!" from Isa. 9:6) was the polar opposite of the rough-barbed warnings of our rustic from Moresheth. A historical parallel would be the AD 1511 trip of (an equally earthy and forthright) Martin Luther to Rome, which produced parallel outbursts of indignation on his part. Amos trained his megaphone on the Northern Kingdom while Micah did the same against Jerusalem, Judah, and their enemies.

Micah was a master of paronomasia, or sophisticated and potent wordplay (Mic. 1:10–16 and elsewhere). This is a skill common among contemporary rappers today. Most English translations do not bring this across well, and The Passion Translation makes a humble attempt to correct that.

Micah's communication style can be described in the following way:

> Vividness and emphasis, lightning flashes of indignation at social wrongs, rapid transitions from threatening to mercy, vehement emotion and sympathetic tenderness, rhetorical force, cadence and rhythm at times elevated and sublime,—these

> are among the prophet's outstanding literary characteristics.[a]

Micah focused his wrath like a laser beam on Jerusalem, but his prophecies break outward like ripples in a pond to all Israel and her enemies, skipping out into the New Testament era and even into our present day, with restorative Messianic and kingdom passages, hopes which continue to anchor our souls.

The direct targets of his prophecy, however, were the leaders of the tribe of Judah, including kings, prophets, priests, and all insiders (especially in chapters 3, 6, and 7). As only an outsider can, Micah called these leaders to account for their corruption. It's a good thing when capable people rise to the top in any system, but it's all too common that they bend the rules to benefit themselves when they get there. Those of us who are financially and socially secure must ask ourselves, *Now that I have some political and/or economic power, am I misusing this strength to keep others from upward mobility?* Corruption has always and will always tempt those with access to the levers of influence.

But Micah was not all about condemnation. As is common in other prophetic books, these pages express a mixed message of both threat and promise. "Micah, like other contemporary prophets, alternates oracles of doom and denunciation with oracles of hope and salvation."[b]

MAJOR THEMES

Corruption and Failures of Leadership. The spiritual, economic, and moral corruption of Israel's and Judah's

---

a George Livingston Robinson, *The Twelve Minor Prophets* (New York: Harper and Brothers Publishers, 1926), 104.

b Juan I. Alfaro, *Justice and Loyalty: A Commentary on the Book of Micah*, ITC (Grand Rapids, MI: Eerdmans, 1989), 8.

leaders is one of the dominant features of the book of Micah, highlighted particularly in 1:3–2:11; 3:1–12; 6:1–16; 7:1–6. Although the general population of Israel and Judah were included in this indictment, the prophet laid key responsibility for the corruption squarely at the feet of the nation's civil and spiritual leaders. Micah denounced the nation's prophets and condemned them for their false teaching, lying, and deception (2:6–11; 3:5–7). Then he condemned the civil leaders for their cruel exploitation of the people, reducing them to poverty, denying them justice in the courts, and generally making their lives miserable (3:1–4, 8–12).

Micah also explicitly indicted the priests, alongside civil leaders and prophets, for demanding money from the general population in return for their services. Not only did they disdain and shirk their obligations under the law, but on top of that they brazenly claimed that they were immune from YAHWEH's displeasure and judgment (3:11–12).

Those in authority have the responsibility to act justly (6:8) and to do the right thing even when it is to their disadvantage. And there is much at stake here. Why should God protect a corrupt society against a foreign invader? Many of you reading this may be in positions of leadership, everything from leading a family or a Bible study group to running a large corporation or sitting in a national legislature. Those of us who are leaders should read Micah with extra care, seeking to walk humbly under God's authority as we exercise authority ourselves. The indisputable guilt of the population in general for their spiritual, economic, and moral corruption is also emphasized in 6:9–16.

YAHWEH's Legal Indictment against Israel. Micah calls for intelligent, differentiated justice. This is a constant biblical theme. Human beings often tend toward selfishness. The principal Hebrew word for "justice" (*mishpat*) also carries a sense of discernment and wisdom, not just equality for equality's sake.

In the book of Micah, however, a certain component of the divine administration of justice is particularly significant. It is bound up in the concept of the *rib*. This Hebrew term can have several meanings, the most common of which are "dispute," "quarrel," and "charge" or "case [at law]." It is the last of these denotations that is especially relevant for Micah: where a *rib* (case at law) of God's is concerned, it usually includes a legal, divine indictment that takes place in the heavenly courtroom. This concept is especially significant in the Hebrew canonical prophets, such as, for example, Jeremiah 25:31, Hosea 4:1 and 12:2. And likewise, here in Micah 6:2, YAHWEH declared—twice—that he was taking his people to court. YAHWEH affirmed through the prophet, ". . . for I, YAHWEH, have an indictment [*rib*] against my people, and I will prosecute my case [*rib*] against Israel." Conversely, there is also a "positive" use of this term in Micah 7:9, where the prophet declared, "I must endure YAHWEH's anger for a while because I have sinned against him. Yet he will still defend my cause [*rib*]." The basis of this positive, divine defense of Micah and his people is YAHWEH's steadfast faithfulness to his covenant promise to never ultimately abandon his people.

It may be observed at this stage that these first two themes emerging in the book of Micah are closely related. The very reason for the injustice and corruption in Judah that constituted YAHWEH's *rib* was the leadership's failures (see notes on this theme in previous section).

The Coming Royal Messiah. Micah was not just a prophet of doom, calling everyone to account for their sins. He was also a prophet of hope. The Assyrian army was bearing down on Judah. The Babylonians were right behind them. Nevertheless, even if Judah failed to turn around in renewal and restoration, even if the royal line were cut off, even if Jerusalem were destroyed, God would find a way to forgive their sins (7:18–20) and restore "anointed" (literally, "Messianic") rule to the faithful remnant.

We get the word *Christ* from the verb meaning "christen" or "anoint with oil." Micah found himself living through a difficult chapter of God's story with his people, but this rustic prophet never lost hope that God would end the story on his victorious terms through his Anointed One (see Ps. 110:1, the Old Testament verse that is most quoted in the New Testament). And this Messiah was not some vague concept; he would emerge as a flesh-and-blood baby in Bethlehem (Mic. 5:1–5a), born to be the heavenly King of kings over the people of God—past, present, and for all eternity. This would take place some seven hundred years from the time of Micah's prophecy (2:13; 4:1–9; 5:2–8; 7:1–7).

Chesed. *Chesed* (often transliterated *hesed*) is one of the richest—if not *the* richest—theological terms in the entire Old Testament. This word has a number of simultaneous meanings when describing the *chesed* of God, such as "mercy," "kindness," "loving-kindness," "goodness," "grace," "favor," and "love." Therefore, it is easy to see why this complex, multifaceted Hebrew word, with no *one* English equivalent, is arguably the most potent word in the Bible. We can describe David's psalms, for example, as a pursuit of God's *chesed*—his unearned, unconditional, unceasing love and protection emanating from the heavenly realm.

Although *chesed* is found only three times in the book of Micah (6:8; 7:18, 20), its meaning pervades the entire spectrum of God's promises of mercy and grace found in the prophecy. In particular, it leads off the central "memory verse" of the prophecy: Micah 6:8, where Micah called the leaders to mirror, to those over whom they had authority, the love that YAHWEH had shown them. It then concludes the book in a heartwarming description of the mercy (*chesed*, 7:18, 20) and grace of God, who promised to pardon his people for their sin, renew them in his love, and remain faithful to his covenant promises given to the patriarchs of the nation, Abraham, Isaac (implied), and Jacob, along with their descendants. That, of course, is an immutable guarantee of the fulfillment of the redemptive promises of God that came to ultimate fruition in the gospel, the person and work of Jesus Christ.

Visions of Hope and Renewal. Visions of hope and renewal constitute the powerful contrasts to the oracles of judgment and catastrophe in the book of Micah. They are set in juxtaposition with those oracles of doom. These hopeful visions are found in 2:12–13; 4:1–13; 5:5–15; 7:7–17. They carry not only the divine promises of physical restoration of the land of Israel and Judah and socioeconomic renewal but also guarantees of pardon for the people of God and the spiritual renewal of the nation's relationship with her covenant Lord.

The Day of YAHWEH. References to the "day of YAHWEH" are not numerous in Micah, but as has been noted in the discussion of *chesed*, the infrequent usage of a term does not necessarily demonstrate a lack of significance. As with *chesed*, the significance of the day of YAHWEH permeates the entire book. References to this phenomenon deal with both the timing of YAHWEH's wrathful judgment against his people for their sins (2:4; 7:4) and the extending of his rich blessings toward them: deliverance from their enemies—Assyria and Babylon—as well as their promised spiritual renewal (4:1, 6; 5:10; 7:11–12).

YAHWEH's Covenant Faithfulness. The concluding three verses of the book of Micah (7:18–20) serve as a fitting climax to the powerful contrasting themes of the prophecy.

The sole foundation of Israel and Judah's hope of deliverance from the wrath of YAHWEH, along with the prospect of their forgiveness and spiritual renewal, lies in the faithful promises of their covenant Lord and God. And it is not a vain hope but an absolute certainty, a hope that is grounded in the promised anticipation of the coming Messianic King (5:1–5a), which constitutes the final major theme of the book of Micah.

Seeing Jesus in the Book. There is no doubt that the climactic prophetic oracle of the book of Micah is in the opening five verses of chapter 5. The whole focus of this Messianic prophecy is to guarantee the people of Israel and Judah that YAHWEH, their covenant God, will provide them with a royal leader who will guarantee their everlasting peace, joy, and—in the context of the prophecy as a whole—their forgiveness. The pinpoint accuracy of this prophetic oracle can be fully appreciated when one considers that there are, in fact, two towns of Bethlehem within Israel and Judah. One is located in the northern region of Galilee near the town of Nazareth, where Jesus spent his boyhood; the other is Bethlehem in Judea (i.e., Ephrathah), not far from Jerusalem, the place to which Mary and Joseph were directed to go for the census of Caesar Augustus and, of course, where Jesus was born. The Micah prophecy is quite explicit in naming the latter location as the birthplace of the future Messianic King of the Jews, and the Gospel accounts of Jesus' birth (Matt. 2:6; Luke 2:4–5) make Micah's prophetic reference to Bethlehem in Judea undeniably accurate. In addition to the prophecy of Micah 5, there is another likely Messianic prophecy to be found in Micah 4:8, where YAHWEH declares that "His kingship will come to you, Daughter Jerusalem," and the Messianic age is hinted at in 2:13; 4:1–9; 5:2–8; 7:1–7.

MICAH

Justice and Mercy

Impending Judgment

1 This is the prophetic message Yahweh revealed to Micah of Moresheth. He delivered these prophecies during the reigns of Jotham, Ahaz, and Hezekiah, kings of Judah. These are his supernatural visions[a] concerning Samaria and Jerusalem.[b]

2 Listen, you peoples—all of you!
Earth, pay attention[c]—and everyone on it.
From his holy temple,
the Lord Yahweh himself
will testify against you.
3 For behold, Yahweh is leaving his dwelling place.
Here he comes to tread upon the high places of the land.[d]
4 Mountains melt beneath his feet,
like wax melting near a *raging* fire.

---

a 1:1 The Lord used some spiritual experiences to show Micah what he wanted Micah to say. The Hebrew expresses it as "to see a word."

b 1:1 These two cities were the capitals of the Northern Kingdom of Israel and the Southern Kingdom of Judah respectively. They are mentioned as representing the two kingdoms.

c 1:2 The Hiphil imperative verb form of *qashab* employed here carries a significantly stronger meaning than simply "listening." It denotes "to give attention to." This sentence indicates that Yahweh regards this divine communication as critically important.

d 1:3 See v. 5; Deut. 32:13. The high places were locales of idol worship.

Valleys are split wide open,
like water pouring down a steep slope.
5 All of this is because of the rebellion of Jacob's *tribes*,
the sin of the people of Israel.
So who is to blame for the rebellion of Jacob?
Is it not *the people of* Samaria?[a]
Who is to blame for *the idolatry of* the high places[b] of Judah?
Is it not *the people of* Jerusalem?[c]

6 "So I will wrestle Samaria to the ground,
and she will become nothing more than an open field for planting vines.
I will roll the stones of her *buildings* down into the valley
until I have laid bare her foundations.
7 I will hammer to pieces all her gilded pagan idols,
all the gifts given to her *sacred* prostitutes[d] will be scorched by fire.
I will turn all her precious idols into a pile of rubble.
For she—Samaria—gathered her treasured idols
as a prostitute collects her fees,

---

a 1:5 Historically, due to the influence of Queen Jezebel (during King Ahab's reign in 874–853 BC), Samaria became a center for the worship of the fertility gods Baal and Asherah. Samaria thus was a major source of religious corruption throughout Israel. See 1 Kings 16:29–33.

b 1:5 Or "sin" (LXX, Targum).

c 1:5 Or literally "What is the high place of Judah? Is it not Jerusalem?" The nominating of the people of Jerusalem as the ones responsible for constructing this idolatrous place of worship in the sacred city is a paraphrase that is clearly implied by this expression.

d 1:7 The Hebrew noun *'etnan* denotes the hire, or wages, of a prostitute. The context here clearly indicates shrine prostitutes. The exact nature of these hires or fees is not specified, but the context makes it clear that they will be destroyed by fire. See Deut. 23:18; Hos. 4:14.

and now these idols will become a prostitute's wages
again."[a]

Micah's Lament for Jerusalem and Surrounding Villages

8 I will mourn and wail because of this.[b]
I will walk around barefoot and bare[c] *to show my sorrow.*
I will howl like a jackal
and mourn like an owl.[d]
9 For her wound is incurable,
and *her infection* is spreading to Judah.
It has even reached the gateway of my people,
to Jerusalem itself.
10 Show no tears in *Showtown* (Gath).[e]
People of *Dusty House* (Beth Leaphrah),[f]
wallow in the dust *of your despair*!

---

a 1:7 That is, the idols on which Samaria had spent its wealth will be taken away by its invaders to be used for temple prostitutes elsewhere.

b 1:8 Verses 8–16 contain prophecies of coming disaster to twelve towns in Judah and Philistia. The prophecies are likely a reference to Sennacherib's invasion of the land in 701 BC.

c 1:8 That is, naked.

d 1:8 Or "ostrich." The ways in which Micah showed his sorrow may seem strange to us today, but they were in his day common expressions of deep sorrow and grief.

e 1:10 The Hebrew contains a wordplay lost in translation. The Hebrew word for "show" is nearly identical to *Gath*. The play on words blends the Hebrew plosive consonants *d* and *th*. This translation of vv. 10–16 will attempt to convey the hidden wordplays of the Hebrew.

f 1:10 See Jer. 6:26. The Hebrew contains another wordplay lost in translation. The Hebrew word for "dust" is *ʿaphar*, which sounds like the last part of *Leʿaphrah*. The name *Beth Leaphrah* means "house of [to] dust."

11 You'll take a different path, *Glamour-Girl-Town*
(Shaphir);[a]
you'll go into exile naked and ashamed.
You citizens of *Outbound City* (Zaanan)[b]
are stuck at home.
Your *next-door neighbor* (Beth Ezel) is in mourning
and will no longer be able to help you.[c]
12 The women of *Bitterville* (Maroth)[d]
writhed in labor pains, hoping for good to come.
Instead, YAHWEH sent down disaster
all the way to the gates of Jerusalem itself.
13 Start up your chariots,
you people of *Ponytown* (Lachish),[e]
for the sin of the daughter of Zion
can be traced back to you, where Israel's sin began.[f]

---

a 1:11 *Shaphir* is the Hebrew word for "pleasant," "beauty," or "glamour."

b 1:11 The Hebrew contains a wordplay lost in translation. The words for "come out/outbound" and "Zaanan" sound similar in Hebrew. *Zaanan* may be a variant spelling of the Zenan mentioned in Josh. 15:37.

c 1:11 Or "The wailing of Beth Ezel ["house of proximity" or "neighbor"] will take away from you its standing place" or "He takes from you what he desires." The meaning and interpretation of this sentence are uncertain.

d 1:12 Maroth is perhaps the Maarath mentioned in Josh. 15:59. The name means "bitterness" (see Ruth 1:20 and the first footnote). There may be a wordplay here since bitterness is unpleasant and gives no encouragement to wait for anything good.

e 1:13 The Hebrew contains a wordplay between *Lachish* and "start up your chariots" (lit. "harness the chariots to the horses"; *larekesh* means "to/for [a team of] horses").

f 1:13 Lachish was the first town in Judah that imitated the sins of the Northern Kingdom of Israel.

[14]*People of Judah*, give gifts[a] to Moresheth Gath,[b]
as you would to a daughter who is leaving home *to be married.*
The *Domiciles of Deception* (Beth Achzib)[c]
will deceive the kings of Israel.
[15]People of Mareshah,[d] YAHWEH will again bring a conqueror against you,
and the glory of Israel
will flee to *the cave of* Adullam.[e]

---

a 1:14 Or "a dowry." Micah saw a similarity between parents saying goodbye to a daughter when she married and the people of Judah saying goodbye to Moresheth. The sobering, implicit contrast is that in saying farewell to Moresheth Gath, the prophet recognized that this town would soon be wedded in a sense to a godless gentile husband who would act brutally toward her.

b 1:14 The name *Moresheth* is nearly identical to the Hebrew word for "fiancée." Moresheth was Micah's home village (see 1:1). Micah implied that his hometown would fall into enemy hands and no longer be part of Judah. No doubt, this was a painful prophecy for Micah to deliver.

c 1:14 There is a wordplay in the Hebrew that is lost in translation. The town name *Achzib* is nearly identical with the Hebrew word *'akzab*, which means "deceitful" (see Jer. 15:18). Achzib is also mentioned in Josh. 15:44.

d 1:15 The name *Mareshah* and the Hebrew word *yoresh*—meaning "conqueror" or "prince"—sound similar. Although it is possible that Mareshah is an alternative form of Moresheth, it is more likely another village in Micah's home area (see Josh. 15:44).

e 1:15 Adullam was a cave in which David took refuge when he was fleeing both from King Saul and from Achish, the Philistine king of Gath (see 1 Sam. 22:1). It thus became a symbol for the last hope in a desperate situation. Micah was saying, in effect, that the leaders of Israel ("the glory of Israel" is likely a metaphor for Israel's princes) would go and hide in the cave at Adullam because of their hopeless, desperate situation, just as David did.

16 Cut off your hair and make yourselves bald,[a]
for your delightful children *are taken away*.[b]
Make yourselves as bald as a vulture,
for your children have been taken away from you into exile.[c]

God Will Punish Those Who Oppress the Poor

2 Disaster is ahead for those who plot evil. They're as good as dead!
Disaster is ahead for those who scheme as they lie on their bed.
No sooner is it dawn than they act on their plan
just because they can.
2 They covet someone's field and seize it for themselves,
and they take over his house as well.
They defraud a man of his home[d]
and another man of his inheritance.
3 So here's what Yahweh has to say about that:
"Now I am the one plotting a disaster

---

a 1:16 Or literally "Enlarge the cutting off of your hair, just like the vulture." The action represented here constitutes a total tonsure of the head—that is, full baldness, just like a griffon vulture. In the context here, this action denotes extreme anguish, as in a state of desperate mourning.

b 1:16 Their "delightful children" may also be a metaphor for the people of the surrounding villages and towns in Judah.

c 1:16 The Hebrew verb *galu* is in the form of the Qal Preterit and can be translated as either an English future or perfect tense. In this context, such an expression is known as a "prophetic perfect." In other words, while the populations of these towns have not yet experienced the trauma of being dragged off into captivity, it is certain that they soon will be. Therefore, their fate is expressed as if it has already taken place.

d 2:2 Or "household." This may be a reference to people being forced to sell themselves into slavery to pay their debts.

for those who plot to defraud others,
a disaster from which you cannot escape.[a]
You will no longer walk with heads held high,
for a catastrophe will bring you low.
4 And when that time comes,
people will adopt a taunting proverb about you
and sing this mournful song to mock your sad experience:
'We have lost everything!
God has divided up our people's lands
with no one left to restore it to our hands.[b]
Our property has been seized
and given to our captors—the traitors.' "[c]
5 Because of this, when YAHWEH restores the land to his people,
those *corrupt leaders* will have no stake in YAHWEH's assembly
nor have any part in the distribution of land.[d]

Hostility to Micah's Message

6 They berate me continually. "Don't prophesy," they say to me.
"Don't keep prophesying on and on about these things!
Disgrace will not overtake us."
7 Should Jacob's descendants even be asking,

---

a 2:3 Or "which you cannot remove from your neck." The Hebrew hints of a metaphor of an ox yoke that will be put on the rich, which they will not be able to remove.

b 2:4 Or "How could God take them [lands] from me?"

c 2:4 Or "Our property has been assigned to infidels [Babylonians/ Assyrians]."

d 2:5 That is, the rapacious, wealthy landowners will have no part in any future redistribution of the land.

"Is the Spirit of Yahweh really so short-tempered
that he would do such things *to us*?"[a]

Yahweh Responds

"When I speak, don't my words produce good
within the one who obeys them?
8 But you *wealthy oppressors of the poor*
have become like enemies attacking my people.[b]
When men return home from war
and think they are finally safe at home,
there you are, ready to snatch the coats off their backs
as security for the money they owe you.[c]
9 You wrongly evict the women of my people[d]
from the very homes they love,
forever depriving their children
of the honor of their inheritance.[e]
10 Get up and get out!
This is no longer your resting place.
Because of this defilement, I will completely destroy you,
and your destruction will be severe beyond measure.
11 If a lying windbag comes to deceive you, saying,

---

a 2:7 In this context, the rich who oppressed the poor were distorting the truth of God's patience, mercy, and tolerance (see Ex. 34:6) to give themselves an excuse for continuing their evil conduct. They could not believe that the Lord would really lose his patience and bring back their evil upon their own heads. But God is not mocked. We will reap what we sow. See Gal. 6:7–8.

b 2:8 Or "Lately, my people have risen up like enemies."

c 2:8 See Ex. 22:26–27. The Hebrew text of this verse contains a number of difficulties, and a literal translation of it is almost unintelligible without some emendation.

d 2:9 These women were most likely widows.

e 2:9 Or "from their children you take my glory forever."

'I prophesy wine and liquor[a] will flow for you,'
he would be the ideal prophet for a people like this."

YAHWEH's Promise of Restoration

12 "I will regather the tribes of Jacob.
Yes, I will regather the remnant of Israel.
I will bring you together like sheep in a fold,
like a flock within their pasture,
a noisy, excited multitude.

13 "The Barrier-Breaker will lead them out *into freedom*.[b]
They will all break out,
passing through the *enemy's* gates.
Their king will advance before their eyes
with YAHWEH himself leading the way!"[c]

Micah Prophesies against Judah's Leaders

3 Then I said,
"Listen, you leaders of the tribes of Jacob,
you princes among the people of Israel.
Is it not your duty to see that justice prevails?
2 Yet you hate what is good and love what is evil.
You skin my people alive, pulling the flesh off their bones.

---

a 2:11 Or "beer." The Hebrew term *shekar* denotes any strong, intoxicating drink.

b 2:13 Or "A breaker will ascend before them." The same one who punished them for their rebellion and allowed Israel to go into exile will be the one who rescues them and leads them back to their own land. Jesus, the Messiah, is the one who broke through the gates of death, passed through the torn veil, and ascended to the Father. Our Shepherd-King leads the charge, and those who follow him likewise pass through every barrier. He breaks out ready to conquer (see Rev. 6:2). Jesus is the Barrier-Breaker who lives in us.

c 2:13 Or "YAHWEH at their head."

3 *Like butchers*, you tear the skin off my people.
You break their bones and chop them up
like stew meat for the pot.
Like wild animals, you rip the flesh off their bones
and devour my people.[a]
4 Then you will cry out to him, but he will not answer
your prayers.
Yahweh will hide his face from you rulers
because you have totally misused your power."

Micah Prophesies against False Prophets

5 Here is what Yahweh says against the prophets
who lead my people so far from the truth:
"So long as they pay you, you prophesy peace.
But if they don't, you threaten war.[b]
6 So, darkness will close in around you,
and you will receive no prophetic visions.
A shroud of darkness will bring your predictions to an
end.
The sun will set for the prophets,
and the daylight will go dark for them.
7 Then shame will silence the seers.
Confusion will cover those who predict the future.

---

a 3:3 See Ps. 14:4.

b 3:5 Or "When you have something to eat [literally "when you bite with your teeth"], you promise peace, but if they don't put food in your mouth, you declare war against them." In the time of Micah, prophets were paid not only with cash payments but also with food. In the final clause—"you threaten war"—the Hebrew verb used is *qadash*, which has the predominant sense of "sanctify" or "consecrate." The underlying sense here is that war conducted by God's people against their pagan enemies was routinely preceded by certain sacred ritual ceremonies (see Josh. 3:5; 1 Sam. 13:8–12).

Humiliated, they will all put their hands over their
mouths[a]
because there is no word from God."
8 Not so with me, for I am full of power!
YAHWEH's breath[b] fills me with a sense of justice
and courage to expose the rebellion of Jacob's *tribes*
and the sin of the people of Israel.[c]

9 Now hear this, you leaders of the tribes of Jacob,
you princes of the people of Israel:
You hate justice
and distort right into wrong.
10 Indeed, you build up Zion and Jerusalem
but upon an *immoral foundation* of murder and
malice.
11 Her judges render verdicts for the highest bidder,
her priests preach for a price,
her prophets prophesy[d] for a fee,
and yet they pretend to depend upon YAHWEH.
"Isn't YAHWEH on our side?" they say.
"How could any disaster come upon us?"
12 That is why, thanks to you,
Zion will return to farmland,
Jerusalem to a pile of rubble,

---

a 3:7 Or "they will all cover their lips/mouths/lower part of their faces." This action was associated with classic mourning in ancient Israelite culture, indicating profound grief, shame, or humiliation—or all three (see Ezek. 24:17). Of course, the reason for this was that, as a judgment from God for their wickedness, they had lost their ability to predict the future. They were confronted with a profound divine silence.

b 3:8 Or "YAHWEH's Spirit."

c 3:8 God's prophets have heaven's strength, the breath (Spirit) of God, a passion for justice, and boldness to speak truth to power.

d 3:11 Or "tell fortunes."

and the Temple Mount will be *deserted*—
overgrown with thickets.[a]

Future Glory of Zion

4 In the future,[b] the mountain of YAHWEH's temple
will be raised up as the head of the mountains,[c]
towering over all the hills.
A sparkling stream of every nation will flow into it.[d]
2 Many peoples will come and say,

---

a 3:12 Micah was the first of the prophets to prophesy the overthrow of Israel and destruction of Jerusalem. During the reign of Hezekiah, the king heeded Micah's words and carried out religious reforms (see 2 Kings 18:1–8; 2 Chron. 29–31).

b 4:1 Or "At the end of days." This phrase, often used by the prophets of the Old Testament, refers to our current time in human history between Pentecost and the return of Christ to the earth. See Heb. 1:2; 1 John 2:18. Micah 4:1–3 is nearly identical to Isa. 2:2–4.

c 4:1 The mountain of YAHWEH's temple can be understood in several ways. Some view it as Jerusalem, others as a mountain in the heavenly realm; still others view this mountain as a metaphor for the people of God, his dwelling place (see Eph. 2:11–22). God's grace will fully establish his people as the mountain rising above every other mountain. Mountains in the Bible are often used metaphorically for kingdoms. Kingdoms and governments are like mountains and hills on the landscape of history. The mountain-kingdom of God will be the chief of all mountains, the highest of all hills. The secular world sees Christ's kingdom as irrelevant and powerless. But one day, the kingdoms of the earth will be leveled, and the King's mountain will be high and exalted. See Isa. 25:6–8.

d 4:1 Or "All the nations will flow as a river to it." The Hebrew word *nahar* can be translated "stream [river]," "to sparkle," or "to be cheerful." In Isa. 60:5, it is translated "radiant." A cheerful, sparkling stream of people will come into divine radiance as they come up the mountain of the Lord. This speaks of the uphill flow of the river of God—a supernatural magnetism bringing the nations into the kingdom of Christ. This is the reversal of the dispersion of the people at Babel (see Gen. 11:1–9).

"Everyone, come! Let's go up higher to YAHWEH's
mountain,
to the house of Jacob's God; then he can teach us his
ways,
and we can walk in his paths."
Zion[a] will be the center of instruction,[b]
and the word of YAHWEH will go out from Jerusalem.
3 He will judge fairly between strong, distant nations
and settle disputes among many peoples.
The swords they used *against each other*
they will beat into plowshares, and their spears into
pruning hooks.[c]
No nation will take up weapons against another,
nor will they prepare for war anymore.
4 But everyone will relax
under their own fig trees and vineyards
with no one to trouble them.

---

a 4:2 Zion today is more than a location; it is a realm where God is enthroned (see Pss. 2:4–6; 87:5). Zion is a synonym for the people of God, the dwelling place of his Spirit (see Pss. 9:11; 74:2; 76:2; Heb. 12:22–24). The perfection of beauty is in Mount Zion, where the light of God shines (see Ps. 50:2). Perfected praise rises to the Lord in this place of perfect rest (see Ps. 65:1–2). The Mountain of Zion is where the Lord is known in his greatness (see Ps. 99:2; Isa. 12:4–6). It is the hope of all the afflicted (see Ps. 102:16–22; Isa. 14:32; 51:11).

b 4:2 Although the Hebrew word *torah* is used here, it means more than "the law." This word also can be translated "instruction" or "teaching." This is not the law of Moses, for that came from Sinai. This is revelation of the gospel and the instruction of God out of the Zion realm that overcomes every work of darkness within us and around us. From Jerusalem the gospel light and the twelve mighty apostles went forth to change the world.

c 4:3 Or "sickles" (LXX). Weapons that the people turned on one another will now be used for the harvest. See Isa. 2:1–5.

For YAHWEH, Commander of Angel Armies, has
decreed it.

5 Though all the nations walk in the name of their own
gods,
we will walk in the name of YAHWEH, our God, forever
and ever.

The Scattered Flock Returns to Zion

6 I, YAHWEH, declare:
"In that day *of hope* I will gather the lame
and bring together the wandering outcasts
and those whom I have bruised.
7 I will make a new beginning
with those who are crippled and far from home.
My remnant will be transformed into a mighty
nation.
And I, YAHWEH, will reign over them on Mount Zion[a]
from now and throughout eternity.

---

a 4:7 See the first footnote for v. 2.

8 “And to you, Tower of the Flock,
where the daughter of Zion is lifted up,[a]

---

a 4:8 Or “the hill of Daughter Zion.” *Hill* is taken from the triliteral Hebrew root *ʿpl*, which means “to lift up” or “to swell.” One of the possible meanings is “stronghold [fortress, mound].” Traditionally, this is seen as a metaphor for Jerusalem as the place where God, like a shepherd from his lookout tower, watches over his people. However, “Tower of the Flock” (Hb. *Migdal ʿEder*) is a historical location on the road between Jerusalem and Bethlehem and only yards away from the border of Bethlehem. This was the place where Rachel was buried after giving birth to Benjamin and where Jacob pitched his tent to mourn her passing. Migdal Eder was known to have a two-story stone watchtower where Levitical shepherds would stand watching over the flock to make certain that the wild animals did not harm the sheep. These were the flocks raised to be sacrificed in the temple just four miles away. Migdal Eder was like a holding pen for these special Passover lambs. It is possible that the shepherds, on the night Jesus was born, were near Migdal Eder. This would fulfill both the prophecies of Mic. 5:2 and 4:8. The birthing of the Passover lambs would take place at the lower floor of the watchtower (Migdal Eder). Selected ewes that were about to give birth would be brought there. After the birth of the lambs, the priestly shepherds would wrap the lambs in cloth and lay them in the manger lined with soft hay, for Passover lambs must be unblemished with no bruises or broken bones. The miracle sign for these priestly shepherds would be a baby boy lying where the Passover lamb should be—in *the* manger (not *a* manger, but *the* manger where sacred lambs would be placed). Based on the prophecy of Mic. 4:8, the Jewish Midrash concluded that the arrival of the Messiah would be declared first at Migdal Eder. Jesus was not born in a cave or in a stable but in the lower floor of Migdal Eder and placed where a sacrificial lamb belonged. See Alfred Edersheim, *The Life and Times of Jesus the Messiah*, Book 2, chapter 6; Luke 2:1–20.

your royal dominion[a] will arrive.
His kingship will come to you, Daughter Jerusalem."

The Siege and Exile of Jerusalem

9 Why are you wailing?
Why are you writhing like a woman in labor?
Have you no king to help you?
And your wise leader,[b] has he perished?
10 Groan and writhe in anguish,
like a woman in hard labor, daughter of Zion,
for now, you must leave the city
and live out in the open field.
Off to Babylon you must go!
Yet, one day you will be rescued from there,
for YAHWEH will deliver you
from the clutches of your enemies.

Jerusalem under Siege

11 Many nations have now gathered to attack you.
They say, "Let's destroy Jerusalem
so that we can gloat over capturing Zion."[c]

---

a 4:8 Or "your first rule [dynasty] will come." Traditionally this was understood as the return of David's kingly rulership to Israel; however, seen from the vantage point after Christ's time on earth, the hints of the coming Messiah to take "dominion" as the first and foremost King are clear.

b 4:9 Or "counselor." These two rhetorical questions can be interpreted in two ways: first, in referring to God as their King and Counselor who is always there to help them and, second, in referring to Hezekiah and his prophetic adviser, who could not be counted on to save them.

c 4:11 Or "Let her be profaned [violated] and let our eyes gaze upon Zion." This seems to imply overtones of a violent man about to rape a girl, which is in keeping with the larger context, for Jerusalem is referred to as the "daughter of Zion" (vv. 8, 10, 13).

12 But they do not know YAHWEH's plans,
and they do not understand his strategy:
he has brought them together to punish them,
like grain is brought to be beaten on the threshing floor
to separate the good from the worthless.

YAHWEH's Promise

13 "Arise, start your threshing, daughter of Zion,
for I will make you *strong as a bull*
with iron horns and bronze hooves
so that you can crush many peoples.
And you must devote to YAHWEH what they have stolen
and bring their wealth to me, the Lord of the whole earth."

The Future Glory of the Davidic Dynasty

5 Now you are walled in.[a]
They have laid siege against us.
They smack the ruler of Israel's face with a rod.[b]

---

a 5:1 As translated from the Septuagint. The meaning of the Hebrew text, "Gather in the troops, daughter of troops," is uncertain. In the Hebrew Bible this verse is numbered 4:14 and ch. 5 begins with v. 2.

b 5:1 To "smack [strike]" someone upon the cheek was considered a symbolic way to humiliate a person. See 1 Kings 22:24; Job 16:10; Lam. 3:30.

[2]"But you, Bethlehem Ephrathah,[a]
so small among the clans of Judah,
from your people will come a ruler
who will rule Israel for me.
He will burst forth from the *first* sunrise[b]
from the days of eternity!"[c]

---

a 5:2 Or "But you, fruitful Bethlehem." See Matt. 2:6. Jewish tradition places ancient Bethlehem Ephrathah northeast of the current city and about four miles (six kilometers) south of the Old City of Jerusalem. This puts Migdal Eder (see Mic. 4:8 and the first note there) very close to the modern-day marker of Kever Rakhel—the tomb of Rachel. Bethlehem was the ancestral home of David. *Ephrathah* means "fruitful." It is likely the name for a neighborhood attached to Bethlehem, and it comes from the name of Ephrath, one of the clans that made up the tribe of Judah (see Ruth 1:1–2). David's family was part of this clan (see 1 Sam. 17:12). *Bethlehem* means both "house of bread" and "house of warriors." Jesus, who was born in Bethlehem, is our Living Bread and our Mighty Warrior. The Hebrew alphabet contains picture meanings with each letter. So, if we do a Hebrew word study on the pictographic Hebrew letters, it will display a deeper meaning: *Bet* has a picture of a house and means "a house," "son," or "Son of God." *Yod* is a picture of a hand and means "to work" or "to do a mighty deed." *Taw* is a cross and means "to seal" or "to make a covenant." *Lamed* pictures a staff and means "to control" or "to have authority." *Het* is an inner room and has a picture meaning "to separate," "a fence," or "a sanctuary." *Mem* pictures the waters and means "liquid," "massive," or "chaos." From their pictographs, *Bethlehem* translates as "The Son of God is going to do a mighty deed. This deed will seal a covenant and be identified with the sign of a cross. He will have the authority to provide a sanctuary of safety where he will give those who have received him the water of eternal life."

b 5:2 Or "his goings out" or "his rising." The Hebrew word *motsa'otaw* is derived from a root word meaning "fountain."

c 5:2 The Hebrew word *ʿolam* can be translated "ancient [times]"; however, it is most frequently associated with eternity. This is a clear statement of the eternality of the Savior who was born in Bethlehem.

[3]Therefore, *Yahweh* will hand Israel over to her
enemies
until the labor pains are over and the child is born.[a]
And then the remnant of his brothers *in exile*
will be reunited with the Israelites.
[4]He will take his stand and will lead and feed his flock
with the strength that comes from Yahweh
and with the majesty of the name of his God.
With this shepherd, they will live in safety,
for his greatness will extend to the ends of the earth.
[5]He himself will be their peace.[b]

Yahweh Will Deliver Israel from the Assyrians

When the Assyrian army sets foot on our soil[c]
to invade our land,
we will raise up more than enough
mighty captains to conquer them.[d]
[6]They will shepherd the Assyrians with the sword,
the land of Nimrod[e] with the drawn sword.[f]

---

a 5:3 See Isa. 7:14; 9:6. Although the language used is somewhat mysterious, the implication of the text is that the child born from this labor will be the deliverer of the nation. The labor pains will birth the hope of deliverance and restoration in the future.

b 5:5 The Hebrew word *shalom* means "peace," "abundance," "prosperity," and "wholeness." See Isa. 9:6; Eph. 2:14.

c 5:5 As translated from the Septuagint and Syriac. The Hebrew is "treads upon our palaces/fortresses."

d 5:5 Or "we will raise up seven shepherds [rulers] against them and eight princes of men." This is a figure of speech saying that they raise up not two or three but more than enough (seven or eight) forces to defeat them. This figure of speech—giving one number followed by another number that is greater by one—is frequently found in Scripture (see Prov. 6:16; 30:15; Amos 1:3, 6, 9, 11, 13).

e 5:6 The "land of Nimrod" is synonymous with Assyria.

f 5:6 Or "at its borders [entrances]." A slight emendation of the text gives *peticha*, "drawn sword."

And *Yahweh* will deliver us from the Assyrians,
when they invade our land
and tread on our territory.

The Remnant

7 Then the remnant of Jacob
will be scattered among many peoples.
They will be like the refreshing dew from Yahweh,[a]
like raindrops on the meadows,
which do not wait on man's command
and are beyond human control.
8 Then the scattered remnant of Jacob will live among
the nations.
They will be like lions among the animals of the
forest,
like fierce lions among flocks of sheep,
they will pounce on their prey with no one to rescue.
9 You will be victorious over your foes,
and all your enemies will be torn to pieces.

Yahweh Will Destroy Their Idols

10 "When that day comes," declares Yahweh,
"I will destroy your horses and demolish your
chariots.
11 I will destroy the cities of your country
and tear down all your strongholds.
12 I will dismantle the witchcraft[b] in your land,
and you will no longer cast spells.
13 I shall tear away your idols
and your sacred stone pillars from among you.
You will no longer worship things

---

a 5:7 The dew was considered to be a gift from the Lord (see Gen. 27:28; Deut. 33:28; Hos. 14:5).

b 5:12 Or "I will remove the magic charms from your hands."

that your own hands have made.
14 I will uproot your sacred poles[a]
and level your cities.
15 I will punish with furious anger
the nations who have disobeyed me."

Yahweh's Indictment of Israel

6 Now listen to what Yahweh says:
"Stand up and state your case.[b]
The mountains *will be your witnesses*,[c]
so let the hills hear your *defense*.[d]
2 Listen, mountains, to Yahweh's accusation;

---

a 5:14 Or "Asherah poles," which were idols used in the worship of the goddess Asherah.

b 6:1 The reading "state your case" translates the Hebrew verb *rib*. Micah 6:1–5 constitutes what Old Testament scholars call a "*rib*-oracle"—that is, a "covenant lawsuit." The Hebrew term *rib* occurs as both a verb and a noun. In a number of contexts, the verb *rib* carries the meaning "to conduct [or mount] a legal case [or lawsuit] against someone." As a noun, *rib* denotes a "lawsuit," "[legal] charge/case," plus other synonymous terms. The essential significance of such an oracle in this context is that Yahweh was launching a formal legal indictment against his people Israel for their violation of the divine covenant law. The assumed setting for such a divine legal prosecution is the heavenly courtroom. In addition, there is the significance of the canonical prophet functioning as a divinely appointed prosecuting attorney, pleading Yahweh's case against his wayward people. Micah fulfilled this role here, *formally*, in ch. 6, and it may also be argued that he executed this role *informally* throughout his entire prophetic work. The same may be said for the prophet Hosea, who participated in another *rib*-oracle against Israel in Hos. 4–5. For similar uses of the term *rib*, see Ex. 23:2–3; Deut. 25:1; Jer. 25:31.

c 6:1 In vv. 1–5, God convenes his courtroom and summons the age-old mountains to be the witnesses to Israel's waywardness. God often met with his people on mountains (Sinai, Nebo, Ebal, Gerizim, Zion, Carmel, Calvary).

d 6:1 Or "your voice."

pay attention, you enduring foundations of the earth,
for I, YAHWEH, have an indictment against my people,
and I will prosecute my case against Israel.
3 My people, what have I done to *deserve* your *neglect*?
How have I made you tired of me? Answer me!
4 *Did* I *not* rescue you from Egypt
and ransom you from slavery?[a]
I sent Moses, Aaron, and Miriam to lead you.[b]
5 Please remember this, my people:
King Balak of Moab planned *to curse you*,
and how did *the prophet* Balaam son of Beor answer him?[c]
He spoke YAHWEH's blessing over you!
Remember how I parted the Jordan
so that you could cross over from Acacia to Gilgal.[d]
Now you should know *through all my saving acts*
that I have treated you fairly."[e]

Micah's Response

6 What should I bring when I enter YAHWEH's presence
and bow down before God Most High?

---

a 6:4 Or "the house of slavery."

b 6:4 Israel was led out of slavery, in part, by a woman—Miriam. She was the older sister of Moses and a prophetess. See Ex. 15:20; (Talmud) Megillah 14a. Another "Miriam" had a role in leading us out of our former slavery to sin, for the mother of Jesus was named Miriam (Mary).

c 6:5 See Num. 22–24.

d 6:5 This sentence in Hebrew reads simply: "From Shittim [Acacia] to Gilgal." Shittim is short for Abel Shittim (Hb. *ʾabel hashshittim*), which translates to "Acacia meadow." Most scholars see a lacuna, a gap, in the Hebrew text here. The obvious inference is a reference to the miracle-crossing of the Jordan so that Israel could go from her last camp in the wilderness (Acacia) to her first camp in the promised land (Gilgal; see Josh. 3:1–4:19).

e 6:5 Or "righteously."

Should I approach him with burnt offerings,
with year-old calves *to sacrifice*?
7 Will he be pleased with thousands of rams
and with endless streams of olive oil?
Should I offer him my firstborn for my wrongdoing,
my own offspring for the sins of my life?[a]
8 *No! Listen*, O Adam's *offspring*,
Yahweh has made it plain to you what is best.
He has shown you what he really is longing for from you—
only to promote justice,[b] to love kindness,[c]
and to walk humbly with your God.

Yahweh's Punishment

9 Yahweh's voice is calling out to the city.[d]
Wise is the one who fears the name of Yahweh.
"So pay attention, O tribe,
to the one who called you together![e]
10 Can I overlook the treasures that fill the homes
of evil people who cheated others?
They use false measures, which I despise.[f]

---

a 6:7 Or "soul." The Hebrew term *nepesh* has a very broad semantic range. Possible meanings can include "life," "soul," "living being," "self," "person," "desire," "appetite," "emotion," or "passion," all with various shades of meanings.

b 6:8 Or "to act from a sense of wise [discerning] justice."

c 6:8 Or "to [demonstrate] unfailing love [mercy]." This is the almost untranslatable Hebrew word *chesed* (or *hesed*), which includes the meanings of "loyalty," "goodness," "kindness," "mercy," "faithfulness," "love," "graciousness," and more. Many commentators view Mic. 6:8 as one of the greatest sayings in all the Old Testament. See Mark 12:32–33.

d 6:9 See Prov. 1:20–21.

e 6:9 The Hebrew of this sentence is uncertain.

f 6:10 The Hebrew of v. 10 is uncertain.

11 Do you really expect me to forgive those who cheat others
with a bag of wrong weights and dishonest scales?
12 The wealthy are steeped in violence,[a]
and the people are liars and speak deceitfully.[b]
13 As for me, I will deal you a crippling blow
to ruin you for your sins.
14 You will eat but not be satisfied;
you will still be hungry.[c]
You will acquire but save nothing
because what you save,
I will send your enemies to destroy.
15 You will plant crops but not reap a harvest,
press olives for its oil and never be able to rub it on yourselves,
and tread grapes but never drink the wine.
16 For you live by the standards of the dynasty of Omri[d]
and follow the evil ways of Ahab and his household.[e]

---

a 6:12 The Hebrew word for violence is *chamas* (or *hamas*, in an alternate transliteration style). This implies more than just physical violence. It also involves economic coercion or force. The powerful often seek a monopoly on the use of force.

b 6:12 See Ps. 116:10–11; Rom. 3:4.

c 6:14 Or "your filth is inside you." The Hebrew verb form *yeshacha* is a hapax legomenon, found only here in the Scriptures. Consequently, Old Testament scholarship recognizes that there is no way to ascertain the true meaning of this term.

d 6:16 Omri ruled the Northern Kingdom of Israel from 885 to 874 BC, and his son Ahab followed him from 874 to 853 BC. The Omride dynasty held the throne longer than any other family in the Northern Kingdom, yet they were outstanding for their wickedness.

e 6:16 Or "the house [family] of Ahab." Ahab and his wife Queen Jezebel encouraged people to worship foreign gods. See 1 Kings 16:23–24; 21:25–26. Ahab's evil sons ruled after him, first Ahaziah, then Jehoram. See also 1 Kings 22:52; 2 Kings 3:2. Micah's ministry began more than one hundred years after the Omride dynasty ended.

Because you walk after their example,
you force me to make an example out of you!
I will hand you over to ruin
and make you a laughingstock *among the nations*.
People everywhere will treat you with contempt."

Micah's Lament over Judah's Wickedness

7 I'm so depressed and disappointed,[a]
like a hungry man who went to the field
after the harvest had been gathered
and found nothing remaining, not even the
gleanings—
nor a single cluster of grapes
nor any of those firstfruit figs I love.
2 The godly[b] have vanished from the land:
there is not a decent person left.
They are all out for each other's blood,
they hunt each other with a net.
3 Concerning evil, both hands do it well.[c]
Officials and judges ask for bribes,
the man in power pronounces whatever he pleases,

---

a 7:1 Or "Woe is me." The prophet Micah was sad as he saw the wickedness of the people. He felt as though he had wasted his life in trying to bring his people back to following YAHWEH.

b 7:2 This is the Hebrew word *chasid* (or *hasid*), which is taken from the same root word as *chesed* (*chesed* means "merciful," "loyal love," "loving-kindness," or "tender love"). To be godly is to be loving and kind, a person of *chesed*.

c 7:3 This was off-putting imagery meant to revolt the original Jewish hearers. They had a strict cultural regulation of the uses of the right and left hands: food was eaten only with the right hand, while the left was used for less sanitary tasks. The Hebrew word translated "hands" here is *kap*, which refers more specifically to the hollow of one's palm. The implication is that not only were the people doing evil acts with both hands, including the left hand reserved for filthy tasks, but they were cupping their hands to scoop up evil.

and the prominent plot as one.
4 The best and brightest is like a briar bush,
the most honest of them like a thorn hedge.
Now here comes the punishment your prophets
proclaimed.[a]
Confusion confronts you!
5 Don't dare to trust in a neighbor
or place your confidence in a friend.
Watch your words even with the wife you love.[b]
6 For the son insults his father,
the daughter rebels against her mother,
and the daughter-in-law quarrels with her
mother-in-law.
One's enemies come from within your own household.[c]
7 But as for me,
I will keep watching for YAHWEH *to break through.*
I will wait for the God who will save me,
and I know my God will hear my cry.

YAHWEH Will Vindicate His Own

8 Listen, my enemy.
Don't gloat over me when I fall,
for I will get back up *even stronger.*
Whenever I feel darkness around me,
YAHWEH himself will be the light that surrounds me.
9 I must endure YAHWEH's anger for a while
because I have sinned against him.

---

a 7:4 Or "the day of your watchmen [the prophets], your appointed [time of punishment], is coming." The prophets were viewed as Israel's "watchmen" because they were to see prophetically when trouble was coming and were supposed to warn the people so that they could change their evil ways and be delivered. See Jer. 6:17; Ezek. 3:17–21; Hos. 9:8.

b 7:5 Or "the one who lies in your bosom."

c 7:6 See Matt. 10:21, 35–36; Mark 13:12; Luke 12:53.

Yet he will still defend my cause
and right every wrong done to me.
He will *expose it all and* bring me out into the light,
and I will experience firsthand his vindication.[a]
10 When my enemy sees this,
she will be disgraced and covered with shame—
she who sneered, "Where is this God of yours,
Yahweh?"
I'll see it with my own eyes
as she is trampled down
like mud in the streets.

A Prophecy of Restoration

11 What a day that will be! A day for rebuilding your
walls!
A day for expanding your borders!
12 A day when people come to you from everywhere—
from the cities of Assyria, Egypt, and Tyre
and all the way from the river *Euphrates*,
from across the seas, and from every mountainous
land.[b]
13 Those lands will become desolate
because of the corruption of their inhabitants.

Micah's Prayer

14 *Our kind* Shepherd,
watch over us, the flock that is your special
inheritance.
With your staff,[c] lead your people to pasture.[d]

---

a 7:9 Or "I will see his righteousness."

b 7:12 Or "from sea to sea, mountain to mountain," a poetic way of saying "from all over the world."

c 7:14 Or "scepter."

d 7:14 See Ps. 23; John 10:1–16.

For we are like a flock confined to live in a forest
with meadowland all around us.
Let us graze again in *the fertile fields of* Bashan and Gilead
as in the days of old.[a]

15 "I will show you mighty miracles
as in the days when you came out of Egypt."[b]

16 When the nations see your miracles,
they will be ashamed, seeing that their power counts for nothing.
They will put their hands over their mouths,
too dumbfounded *by your might* to even speak,
and their ears will become deaf.
17 Let them lick the dust like snakes,
like the crawling things of the earth.
Let them come slinking out of their strongholds,[c]
trembling in terror before you, YAHWEH.

Micah's Psalm

18 Who is a merciful God like you?[d]
Your *grace* wipes the slate clean of guilt

---

a 7:14 Bashan and Gilead were regions on the east of the river Jordan and were among the first areas to come into the possession of the Israelites at the conquest. Invaders in the 700s BC captured their land. In effect, Micah was praying for the restoration of the territory God had once given them. Micah asked for a future that would be as glorious as their past, like it was under the united monarchy during the days of King Solomon.

b 7:15 It appears that God interrupted Micah's prayer with a declaration and a promise to God's people. God is faithful to answer our prayers.

c 7:17 See Ps. 18:45.

d 7:18 The prophet Micah's name means "Who is like YAHWEH?"

and pardons the rebellion[a] of the remnant of your
people.
You don't hold your anger against us forever,
but you delight in showing faithful, tender love.
19 Once more we ask:
have tender mercy[b] on us,
tread our iniquities under your feet,
and hurl all our sins to the bottom of the sea.[c]
20 You will demonstrate endless faithfulness to Jacob's
tribes
and to Abraham's *descendants* your constant love,
just like you swore to our ancestors
in ancient times.[d]

---

a 7:18 Or "passes over our crimes [transgressions]." See Ex. 34:6.

b 7:19 This is the nearly untranslatable Hebrew word *racham*, a homonym for "womb." It conveys the thought of mercy, pity, compassion, and a tender love like that of a mother for the child inside her womb. God has "womb-love" for you. Although righteous anger at evil is a part of God's character, his delight is in showing tender love and mercy, which always triumphs over judgment.

c 7:19 See Ps. 103:12; Isa. 43:25; 44:22; 2 Cor. 5:19; Heb. 8:12.

d 7:20 Our Jewish friends read vv. 18–20 on Sabbath Shuvah (the Sabbath of Repentance) and publicly recite them on Yom Kippur (the Day of Atonement) after the book of Jonah. On the first day of Rosh Hashanah, the Tashlik liturgy is performed near a body of water. *Tashlik* is the Hebrew word for "cast," "throw," or "hurl" found in v. 19. This liturgy involves symbolically casting off the sins of the previous year by tossing pieces of bread or another food into a body of flowing water. Just as the water carries away the bits of bread, so, too, are sins symbolically carried away. Since Rosh Hashanah is the Jewish new year, in this way, the participants express hope to start the new year with a clean slate.

THE BOOK OF

NAHUM

YAHWEH, the Divine Warrior

BroadStreet
PUBLISHING

NAHUM

Introduction

AT A GLANCE

Author: Nahum the prophet

Audience: The people of Judah before and after the fall of Nineveh, the oppressing Ninevites, and any people elsewhere who exercise military oppression or who are facing such oppression

Date: Sometime between 661 and 612 BC

Type of Literature: Prophecy

Major Themes: Divine judgment is inevitable for all who oppose YAHWEH; YAHWEH's plan of salvation is inevitable; YAHWEH's preservation of his faithful remnant is inevitable; seeing Jesus in the book

Outline:

- I. Superscription: author and setting — 1:1
- II. The character of YAHWEH is revealed in his judgment against Nineveh — 1:2–14
  - a. YAHWEH is a jealous and avenging God, just, slow to anger, and supremely powerful — 1:2–8
  - b. Plotting against YAHWEH can never succeed — 1:9–14
- III. YAHWEH promises peace, deliverance, and joy for Judah — 1:15
- IV. The siege of Nineveh — 2:1–13
- V. Nineveh's total destruction — 3:1–19
  - a. Nineveh's sins and military aggression are the reason for her fall and utter ruin — 3:1–11

b. Nineveh will be totally defenseless against her attacking enemies — 3:12–17

c. Nineveh's population will be either scattered or killed, and the city will never be rebuilt — 3:18–19

ABOUT THE BOOK OF NAHUM

The Northern Kingdom, with its ten tribes, had been destroyed by Assyria (722 BC) about a century before the writing of Nahum. Judah, with its capital at Jerusalem, home of YAHWEH's temple, stood alone against Assyria, the "evil empire" of that era. The situation seemed hopeless, but Nahum rebuked Assyria in no uncertain terms and claimed that God's people would outlive their potent enemy.

At the heart of YAHWEH's condemnation of the Assyrian Kingdom is the gross idolatry practiced by the city of Nineveh. (Note: The terms *Assyria* [nation] and *Nineveh* [capital of Assyria] are often used interchangeably.) It was in response to this stance of profound disdain for the one true and living God that YAHWEH poured out his anger and judgment on the Assyrians (Nah. 3:5–7).

Poetically, the little book of Nahum is one of the finest in the Old Testament. Calvin wrote about Nahum in superlative terms. Its descriptions are vivid and distinct. The poetry glows with passionate joy as it contemplates the ruin of cruel and victorious Assyria. Nahum's writing is full of descriptive power and expressive turns of phrase that the reader can easily understand. In Nahum, Nineveh is an object lesson to the world of God's sovereign power to judge nations that oppose his vision for how we are to live together; he can and will remove oppressive despots who attempt to bypass his eternal plan for his creation.

Nahum and Jonah were the two prophets assigned to speak God's truth about and to Nineveh. When Jonah prophesied, the people repented, and God spared them from judgment. Nahum came on the scene about one hundred fifty years later at a time when Nineveh had reverted to its old ways and had grown even more oppressive than before, during the apex of Assyrian power. These are Nahum's spoken prophecies; they could have been collected in written form by him or by a later editor. Some propose that they were collected to celebrate Babylon's eventual victory over Assyria (612 BC), affirming, after the fact, what Nahum had predicted beforehand: that YAHWEH would be faithful in bringing Nineveh down. Listed below are some important dates on a timeline that will help readers orient themselves:

- 722 BC — The fall of the Northern Kingdom of Israel, which thereafter became known as the "ten lost tribes." Assyrian troops obliterated the nation.
- 701 BC — The Assyrians' failed attempt to besiege Jerusalem during the reign of Hezekiah (2 Kings 18:13–19:37).
- Between 663 and 661 BC — The battle between Assyria and Thebes in Egypt mentioned in Nahum 3:8–19. The book of Nahum must have been written after this date.
- 640–609 BC — The reign of the reformer King Josiah in Jerusalem.
- Sometime between 661 and 612 BC — The Lord spoke through Nahum.
- 612 BC — The fall of Assyria. Babylonians, Medes, and Persians besieged and razed Nineveh.
- 586 BC — The fall of the Southern Kingdom of Judah. Babylon destroyed Jerusalem and the temple.

PURPOSE

Nahum's purpose was to encourage the people of Judah to stand firm against their seemingly omnipotent enemy, the Assyrian Empire. YAHWEH gave Nahum the words that formed a spiritual shield for the people. It is a classic David (Judah) and Goliath (Assyria) rematch. And YAHWEH is never on the side of the oppressor.

Then, as a supplement to this overriding purpose, it may be noted that the words and written message of the prophet Nahum were designed to instill into his hearers and readers the certainty that the promises of God will always come to pass. The prophecy also serves as undeniable proof that God will have victory over his enemies, such as the Assyrians. And finally, the prophecy serves as a reminder that God's characteristics never change, neither those that facilitate blessings nor those that deliver judgment.

AUTHOR AND AUDIENCE

We know nothing about Nahum except that he was from Elkosh. Nahum's name means "to sigh" (in a positive sense) or "to comfort others." He was an enthusiastic, optimistic Israelite with strong patriotic tendencies. Nahum was obsessed with rooting out discouragement and defeatism in Jerusalem. Unlike Jeremiah, who took the baton of prophecy from Nahum and dealt with the next generation of issues, Nahum did not look at the internal sins of God's people but rather only condemned Assyria, outside of Israel.

Nahum understood that courageous, well-spoken words are more powerful than chariots or weapons of iron. Truth spoken forth boldly can rally a nation regardless of terrible odds. Every nation can have its finest hour in the face of a powerful enemy.

Nahum was a contemporary of the prophets Joel and Habakkuk,[a] and his life possibly overlapped with Jeremiah's.

---

a See Seder Olam Rabbah 20.

Elkosh was perhaps the birthplace, main residence, or burial city of the prophet. There are three or more proposals for the location of Elkosh: in Mesopotamia near present-day Mosul, in Galilee (Capernaum, the Village of Nahum), or perhaps near Eleutheropolis (Semitic: Beth Gabra of Judah), or somewhere else in Judah. There is no scholarly consensus, just educated guesses as to where Elkosh was. Nahum may have been one of the captives of the Assyrians who later died somewhere on the banks of the Tigris River near Nineveh (modern Mosul). Some claim that his tomb is there.[a]

The audiences for the book of Nahum can be separated into five categories, starting with the people of Judah before the fall of Nineveh. These prophecies were intended to encourage them that their adversary would not always oppress them.

Second, the people of Nineveh. It would be hard to believe that no one in Nineveh knew about the fiery warnings that Nahum spoke against them.

Third, the people of Judah after the fall of Nineveh. The words of Nahum could be read aloud at celebrations marking Assyria's demise, confirming that YAHWEH had kept his promises.

Fourth, oppressors anytime, anywhere. The example of YAHWEH's righteous wrath and judgment on the violent, idolatrous, and cruel Assyrians provides a strong warning to anyone who trusts in the militarism of coercive empires. Such cultures should not be lulled to arrogant security because God's judgment does not immediately

---

a According to tradition, the synagogue in the town of Alqosh in Iraq houses the tomb of Nahum. This structure is not sound and was temporarily stabilized in 2018. Alqosh is a possible location for Elkosh, the home of the prophet, and lies near modern Mosul.

punish them. Although Yahweh is slow to anger, his just vengeance is inevitable and inescapable.

The final audience is anyone facing a "Nineveh." Nahum provides hope for all little nations facing a Nineveh and any David facing a Goliath. We all encounter malevolent forces during the span of our lives, and the words of Nahum remind us that God will always restore his faithful people. Looking at history, the faithful remnant, against staggering odds, has always inherited God's promises and found creative ways to thrive, flourish, and move forward into new situations. The faithful remnant has never been wiped from the face of the earth—and they never will be.

MAJOR THEMES

Divine Judgment Is Inevitable for All Who Oppose Yahweh. The continuous human cycle of empire building, overreach, corruption, internal rot, and eventual collapse has repeated countless times in history. Emperors attempt to build a systemic human pyramid of coercion, ignoring the fact that while they can, indeed, physically control people, they cannot control human thought. God is certainly capable of controlling people's actions, and although he is theoretically able to control human thought, he chooses to allow humankind a freedom of moral decision-making. However, should any people choose to oppose and rebel against him and refuse to change their stance, they will *inevitably* be subject to divine judgment. Human effort and strategies may play a part in preventing despots from "ruling the world," but only God has the power and authority to thwart such autocratic activity in an absolute sense. While oppressive cultures and empires may persist for a generation or even centuries, God will eventually empower agents of his will to bring about their destruction.

This is true of any human civilization—past, present, or future—and the Assyrians, as represented by the population of Nineveh in Nahum's day, were no exception. As Jesus said, "All those who embrace violence will die by violence" (Matt. 26:52). The Assyrian Empire was built on naked force and aggression, their violence swallowing up neighbors one at a time. They truly believed they were invincible. God gave to Nahum the prophetic opportunity and mandate to denounce the wicked and idolatrous culture of Assyria and the Ninevites and to threaten divine destruction of that godless empire. Then God brought it to pass. The Assyrian Empire came to a catastrophic, irrevocable, and brutal end. Such will be the fate of all who imagine they can win any struggle against the one true and living God. The language of Nahum's prophecy is the language of the certainty that God's judgment would undoubtedly prevail, and nothing the Ninevites did would ever be able to prevent it. Yahweh is sovereignly powerful over all his enemies. He cannot be beaten. Nineveh, and all that it represents, will (always) fail.

Yahweh's Plan of Salvation Is Inevitable. While the book of Nahum is primarily a record of Yahweh's plan to pour out a terrifying and devastating judgment upon evildoers, equally important are the few but powerful expressions of Yahweh's redemptive grace and promises of deliverance directed toward his people. There are three occasions in the book where this emphasis carries a dramatically powerful impact.

In the first instance, Nahum 1:7, after the initial prophetic salvo describing the terrifying impact of Yahweh's righteous anger and avenging judgment on his enemies in verses 1–6, the prophet affirmed that Yahweh is good, a refuge in times of trouble, and that he cares for those who trust in him. Then Nahum 1:15 contains the iconic prophetic declaration of the coming Messianic Ruler and Deliverer, who comes down from the mountains proclaiming peace and bringing "good news." The action of "coming . . . to announce good news and to proclaim peace" is an anticipation of the gospel of redemption. Nahum directed this prophecy of hope and salvation explicitly toward the people of Judah, exhorting them to celebrate their festivals and fulfill their vows. They could do so because the destruction of their enemies was a certainty. And finally, Nahum 2:2 records the prophecy that YAHWEH will "restore the majesty" of the entire Israelite nation.

Never miss an opportunity to encourage someone with the promises of God's Word when he or she is going through a rough time. Nahum's courageous declarations brought hope to a people who felt they had very little reason for any hope at all. Think of the times when someone's uplifting words to you changed the course of your life. You can be that person for others, over and over. The more difficult the circumstances, the more your words of encouragement have the power to heal and revitalize the weary among us with the reminder that God's plan of promised forgiveness and redemption for his chosen people will always succeed.

YAHWEH's Preservation of His Faithful Remnant Is Inevitable. Why should a tiny, faithful remnant in Jerusalem have any hope against the power of Assyria?

Nineveh was once the greatest city of the ancient Near East, being one and a half times larger than its rival Babylon and about twice as large as Rome at its greatest extent. It was the great King Sennacherib (705–681 BC) who turned Nineveh into the capital city of Assyria and made it more glorious than any city of his era. His son, Ashurbanipal (669–626 BC), became the last great king of Assyria. He left an extensive library, which archaeologists discovered at Nineveh, to carefully detail the history of Nineveh.[a]

In any age, it might seem like the current trends will continue forever. But that is not true. The path of history can take radical and sudden turns. Just because Assyria may be on top today does not mean that this will always be the case. The one quality that all people of all times have shared with their Creator, which stands out here in opposition to "trends," is creativity. We are made in God's image and will always find, with his help, a way out from under attempts at human oppression.

Nahum's certainty about this deep truth underlies everything he wrote in his magnificent, Spirit-infused rebuke of abusive political and military power.

Seeing Jesus in the Book. There are two explicit prophecies in the book of Nahum that point forward to the climax of God's redemptive program in the coming of the Messiah, Jesus Christ, God's Son. These prophecies have already been noted in the previous theme discussions. The following observations supplement that commentary.

In the first instance, Nahum 1:15 makes an unambiguous reference to the coming Messianic Redeemer. He brings good news on his journey through the mountains of Jerusalem and Judah, and he proclaims peace. This prophecy is partially repeated in Isaiah 40:9, in the context of the promise that Yahweh will deliver that good news along with his supreme power and authority. He will both exercise his sovereign power and gather his flock like a protective shepherd does, offering his people peace and security wherever they go. Similarly, Isaiah 52:7–10 repeats the Nahum prophecy but this time almost verbatim. And the accompanying

---

a See Michael Roaf, *Cultural Atlas of Mesopotamia and the Ancient Near East* (New York: Facts on File, 1990), 186–91.

context, as in Isaiah 40, likewise promises that YAHWEH will return to Jerusalem, victorious over his enemies, and bring comfort to his people. Then the nations of the earth will bear witness to the salvation he brings to those who belong to him.

Romans 10:15 confirms beyond any doubt that the prophecies of Nahum 1:15 and Isaiah 40:9 and 52:7–10 find their ultimate fulfillment in Jesus Christ. Here, the apostle Paul cited the essence of these Old Testament prophecies and explicitly linked them with the gospel ministry of Jesus during his time on earth. Our Lord's message of salvation was then taken up by his apostolic messengers who proclaimed the gospel—the "good news"—to the world at large. The "precious feet of the messenger coming over the mountains to announce good news" began with the old covenant prophets, who prophetically anticipated the arrival of the climactic stage of God's plan of redemption. That plan was consummated in the person and work of Jesus Christ and then proclaimed to the whole world by those who obeyed Jesus' command to take the gospel to the ends of the earth.

In the second instance, Nahum 2:2 provides another specific promise of salvation that is linked to the person of Jesus. This verse predicts the restoration of the entire land of Israel—a prophecy that finds fulfillment in two stages. We see the first of these in the literal, historical return of the people of Judah from their exile in Babylon in 538 BC, around one hundred years after the time of Nahum's prophetic ministry. While it is true that the reunification and establishment of God's people were only experienced in an earthly political and cultural sense by the Southern Kingdom of Judah, the second and final stage of the fulfillment of this prophecy began to take place only after Jesus had completed his earthly mission. There is no doubt that the New Testament interprets the manifestation of the worldwide community of the Christian church as the spiritual fulfillment of the nation of Israel in the Old Testament. The church of Jesus Christ—the gathered community of God's people in the new covenant age—has been initiated, enabled, and empowered by the indwelling Spirit of God in the lives of his people as an ongoing, never-ending spiritual kingdom.

NAHUM

Yahweh, the Divine Warrior

Yahweh's Judgment of Nineveh

1 This is the book of the vision of Nahum who was from *the village of* Elkosh.[a] A prophecy concerning Nineveh:

2 Yahweh is a God who tolerates no rivals.[b]
Lord Yahweh will take vengeance on *his foes*.
He punishes his adversaries
and keeps wrath for his enemies.[c]

---

a 1:1 *Nahum* means "full of comfort." *Elkosh* means "God is my bow." Nahum had a vision in which he saw the events that he described in these three chapters. He may have received his message while in a trance or some similar state.

b 1:2 Or "Yahweh is a jealous God." The English word *jealous* most often carries a negative connotation of being envious of what someone else has. This is not the full sense of the Hebrew word *qanno'*, which is best understood as God's burning passion to fully possess what is his. God is jealous over those whom he loves and wants them to be fully his. And God is vengeful toward anyone who would harm those who belong to him. See Ex. 20:5; 34:14; Deut. 32:21; James (Jacob) 4:5.

c 1:2 Verses 2–8 are in the form of an alphabetic poem, known as an acrostic. An acrostic poem begins each line in Hebrew with a different letter of the Hebrew alphabet in alphabetical order. In this case, the poem goes only halfway through the alphabet, up to the eleventh of the twenty-two letters. This type of poem is found in several places in the Old Testament (see Pss. 25; 34; 37; 111; 112; 119; 145; Prov. 31:10–31; Lam. 1–4).

[3]YAHWEH is very slow to anger[a] but so great in power;
YAHWEH will not let the guilty go unpunished.
He marches out in the whirlwind and storm,[b]
and the clouds are the dust of his feet.
[4]He rebukes the sea and dries it up
and makes all the rivers run dry.[c]
At his rebuke, *the lush meadows* of Bashan and Carmel wither;
the flowering fields of Lebanon fade.[d]
[5]In his presence, the mountains quake
and the hills melt away.[e]
When he appears, the earth heaves,
and the world and all who dwell in it *are laid waste.*
[6]Who can stand before an angry God?
Who can face his fiery fury?[f]
When his wrath erupts, it pours out like lava,
and boulders are broken to bits as he approaches.

God, Our Hiding Place

[7]The goodness of YAHWEH is *beyond belief*!
For when trouble comes, we run into *his heart* and hide.

---

a 1:3 Or literally "YAHWEH is long of nostril," a figure of speech for "YAHWEH does not easily become angry." See Ex. 34:6; Num. 14:18.

b 1:3 Or "His way is in the whirlwind and storm." That is, where the Lord walks, great storms begin to blow. God will use the storms of our lives to reveal himself and his ways to us.

c 1:4 The Jewish reader would immediately see the reference to the miracle-crossings of the Red Sea (see Ex. 14; Ps. 106:9) and the river Jordan (see Josh. 3:16–17; 4:23).

d 1:4 Bashan, Carmel, and Lebanon represent the most fertile parts of the land (see Isa. 33:9; 35:2).

e 1:5 See Judg. 5:4–5; Mic. 1:4; Hab. 3:6.

f 1:6 See Jer. 7:20; 42:18; 44:6.

He always cares for those[a] who seek refuge in him.
[8]But with an overwhelming flood,[b]
he will make a complete end of *Nineveh*,[c]
and darkness will overtake his enemies.[d]

Prophecy concerning Assyria

[9]Whatever evil plot you hatch against YAHWEH,
he will so completely thwart
that it will not rise up a second time.
[10]They will be like drunkards from their carousing—
like entangled thorns, they will be consumed as dry stubble.[e]
[11]From you, *Nineveh*, came one

---

a 1:7 Or "he knows those." This knowledge (Hb. *yada'*) is more than understanding us. It is also caring and protecting us. He knows us fully and protects us when we turn to him, for we are one with him in Christ. We best see God's goodness in times of trouble.

b 1:8 Linguists are divided over where this phrase connects. Some connect it to the previous line: "He cares for those who seek refuge in him in [the time of] an overwhelming flood." Others to what follows: "With an overwhelming flood, he will make an end of Nineveh." Perhaps this ambiguity is intentional, and the phrase connects to both. See D. T. Tsumura, "Janus Parallelism in Nah 1:8," *Journal of Biblical Literature* 102 (1983): 109–11.

c 1:8 Or "her place."

d 1:8 This "darkness" may be a metaphor of calamity or even destruction (see Job 18:18).

e 1:10 This verse is recognized as the most difficult verse in Nahum to translate. Some view it as the most difficult verse in the Bible. Some modern translations omit the words "like drunkards from their carousing." See J. M. Powis Smith, *A Critical and Exegetical Commentary on Micah, Zephaniah, Nahum, Habakkuk, Obadiah and Joel* (New York: Charles Scribner's Sons, 1911), 294.

who plotted evil against YAHWEH,
a wicked, worthless strategist.[a]

Prophecy concerning Judah

12 YAHWEH says,

"Although your enemies are many and secure in their alliances,
they will nonetheless be mowed down and pass away.
Though I have afflicted you, *my people*,
I will not do it again.
13 And now I will break his yoke of bondage from *your neck*
and tear away your shackles of *Assyrian* oppression."

Prophecy concerning the King of Nineveh

14 YAHWEH has decreed against you, Nineveh:

"Your dynasty is over![b]
Every idol in the temple of your gods I will destroy,
your carved and engraved idols.
I will dig your grave, for you are nothing to me."

Prophecy concerning Judah

15 What a *beautiful* sight to behold—
the *precious* feet of the messenger
coming over the mountains to announce good news
and to proclaim peace!

---

a 1:11 This is likely a reference to King Sennacherib, who ruled over Assyria from 705 to 681 BC and who besieged Jerusalem in 701 during the reign of Hezekiah, king of Judah (see 2 Kings 18:13–19:37).

b 1:14 Or literally "it will not be sown from your name anymore." The culture of that time regarded the lack of descendants and loss of the family name as a serious matter (see Deut. 7:24; 29:20; 1 Sam. 24:21).

People of Judah, celebrate your feasts,
keep your solemn promises *to God*,[a]
for the wicked one[b] will never pass through you
again;
he is completely cut off.

The Siege of Nineveh

2 Nineveh, an attacker[c] is poised to advance against
you.
Place your guards along the top of the walls;
set lookouts on the road.
Go ahead, get ready for battle;
gather all your forces,[d] *but it will be in vain.*
2 For YAHWEH is about to restore the majesty of Jacob
and Israel her glory.
For you have plundered everything
and ruined their vineyards.[e]
3 The *invading* soldiers' shields are scarlet,
each warrior robed in red.[f]
The metal of the *Babylonian* chariots gleams like fire
on the day they are made ready *for battle*,

---

a 1:15 See Pss. 22:25; 66:13. Verse 15 is 2:1 in the Hebrew Bible.

b 1:15 Or "Belial." *Belial* means "the wicked one" or "the worthless one." This is a reference to both the demonic power coming against God's people and the king of Assyria, who will never invade the land again.

c 2:1 Or "the scatterer."

d 2:1 Or "make strength exceedingly firm."

e 2:2 The ten northern tribes were the victims of scorched-earth warfare by the Assyrians, who were ruling the remaining peasants with a rod of iron. This judgment is God avenging the destruction of the Northern Kingdom (Jacob/Israel) in 722 BC.

f 2:3 The Medes and Babylonians who captured Nineveh were noted for wearing red uniforms (see Ezek. 23:14–15).

and the wooden spears are brandished *in anticipation.*[a]
4 The chariots race madly through the streets *of Nineveh*;
they dash wildly through the public squares,
gleaming like torches, darting like lightning.
5 *The king of Assyria* summons his elite commanders,
but they stumble while attempting to advance.
The attackers run swiftly to the city wall;
the protective canopy for the battering ram is set up.
6 The floodgates are opened;[b]
the royal palace is inundated *by the surging torrent* and collapses.
7 *Nineveh*[c] is stripped, taken captive, and carried into exile.
Her maidservants moan like doves
and beat their breasts *in sorrow.*[d]
8 *The people rush out of* Nineveh
like water pours out of a broken dam.[e]
The officers shout, "Stop! Stop!"
but no one turns back.

---

a 2:3 Or "their horses quiver with excitement" (LXX).

b 2:6 Archaeologists have discovered sluice gates and dams around Nineveh to control the river waters that flowed through the city. See R. C. Thompson and R. W. Hutchinson, *A Century of Exploration at Nineveh* (London: Luzac, 1929), 120–32.

c 2:7 Or "Its mistress," a hapax legomenon. This is the Hebrew word *hutsab*, which may be the name of the queen of Nineveh or a name for the goddess Ishtar worshiped in Assyria. There is no scholarly consensus on its actual meaning.

d 2:7 Verse 7 has several translation difficulties with a number of possible emendations.

e 2:8 Or "Nineveh is like a pool, and its waters are draining away." However, this clause, in the context of the imminent destruction of the city, is most likely a metaphorical expression for the terror-stricken Ninevites fleeing the city as fast as they can.

9 Plunder the silver,
plunder the gold!
Look! There is no end of the treasure[a]—
heaps of every precious thing.
10 Desolation! Devastation! Destruction!
Hearts melting, knees knocking,
stomachs churning,[b] faces turning pale.

11 What has happened now to the lions' den[c]
where the fierce lions[d] were fed,
where the lion and lioness once lived,[e]
where the cubs frolicked, cozy and fearless?
12 Like a lion, *Assyria* once killed his prey
and tore it to pieces,
filling his cave with meat
for his mate and her cubs.

13 "Behold, I am your enemy," declares YAHWEH,
Commander of Angel Armies.
"I will burn your chariots to ashes,
and the sword will slaughter your young lions.
No longer will you prey upon the land,
and your messengers will announce no more
victories."

The Destruction of Nineveh

3 Doomed is the city of bloodshed,
embodiment of treachery and thievery,

---

a 2:9 Or literally "store," denoting the hoarding of a vast quantity of treasure.
b 2:10 Or "all the loins are shaking."
c 2:11 The lion was a common emblem of Assyrian culture; thus the city of Nineveh is described metaphorically as a lions' den.
d 2:11 Or "young lions," a metaphor for the Assyrian soldiers.
e 2:11 Or "where the lion brought his prey."

where the murdering never stops!
2 *Listen to* the crack of the whip,
the rumble of the chariot wheels,
the thunder of horses' hooves,
and charging chariots.
3 Horsemen advancing,
gleaming swords and glistening spears,
hosts of slain, heaps of corpses,
dead bodies, too many to count.
People stumble over the carcasses.

4 *This is because* you lustfully lured the nations
like a wanton whore.
You acted so gracefully, yet you are a mistress of witchcraft.
You sold entire nations into the sex trade
and bewitched whole families into slavery.
5 Behold, YAHWEH, Commander of Angel Armies,
declares to you:
"I am your enemy!
I will lift up your skirt over your face,
and I will make nations gawk at your nakedness
and kingdoms at your shame.[a]
6 I will pelt you with filth
and make you an object of scorn
and will treat you with contempt.
7 And all who look at you
will turn their backs on you and say,

---

a 3:5 Nineveh had acted like a prostitute by luring other nations into her treacherous schemes. In the culture of that day, communities would punish a prostitute by stripping off her clothes, publicly exposing her shame. So Nineveh would endure public disgrace as a prostitute. See Jer. 13:26; Ezek. 16:36–38; Hos. 2:10.

'Poor Nineveh is a pile of rubble; who will grieve for
you?
Who will have sympathy for you?' "

8 Are you any better than Thebes,[a]
which once sat by the Nile surrounded by water,
her moat[b] of defense, a mighty river?
9 Ethiopia[c] and Egypt were her endless strength;
Somalia and Libya[d] were her helpful allies.
10 Yet *the people of Thebes* became exiles
and were carried off into captivity.
Their infants were dashed to pieces on every street
corner.
They cast lots for her honored men—
all the best and brightest were bound in chains and
taken captive.
11 You will fall into a drunken stupor.
You will go into hiding
and seek refuge from the enemy.

---

a 3:8 Or "No-Amon." *No-Amon* means "the city of the god Amon." Thebes is the Greek name for the Egyptian capital, once considered the greatest city of the ancient world. It was situated on the Nile River about 400 miles (650 kilometers) south of Egypt's present capital, Cairo. The massive temple ruins of Thebes can still be seen at Karnak and Luxor.

b 3:8 Or "walls."

c 3:9 The Egyptian Empire included the land south of Thebes called Cush (or Kush) in Hebrew. This region was called Ethiopia in Greco-Roman times and is recognized as such in the Septuagint. Cush also included most of modern Sudan and part of present-day Ethiopia (Abyssinia).

d 3:9 Or "Put." Most scholars believe that Put (or Phut, the third son of Ham) was a region located along the African coast at the southern end of the Red Sea that would have included portions of modern Libya and Somalia.

Assyria Will Crumble

12 All your fortified cities are like fig trees
with first-ripe figs: shake the tree and they fall
right into the open mouth of the eater.
13 Behold, all who remain in the midst of your cities
are the women.
The borders of your land
are wide open to your enemies.
Fire will devour your fortresses.[a]
14 *Go ahead and* draw plenty of water
and prepare for the siege.
Strengthen your defenses.
Get mud, trample the clay, make more bricks.
15 Yet the fire will devour you there.
You will be slaughtered by the sword.
It will consume you like locusts.
You multiplied like hopping locusts
and like swarming grasshoppers.
16 Your merchants multiplied
until they were more than the stars in the sky.
Like locusts they stripped the land,
spread their wings, and flew away.
17 Your officials[b] were as numerous as grasshoppers,
your scribes[c] like a swarm of locusts.
On a cold day, they settle on the stone fences,

---

a 3:13 Or "bars [of your gates]."

b 3:17 The Hebrew term *minzarayik* is a hapax legomenon [lit. "spoken only once"]. Consequently, its meaning cannot be ascertained with any certainty. Only the context can be a guide. In this case, the rendering "your officials" or "your guards" is a reasonable hypothesis.

c 3:17 The Hebrew term *tipsarayik* here is likely an Assyrian loanword. It may be translated "your scribes" or "your marshals," denoting those professionals employed by the military for their skills in writing.

but when the sun appears, they *abandon you* and fly
away;
no one knows where they are.[a]
18 Emperor of Assyria, your shepherds slumber,
your nobles nod off to sleep soundly.
All your people are *like sheep* scattered on the
mountains
with no one to bring them home.
19 There is no remedy for your injuries;
your wound is fatal.
All who hear the news about you
applaud for joy over your downfall.
For whoever was untouched
by your endless evil?

---

a 3:17 Nahum was saying that the officials and scribes of Nineveh would all run away when the city was attacked.

THE BOOK OF

HABAKKUK

Triumphant Faith

BroadStreet
PUBLISHING

HABAKKUK

Introduction

AT A GLANCE

Author: Habakkuk the prophet

Audience: Primarily, this was a discussion between Habakkuk and God. Habakkuk then wrote these prophetic conversations down and shared them with the people of Jerusalem.

Date: Sometime between 612 BC and 586 BC. The action of the book occurs after the Babylonians came to full power in the region around 612 BC but before Babylon captured Jerusalem and exiled the Jews in 586 BC.

Type of Literature: Prophecy

Major Themes: The problem of evil; the cycles of coercion and empire; things are not as they should be—how are the righteous to live in such conditions?; triumphant faith; seeing Jesus in the book

Outline:

I. Superscription: author and setting — 1:1

II. Habakkuk's first question: Why does it seem like Yahweh allows evil in Judah to go unpunished? — 1:2–4

III. Yahweh's first response: he will raise up the ruthless, godless Babylonian nation to invade Judah — 1:5–11

IV. Habakkuk's second complaint: How can a just and righteous God use a wicked nation to punish a people who are more righteous than the invaders? — 1:12–2:1

a. The prophet's question — 1:12–17

   b. The prophet is determined to watch and wait for an answer from YAHWEH — 2:1
V. YAHWEH's second response — 2:2–20
   a. YAHWEH declares that the prophet will receive a definite answer although it will come in God's timing — 2:2–3
   b. God contrasts the terrible fate of the godless, arrogant Babylonians with the blessed destiny of the righteous, who live by faith in God and his promises — 2:4–5
   c. YAHWEH's "woe-oracles" against the idolatrous, brutal decadence of the Babylonian nation — 2:6–20
VI. Habakkuk's prayer, expressing confidence and joy in YAHWEH's deliverance — 3:1–19
   a. Habakkuk petitions YAHWEH to remember mercy in the outpouring of his divine wrath — 3:1–2
   b. Habakkuk rehearses the spectacular actions of YAHWEH in history — 3:3–15
   c. Habakkuk awaits patiently and in fear the climactic divine judgment on Babylon — 3:16
   d. Habakkuk rejoices in the salvation YAHWEH will bring to his people even if God punishes them with suffering and loss — 3:17–19

ABOUT THE BOOK OF HABAKKUK

The books of the twelve Minor Prophets are often overlooked by readers today, but they contain incredible passages addressing timeless themes such as God's mercy and judgment, his covenant with Israel, the day of YAHWEH, and the coming of the Messiah. Habakkuk[a] is no exception to this display of incredible richness and depth in

---

a There are two primary pronunciations of *Habakkuk*: The first one places the emphasis on the second syllable, *bak* (as in *tobacco*). The second places the emphasis on the first syllable, *ha* (as in *habit*).

a comparatively short book. Of the literary prophets (as opposed to Jonah, for instance, which is more narrative), Habakkuk fits into the timeline between Nahum and Zephaniah (earlier) and Jeremiah and Ezekiel (later).

Prophecy is unique to ancient Israel, at least as it is shown in the actions of the prophets and the corresponding literary form in the Old Testament. There are no true parallels to this literature within the "superior" cultures of Israel's neighbors (and their vast empires) that inhabited the lush, fertile lands of the Nile, Euphrates, and Tigris Rivers. One searches in vain for true counterparts and equals to Habakkuk (and his prophetic colleagues) in Greece, Egypt, and Mesopotamia. Israelite prophecy is truly an exclusive and potent contribution to world literature and spiritual history. Biblical prophecy calls out in a voice that has no echo in the ancient Near East.

The task of the prophets was to call the leadership of Israel to live up to the very best aspects of their special identity, distinct in all the world, as partners with Yahweh. In the end, this centuries-long effort was a failure, and Jerusalem was sacked in 586 BC by the Babylonians.

But that same robust prophetic voice calls out to all of us today, believers and unbelievers alike, to live our best and most virtuous lives. That vigorous, primal, unvarnished cry of uncomfortable truth has outlived its speakers and even the culture from which it burst forth. Prophecy's eternal usefulness and raw beauty can and will, even in the twenty-first century, challenge and elevate us to be more of what God created us to be.

Habakkuk spoke and wrote with considerable eloquence and literary ability. He also was able to thread the needle of challenging God without being inappropriately disrespectful. This tension is beautifully maintained during the opening dialogue between the prophet and

Yahweh. He "dares to go there" but doesn't overstep. He provides a role model for all of us during those seasons in our prayer life when things don't make sense to us and clouds of negativity start to gather.

All of us who think deeply have been troubled by the problem of evil. If God is totally good and all-powerful, from where do suffering and malice come? It's never enough just to answer with "human free will" because some terrible things happen that have nothing to do with human choices. Habakkuk wrestled with God (Jerome's insight) because of this very issue. It is also a valid question for us today: How do we, as people of faith, live with integrity when we are in an unjust social structure or when the tides of history do not seem to be aligning with what a benevolent God would ordain in the first place?

The middle section of the book (Hab. 2:5–20) deals with curses and woes against the oppressor Babylon. The original hearers of Habakkuk's prophecies would have known exactly about whom he was talking. And these curses apply, even today, to any malicious oppressor.

The third section of the book (3:1–19) is a prayer, breaking out in song, which beautifully showcases Habakkuk's new insights after wrestling with God. He used potent imagery of God's mighty acts in the exodus to remind the people of God's faithfulness and power and petitioned Yahweh to remember mercy in the carrying out of his wrath. Thus, no matter what the current circumstances (i.e., with the enemy Babylon at the doorstep), the prophet would live by faith in Yahweh, the Savior of Habakkuk and the people of Judah, and would trust the divine vision and purpose for creation.

PURPOSE

As a result of his direct, urgent interactions with God during a harrowing historical moment in time, Habakkuk rose to a new level of understanding. The purpose of the book is to share that fresh insight, that "the righteous will live by his faith" with everyone who reads it (2:4).

God's people were in deep trouble. There was corruption within Israel. But emerging in the East was an even greater evil, oppression, and coercion headed their way. The new superpower empire of Babylon had set its plundering sights on Jerusalem. With fatal forces at work and accelerating within and without, God's people were headed straight over the cliff.

Terror gripped Habakkuk, and he started the book with "Yahweh, how long must I cry for help and you turn a deaf ear?" (1:2).

Much to Habakkuk's chagrin, Yahweh let him know that he was going to use Babylon, of all possible tools, to punish Judah and Jerusalem for their corruption and idolatry. This did not sit well with Habakkuk, who reminded God that the Babylonians were far worse than the Israelites. How could this be fair? Habakkuk mounted his watchtower to await a response from God.

Yahweh was quick to respond and show Habakkuk the bigger picture. There is an endless cycle of people living luxuriously from the labors of other people and using force and violence to keep it that way. Empires craft level upon level of mandatory service to those closer and closer to the top, where the ruler puts himself or herself in the place of God. This is not sustainable, and empires must gobble up nearby nations to feed the system. To bring down these corrupt systems, God uses other corrupt systems (like the Babylonian Empire) to dispense justice. After all, there are no perfect people or nations in the world. But in the end, Yahweh painted a solid vision of a time when true justice and righteousness will prevail and people will be free to enjoy the blessings of the salvation he will bring. God has done it before—at the time of the exodus from Egypt when he set his people free from

Egyptian captivity—and he can do it again. He encouraged Habakkuk to wait patiently, trust this vision, and live his life in alignment with it even when there was no apparent evidence to back it up.

This insight brought Habakkuk to the point where he chose, despite the messed-up world in which he lived, to set his sights on Yahweh's vision and his redemptive activity and to set his heart, mind, and actions in the direction of that vision. The righteous will live by his *faith*.

The Creator will have his way with his creation. We all have a choice to focus on the brokenness of the world or aim our lives toward the promise of God's coming and lasting restoration. This one choice determines virtually everything about how we speak, act, and live our lives.

AUTHOR AND AUDIENCE

Habakkuk referred to himself as a *nabi'*. Although Jewish tradition includes all of those who speak for God under the banner of *nabi'*, or "prophet," very few of those prophets called themselves by this title. The word *nabi'* (pronounced "nah-bee" or "nah-vee") carries the rich root meaning of "bubbler" or "one through whom the Word of Yahweh springs forth like a fresh spring." Have you ever experienced a brand-new truth from God—one that you could not have learned in any conventional way—spring up from inside you? The apostle Paul encouraged all believers to be receptive to this phenomenon (1 Cor. 14:5). That is the heart of prophecy.

As with most of the prophets (except, most notably, Jeremiah), we know very little about Habakkuk outside of his book. He lived and worked during the twilight of the kingdom founded some four centuries earlier by Saul, David, and Solomon. The storm clouds of disaster were gathering, and the final catastrophic sunset (586 BC) of First Temple Jerusalem was at hand.

His name is taken from the triliteral verbal root *hbq*, meaning "to enfold," "to embrace," or "to caress." Jerome suggested that this is at least a hint of the close, affectionate relationship between YAHWEH and his prophet.[a] Martin Luther, apparently in agreement with Jerome over the meaning of the name, discussed how appropriate the name was for Habakkuk's task, saying that in a sense he embraced his people comfortingly through his prophecy. And seen another way, the book of Habakkuk is the honest struggle of a man who learned to embrace the ways of God.

Primarily, Habakkuk was speaking to God, and God was responding. However, by writing these conversations down, he certainly intended a larger audience. Interestingly, much as with compounding interest, the book seems to mean more and more to people as the generations pass. It speaks to a universal audience of people of faith everywhere who are trying to do the right thing and attempting to make sense of a world that sometimes makes no sense.

Although, undoubtedly, many felt the force of Habakkuk's written words before the fall of Jerusalem in 586 BC, his prophecy took on special meaning to Jews in Babylonian captivity. The situation seemed upside down. If their God, the Creator of the universe, let pagans destroy his temple and enemies take his people prisoner in a foreign land, what, then, is the correct way for people of faith to live out their lives and to relate to a God who allows such things to happen? Habakkuk's prophecy and his emotionally transparent wrestling with God took on a new and elevated meaning during this season of Israel in exile.

---

a J. Migne, *Patrologia Latina*, vol. 25, col. 1273.

Israel had so many occupiers between 586 BC and AD 1947 that Habakkuk has continued to carry a strong resonance throughout the centuries among the Jewish people, who were virtually always living under the authority of some other nation. Those of the Qumran community (living in the first century before Christ) in their commentary Pesher Habakkuk (1QpHab) likely saw their Roman conquerors in the place of the Babylonians in Habakkuk's prophecy, at least symbolically.

Even though the book meant a certain thing during its composition, Habakkuk continues to mean a great deal to those who, for whatever reason, are wrestling with God and trying to make sense of what he has done in history and is doing now.

MAJOR THEMES

The Problem of Evil. Philosophically, this problem has never been solved to everyone's satisfaction. If God is all-good and all-powerful, from where did evil emerge? There are four typical answers:

One: God is all-loving but limits his power. Some things happen outside of his will. Some or all of the physical universe is left to random chance. Bad things happen, but they are no one's fault.

Two: Human free will is the cause of all evil. This works, partially, for many situations, but what about horrible birth defects or natural disasters that destroy innocent lives?

Three: Everything is truly good, in the ultimate sense, but we just don't understand it yet.

Four: The devil is the cause of all evil (John 10:10). But that still begs the question: How could a good God allow such a being? And if one gives the devil too much power, he becomes a second god with all the powers of a god. The Bible is clear that there is one God (Deut. 6:4).

Habakkuk was facing this very problem of evil when YAHWEH told him that he was going to use Babylon (eviler than Israel) to punish Israel. Habakkuk pushed back firmly but with grace in chapter 2 and went to his watchtower to await an answer.

The Cycles of Coercion and Empire. The book of Habakkuk is a scorching rebuke of invading empires bending other nations to their will. Coercion, like a Ponzi scheme, is never sustainable, and nations resort to occupying and controlling their neighbors to "feed the beast" of empire. Empires eventually (100 percent of the time) collapse under their own weight. Even if YAHWEH used Babylon to punish Israel, in the end, Babylon was going down. The children of Israel are still alive to this day, but it's hard to find a solid Babylonian. It is a common sight around the Arch of Titus in Rome, any day of the week, to see Jewish people chanting in Hebrew, "The children of Israel live!" at the very monument built to celebrate the destruction of Jerusalem by the Roman Empire in AD 70. Much of Rome is still in ruins, yet the children of Jacob continue to flourish all around the world.

Things Are Not as They Should Be—How Are the Righteous to Live in Such Conditions? When we face spiritual, emotional, financial, and other "headwinds" in life, how are we to respond? Many just give up on faith altogether. Habakkuk shows us a different way: to trust that the forces of evil, forever carrying the seeds of their own destruction, will fail in the end and that living by faith, no matter what happens, is the best path forward. The rituals and rules of human religion may have some benefit (for instance, honoring our parents is an eternal truth worth practicing), but when facing the bigger storms of life, we have to build our lives upon a rock. This rock is God himself. And we need to exercise a rock-like faith in a God who saved us before and can save us again.

This latter requirement is of paramount significance. Habakkuk's prayer in chapter 3 begins with a plea for YAHWEH to remember mercy when he dispenses his wrath. Habakkuk also asked YAHWEH to renew his deeds in the prophet's generation. The particular act of redemption singled out by the prophet was YAHWEH's deliverance of his people from their captivity in Egypt. It was a rescue that sounded the death knell of the Egyptian army and forced the surrounding nations to cower in fear before Israel's almighty Lord. Ultimately, YAHWEH's plan of redemption for his people will culminate in the person and work of Jesus Christ our Lord, God's Son. This is the consummate focal point for our saving faith.

Triumphant Faith. Rather than leading to despair, the challenges that Habakkuk and Israel were facing led to a raw and honest back-and-forth conversation with God that, in turn, led to a breakthrough to a higher way of living. This way is characterized by a triumphant faith, one that is certain of final victory, despite the apparent lack of evidence for such an outcome in our current circumstances. God will be victorious with everything. Let's align our thoughts, words, and actions with that victory firmly in mind.

Seeing Jesus in the Book. There are four specific passages in Habakkuk's prophecy that provide us with an insight into how this book may be seen as an anticipation of the climax of God's redemptive plan in Jesus Christ.

First of all, in Habakkuk 2:4, there is the iconic declaration that "the righteous will live by his faith." The context of this declaration is the beginning of YAHWEH's response to Habakkuk's second complaint, where God promises to provide an answer to the prophet's dilemma, although the revelation of that response will be in God's timing—not man's. The outworking of saving faith in the life of the just believer stands in stark contrast to the consequences of the brutal, godless arrogance and wickedness of the Babylonians, who were doomed to destruction, as a punishment for their evil ways, at the hands of a righteous and wrathful God. We can find the ultimate and supreme example of faithful living in the face of an apostate and godless evil world in the person and work of Jesus, the Messiah, who found himself living under the power and authority of the pagan Roman Empire. His faithful dependence on and trust in God his Father was flawless. Furthermore, his perfect obedience and submission to his Father's plan of salvation, as his righteous Son, led to the forgiveness of sin and life everlasting for all those who would place their lifelong faith and trust in him. The destiny of all these righteous followers is everlasting life in the new heavens and the new earth, in intimate relationship with God the Father and his resurrected Son. Today, we "live by faith" by constantly trusting in that faithfulness of Jesus and hoping in that resulting promised renewal—despite our circumstances.

Second, in 3:2, Habakkuk prayed that Yahweh would renew his redemptive actions in history in the prophet's own time. Habakkuk then explicitly asked that God would remember mercy in his wrath. God's ultimate act of redemption was expressed in the death and resurrection of his Son, Jesus Christ, whose sacrifice on the cross atoned for the sins of the world. The spiritual reality at the heart of this redemptive sacrifice is that God turned his back on his Son as the sins of the world were placed upon him just before he died. In effect, Jesus bore the wrath of God so that God might grant his mercy to all who believe in what theologians refer to as Christ's substitutionary atonement—namely, that Jesus died in the place of sinners so that their transgressions may be forgiven.

Third, in 3:3–15, there is an extended discourse on the miraculous divine deliverance of the Israelite people from Egypt, the exodus. This reminder of God's past faithfulness points forward to another exodus: Jesus Christ is the ultimate Passover Lamb, delivering his people from the enemies of God—not earthly enemies but the twin evils of sin and death, along with Satan himself, all of whom were defeated and destroyed by Christ's atoning sacrifice. This victory was a consummate spiritual one, accomplished by Jesus on the cross.

Finally, 3:18 is one of the strongest affirmations of faith in the whole of Scripture, as Habakkuk joyfully declared: "I still have YAHWEH, and I will rejoice in him . . . for I have a Savior-God." And again, the salvation provided by God is consummated in the person of Jesus Christ.

HABAKKUK

Triumphant Faith

Habakkuk's First Question

1 This is the vision[a] of Habakkuk the prophet:

[2]Yahweh, how long must I cry for help
and you turn a deaf ear?
My heart cries out, "Save us from this brutality!"
but you do not save.
[3]Why do you make me stare at injustice?[b]
Why do you tolerate such trouble and wrongdoing?
Destruction and violence surround me;
strife and conflict[c] are everywhere.
[4]Therefore, the law is not enforced,[d]
and so justice never prevails.

---

a 1:1 Or "burdensome vision." The Hebrew term *massa'* denotes primarily an "oracle" or "vision" but may also denote a "burden." It can refer to visionary messages containing either warnings of doom (e.g., Isa. 15:1; 19:1; 22:1) or messages of hope (e.g., Zech. 9:1; 12:1; Mal. 1:1). The text is clear that Habakkuk did not merely receive this vision but "saw" it (Hb. *chazah*) with his own eyes, perhaps in a trance or an ecstatic prophetic encounter.

b 1:3 It is difficult to find an English word equivalent to *'awen*. It has the nuance of "panting/striving for something for naught"—putting a tremendous amount of work into something and having it unravel before your eyes.

c 1:3 The word translated "conflict" here (Hb. *madon*) has a root sense of a capricious, arbitrary use of coercive force by authorities.

d 1:4 Or "the law is slack [feeble, crippled]"—that is, twisted justice goes forth.

The wicked overwhelm the righteous
so that justice is perverted.

Yahweh's Answer

5 "Look at the nations and observe—
you'll be stunned by what you see.
For while you watch, I am about to do something
so surprising in your days that you would not
believe it
even if you were told.[a]
6 I am raising up the Babylonians *to punish you*[b]—
that fierce and fearsome people,
who sweep across the whole earth
to seize houses they do not own.
7 They are a feared and dreaded people.
In their autocratic arrogance,[c]
they become a law unto themselves.
8 Their horses are swifter than leopards,
fiercer than wolves *on the prowl* at dusk.[d]
Their cavalry charges headlong;
their horsemen come from afar.
They soar swiftly like an eagle swooping to devour.
9 Their *armies* invade, intent on violent *conquest*.

---

a 1:5 See Acts 13:41. This is an example of the Holy Spirit infusing with fresh meaning a passage that seemed one-dimensional to the original recipients. The "something" God was about to do in Habakkuk's day was to raise up the Babylonians to invade their land. Yet, the Holy Spirit has a "context of inspiration" and has applied the verse to the miracle of Christ's resurrection as well. We must never limit Scripture to only one interpretation or application.

b 1:6 Or "the Chaldeans," who were originally the inhabitants of southern Babylonia. The Babylonians had lived in lower Mesopotamia for many centuries, but through their recent conquest of Assyria, they had ascended to become a world power for the first time.

c 1:7 Or "In promoting their own honor."

d 1:8 Or "fiercer than evening wolves." See Matt. 7:15; Acts 20:29.

Their *terrifying* hordes advance like a desert wind[a]
and gather prisoners as numerous as grains of sand.
10 They are a people who mock kings
and scoff at those in authority.[b]
They laugh at every stronghold;
they pile up earthen siege ramps and capture them.
11 Then they hurry on, like the wind that blows by and
disappears.
They are guilty men who worship their own power
as if it were a god."

Habakkuk's Second Question

12 YAHWEH, have you not always been the everlasting
God?
You are my God, my Holy One, who will not die.[c]
YAHWEH, you have appointed the *Babylonians* to
execute judgment;

---

a 1:9 The ambiguity of the Hebrew of this line results in uncertainty. The Hebrew term *qadimah* can either denote the meaning of "forward" or refer to the "wind from the east." In the Mediterranean world, the east wind originating from the Arabian desert is highly destructive, given that it is very dry and fiercely hot and can wreak havoc on the agricultural lands of Israel and magnify the impact of devastating bushfires.

b 1:10 See 2 Chron. 36:6.

c 1:12 As translated from an ancient scribal tradition. The Masoretic Text is "we will not die," that is, God would not let them be destroyed. The Hebrew phrase is *lo' namut*, which translates to "we shall not die." This phrase "is one of the eighteen passages in the OT called *tiqqune sopherim*, 'corrections of the Scribes' by the Masoretes [producers of the Masoretic Text]. The scribes were supposed to have corrected the original reading. The original reading of the passage was probably *lo' tamut*—'you shall not die,' referring to God. Even though there is no manuscript or version support for *tamut*, it is probably the best reading" (Ralph Smith, *Micah–Malachi*, Word Biblical Commentary, vol. 32 [Dallas, TX: Word Books, 1984], 103; diacritics removed for consistency).

my Rock, you have raised them up
so they can punish us.
13 Your eyes are so pure that you cannot stand the sight
of evil;[a]
nor do you look on wickedness with favor.
Why then do you tolerate the treacherous?
Why are you so silent while sinners
devour those more righteous than themselves?
14 Have you only made us like fish,
to be caught and killed *by the wicked*;
like swarming *schools of fish* with no ruler?
15 Then the *Babylonians* pull them up with fishhooks
and drag them in with their nets.
Gleefully, they gather them up in their dragnets,
shouting for joy over their catch.[b]
16 They even offer sacrifices and burn incense
in honor of their nets, as if these were gods.
For their nets[c] enable them to live luxuriously
and eat the finest food.
17 How long will you allow them
to *fill and* empty their throw nets?[d]
Will they forever destroy nations without mercy?[e]

Habakkuk Waits for God's Answer

2 I will wait at my watchpost[f]
and station myself on the tower.

---

a 1:13 Or "Your eyes are too pure to look upon evil [favorably]."
b 1:15 Or "He gathers [they gather] them up in his dragnet [their dragnets]; therefore, he rejoices [they rejoice] and is [are] glad." See Isa. 19:8.
c 1:16 The nets in this passage are used metaphorically for the weapons of the Babylonians and their military might.
d 1:17 Or "How long are they going to use their swords?"
e 1:17 See Isa. 14:6.
f 2:1 See Isa. 21:8.

I'll keep watching to see what he'll say to me[a]
and consider the reply
when he answers my argument.[b]

Yahweh's Answer

[2]Then Yahweh replied:
"Write down the revelation;[c]
write it legibly on clay tablets
so that whoever reads it
may run and explain it to others.[d]
[3]The vision still *awaits* an appointed time;
it speaks of the end and will not prove to be false.
When the appointed time comes,
it will happen with breathless haste.[e]
Although it may seem slow, just be patient and wait.
For it[f] will surely come right on time.

---

a 2:1 Or "I will lean forward and see what he'll say in me." See Ps. 85:8; Prov. 8:34.

b 2:1 Or literally "concerning my correction."

c 2:2 We, too, are told to write down the revelation of God—on our hearts. God is looking for something to write on. See 2 Cor. 3:2–8.

d 2:2 Or "so that it can be read on the run." This second clause may also be read as "so that a herald may run with it [and explain it to others]." The implication here is that a herald would routinely take up such a record of divine revelation and would then run with it to various audiences for a public reading. Verses 1–2 give us seven wise principles: (1) Be sure you know and keep your assignment as an intercessor. (2) Be watchful at all times. (3) Believe that God will be faithful to speak to you. (4) Be prepared to hear words of correction. (5) Write down and preserve what God has spoken to you. (6) Be ready to apply his words appropriately. (7) Share what he says so that it may bless others also.

e 2:3 "Breathless haste" is taken from a Hebrew word that means "to puff or pant." To know God's will (plan) doesn't mean that we know his timing. God's plan and God's timing are like a wheel inside a wheel.

f 2:3 Or "he." See Heb. 10:37 where this verse is quoted as "the coming one."

4 "Look at the proud, puffed up with pride!
They are crooked to the core.[a]
But the righteous will live by his faith."[b]

God Will Punish the Wicked

5 "Wealth is deceitful.[c]
The proud are full of themselves but have empty souls.
They are as greedy as the grave.
And just like death itself, they are never satisfied.
They gather and grasp for themselves all *the wealth of* the nations
and take all the people captive.[d]

6 "All these *conquered* nations will one day taunt them, saying,

---

a 2:4 Or "his soul is not right." The Hebrew of this sentence is uncertain.

b 2:4 Or "live by his faithfulness." It is possible that "his" refers to God; that is, the righteous will live by God's faith. See Rom. 1:17; Gal. 3:11; Heb. 10:38. To live by faith is to live with unbreakable loyalty to God, obeying his Word even when outward circumstances make it difficult. Both the Hebrew and Greek words for "faith" mean something "certain." Even surrounded with questions that go unanswered, we live by faith, not by knowledge.

c 2:5 Or "Wealth is treacherous," as translated from the Dead Sea Scrolls. Instead of "wealth," the Masoretic Text reads "wine."

d 2:5 Or literally from the Masoretic Text: "When *the enemy [Babylon]* crosses the line with wine, he sees himself as a mighty hero and no longer tends to his own home but rather inflates his hungry soul, *just like insatiable* death and Sheol, and collects for himself *entire* nations and peoples."

'You are doomed,[a] you who pile up stolen goods!
How long will you amass wealth by extortion?'[b]
7 Will not your creditors[c] suddenly arise?
Will they not wake up and terrify you?
Before you know it, you will become their prey.
8 Since you have plundered many nations,
the peoples who are left will plunder you.[d]
For you have killed many people;
you have acted violently against lands and cities
and everyone within them.

9 "You are doomed, you who enrich your family by
cheating others!
You build your *luxurious* home on high
thinking you'll be safe from harm's reach.
10 Your schemes to ruin the lives and homes of
others
bring shame upon your own house.
You are as good as dead for doing this.[e]

---

a 2:6 Or "Woe to him!" The Hebrew term *hoy* is traditionally translated "woe" and serves as a descriptor title for oracles of divine judgment in the Old Testament, especially in the canonical prophets. Here, in 2:6–20, there are five of these "woe-oracles," found in vv. 6, 9, 12, 15, 18–19. The term *woe* is a classic denotation of divine judgment and condemnation, although the word itself is rarely found in contemporary, everyday English usage. Outside of the biblical context, *woe* refers generally to painful human experience and emotions such as anguish, grief, and affliction.

b 2:6 Or "Will you weigh them down with the burden of heavy debt?"

c 2:7 The Hebrew word for "creditor" is *noshek* and means "one who bites."

d 2:8 See Isa. 33:1. This verse was fulfilled about twenty-five years later after Nebuchadnezzar died. The Persian king, Cyrus, rose up and plundered Babylon and made it part of his empire.

e 2:10 Or "You bring shame upon your own house [kingdom] by destroying many other peoples and thus forfeiting your own lives."

[11]The stones of the wall will cry out to accuse you,
and your wooden rafters will echo it.

[12]"You are doomed, you who build a city with bloodshed
and establish it upon evil!
[13]I, YAHWEH, Commander of Angel Armies, have decreed:
The efforts of the nations are nothing but fuel for the fire,
for all they have built will go up in smoke.[a]
[14]Yet the entire earth is being filled[b]
with the revelation of the glory of YAHWEH,[c]
just as waters fill the sea.

[15]"You are doomed, you who delight to mix drinks for neighbors,
pouring wine from pitchers[d] until they are dead drunk
just so that you can gaze on their naked bodies!
[16]Now you will be drunk with shame instead of honor.
Now it is your turn! Drink your fill
and let your nakedness be exposed.[a]

---

a 2:13 The words of Habakkuk (and Jer. 51:58) were possibly a proverb or popular saying among the people.

b 2:14 The Hebrew imperfect in poetry denotes imperfective aspect (ongoing action) and therefore can be translated with present tense. See Bruce Waltke and M. O'Connor, *An Introduction to Biblical Hebrew Syntax* (Winona Lake, IN: Eisenbrauns, 1990), 559–60; R. B. Chisholm, *A Workbook for Intermediate Hebrew: Grammar, Exegesis, and Commentary on Jonah and Ruth* (Grand Rapids, MI: Kregel, 2006), 275.

c 2:14 The context shows that the nations strive in vain for their plans to be fulfilled, yet God's plan is to fill the earth (and its people) with a glorious understanding of who he truly is.

d 2:15 Or "you pour out your wrath" (MT). The neighbors getting drunk is a reference to the neighboring nations who were conquered by the Babylonians.

The cup *of punishment* that YAHWEH holds in his right hand[b]
is now coming around to you.
Your *former* glory will be covered with your vomit of disgrace.
17 Your violent acts against Lebanon will *violently* overwhelm you.
Since you killed its animals, animals will terrify you.
For you have killed many people
and acted violently against lands and cities and everyone in them.

18–19 "You are doomed, you who say to a piece of dead wood, 'Come to life!'
Or to lifeless stone, 'Get up!'
Can something dead give revelation?
Even though it is covered with gold and silver,
there is no breath in it.
Of what use is an idol carved by a craftsman?
Or a metal image that gives misleading oracles?[c]
For the one who makes it trusts the work of human hands;
a god that cannot even talk."

---

a 2:16 As translated from the Masoretic Text. The Dead Sea Scrolls (1QpHab), the Septuagint, and other versions read: "Drink your fill and stagger." See Jer. 25:16; Lam. 4:21; Nah. 3:5–6. The true pagan nature of the Babylonians is also emphasized here, in that the Hebrew verb form *heʿaral* literally denotes "exposing your uncircumcision."

b 2:16 The "cup" in YAHWEH's right hand is a common symbol of divine retribution (see Isa. 51:17, 22; Jer. 25:15–17; Lam. 4:21; Rev. 14:10; 16:19; in all these references, the divine right hand is assumed).

c 2:18–19 Or "a teacher of lies."

[20] YAHWEH is in his holy temple;
let everyone on earth be silent before him.[a]

Habakkuk's Prayer

3 This is the passionate[b] prayer of Habakkuk the prophet.

[2] YAHWEH, I know the things that have made you famous.
I am stunned when I consider your miracles.[c]
Do them again in our day![d]
Let this generation experience your mighty deeds.
YAHWEH, show us your mercy
even in this time of turmoil.

---

a 2:20 See Ps. 11:4. We silence our hearts before God to listen to what he will say to us (see Mic. 1:2–3; Zech. 2:13). In this chapter, Habakkuk saw three absolutes, three life-altering things: (1) The righteous will live by faith (see v. 4). (2) The whole world will be filled with the knowledge of God's glory (see v. 14). (3) God is in his holy temple, ready to solve the issues of life (see v. 20).

b 3:1 Or "upon *shiggaion*." Although the meaning of *shiggaion* is uncertain, the most likely meaning is "a loud cry," taken from a Hebrew root word that means "roar." See Ps. 7. Habakkuk's psalm is wild and passionate. Have you ever been under such pressure that you felt like roaring? That is a "shiggaion." Other scholars believe the central thought of the word is that of wandering. It may also indicate the style of music to which the song was to be sung.

c 3:2 Or "in awe [fear] of what you accomplished."

d 3:2 Or "In the midst of [our] years revive it!"

A Theophany: The Manifestation of God

3 God came from Teman,
the Holy One from Mount Paran.
Pause in his presence[a]

The heavens[b] blazed with the brightness of his glory
while the earth echoed his praises.[c]
4 The brilliance of his glory is bright as the sun;[d]

---

a 3:3 Or "*Selah*." This Hebrew term cannot be translated with any certainty, and there is no scholarly consensus as to its meaning. It is found frequently in the Psalms (thirty-nine times) and may be a liturgical notation denoting a pause. In relation to this context, the word *Teman* means "the south." Teman was both a person (the grandson of Esau) and a city of Edom (Adam). Teman was the home of Eliphaz, the friend of Job (see Job 2:11). Paran is a barren and mountainous region in the Sinai peninsula. The verse describes God coming up from Teman and Paran—that is, from the area where he made himself known to his people in the wilderness and where he gave them the Torah (see Ps. 68:7–8). See J. L. Mihelic, "Paran," *Interpreter's Dictionary of the Bible*, vol. 3, ed. G. A. Buttrick (Nashville, TN: 1962), 657. The word *Paran* is taken from a root word for "to beautify" or "to glorify." Mount Paran can also be a metaphor of the holy realm of beauty and glory that transforms the human heart. God is the Holy One (see Isa. 1:4; 6:3; 40:25); "holy" is the Hebrew word *qadosh*. This may be a hint of a third location, Qadesh Barnea. Truly, there is much in the Hebrew text that would cause one to "pause in his presence."

b 3:3 The Hebrew word for "heavens" is *shamayim*, which more literally means the "sparkles on the water." It is a metaphor used to describe the heavenly realm, the source of everything.

c 3:3 Or "His glory covers the skies, and the earth is filled with his praises."

d 3:4 Or "blinding as lightning." See Pss. 4:6; 44:3; 89:17; Prov. 4:18; Isa. 60:3; Heb. 1:3.

twin bolts of lightning flash from his hand[a]—
there is the hiding place of his power.[b]
5 A plague marched in front of him;[c]
a consuming pestilence followed at his heels.[d]
6 When he stood up, the earth shook.[e]
At his glance, nations trembled, mountains crumbled,
and age-old hills collapsed,[f]
but his paths are everlasting.

---

a 3:4 See Deut. 33:2–5; Ps. 18:12, 28; Ezek. 1:4, 28; 10:4. God is radically and dangerously transcendent. The Hebrew for "twin bolts of lightning" can also be translated "two horns." The Hebrew root in its verbal form is used to describe Moses' face shining in Ex. 34:29–30. Most modern translations render it similar to "rays of light [stream from his hand]."

b 3:4 God hides his power in the palms of his hands. To experience God's power in your life is to take the hand of God in yours. In his sunlit splendor resides his triumphant power. God's glory both reveals his transcendence and conceals his power. Moses found the hiding place of God's glory (see Ex. 33:18–20). Jesus' hands took our nails. The crucified hand of Christ is the hiding place of his power.

c 3:5 This occurred in Egypt as a plague came over the land (see Ex. 7:2–4). For references of God using a plague to combat his enemies, see Ex. 5:3; 9:15; Lev. 26:25; Num. 14:12; Deut. 28:21; 2 Sam. 24:15; Jer. 14:12.

d 3:5 The army of Sennacherib experienced this (see 2 Kings 19:32–35). The Hebrew for "pestilence" can also mean "a darting flame" and can be used for arrows and lightning (see Ps. 78:48). See E. R. Clendenen, "Religious Background of the Old Testament," in *Foundations for Biblical Interpretation*, ed. D. S. Dockery et al. (Nashville, TN: Broadman & Holman, 1994), 297.

e 3:6 Or "he measured the earth."

f 3:6 See Pss. 97:4–6; 104:32.

[7] *In my vision*, I saw the tents of Cushan trembling in distress[a]
and the tent curtains of the Midianites shaking in anguish.
[8] YAHWEH, was it the rivers that made you angry
or stirred up your rage?
Was it the sea that made you furious
when you rode your horses
and chariots of salvation?[b]
[9] Your bow is strung and ready for action,[c]
and with a word, you commission your arrows
to hit their mark.[d]

Pause in his presence

You carved open the earth with rivers.
[10] The mountains saw you and trembled.
Torrential rains flooded the earth;
the *ocean* depths roared

---

a 3:7 Cushan was likely a Midianite nomadic tribe (clan) that lived in southern Transjordan. See O. Palmer Robertson, *Nahum, Habakkuk, Zephaniah*, New International Commentary on the Old Testament (Grand Rapids, MI: Wm. B. Eerdmans, 1990), 228; D. W. Baker, "Cushan," *Anchor Bible Dictionary*, vol. 1 (New York: Doubleday, 1992), 1219–20.

b 3:8 Horses may represent the Lord as he comes riding upon clouds bringing deliverance and victory. See Deut. 33:26; Pss. 18:9–11; 68:33; 104:3–4; Isa. 19:1. God's chariot can be a picture of the ark of the covenant as it marched through the wilderness. The Shulamite bride of Christ rides with him in his chariot of salvation (see Song. 3:6–11).

c 3:9 Or literally "nakedness your bow is laid bare." The bow is a picture of God's might and power in warfare.

d 3:9 Or "sworn in are the arrow-shafts with a word." This line is difficult to translate. For a thorough discussion of the problems in translation, see B. Margulis, "The Psalm of Habakkuk: A Reconstruction and Interpretation," *Zeitschrift für die alttestamentliche Wissenschaft* 82 (1970): 409–20.

and lifted their waves[a] on high.
11 Sun and moon stood still in the sky[b]
when your speeding arrows flashed
and your glittering spear gleamed.[c]
12 In your fury you marched across the earth,
and in your anger you trampled the nations.
13 You came to save your people,[d]
to win the victory with your Messiah.[e]
You crushed the head of the house of wickedness
and stripped him from head to toe.[f]
Pause in his presence

14 You pierced his head with his own arrows[g]
when his warriors stormed out to scatter us,
gloating as they slaughtered their wretched victims in hiding.
15 You trampled the sea with your horses,
churning the great waters.

16 I hear all this, and my heart pounds;
my teeth chatter with fear at the sound.
My body goes limp,
and my legs tremble.
Yet my heart quietly rests.[h]

---

a 3:10 Or "hands."
b 3:11 See Josh. 10:12–13.
c 3:11 God's arrows and spear are likely symbols of lightning flashes streaking across the sky.
d 3:13 The Hebrew for "save" is quite similar to the name Yeshua. See Matt. 1:21 and the first footnote.
e 3:13 Or "to deliver your anointed one."
f 3:13 See Gen. 3:15; Col. 2:15. At the cross, God struck down the leader of the land of wickedness (Satan) and stripped him of his weapons.
g 3:14 Or "spears." The Hebrew term *matteh* may carry the underlying meaning "shafts," which could refer to either arrows or spears.
h 3:16 See Ex. 33:14; 1 Kings 5:4; Isa. 28:12.

I know the day of trouble is ahead
for the people invading us.

Triumphant Faith

17 Even if *my* fig trees do not blossom
and *my* vines grow no grapes,
if *my* olive crop fails
and *my* fields produce no harvest,
and even if all *my* sheep die
and I'm left with no cattle in my barn,
18 I still have YAHWEH,
and I will rejoice[a] in him.
Yes, I will dance with joy[b] *no matter what*,
for I have a Savior-God!
19 YAHWEH is the Lord of my strength;
he makes my feet sure-footed as a deer
bounding upon the high places.[c]

These are the lyrics for the conductor[d] of my string ensemble.

---

a 3:18 The Hebrew word for "rejoice" is *ʿalaz*, which can also be translated "triumph." There is a joy full of glory that triumphs over loss.

b 3:18 The Hebrew word for "dance with joy" is *gil*, which means "to spin in a circle with joy." It could be expressed by being so powerfully overtaken with joy that one sings, shouts, and spins, crying out with joyous shrieks. There is an ecstatic joy that can be found in our love relationship with God, for even if all our creature comforts are taken from us, he will never leave us.

c 3:19 See Song. 8:14.

d 3:19 Or "musical director" (Hb. *menatseach*), which comes from a Hebrew root that means "to conquer." This is how we fight our battles—with joy in our Savior-God, who always leads us in triumph (see 2 Cor. 2:14). The Greek Septuagint sees no line break between the last two lines of this verse. It reads "He will cause me to ride upon the high places so that I might conquer with his song."

THE BOOK OF

ZEPHANIAH

The Day of YAHWEH

BroadStreet
PUBLISHING

ZEPHANIAH

Introduction

AT A GLANCE

Author: Zephaniah delivered these prophecies, although they may have been published by others

Audience: The Kingdom of Judah and the surrounding nations

Date: During the time of King Josiah, about 640–609 BC, especially 630–622 BC

Type of Literature: Prophecy

Major Themes: The day of YAHWEH; the indictment against Judah's idolatry; YAHWEH's avenging anger; catastrophic divine judgments against the nations; inevitable punishment for corruption in Jerusalem; promised hope for the future; seeing Jesus in the book

Outline:

I. Superscription: author and setting — 1:1

II. The destruction of the day of YAHWEH — 1:2–18
- a. The inevitable day of YAHWEH's punishment for Judah's idolatry — 1:2–13
- b. The inescapable wrath of a holy God, poured out on a sinful world — 1:14–18

III. YAHWEH's judgment against the nations — 2:1–3:8
- a. A call to the nation of Judah to repent — 2:1–3
- b. Judgment against the nations — 2:4–15
- c. Indictment of Jerusalem for her rebellion against YAHWEH — 3:1–5
- d. Jerusalem's refusal to repent — 3:6–8

IV. The ultimate promised blessing of the day of YAHWEH — 3:9–20
   a. The purifying of the nations — 3:9–10
   b. The spiritual renewal of the remnant of Israel and Judah — 3:11–13
   c. The redemption of the people of Israel and Judah — 3:14–17
   d. The restoration of the nation of God's people to their homeland — 3:18–20

ABOUT THE BOOK OF ZEPHANIAH

The scene depicted in the book of Zephaniah stands in stark contrast to how the authors of Kings and Chronicles portrayed Josiah's reign. Those writers called Josiah the last "good king" in David's royal line. This tension shows that there are at least two ways of looking at every complex situation, depending on one's perspective. During times of rapid social decline, a polarization of opinions tends to emerge. Granted, Zephaniah did not call Josiah out by name, but he painted a much bleaker, more critical picture of the era than the composers of Kings and Chronicles. The Bible expresses many such tensions, and Scripture is full of paradox. This gritty authenticity rings truer than some artificially sanitized history of God's people.

Zephaniah started at home, speaking truth to the powers that be in Judah. He then broadened his warnings to the surrounding nations. He closed, as prophets often do, with a message of hope. Later readers (after the destruction of Judah and the rebuilding of the Second Temple) could see fulfillment in both Zephaniah's scathing critique and his prospect of promise, fulfilled as the remnant returned from exile to rebuild the nation.

It is hard to find explicit New Testament references to Zephaniah, except perhaps in Matthew 13:40–52.

Matthew 13:44 could be an allusion to the Hebrew meaning of Zephaniah's name: "the Lord hides" or "the Lord treasures."

Zephaniah wrote totally in poetry. Zephaniah's poetic style is characterized by the use of staccato exclamations, rapid changes of vantage point and voice, discourse, rhetorical questions, and frequent wordplay and metaphors.

Zephaniah's language was graphic, potent, and pointed. Perhaps no other prophet has painted the picture of Jerusalem's decline more realistically. He described a time of terrible gloom with inevitable cataclysmic judgments on the horizon, coupled with a glorious promise of hope and salvation for his people. With burning eloquence, he alternated his prophecies between stern warnings and soothing comforts.

PURPOSE

We cannot limit the book of Zephaniah to any single interpretation. Much like any gifted writer, Zephaniah cloaked his words in just enough mystery to fit broader applications of universal truth. The prophet Zephaniah may have been the greatest master of creating word art of such unlimited relevance; his message often applies to today's situations as well as it did millennia ago, even when totally detached from the context that brought it forth. As an example, Zephaniah's enemy from the North could fit various invaders, from Scythians (who raided the area during this time) to the superpowers of Babylon and Persia.

However, what *is* clear is that the multifaceted applications of Zephaniah's prophecy are fully consistent with the dominant, overarching theme of the book: the day of Yahweh. This phenomenon is one of the richest and most complex of all scriptural prophetic motifs. Hence, it follows that the prophecies of blessings of the day of Yahweh contain multiple levels of fulfillment. The first iterations of fulfillment occurred comparatively shortly after the prophecies were given, in the return of God's people from exile to their land. Then a more climactic fulfillment appeared in the person and work of Jesus Christ. What has yet to follow is its absolute consummation at the end of time, when Jesus will return to usher in the new heavens and the new earth in the eternal heavenly kingdom.

Zephaniah held law and gospel (in Christian theological terms) in balance. God speaks his no. God speaks his yes. We are to take both with utter sobriety and seriousness. The promise of yes prevails in the end but is born out of that uncomfortable tension between law and gospel, the paradox in which we live our daily lives. And God's greatest promise did not come to us without a cost: it required the crucifixion of Jesus. Like a good surgeon, Zephaniah didn't pretend that healing would come without the use of a sharp scalpel. He reminded us that healing means blood will be shed, as it was in Jesus' sacrifice.

Zephaniah wrote to reveal God's passion for righteousness, justice, and virtue among his people. If these prophecies took place *before* Josiah's reform, they may well have catalyzed that renewal. Because of Zephaniah's universalizing writing style, it stands to reason that he intended his words to help warn people at any time and in any place and give them hope in all kinds of situations.

AUTHOR AND AUDIENCE

The book gives us few clues about Zephaniah himself. We see him as a man of passion and integrity, a man of joyful song (Zeph. 3:14), who possessed great courage and boldness as a prophet (1:8).

The introduction in 1:1 seems to imply that he was descended from King Hezekiah. Some scholars think that this could be any Hezekiah, but that would require a qualifier, especially with another king (Josiah) being mentioned in a parallel manner. Likely he was very comfortable among the ruling class and not some radical outsider like Amos. Critique from *inside* the system can be especially effective. He and Josiah may even have been cousins.[a]

Zephaniah was a contemporary of Nahum, Jeremiah, and Huldah the prophetess. His name means "the Lord hides" or "the Lord treasures." Both Zephaniah and you are treasured by the Lord and hidden in his heart (Col. 3:2–3).

MAJOR THEMES

The Day of Yahweh. The theme of the day of Yahweh is an overarching one and pervades the entire book. Each of the following major themes listed in this section illustrates an element of either the judgment or blessing of Yahweh in the multifaceted manifestations of that complex day.

The hearers of Zephaniah's message did not receive the warning of this ominous day as good news. Back then, as well as today, evildoers often appear to go through life with as much favor as good people. But God will balance the cosmic checkbook. A holy God cannot tolerate evil. Justice must be served. However, it is also equally true that the grace and mercy of God can never be extinguished. His promised plan of eternal redemption and renewal for humankind—accomplished via the supreme sacrifice of his Messianic Son and King, Jesus Christ—is as certain as the doom of Satan and the total destruction of sin

---

a See R. B. Dillard and T. Longman III, *An Introduction to the Old Testament* (Grand Rapids, MI: Zondervan, 1994), 415; R. K. Harrison, *Introduction to the Old Testament* (Grand Rapids, MI: Eerdmans, 1969), 939.

and death. These two phenomena constitute the ultimate fulfillment of the day of YAHWEH.

The Indictment against Judah's Idolatry. The people of Israel have struggled to maintain an intimate relationship with God since the day they created the golden calf, an inert, artificial barrier between them and their Creator. An idol can be measured and weighed. It has no life and no mystery to it. The worshiper can carry it around or discard it. People use idols to avoid the vulnerability they must risk in any intimate relationship, with others or with God. Thus, idols are a form of spiritual "pornography," which keeps us from the real God. God was not angry because Israel was breaking some arbitrary idol rule but because she was avoiding a deep relationship with him and settling for a false substitute.

Arguably, the sin of idolatry was the most egregious act of rebellion against God that Israel (and Judah) had ever committed. First and foremost, it was both a denial and a betrayal of his unparalleled uniqueness. YAHWEH was Israel's supreme covenant Lord, the one true and living God who had delivered them single-handedly out of their four-hundred-year captivity in Egypt. And in return, God demanded an exclusive, wholehearted devotion from his people as a mandatory response of gratitude for the love and mercy he showed to them. God encapsulated this exclusive worship in the first and greatest of the Ten Commandments, wherein God commanded the people to have no other gods except God himself (Deut. 5:7); in fact, this command lay at the heart of the entire covenant with Israel. Violation of this stipulation would result in the direst consequences for the people of God, and sadly, the history of Israel reveals an all-too-tragic willingness on their part to ignore that solemn requirement. It is, therefore, no surprise that Zephaniah recorded the terrifying denunciation of the people of Judah in the opening chapter of his prophecy, showing that their worship of pagan idols would result in catastrophic punishment at the hands of their God. And, to reinforce the severity of this judgment, God described it as an outworking of the day of YAHWEH against them.

In conclusion, a profound contrast is notable here. In that deep, exposed relationship between two mysteries, the complex depths of our souls and the boundless power of God, true love and grace (*chesed* in Hebrew) are generated. This also provides us with what we need to love others graciously. However, if ever we choose to turn our backs on this wonderfully unique relationship with our God—when we turn to idolatry—we do so at our peril, just like Israel and Judah of old.

YAHWEH's Avenging Anger. Several Hebrew terms denote the anger, or wrath, of God in Zephaniah (Zeph. 1:18; 2:2–3; 3:8). In every instance—as is the case throughout the whole of Scripture—this divine anger is a holy, righteous wrath. It is always triggered by the sinful, rebellious actions of humankind—in particular, when God's own people rebel against him. We should never equate YAHWEH's anger with sinful, human passions. His anger is always a just and righteous reaction to any affront to his moral perfections or to violations of his sacred commands and statutes. This is the case regardless of whoever is guilty of such transgressions—pagan nations or his own people.

One particular term is worthy of special note here—namely, the noun *qin'ah*, which is often translated "jealousy" or "anger." However, the English word *jealousy* has connotations inappropriate for a holy God, as if he were insecure in his relationship with us. Some translations use *zeal*, but that doesn't convey the righteous anger to which YAHWEH has every right. "Avenging anger" is perhaps the best translation of this Hebrew term, as it reflects the solemn severity of such a terrifying divine response, especially as it characterizes a fearful outworking of a day of YAHWEH's judgment.

Catastrophic Divine Judgments against the Nations. One significant element of this particular manifestation of the day of YAHWEH is that the account of the devastating punishments God will hand down to the nations of Philistia, Moab, Ammon, Cush, and Assyria is bracketed by the terrible indictments directed against the "shameless people" of Judah (2:1–3) and Jerusalem, "the filthy and foul city—the city of oppression!" (3:1–8). These judgments include a call for the people of Judah to repent of their unrighteousness if they are to avoid bearing the full brunt of YAHWEH's wrath (2:3). There is also condemnation for Jerusalem's refusal to repent of her social, economic, moral, and spiritual corruption (see further discussion under the following theme), including her profaning of the sanctuary (3:1–8). In light of these covenant violations, God deemed it appropriate to include Judah and Jerusalem in the list of nations that were to be on the receiving end of YAHWEH's wrath. However, it is important to recognize the ray of hope in the midst of these judgments. In 2:6–7, God declared that the once-populous cities of the Philistines would return to pastureland. And it is here that the remnant of Judah would eventually return. This is a brief but shining anticipation of the redemptive climax of the day of YAHWEH for the people of YAHWEH in the second part of chapter 3.

Inevitable Punishment for Corruption in Jerusalem. By taking on responsibilities and getting things done, some people will inevitably rise to positions of authority. They will then have enhanced access to resources that are unavailable to others. At this point the great temptation always arises to use that authority to one's own benefit at the expense of those who have less authority. We call this corruption, and virtually all the prophets rage against it. Most nations do not fall because of enemies from without but rather from the rot of corruption from within. Once at the "top," leaders often use force and coercion to rig the game in their favor, making upward mobility hard or even impossible for others. Zephaniah, in no uncertain terms, came down on this (3:1–5).

What made Jerusalem's corrupt activities more heinous in the sight of God was the corruption of civic leadership in the city. The common characteristic of the ruling classes in Jerusalem was their arrogant shamelessness, which they showed in their blatant oppression and extortion of others and their utter scorning of the worship of YAHWEH. It is no wonder that God condemned the officials, rulers, priests, and prophets of Jerusalem at the outset of the indictment in 3:1 as a corporate gathering of rebels, oppressors, and those who profane the sacred worship of their Lord. Therefore, the rationale for YAHWEH pouring out his righteous anger on both the godless nations and Jerusalem was essentially the same.

Promised Hope for the Future. As is the case with the majority of the canonical prophets, oracles of divine judgment and wrath—directed at the godless nations neighboring Israel and Judah as well as the people of God themselves—precede the promises of YAHWEH's grace and mercy. Such promises focus on the renewal, restoration, redemption, and forgiveness of his people and, for the most part, come at the conclusion of the books of prophecy. Zephaniah fits into this pattern.

There is no doubt that the prophet primarily expressed the various manifestations of the day of YAHWEH to both Judah and the godless nations around her as retribution for rebellion against, and violations of, the divine covenant. However, at the conclusion of Zephaniah (3:9–20), there is a glorious and dramatic reversal in the outworking of the day of YAHWEH for both the nations and the faithful remnant of Israel. There is always hope for the faithful remnant. God's promises of salvation routinely follow his avenging anger with regard, initially, to his chosen people. Most certainly, this is also a word for us today.

Zephaniah expresses this final manifestation of the day of YAHWEH as a powerful and comforting hope. Not only will YAHWEH completely remove punishments for all sins his people committed in the past (3:15), but he also will totally renew the remnant of Israel so that they will no longer utter lies and speak deceitfully (3:13). And they will experience the love of God and his rejoicing over them in a manner they never experienced before (3:17). Such redemption and renewal will include a joyful restoration—a return to their homeland. Such a return will precipitate an expression of honor and praise from all the nations of the world.

One must also not overlook the promise of renewal given to the peoples of the earth in 3:9. Here YAHWEH promised to purify the lips of the peoples so that they would call on his name.

This wonderful and joyful conclusion to the book of Zephaniah is nothing less than an anticipation of the glorious, positive climax of the day of YAHWEH—one that points forward to the coming of the Messiah, Jesus Christ.

Seeing Jesus in the Book. The key to understanding how Zephaniah anticipates the coming of the Messiah, Jesus Christ, lies in the final section of the prophecy in 3:9–20. It is in this concluding oracle of hope, outlining the future renewal, restoration, and redemption of the people of YAHWEH, where the prophet revealed the glorious climax of the day of YAHWEH.

As is most often the case with prophetic oracles that anticipate the coming of Jesus to earth, such predictions can have multiple, partial levels of fulfillment embedded in the historical experiences of the people of Israel and Judah. And in each of these progressive stages, the history of God's people points to the consummate stage of fulfillment in the Messianic gospel age.

In Zephaniah 3:9–20, God promised, first of all, to purify corrupted worship, including that of the nation of Judah (3:9–11). It was Jesus who restored true worship of God at the Jerusalem Temple. Then, in 3:13, God promised to renew the speech of his people so that they would always speak the truth. It was one of Jesus' primary characteristics that he spoke the truth—in the name of God his Father—at all times. He never feared the consequences that his truth-speaking might provoke. Then in 3:14–15, the prophet exhorted the remnant of Judah to rejoice because YAHWEH removed their punishment and turned back their enemy. He also promised to bring them back to their homeland (3:19–20). At the same time, God promised to be with them, to save them, and to take great delight in them with love and rejoicing (3:17).

The climactic fulfillment of these promises of renewal, restoration, and redemption all take place in the atoning sacrifice of Jesus Christ on the cross. It is Jesus' death and resurrection that offer a guarantee that all those who put their faith and trust in him will be wholly renewed, restored, and redeemed—for all eternity. The restoration of the earthly kingdom of Judah was only a partial fulfillment of these promises. When Jesus rose from the dead and ascended to heaven, he returned to God, his Father, and claimed the throne of an everlasting kingdom that would never be defeated. This is the absolute, consummate blessing of the day of YAHWEH that is yet to come, and it offers a stark, contrasting parallel to the consummate destruction of all the enemies of God and his people.

ZEPHANIAH

The Day of Yahweh

The Day of Yahweh

1 This is the prophetic message Yahweh gave to Zephaniah son of Cushi,[a] grandson of Gedaliah, great-grandson of Amariah, great-great-grandson of Hezekiah. Zephaniah received this message during the time when Josiah, the son of Amon, ruled Judah.

2–3 "I, Yahweh, declare that I will certainly sweep away
every *living* thing from the land—
animals and humans, birds and fish.

---

a 1:1 Or "The word of Yahweh came to Zephaniah, son of Cushi." *Zephaniah* means "the Lord hides" or "the Lord treasures." Both Zephaniah and you are treasured by the Lord and hidden in his heart (see Col. 3:2–3). Cushi (see Jer. 36:14) is not to be confused with the land of Cush, which was called Ethiopia in Greco-Roman times and included portions of modern Sudan and part of present-day Ethiopia. It is possible, however, that Zephaniah's father was Ethiopian or Sudanese and that Zephaniah himself was a Black man.

I will topple the wicked and their idols[a]
and sweep away man[b] from the land."

Judah's Idolatry Punished

4 "I will punish Judah and all who live in Jerusalem.
I will wipe out every trace of Baal from the land
along with the names of the pagan priests
or any priest *who has turned away from me*.
5 I will punish those who bow down on their rooftops
to worship the *sun, moon, and stars*[c]
and those *with divided loyalties* who bow before
YAHWEH
and swear allegiance to me
but also swear their oaths in the name of their king.[d]
6 I, YAHWEH, will punish those
who have turned their back on me,
who do not seek me nor pray for me to guide them."

---

a 1:2–3 Or "I will sweep away these stumbling blocks with the wicked." The context implies that the idols (stumbling blocks) are images of previously mentioned "animals and humans, birds and fish." See J. J. M. Roberts, *Nahum, Habakkuk, and Zephaniah*, Old Testament Library Series (Louisville, KY: Westminster/John Knox Press, 1991), 167; Adele Berlin, *Zephaniah*, Anchor Yale Bible Commentaries, vol. 25a (New Haven, CT: Yale University Press, 1994), 73–74.

b 1:2–3 Or "Adam." There is a powerful wordplay in Hebrew: "I will cut off Adam from the very *'adamah* [dirt] from which he came."

c 1:5 Or "the host [armies] of heaven." See Deut. 4:19; 17:3–7; Jer. 19:13; 32:29.

d 1:5 This "king" is likely a reference to the pagan god they worshiped, possibly Baal or Molech or a Canaanite god known by the Ammonites as Milcom. See E. R. Clendenen, "Religious Background of the Old Testament," in *Foundations for Biblical Interpretation*, ed. D. S. Dockery et al. (Nashville, TN: Broadman & Holman, 1994), 298–99. See also Deut. 6:13; 10:20.

The Day of Yahweh Is Near

7 Be silent before the Lord God,
for the day of Yahweh is near.

"I have prepared a sacrifice[a]
and have consecrated my invited guests.[b]
8 On the day of Yahweh's sacrifice,
I will punish the royal family, your officials,
and all who dress like pagan priests.[c]
9 At that time, I will punish
all who *worship Dagon*[d]
and fill the palace of their rulers
with violence and deception.

10 "I, Yahweh, declare:
A cry for help will be heard from the Fish Gate *in Jerusalem*,[e]
wailing from the *wealthier*, newer part[f] of the city.

---

a 1:7 The Hebrew word *zabach* means both "sacrifice" and "slaughter."

b 1:7 This passage describes the day of Yahweh with stinging irony, using the technical language of sacrificial ritual. God's metaphorical banquet is his punishment, the sacrifices are his people, and the invited guests are Israel's enemies whom God uses to punish his people. See Isa. 34:6; Jer. 12:3; 46:10; Ezek. 39:17.

c 1:8 Or "in foreign attire," likely a reference to the cultic clothing of pagan religions. See 2 Kings 10:22.

d 1:9 Or "who leap over the threshold," likely a reference to the superstitious custom of those who worshiped the fish-god Dagon. See 1 Sam. 5:4–5.

e 1:10 The Fish Gate was on the northern side of Jerusalem, the closest gate both to the fishing port of Tyre and to Lake Galilee, where fishermen caught, dried, and sold fish in Jerusalem. Jewish scholars believe the Fish Gate was also called the Ephraim Gate.

f 1:10 Or "Second Quarter" or "Mishneh," a section of the city possibly near the Fish Gate. See 2 Kings 22:14.

A loud crash will echo from the hills.[a]
11 Wail, you who live in the market area[b]
because all the merchants will be dead,
and those who weigh out silver will be wiped out.

12 "When that time comes,
I will search Jerusalem with lamps[c]
and punish those stagnating
in their self-satisfied smugness.[d]
They say in their hearts,
'Yahweh *is aloof* and can do nothing for us,
either good or bad.'

---

a 1:10 The approaching armies coming to attack Jerusalem are the cause of the uproar, the wailing, and the crashing (of buildings) on the hills surrounding the city.

b 1:11 Or "Makhtesh." Probably the lower area later known as the Tyropoeon Valley that separates the Upper City from the Temple Mount. The word means "mortar" or "depression." According to this verse, the merchants conducted their business here. The Targum reads "Kidron wadi." See Berlin, *Zephaniah*, AYBC, 87.

c 1:12 Or "I will illumine Jerusalem with lamps," a figure of speech for light exposing what is taking place in the dark. The lamp of God's Word and his holy gaze will uncover what is hiding in people's hearts.

d 1:12 Or "those who are thickening upon their lees [sediment]," a metaphor referring to the process of making wine. During fermentation, wine must be poured from one vessel to another to separate the lees or sediment (see Jer. 48:11). Failure to do this ruins the wine. Those who are "thickening upon their lees" are entrenched in their smugness; they are the self-satisfied wealthy who are overconfident in themselves. The Hebrew words for "search" and for "lees" sound nearly the same when spoken. During the days of Zephaniah, the people of Jerusalem worshiped the god Dionysus along with Yahweh. Dionysus was the god of wine and pleasure. The Romans called this god Bacchus. This religious syncretism was offensive to God, so he told them that his searchlight would uncover the darkness of their syncretism so that the people could see it for what it was.

13 Yet all their *hoarded* wealth will be looted
and their houses leveled.
They will build houses but never move in,
plant vineyards but never drink the wine."

Judgment Day

14 The great day of Yahweh is near,
right around the corner, closer than you think and
coming fast.
How bitter will be the sound of the day of Yahweh,
when even the brave warriors weep in anguish.[a]
15 It will be a day of wrath,
a day of terror and trouble,
a day of desolation and distress,
a day of darkness and gloom,
a day of clouds and thick darkness,
16 a day of shofar[b] blasts and battle shouts
against fortified cities
and all the lofty towers.[c]

17 "I will bring such distress on people
that they will grope their way like the blind
for having sinned against me.

---

a 1:14 This sentence in Hebrew is somewhat uncertain. It is literally "the sound of the day of Yahweh, bitter [is] one crying out there, a warrior."

b 1:16 Or "trumpet" or "horn." The *shopar* (or *shophar*) is a ram's or goat's horn that one blows as one would a trumpet.

c 1:16 Zephaniah employed many Hebrew words that sound similar and filled vv. 15–16 with wordplay. This is a brilliant literary stanza. "This passage [vv. 15–16a] is probably the most classical description of [the day of Yahweh] in Israelite literature. . . . Each saying has 7 syllables and the word *ywm* [day] occurs 7 times. A complete stanza is thus formed" (P. J. Nel, "Structural and Conceptual Strategy in Zephaniah, Chapter 1," *Journal of Northwestern Semitic Languages* 15 [1989]: 164).

Their blood will be poured out like dust,
yes, their flesh like dung.
18 On that day, I will display my great anger,
and none of their silver or gold will save them.
My avenging zeal will burn like a fire on that day,
to consume the entire land.
For I will bring a terrible and sudden end
that will destroy everyone living in the land."

A Call to Repentance

2 Go ahead and gather yourselves together,[a] you shameless people!
Gather yourselves together *and turn back to* YAHWEH
2 before the appointed time arrives.[b]
Repent before you are blown away like chaff,
which is swept away in a day,
before YAHWEH pours out on you his fiery anger—
the day of YAHWEH's burning fury.

3 All who are meek and humble on earth,[c]
seek *the mercy of* YAHWEH.
All who obey his commands,
pursue righteousness and discover *true* humility.
For maybe, *just maybe*, YAHWEH will shelter you
on the day of his anger.

---

a 2:1 The Hebrew verb for "gather" is taken from the same root word for "straw" or "stubble." The verb is used for gathering straw (see Ex. 5:7, 12) and gathering sticks for firewood (see Num. 15:32; 1 Kings 17:10). Zephaniah's play on words would not be lost upon the Hebrew reader. Straw would easily burn in a day of God's fiery anger.

b 2:2 Or "before the birthing of a decree [of judgment]."

c 2:3 See Matt. 5:3, 5–6.

The Doom of Israel's Enemies

4 "For Gaza will be deserted,
and Ashkelon devastated.
Ashdod will be driven out in broad daylight,
and Ekron left desolate.[a]
5 Doom to you who live on the seacoast,
to the nation of Cherethites![b]
And Canaan, land of the Philistines,
the word of YAHWEH is bad news for you.
I will destroy and annihilate you.
6 Your coastal lands will be reduced to pastureland,
to grazing grounds[c] for shepherds
and folds for flocks.
7 Your land will be occupied
by the remnant of the people of Judah.
During the day, they will find pasture by the sea,
and at night, they will rest in the houses of Ashkelon.
YAHWEH their God will care for them,
and make them prosper again."[d]

Moab and Ammon

8 "I, *YAHWEH*, have heard the crude taunts of Moab
and the vile insults of the Ammonites

---

a 2:4 Four of the five major cities of the Philistines are mentioned here. Gath had already been destroyed by the Assyrian king Sargon II in 711 BC.

b 2:5 The Cherethites were originally from Crete and settled along the southern coast of Israel with the Philistines. See Ezek. 25:16.

c 2:6 Or "hand-dug shelters [caves] for shepherds."

d 2:7 Or "and return their captives." The meaning of the root Hebrew expression *shub shebut* is disputed. There are two possible readings: either "to restore their fortunes" or "to turn their captivity" (i.e., "return their captives"). It may be argued that these two readings are related, providing a dual perspective on God's gracious restoration of his people.

as they scorned my people
and boasted that they would annex the land of Judah.
9 For as surely as I live, I, Yahweh,
God of Israel, Commander of Angel Armies, decree:
Moab will become like Sodom
and the Ammonites like Gomorrah.
The remnant of my people will plunder them;
the survivors of my nation will possess them.
Their lands will become barren forever,
a land of nothing but salt pits and piles of weeds.
10 This will be the price of their pride,
of having taunted and boasted
against the people of Yahweh, who commands angel armies.
11 I, Yahweh, will be terrifying to them,
for I will make all the gods of the earth vanish.
And the people of every nation
will bow down and worship me wherever they live."[a]

Ethiopia

12 "You Ethiopians,[b] too,
will be killed by my sword."

Assyria

13 "I will attack the northern land of Assyria
and destroy it all.

---

a 2:11 See Phil. 2:10–11.

b 2:12 Or "Cushites," those living south of Egypt in the Upper Nile region, which included parts of modern-day Ethiopia and most of Sudan.

Nineveh will be left as desolate and dry as a desert.[a]
14 It will be *nothing more than* a resting place for flocks
and herds,
along with all creatures of every kind.[b]
The vulture and owl[c]
will nest at night in its ruins.[d]
Owls will hoot from the windows,
and crows will caw in the doorways—
for all their once-fancy cedar woodwork
will be exposed to the elements.[e]
15 This is the once-proud city,
living so happy and carefree
and thinking to herself,
'I am *so amazing*, and I have no rival!'
Yet look at her now! What has she become?

---

a 2:13 The river Tigris flowed through the land of Assyria, and the city of Nineveh was known for its canals and waterways. The great city of Nineveh was conquered and leveled by the Medes and Babylonians in 612 BC, so it is likely that Zephaniah lived to see his prophecy fulfilled. In 401 BC, the Greek traveler Xenophon visited its site and wrote that he could find no trace of it, so complete was its destruction.

b 2:14 Or "all the beasts of the nations" or probably "animals of every species."

c 2:14 The meaning of the Hebrew word used for the first bird, *qa'at*, is uncertain. It could be translated "cormorant," "pelican," "jackdaw," "screech owl," "horned owl," "desert owl," or "vulture." Regardless of this bird's exact identity, we know it is an unclean bird mentioned in Lev. 11:18 and Deut. 14:17 that is known for inhabiting deserted places (see Ps. 102:6; Isa. 34:11). The second animal is mentioned with the word *qippod*, which can be translated "owl," "hedgehog," "bittern," "heron," "porcupine," or "ruffed bustard." Zephaniah was not giving us a scientific definition of species but informing us that the land will be occupied only by wild animals that live in desolate places.

d 2:14 Or "on its [broken] pillars."

e 2:14 Or "will be laid bare."

Nothing but a pile of rubble and a lair for wild beasts.
Everyone who passes by
will hiss with scorn and shake their fists."

Jerusalem Will Be Punished

3 Doomed is the filthy[a] and foul city—
the city of oppression!
2 Her people do not listen to the voice *of God*
and will not accept correction.[b]
They do not trust in YAHWEH anymore
and do not want a close relationship with their God.[c]
3 Her rulers are roaring lions,
and her judges are ravenous wolves who *hunt* in the evening,[d]
too greedy to leave even a bone till the morning.
4 Her prophets are proud, reckless impostors.[e]

---

a 3:1 Or "rebellious." The Hebrew word *mor'ah* is taken from the root word for "excrement." Zephaniah was saying that the city is full of rebellion and filth. There are three Hebrew terms that qualify her spiritual and moral corruption in this opening verse: *mor'ah*, *nig'alah*, and *hayyonah*—participial adjectives. The first of these derives from the verb *mara'* or *marah*, which means "rebellious." The second derives from the verb *ga'al*, with the sense of "polluted" or "defiled"—and it is this latter meaning that is particularly appropriate for Jerusalem since it accurately describes the extent of both her ceremonial and moral impurity. And the third participle derives from the verb *yanah*, meaning "oppressive."

b 3:2 See Jer. 7:28.

c 3:2 This is perhaps the whole issue of the golden calf, that which stood in the way of intimacy between God and Israel. Intimacy requires acknowledgment of the total "otherness" of God and our inability to fathom him and his grace toward the depths of our beings, which we will never fully understand. This grace relationship with God allows us to go forth and love others with the same graciousness.

d 3:3 Or "evening wolves."

e 3:4 Or "irresponsible and treacherous."

Her priests profane the holy *place*[a]
and openly break the Law.[b]
5 *In spite of all this*,
Yahweh the Righteous *resides* in *Jerusalem*,
and all he does is just and true.
Morning by morning, he brings justice to light,
and day by day, he never fails.
Yet the wicked are shameless.

Yahweh Judges the Nations

6 "I have destroyed *proud*[c] nations
and toppled their high towers.
I filled their streets with rubble
so no one walks through them.
Their cities have been demolished.
Everyone is gone. Not one is left.
7 I thought, 'Certainly, now you will revere me.
Now you will yield to my correction.'
Then I would not need to punish them again
and destroy their homes.
But no, they were just as eager
to do whatever was evil.

8 "So wait patiently for me," declares Yahweh.[d]
"Wait for the day when I rise to seize the prey.[e]
For I have determined to gather the nations
and assemble the kingdoms
so that they will experience my fury
and know how great my anger is.

---

a 3:4 See Lev. 10:10.

b 3:4 Or "wage war [Hb. *chamas* or *hamas*] against the Torah."

c 3:6 As translated from the Septuagint.

d 3:8 Most commentators believe that this verse is addressed to those in Jerusalem who remained faithful to God.

e 3:8 Or "when I rise up to accuse" (LXX, Syriac).

For the land will be consumed
by the fire of my avenging zeal."

A Time of Restoration

9 "For then I will change the impure speech of all the people[a]
to the pure speech *of praise*[b]
so that all may worship my name together
and serve me shoulder to shoulder.[c]
10 From beyond the rivers of Ethiopia,[d]
my worshipers from distant lands will bring me gifts."[e]

The Humble Remnant of Israel

11 "When that day comes,
you will never again be put to shame
over your former acts of rebellion.
For I will remove from your midst
all who are arrogant and who boast in their self-importance.
You will never again strut about in pride
on my holy mountain.
12 But I will leave a remnant among you:
a humble and lowly people
who will find their hiding place

---

a 3:9 Or "nations."

b 3:9 In the context, God promises to convert the people of the nations from speaking the names of impure gods to offering pure speech (lit. "pure lip") to him.

c 3:9 Or "with one shoulder."

d 3:10 A possible figure of speech for "from the remotest parts of the earth." See footnote on 2:12.

e 3:10 Or "From beyond the rivers of Ethiopia [Sudan] they will bring my worshipers, the daughter of my dispersed, as an offering unto me."

in the *beautiful* name of Yahweh.
13 They will do no wrong and only speak the truth,
nor will they use any form of deceit.
They will be content like grazing sheep.
They will rest, and no one will frighten them."

Songs of Joy in Zion

14 Go ahead, sing for joy, daughter of Zion.
People of Israel, get excited and shout aloud.
Rejoice, let blissful praise fill your heart,
fair daughter of Jerusalem.
15 Yahweh has canceled out his judgments against you.
He has turned your accuser away.
Yahweh, your King, is here within you,[a] Israel;
you have nothing more to fear.
16 On that day, the message for Jerusalem will be:
Zion, do not yield to fear.
Don't let your heart be discouraged.[b]
17 Yahweh, your God, is inside you.[c]
He is the Warrior-Savior
who takes such delight in you
that it will make him leap for joy
and shout with great gladness.
Yes, he will soothe you with his love.[d]
He will sing over you his song of praise.[e]

---

a 3:15 Or "among you." See v. 17.

b 3:16 Or "Don't let your hands grow weak [limp]."

c 3:17 Or "in your midst."

d 3:17 Or "quiet you with his love" or "seal [engrave] you with his love." To rest in God's love is a silent ecstasy. God's love both renews and soothes the troubled soul.

e 3:17 The word for "song" is *ranan*, which is a song of praise. See 1 Cor. 4:5.

18 "I will remove the sadness over your appointed
feasts,
and you will not be ashamed about them again.[a]
19 Behold, at the right time,
I will deal with those who mistreat you.
I will rescue the weak
and regather the scattered ones.[b]
I will turn their shame into praise
when I restore their honor across the land.
20 On that day, I will be your guide to bring you home;
at that time, I will gather you together.
You can be sure of this:
I will give you a good name,
and you will be admired among all the peoples of the
earth
as I restore your fortunes before your own eyes.
I, YAHWEH, have spoken."

---

a 3:18 Or "I will gather together those who mourn for the appointed feasts—those people belong to you, so you will no longer suffer reproach." The Hebrew verb *ʾasap* or *ʾasaph* can mean either "to gather" or "to remove," depending on the context. The precise meaning of the Hebrew of this sentence is uncertain.

b 3:19 See Mic. 4:6–7.

POSTEXILIC TIMELINE

An understanding of the postexilic time is absolutely necessary for laypeople as well as pastors and scholars. Otherwise, the power and passion of the six postexilic books—Ezra, Nehemiah, Esther, Haggai, Zechariah, and Malachi—will be cut off from the pathos of their context. The events and prophecies of these six books took place during the emotional era surrounding the rebuilding of Jerusalem and the temple after their catastrophic destruction by the Babylonians in 586 BC.

In fact, many doctoral Old Testament scholars can't keep the chronology of these books straight in their heads. For obvious reasons, the narrative from Adam and Eve to 586 BC (a fairly clean historical line) shatters at this point in Israel's story. It's similar to someone who kept a daily journal on a vacation and then was involved in a car crash. There will be a gap between entries.

Unfortunately, the order of the English Bible puts these books in two different places. Ezra, Nehemiah, and Esther are listed with the history books, while the three postexilic prophets appear at the end of the Old Testament. Few lay readers connect the dots and accurately assemble those three history books with Haggai, Zechariah, and Malachi into the historical narrative they create together.

Historic Context of the Postexilic Books

The assigning of specific year-dates to people and events from the pre-Christian era is not a precise science. In most cases, the dates are approximate and accurate within a timeframe of one to three years. However, for the sake of simplicity, the following timeline and the footnotes throughout TPT will employ specific year-dates, apart from references to periods within a particular century.

- First Temple Judaism: approximately 1,000–586 BC (over four hundred years)
- Israel in exile (the time between the temples): 586–536 BC (about fifty years)
- Second Temple Judaism (construction started in 536 BC, but it took a while to finish): 536 BC—AD 70 (about six hundred years)

A small, initial Babylonian incursion and deportation from the nation of Judah took place in 605 BC. This was the time when Daniel was taken into exile along with other specially selected young Jewish men. Daniel subsequently rose to fame and influence at the royal Babylonian court, primarily because of his extraordinary divine gift of dream interpretation. The once-mighty nation of Israel had already disappeared in 722 BC at the hands of the Assyrians, and the nation of Judah was coming apart from 597 BC to 586 BC in the face of internal corruption and the invasion of the Babylonian Empire.

The first major deportation took exiles to Babylon in 597 BC. About ten years later, the city of Jerusalem and its temple were utterly destroyed (586 BC). The second wave of exiles to Babylon followed this devastating event. The third and final deportation took place in 582 BC.

The Babylonian captivity lasted approximately seventy years (measured from the time the first exiles were taken into captivity), until 539 BC, at which point the Persian Empire destroyed Babylon. The Persians inherited the Israelite exiles, and Cyrus, the Persians' leader, issued a proclamation in 538 BC allowing the Israelites to return to rebuild the temple in Jerusalem if they wanted to (Ezra 1).

The next era is the Persian age. It lasted over two hundred years, from 539 until the Greeks conquered Persia in 332 BC. It was during this time that work on rebuilding the temple commenced (536 BC), which gave rise to the designation Second Temple Judaism—a period that lasted until AD 70. It was in this Second Temple that Jesus, as a young boy, stayed behind, causing his parents to search frantically for him (Luke 2:41–52).

During the Persian age, the Jews looked both to the past and to the future. They gathered hope and wisdom from the wealth of their rich heritage, from the visions of the canonical prophets, and from the corresponding anticipation of a renewal of the land and kingdom of Israel, along with the new covenant age. This also involved the cultivation of a future hope for a Messiah who would restore Jerusalem and David's kingdom.

A great deal of tension existed within Second Temple Judaism. One contentious issue involved how the newly returned exiles should relate to the foreigners surrounding them. Two opposing opinions arose regarding this issue.

On one side of the divide were those who maintained that the Jews must keep separate from the ethnicities around them. The Jewish remnant was so small that many worried they would disappear if they diluted their culture. This train of thought permeates the books of Ezra and Nehemiah, in which intermarriage with outsiders was seen as troublesome and undesirable. It sounds bigoted to our modern ears, but in their defense, the Jews were a tiny, disorganized remnant, and they happened to be in a rough neighborhood full of hostile tribes and peoples. Additionally, the syncretism (the blending of Israel's faith with the pagan religions of their neighbors) of the past had sped the destruction of the First Temple and Jerusalem. The Jews were especially bitter about the Edomites, their brother tribe descended from Esau, who failed to come to their aid when Babylon invaded. Instead, the Edomites looted Jerusalem (Obad. 10–14).

During this time, some also held the opposite (less defensive and more open) point of view. The stories of Ruth and Jonah reminded the Jews that outsiders are often more receptive to God than Jewish insiders. Jesus championed this theme in his ministry. The book of Haggai talks about God's plan to bless all nations through the Jewish people.

The mighty Israelite literary and spiritual tradition of prophecy (unique among all civilizations), whose prophets shouted forth the declarations of YAHWEH, began to sputter out and eventually die during the early Second Temple period.

Many priests and scholars of that time held the conviction that the Holy Spirit's voice had departed after Malachi. Now this was indeed the reality, for canonical prophecy did cease after Malachi and did not resume until the arrival of John the Baptist, some four hundred years later. The only prophetic phenomenon believed to be left was the *Bat Kol*, literally meaning "daughter of a voice." *Bat Kol* referred to a heavenly voice that was thought to proclaim God's will or divine judgment in a legal dispute.

The season of scholars, sages, and rabbis emerged to replace the prophets. Footnoters and commentators diluted and obscured the fire and passion of Jeremiah and Amos. A culture of scholastic legalism started taking shape. By the time Greek rule emerged in the Holy Land (332 BC), the genres of wisdom and apocalyptic literature had replaced the prophetic tradition.

No longer an independent nation, Judah was reduced to a vassal state of Babylon, Persia, Greece, and Rome (in succession, for centuries) without an anointed descendant of David ruling from Jerusalem. The people of God even forfeited their holy language, Hebrew, which was confined to the synagogue and studied by scholars. They had adopted Aramaic, the language they learned from their Babylonian captors in exile. We see the shift from Hebrew to Aramaic in the original version of the book of Daniel,[a] the action of which takes place during that season of exile.

The Postexilic History Books

It's easy to confuse the books that bear the names Ezra and Nehemiah with the personal activity of these two Bible characters. In the Hebrew Bible, there is just one book: *Ezra-Nehemiah*. The text covers much more ground than just the workings and doings of Ezra and Nehemiah themselves. For instance, there is a gap of nearly sixty years between Ezra chapter 6 and Ezra chapter 7. The unified book of Ezra-Nehemiah covers over one hundred years of history (538–433 BC). Between Ezra 1–6 and Ezra 7 through Nehemiah 13, six decades of silence ensue. This fact is often lost on the casual reader.

Ezra-Nehemiah Timeline:

- The events in the book of Ezra start not with Ezra but with the Edict of Cyrus (538 BC).
- The first group of exiles returned to Jerusalem (538 BC).
- The prophets Haggai and Zechariah prophesied during the events of Ezra 5 (520 BC).
- The temple was rebuilt and Passover celebrated in Ezra 6 (516 BC).
- Ezra showed up for the first time in Ezra 7, many decades later (458 BC). The second wave of exiles came with him to Jerusalem, and a spiritual awakening ensued.
- Nehemiah arrived with a third wave of exiles to rebuild the city wall of Jerusalem (445 BC).

---

a Daniel 1:1–2:3; 8:1–12:13 were written in Hebrew; 2:4–7:28 was written in Aramaic.

In one sense, the book of Esther is not technically a postexilic book, as Esther and Mordecai were still in exile. But it recounts events in Persia long after the Edict of Cyrus, right before Ezra's return to Jerusalem. There was no single return from exile. It happened in waves. Scholars cannot pinpoint the date of Esther's composition with any certainty; see the following timeline for the possible date range.

Dates from the Persian Age (539–332 BC)

- 559–530 BC: Cyrus reigned in Persia.
- 539 BC: Babylon fell to Persia.
- 539 BC: Judah (mostly destroyed) fell under Persian control.
- 538 BC: Edict of Cyrus was proclaimed (2 Chron. 36:22–23; Ezra 1:1–4; 6:3–5).
- 536 BC: First wave of returnees began work on the Second Temple. Work stopped soon after.
- 521–486 BC: Darius I reigned in Persia.
    - 520–510 BC: Zerubbabel acted as governor in Judah.
    - **520 BC: Haggai prophesied** (encouraged the completion of the temple).
    - **520–518 BC: Zechariah prophesied**.
    - 516 BC: The Second Temple was at least somewhat completed; Passover was celebrated (Ezra 6).
    - **515–430 BC: Malachi prophesied.**[a]
    - Persia and Greece were at war.
        - 490 BC: Battle of Marathon took place.
        - 489 BC: Battle of the Hot Gates took place.

---

a A definitive date is not possible here. The likely period of Malachi's ministry and the recording of his prophecy lies between the building of the Second Temple and the period of the Ezra-Nehemiah reforms (i.e., between 515 BC and 430 BC). Given the similarity between Malachi's concerns and those of Nehemiah, the latter end of that range is the more likely date.

- 486–465 BC: Xerxes I (Ahasuerus) reigned.
  Events of Esther occurred.
- 465–424 BC: Artaxerxes I reigned.
  460–332 BC: Esther was written (the exact date is disputed).
  458 BC: **Ezra returned** (a fifty-eight-year gap spans Ezra 6 and 7).
  445–433 BC: **Nehemiah was governor of Judah**—sent to Jerusalem under Artaxerxes I to rebuild the city.

Dates from the Greek Age (332–64 BC)

- 332 BC: Alexander the Great defeated Persia.
  The rise of apocalyptic and wisdom literature "sages" occurred.
  The Greek language books of the Old Testament Apocrypha were written at this time.
- Mid-200s BC: The Hebrew Torah was translated into Greek in Alexandria. This came to be known as the Septuagint or LXX.
- 100s BC: The rest of the Hebrew Bible was translated into Greek, and the Septuagint was completed. This Greek Bible was most likely the version that the writers of the New Testament preferred.

The Hasmonean Rulers (152–37 BC)

The Hasmoneans were a theocratic, high priestly dynasty.

- 152–37 BC: Leaders included Jonathan Maccabee; Simon; John Hyrcanus; Aristobulus; Alexander Jannaeus; Salome Alexandra (widow of Alexander); Hyrcanus II; Aristobulus II; Antigonus.
- Mid-100s BC: Parties emerged within Palestinian Judaism—Essenes, Pharisees, Sadducees.

Dates from the Start of the Roman Age (63 BC—70 AD)

- 63 BC: Roman general Pompey entered Jerusalem.
- 37 BC: The Romans made Herod the Great king of Judea, replacing Antigonus, the last Hasmonean ruler.
- 6 BC: Judea came under direct Roman rule.
- 4 BC: Jesus was born.
- AD 26–36: Pontius Pilate was governor of Judea.
- AD 30: Jesus was crucified, died, rose from the dead, and ascended to heaven.
- AD 70: The Second Temple period came to an end with the fall of Jerusalem and the destruction of the temple.

THE BOOK OF

HAGGAI

Greater Glory

BroadStreet
PUBLISHING

HAGGAI

Introduction

AT A GLANCE

Author: Haggai the prophet

Audience: Those rebuilding the city of Jerusalem and the temple

Date: The second half of 520 BC, almost seventy years after the destruction of Jerusalem and exile of the Jews to Babylon in 586 BC

Type of Literature: Prophecy

Major Themes: Wrong priorities incur judgment; wholehearted obedience guarantees blessing; YAHWEH's vision for the whole world; judgment on sinful rebellion paves the way for the fulfillment of salvation; seeing Jesus in the book

Outline:

I. Superscription: author and setting — 1:1

II. The first message from YAHWEH: the call to rebuild the temple — 1:2–11

- a. A divine rebuke for wrong priorities: private homes are deemed more important than the temple of YAHWEH — 1:2–4
- b. Economic poverty: the penalty for ignoring the commanded priority of building God's house — 1:5–11

III. The people's response to the divine command: obedience and reverent awe — 1:12–15

IV. The second message from YAHWEH: the glory of the Second Temple will be greater than the glory of the First Temple — 2:1–9
  a. Exhortation for the people to be strong with God's Spirit — 2:1–5
  b. God's promise to fill his new temple with a greater glory — 2:6–9

V. The third message from YAHWEH: a defiled people are cleansed and blessed — 2:10–19
  a. The people are defiled because of their disobedience — 2:10–14
  b. The people's disobedience results in economic impoverishment — 2:15–17
  c. The people's obedient response to rebuild the temple results in economic prosperity — 2:18–19

VI. The fourth message from YAHWEH: a promise to Zerubbabel — 2:20–23

ABOUT THE BOOK OF HAGGAI

While this book is short, it is also an essential link in the story of God's salvation plan for the whole world. It is exquisitely organized in a way that allows us to precisely date the prophecy, as the following quote demonstrates (note how this informs the previously given outline): "Haggai's book stands in a carefully planned chronological order. It has five sections, each exactly dated in 520 according to the months and days of the Babylonian lunar calendar. Using the equivalent dates on the Julian calendar, these five sections and their dates are

1:1–11 from August 29,
1:12–15*a* from September 21,
1:15*b*–2:9 from October 17,

2:10–19 from December 18,
2:20–23 also from December 18."[a]

Because of these provided dates and because of the issues so clearly addressed in the prophecy, we know exactly what the people of God were facing when God was speaking through Haggai. By the time of Haggai, the once-glorious kingdom of Solomon had shrunk to a scruffy twenty-square mile "county." Judah's territory was reduced to a tiny fragment of the massive Persian Empire, a little region in the hill country surrounding the town of Jerusalem. Judah was a shadow of what it had once been.

Solomon's Temple had been destroyed, and the royal lineage descending from King David had been cut off in 586 BC. God's people had survived the exile in Babylon, and a ragtag faithful remnant had returned to make a new start.

This was a very complex time of disorder, and the clean timeline of the Bible narrative (all the way from the garden of Eden) breaks down into random shreds, mirroring the muddled and confused season in which the people lived. Please see the "Postexilic Timeline" preceding the book of Haggai.

The prophets of old had warned Israel that wandering from their covenant with God would lead to destruction. Every civilization needs an organizing principle, an ideal toward which to orient its collective life and values. For Israel, that central guiding structure was the covenant. And, while Israel broke the covenant in many ways, idolatry came to symbolize her wandering away from

---

a Elizabeth Achtemeier, *Nahum—Malachi: Interpretation: A Bible Commentary for Teaching and Preaching* (Louisville, KY: John Knox Press, 1986), 94.

that covenantal bond with YAHWEH that had held Israel together. A kingdom that fights itself is ruined (Matt. 12:25). Even a modern, diverse, multicultural society needs a gravitational center. Divergent loyalties produce a fractured society.

From its peak around the year 1000 BC with David and Solomon, Israelite society slowly unraveled and lost focus on the people's covenant with God, which arose from the exodus, reenacted with the celebration of the Passover. By 586 BC, Jerusalem (and what remained of Israel) had reached the point of no return, and Babylon destroyed the city and took the people into exile.

A generation or two later, however, Persia in turn destroyed Babylon and inherited the Israelite exiles. We see this personally with Daniel, who served both empires. Persia allowed the exiles to return to Jerusalem and attempt to rebuild the ruins of the once-great city. The Edict of Cyrus (ruler of Persia) put this new freedom for the Jews in writing in 538 BC.

We call this the beginning of Second Temple Judaism, the era in which Jesus grew up and which ended in AD 70, when the Romans destroyed the Second Temple.

The history books of Ezra, Nehemiah, and Daniel and the prophetic books of Haggai, Zechariah, and Malachi describe this effort to revive what once was. The returned exiles succeeded in the end, and out of that recovered Second Temple civilization emerged none other than Jesus of Nazareth.

PURPOSE

Haggai addressed several issues in order to bring the remnant community of Judah to the realization that their failure to complete the rebuilding of the Jerusalem Temple was the root cause of their economic woes. In other words, their rank disobedience of God's instructions was their undoing. The prophet's purposes included the following:

- To underscore the dangers of misplaced priorities. The people were putting all their energy into building and refurbishing their own homes and were neglecting the restoration and renovation of God's house.
- To demonstrate that the lack of faithfulness to the covenant was causing problems in the economy. The returning Jews were hardly living in abundance, and Haggai pointed to the cause: they had strayed from the mandatory laws and stipulations that God had laid down in the covenant.
- To remedy the Jews' failure to see the big picture of YAHWEH's vision for the whole world. God didn't create the world just to bless the Jews; he chose the Jews to bless all people.

Haggai spoke powerfully to alleviate discouragement and apathy. Everyone knew that the (under-construction) city and the temple were mere shadows of the past glory that was Jerusalem. Nostalgia can be corrosive and tends to paralyze positive action.

The message of Haggai addresses a significant need in the church today. In our mad, narcissistic pursuit of our own agendas, we have neglected God's plans and purposes. He is calling us back to finish his work. We are to put God's outlook and will ahead of our own designs. In some ways, the ruined, devastated temple of the days of Haggai mirrors our ruined and devastated church today. It is always a good time to repent of these recurring trends and return to our first love.

AUTHOR AND AUDIENCE

Haggai the prophet generated this message and addressed the people of Judah who were rebuilding the city of Jerusalem and the temple. His prophecies all took place in the second half of the year 520 BC. Like Jeremiah, for whom Baruch wrote everything down, Haggai may have had one or more scribes or editors.

Haggai means "festival," "fiesta," "sacrifice," or "my feast." His name may imply that he was born on one of the feast days.[a] Some scholars believe that Haggai was a very old man at the time of his prophecies and that he had been a witness to the destruction of Solomon's Temple.[b] Some scholars believe he spent most of his life in Babylon and was one of the first to leave under the proclamation of Cyrus.[c]

The Septuagint (Greek Old Testament) and the Vulgate (Jerome's Latin Bible) state that Haggai and Zechariah wrote Psalms 111–112, 125–126, 137–138, and 145–149 after their return from captivity.

The people of Haggai's day did not have it easy; they were trying to make things work in a rough neighborhood. They were sandwiched between the Edomites, their "brother" nation descended from Esau (who did

---

a See Joyce G. Baldwin, *Haggai, Zechariah, Malachi: An Introduction and Commentary* (Downers Grove, IL: InterVarsity Press, 1972), 28; Pieter A. Verhoef, *The Books of Haggai and Malachi*, The New International Commentary on the Old Testament (Grand Rapids, MI: Eerdmans Publishing, 1987), 4; Richard A. Taylor and E. Ray Clendenen, *Haggai, Malachi*, The New American Commentary: An Exegetical and Theological Exposition of Holy Scripture, vol. 21A (Nashville, TN: B&H Publishing, 2004), 44.

b See E. B. Pusey, *The Minor Prophets, with a Commentary Explanatory and Practical, and Introductions to the Several Books*, vol. 2 (Grand Rapids, MI: Baker Book House, 1950), 293.

c See Rabbi Eli Cashdan, *The Twelve Prophets* (London: Soncino Press, 1948), 254.

not defend their kindred people when the Babylonians attacked but rather looted the city of Jerusalem), and the Samaritans. And the New Testament makes it very clear what kind of tension there was between the Jews and the Samaritans.

The returning Jews seemed to have had a flurry of rotating leaders; this era is hard for historians to follow because it was not a stable time. In the time of Haggai, the priest Joshua was the spiritual leader, and Zerubbabel, of the royal line of David, was the political leader.

It was time for God to re-create a people, a nation.[a] A new chapter of Israel's history was being written, and Haggai and Zechariah (senior and junior prophets during this era, respectively) inspired the people to act and record what happened. The people responded to Haggai's message, and within a few weeks of his first prophetic words, they began to rebuild God's house. Zechariah strengthened and repeated Haggai's message. However, it was Haggai who catalyzed the effort. Without his prophetic ministry, there might not have been a Second Temple. There was no prophet in Israel whose ministry was more successful than Haggai's except, perhaps, for that of Jonah, but the source of the heartfelt conversion of the Ninevites had his own issues.

MAJOR THEMES

Wrong Priorities Incur Judgment. The returning exiles put more work into decorating their own homes than into rebuilding God's house. That is not to say that God needed a building, but their selfish behavior was reminiscent of what sent them into exile in the first place. The rebuilding of the temple had begun in 536 BC, but the scaffolding had been deserted for half a generation by

---

a See Ezek. 37.

the time of Haggai. The fire-blackened ruins of Solomon's Temple remained as a stain on their conscience, a blot on Israel's national identity, and the root cause of her economic woes (Hag. 1:5–11). Houses of worship today (such as our churches) do not need to be palatial showpieces, but if we say one thing about the priority of our faith and the state of our church buildings show another, the people on the outside will believe our buildings, not our words.

Wholehearted Obedience Guarantees Blessing. The people of Judah were struggling economically, and Haggai named the cause, calling them to a higher path forward. We need to remember that during the era of the law (i.e., old covenant), people measured divine blessing almost exclusively in economic and material terms. If the people of God wished to live prosperously, then they had to live in wholehearted obedience to God's laws and commands. Failure to do so would leave them impoverished—both materially and spiritually. The values that bring human flourishing in the first place are those that are consistent with God's timeless principles of justice, righteousness, compassion, mercy, and the like. A virtuous society is a prosperous society, although we must also recognize that, in the new covenant age, divine blessing is focused primarily on spiritual renewal, peace, and well-being, via the ministry of the indwelling Holy Spirit. In this new covenant era, the parameters of a "prosperous society" are far wider, encompassing more than simply economic well-being.

The wonderfully positive outcome for the people of Judah, as a result of Haggai's preaching, was that they listened and obeyed the voice of God. The text of Haggai 1:12–15 makes it abundantly clear, albeit by undeniable implication, that the indwelling presence of the Spirit of God within the people was the sole reason for their renewed commitment to the will of their Lord.

Some contemporary applications of this principle may be evident in the following examples: An honest, hard-working society that places a premium on God's divinely revealed principles for living will experience higher levels of justice, compassion, equality, and social harmony. There will likely be less need for police and jails. People will keep their contracts and promises, creating more trust and market opportunities. Cheating and corruption will be rare or unknown. A nation with fair judges and courts will lack resentment among its people and the cynicism and violence that it breeds. Generosity takes the edge off poverty. Justice is contagious. To this day, the nations and regions of our world with the lowest crime rates have the highest levels of civilization and human flourishing. In addition, a nation that cares for its land, air, water, and resources is more likely to have sustainable, flourishing harvests.

Yahweh's Vision for the Whole World. There is no doubt that part of Haggai's message was to offer the remnant of the Jewish population in Judah and Jerusalem a guarantee from God that, as a consequence of their renewed obedience to him in rebuilding the temple, they would once again experience abundant economic blessing (2:15–19). However, Haggai didn't call the Jews to this higher path just to generate national prosperity and well-being. He tried to show them that God transforms the whole world through the ones who are faithful to him. Haggai wanted to help the Jews realize that they were not just rebuilding a town and then falling short of what it once was. They were taking all the wisdom and experience of a centuries-long covenant journey with God and adding their own chapter to it. They were forging their own iron link in a long chain of salvation history that would have implications, for better or for worse, for those who came after them and potentially for all creation. The prophet attempted to show them the big picture: that their recommitment to the temple reconstruction would eventually transform the world. He was correct. The Jews did indeed rebuild and thus created the platform for the emergence of Jesus, whose message burst forth at Pentecost to reach all the nations (Acts 1:8). The same can be said for us. We live not just to experience our own salvation but also to add our chapter of faith to the greatest of all stories in which the final chapter will tell of the victory of all that is good over all that is evil.

Judgment on Sinful Rebellion Paves the Way for the Fulfillment of Salvation. One of the major recurring themes of scriptural prophecy is that the outworking of the redemptive purposes of God on behalf of his people very often follows the outpouring of divine judgment, whether it be on the pagan nations of the world, on the people of God for their covenant faithlessness, or both.

Here in the prophecy of Haggai, this pattern of divine activity is once again in evidence. The declaration "I . . . will once again shake the heavens and earth, the land and sea" is declared by God on two occasions: In Haggai 2:6, the whole action is indicated, and in 2:21, only "the heavens and the earth" is recorded—although, no doubt the shaking of "the land and sea" is also implied in the second reference. The particular significance in the context of these two references is that they are both followed by a Messianic prophecy that anticipates the fulfillment of God's plan of salvation for his people all over the world. Further details of this prophetic motif are to be found in the final theme, Seeing Jesus in the Book.

Seeing Jesus in the Book. The anticipation of the Messianic age, in relation to the coming of Jesus Christ to earth, is explicitly indicated in two passages in the second and final chapter of the book of Haggai.

First, in 2:6, the sovereign, divine shaking of the earth and sea is followed by the declaration that "the treasures of the nations will flow in" (2:7). Now this treasure has been interpreted either as something or someone of inestimable value or something or someone that has been expected by peoples all over the world for a very long time. In either case, such an expectation is fulfilled in the person of the Messiah, foretold consistently throughout the prophetic canon of the Old Testament and realized in the Messianic fulfillment texts of the New Testament. What reinforces the viability of such an interpretation is the accompanying prophecy in 2:7 that God "will fill this temple with glory"—a glory that "will surpass the glory of the original" (2:9).

Two passages can illustrate the New Testament fulfillment of such a prophecy. The first is found in Luke 2:27–32, where the infant Jesus is taken by his parents to the temple for the rite of circumcision and consecration in accordance with the law. There, his parents handed him over to Simeon, a faithful temple official, who had been assured by the Spirit of God that he would see "the Anointed One of God" (v. 26) before he died. During the circumcision ceremony, Simeon offered a prayer of praise to God, in which he declared: "With my own eyes I have seen your Word, the Savior you sent into the world. He will be glory for your people Israel, and the Revelation-Light for all people everywhere!" (vv. 29–32).

Then, in the magnificent vision of the heavenly Jerusalem, as experienced by the apostle John on the Isle of Patmos, there is a particularly striking description of the heavenly city in Revelation 21:22–23. Here, John records: "I saw no temple in the city, for its temple is the Lord God, the Almighty, and the Lamb. The city has no need for the sun or moon to shine, for the glory of God is its light, and its lamp is the Lamb." This is undoubtedly the climactic vision of the temple in all of Scripture, and in this vision, God the Father and the risen Lord Jesus Christ—the Lamb King—constitute the eternally glorious lighting of the heavenly city-temple.

The second relevant Messianic text of Haggai is found in Haggai 2:21–23, where God repeats his intention to "shake the heavens and the earth." God then immediately declares that he will overthrow and destroy the power and authority of the kingdoms of the world; namely, all those nations who defy and blaspheme him. God then declares that he will take Zerubbabel, the political leader of the postexilic Judean community, and make him "like a signet ring. For I have chosen you to be mine" (v. 23). In the ancient world, a signet ring worked much like a seal—an identifying signature, if you like. Additionally, it was often regarded as a guarantee of a future payment (i.e., a deposit or down payment).[a] When this metaphor is linked to the action of sovereign divine choosing, its full meaning is further clarified: Zerubbabel was a descendant of King David and is found in the lineage of Jesus Christ, as recorded in Matthew 1:12–13. The point here is that God was declaring, at the end of the prophecy of Haggai, that Zerubbabel was a forerunner of the Davidic Messiah—one who would anticipate the climactic fulfillment of God's plan of salvation in the age to come, in the person of Jesus, the Son of God.

---

a See footnote on Hag. 2:23 in *The NIV Study Bible* (Grand Rapids, MI: Zondervan, 1995), 1397.

HAGGAI

Greater Glory

Yahweh's Message to the Leaders of Judah

1 On the first day of the month of Elul[a] during the second year Darius was emperor *of Persia*,[b] the word of Yahweh was spoken through the prophet Haggai. He delivered this prophecy to the *appointed* governor of Judah, Zerubbabel son of Shealtiel, and to the high priest, Joshua son of Jehozadak.[c]

2 "Yahweh, Commander of Angel Armies, says this: 'These people *procrastinate* by saying that this is not the right time to *finish* rebuilding Yahweh's house.' "

---

a 1:1 This can be calculated as about August 29, 520 BC (Gregorian calendar). The first day of every month was to be a day of feasting, rejoicing, and bringing special offerings to the Lord. But with no temple standing, there was no way to properly observe this feast of the new moon. See Num. 10:10; 28:11–15.

b 1:1 This is Darius I Hystaspes, Persia's king from 521 to 486 BC after the death of Cambyses.

c 1:1 Haggai's prophecy was intended for both the civil and religious leaders of the Jewish community. The governor was Zerubbabel the son of Shealtiel, a grandson of Jehoiachin, the king of Judah who was taken into exile in 597 BC (see 2 Kings 24:15; see also 1 Chron. 3:16–19). Joshua the high priest is also mentioned in Zech. 3:1 and 6:11 and in the books of Ezra (see Ezra 2:2) and Nehemiah (see Neh. 12:1, 26), where his name is spelled in Hebrew "Yeshuwa," or "Yeshua." His father, Jehozadak, was the high priest who had been taken into exile when Jerusalem was captured by the Babylonians in 586 BC.

Rebuking the Self-Absorbed

3Then YAHWEH spoke the following message to the people using Haggai as his mouthpiece: 4"*Really?* Is this the right time for you to be living in your expensive[a] houses while my house lies in ruins?[b] 5So now, I, YAHWEH, Commander of Angel Armies, say to you: You had better be intentional about the path you choose. 6You have planted much but harvested very little. You fill your plates, but you are never full. You drink but are still thirsty. You put on clothes but not enough to keep warm. You earn wages, but your money burns a hole in your pocket and quickly runs out.[c]

7"I, YAHWEH, Commander of Angel Armies, repeat: Be intentional about the path you take. 8Now, go up the

---

a 1:4 Or "paneled." The Hebrew root meaning is "covered," perhaps in contrast to the temple ruins being exposed to open air from above.

b 1:4 Haggai masterfully used the Hebrew word *chareb*, the same word for "drought" in v. 11. *Chareb* can be translated "rubble," "ruins," or "drought." Apparently, the returned exiles had cleared the site of the temple and set up an altar, but they had erected no actual building (see Ezra 3:1–6). There were likely no walls completely constructed, yet the people were warm and cozy in their homes elaborately paneled with cedar. The Lord must be first place in all things (see Matt. 6:33). To apply this to believers today, we need to see ourselves as the house, God's living temple. There is still much "rebuilding" and restoration that God wants to accomplish in his people (see Acts 3:21; 1 Cor. 6:19; Eph. 2:21; 4:11–13).

c 1:6 This is a figure of speech for prices rising faster than their wages. The cost of inflation had made their hard-earned money lose its value. It was like putting money in a pocket with holes.

mountain,[a] cut some timber, and rebuild my house, and I will take pleasure in it and manifest my glory there. It is I, YAHWEH, who say so.

9"You hoped for abundant crops, but instead you gathered little. When you brought in your meager harvest, I caused it to spoil.[b] It is I, YAHWEH, Commander of Angel Armies, asking you, 'Why?' It is because my house lies in ruins while each of you runs to his own house.
10That is why the sky has withheld the rain[c] and the ground its crops.
11I have called down drought on the land and hills—your grain, oil, and new wine. It has affected both people and animals and spoiled all your attempts to grow food."

The People Obey God's Command

12Then Zerubbabel son of Shealtiel, Joshua son of Jehozadak the high priest, and the entire remnant of the people obeyed the voice of YAHWEH their God. They recognized that YAHWEH their God had sent Haggai to them, so they obeyed his words. And the people were filled with holy awe toward YAHWEH.

---

a 1:8 The word for "mountain" in Hebrew is *harar*. The feminine form is *hararah*, the word used for "pregnant woman." The identical terminology for pregnant women and mountains is not a comment on size. Instead, it's because in Jewish culture, when you are on the top of a mountain, you are closer to God, and a pregnant woman was believed to be very close to God as she carried a living child. "Go up the mountain," taken metaphorically, is an urge to draw close to God. This illustrates how Scripture can carry both concrete and symbolic truth.

b 1:9 Or "I blew it away," a figure of speech for destroying (spoiling) their meager harvest, ensuring that whatever harvest remained would not last.

c 1:10 As translated from the Aramaic Targum; the Hebrew is "dew."

13Then the messenger of YAHWEH, Haggai, spoke YAHWEH's promise to the people: "I am with you *to bless you*[a]—declares YAHWEH."

14And YAHWEH stirred up the spirit of Zerubbabel son of Shealtiel governor of Judah, the spirit of Joshua son of Jehozadak the high priest, and the spirit of the entire remnant of the people, and they came together to rebuild the temple of YAHWEH, their God, the Commander of Angel Armies. 15They began their work on the twenty-fourth day of the sixth month.[b]

The Future Glory of the Temple

2 In the second year of King Darius, the twenty-first day of the seventh month,[c] the word of YAHWEH happened[d] through the prophet Haggai as follows, 2"Go and give this urgent message to Zerubbabel son of Shealtiel, governor of Judah, and the high priest Joshua son of Jehozadak, and all the remnant of the people:

---

a 1:13 God's promise to be "with" his people imparts encouragement and hope and brings blessing with success. See Gen. 28:15; Ex. 3:12.

b 1:15 That is, September 21, 520 BC. It was only three weeks after Haggai's initial message to the people before the work on the temple began. Some translations include the words "in the second year of King Darius." However, the Hebrew text allows for placing those words either with the text that precedes or the text that follows. Since, on a discourse level, it is more convincing to place these words with the text that follows, this translation has done so.

c 2:1 That is, about October 17, 520 BC. This was the seventh or last day of the "Feast of Tabernacles" or "Feast of Booths" that began on the fifteenth day of the seventh month (see Lev. 23:34). Because of the festival, Jerusalem would have been filled with worshipers.

d 2:1 Although most translations read "The Word of the Lord came," the Hebrew is very dramatic. It is as if the prophet "experiences" the Word of YAHWEH. It is a collision with the thoughts of God, a "Word event."

[3]"Did anyone from among you see the magnificent glory of the original temple?[a] And how does it look to you now? Does it not seem as nothing in your eyes?

[4]"I, YAHWEH say to you, Zerubbabel, be courageous! Joshua, son of Jehozadak, high priest, be courageous! All you living in the land, take heart! Go to work, for I am with you, says YAHWEH, Commander of Angel Armies.
[5]I, YAHWEH, will keep the covenant that I made with you[b] when you came out of Egypt. My Spirit is still present among you, so be fearless.

[6]"For I declare to you: Very soon,[c] I, YAHWEH, Commander of Angel Armies, will once again shake the heavens and earth, the land and sea.[d]

[7]"I, YAHWEH, Commander of Angel Armies, will shake every nation, and the treasures[e] of the nations will flow in, and I will fill this temple with glory.

[8]"I, YAHWEH, Commander of Angel Armies, declare to you, all the silver and gold is mine.

[9]"I, YAHWEH, Commander of Angel Armies, declare to you, the glory of this new temple will surpass the glory of

---

a 2:3 This question implies that there were some people old enough to remember Solomon's Temple, which had been destroyed sixty-six years earlier in 586 BC. This means that those who were over seventy years old would be able to remember it. Haggai may have been one who had seen the glory of Solomon's Temple.

b 2:5 Or "the word I cut with you." The Semitic contract (covenant) involved cutting an animal in two and walking between the halves together. See Gen. 15.

c 2:6 The Hebrew phrase is literally "Yet once, it is little"; that is, "the action to follow is imminent."

d 2:6 See Heb. 12:26.

e 2:7 Or "desires."

the original, and I will grant peace *and prosperity* in this place.[a]

"I, YAHWEH, Commander of Angel Armies, have spoken."

Haggai Consults the Priests

10In the second year of Darius, on the twenty-fourth day
of the ninth month,[b] the word of YAHWEH was spoken to
the prophet Haggai as follows: 11"I, YAHWEH, Commander
of Angel Armies, say to you: 'Ask the priests for their ruling on this:[c] 12If someone holds consecrated meat from
a sacrifice and carries it in the fold of his *priestly* robe, could his robe then pass on holiness if it comes into contact with bread, stew, wine, olive oil, or any kind of food at all?' "

"No," the priests replied.

13Haggai then said, "If anyone is ritually unclean by contact with a corpse[d] and touches any of these things, would it become unclean?"

The priests replied, "Yes, it is unclean."

14Then Haggai said, "So it is the same with this people. YAHWEH declares: 'The nation is unclean in my eyes. Everything they produce is unclean to me, and everything they offer *at the altar* is also unclean.' "

---

a 2:9 The Hebrew word *shalom* can mean more than "peace"; it also includes the meanings of "well-being," "health," "strength," and "prosperity." This is the temple (later restored by Herod) that Christ taught in. The Greek Septuagint adds these words, "and peace of soul, to save all those who laid the foundations for the rebuilding of this temple."

b 2:10 That is, about December 18, 520 BC.

c 2:11 Or "Ask the priests a Torah saying." It was one of the duties of priests to give rulings about questions over ritual purity and about the law. See Deut. 17:8–12.

d 2:13 See Num. 19:13.

God's Promise of Blessing

[15]"Now consider carefully your recent past[a] before you
started rebuilding YAHWEH's temple. [16]*Stop and remember*
what condition you were in. You would come expecting
to scoop twenty measures of grain but find only ten. You
would come expecting to draw fifty measures of wine
from a vat but find only twenty. [17]I struck the produce
of your labor by sending hail, hot desert winds to wither
your grain, and damp winds to make it rot. Yet you still
would not return to me[b]—declares YAHWEH.

[18]"Today is the twenty-fourth day of the ninth month,
the day the people resumed the building of my temple.
So be intentional from today forward. [19]The seed is still
in the storehouse, isn't it? Until now, the grapevines, fig
trees, pomegranate and olive trees have not produced a
harvest, but from now on, I will certainly bless you, and
your harvest will be plentiful."

God's Promise to Zerubbabel

[20]On that same day, the twenty-fourth day of the ninth
month, the word of YAHWEH happened a second time to
Haggai, as follows: [21]"Tell these words to Zerubbabel governor of Judah: 'I am going to shake the heavens and the
earth. [22]I will topple thrones and destroy the dynasties of
foreign kingdoms. I will crash their chariots and their riders. Horses and their riders will die, for their riders will
kill one another with the sword. [23]I, YAHWEH, Commander
of Angel Armies, declare, when that day comes, I will take

---

a 2:15 Or "consider carefully from this day onward." The Hebrew is literally "Now set your heart from this day and upward."

b 2:17 The Hebrew is literally "and there was not with you." It could possibly mean that they did not bring God an offering of what they had.

you, my servant Zerubbabel son of Shealtiel, and make you like a signet ring.[a] For I have chosen you to be mine. I, Yahweh, Commander of Angel Armies have spoken.' "

---

a 2:23 That is, God will hold his people close to his heart. The signet ring is also a symbol of God's authority (see Gen. 41:42; Est. 3:10; 8:2, 10). Historically, the signet ring was an important possession. It usually contained a small seal or the initial of the owner that would be impressed on wax for sealing important documents (see 1 Kings 21:8). The owner of the ring would jealously guard it by wearing it on a cord around his neck (see Gen. 38:18–19) or on the finger (see Jer. 22:24). Haggai was prophesying to Zerubbabel that the royal authority of the lineage of David would be restored to him.

THE BOOK OF

ZECHARIAH

Affection and Union

BroadStreet
PUBLISHING

ZECHARIAH

Introduction

AT A GLANCE

Author: Zechariah the prophet

Audience: Those living in the aftermath of a partially failed revival of Israelite culture after the Babylonian exile

Date: 520–518 BC

Type of Literature: Prophetic prose oracles[a] and apocalyptic literature

Major Themes: YAHWEH as Commander of Angel Armies; the day of YAHWEH; angelic revelation; God communicating through visions; the prophet as "custodian" of the covenant; promises of restoration and renewal—blessing for Israel and the nations; seeing Jesus in the book

Outline:

I. Superscription: author and setting — 1:1

II. Visions and revelations of hope, rebuke, renewal, and restoration — 1:2–8:23

- a. A call to repentance — 1:2–6
- b. A succession of eight night visions — 1:7–6:8
  - i. The horsemen — 1:7–17
  - ii. Four horns and four craftsmen — 1:18–21
  - iii. The measuring man — 2:1–13
  - iv. Clean clothes for the high priest — 3:1–10
  - v. The lampstand and two olive trees — 4:1–14
  - vi. The flying scroll — 5:1–4

---

a See C. L. Meyers and E. M. Meyers, *Haggai, Zechariah 1–8* (Garden City, NY: Doubleday, 1987), lxiv.

- vii. The woman in a barrel — 5:5–11
- viii. Four chariots — 6:1–8
- c. Three divine revelations from YAHWEH — 6:9–8:23
  - i. The crowning of Joshua as the priest-king — 6:9–15
  - ii. A call for justice, mercy, and compassion, not ritual observance — 7:1–14
  - iii. The divine promise to bless Jerusalem — 8:1–23
- III. Two oracles of promised Messianic deliverance and rule — 9:1–14:21
  - a. The coming of the Messianic King — 9:1–11:17
    - i. The protection of Judah and Jerusalem: destruction of her enemies — 9:1–8
    - ii. The arrival of Zion's King in Jerusalem: rescue and salvation — 9:9–17
    - iii. The restoration of YAHWEH's people to their homeland: security and blessing — 10:1–12
    - iv. The elimination of the godless "shepherd-rulers" in Israel — 11:1–17
  - b. The full inauguration of the kingdom of God — 12:1–14:21
    - i. God's deliverance of Judah and Jerusalem from all enemy nations — 12:1–9
    - ii. A prophecy of national mourning for "the Pierced One" — 12:10–14
    - iii. God's promise to cleanse his people from their sin — 13:1–6
    - iv. The scattering and execution of those who will "strike" the Good Shepherd, followed by the spiritual renewal of the faithful remnant — 13:7–9
    - v. The consummation of the coming kingdom of God, with the arrival of the Messianic Ruler, and the apocalyptic destruction of the enemies of God worldwide — 14:1–21

ABOUT THE BOOK OF ZECHARIAH

Zechariah is one of the longer books of the Twelve (the Minor Prophets) and is one of the most difficult books of the Bible to translate and interpret. Hebrew, as a spoken language, was starting to die and be replaced by Aramaic, the language of the Babylonian conquerors.

The exiles were back in Judah, their homeland, having returned from captivity in Babylon some twenty years previously (538 BC). The last sands of the seventy years of exile predicted by Jeremiah (Jer. 25:11; 29:10) had dropped through to the pile at the bottom of the hourglass.

In this exciting season, the prophets Zechariah and Haggai were encouraging the people to rebuild the temple and restart the Israelite civilization. This revitalization of Israel would come to be known as "Second Temple Judaism" and was the era and culture in which Jesus grew up.

The potent and fiery Old Testament prophetic tradition (unique to Israel) was entering its twilight years, and the season of rabbinic sages and apocalyptic visions was dawning. This fault line runs through the book of Zechariah, which, along with Daniel, expresses the birth of revelatory/apocalyptic language. The book may be divided into two distinct but related parts. The first section is chapters 1–8, which incorporate night visions along with additional revelatory "words of Yahweh." Together, these convey themes of hope, rebuke, restoration, and renewal. The second section is chapters 9–14, containing two prophetic oracles of distinctive apocalyptic language, conveying the primary themes of the divine destruction of the enemies of the people of God, the restoration and cleansing of the postexilic community of Judah, and the coming of the Messianic Priest-King, along with the establishment of the universal, everlasting kingdom of God.

Zechariah's writing is highly cinematic and visual, with the first eight chapters of his book chronicling the eight night visions he experienced. As is often the case with such visions including angels, we occasionally have trouble figuring out who is speaking to whom. This accounts for the plentiful variations among English versions of Zechariah. The literary narratives of such revelatory reveries, much like our own dreams, are distinctly nonlinear.

It is a book of high hopes for an Israelite renaissance, which merges with a prophetic anticipation of the political, cultural, and social turmoil that will erupt in the postexilic community of God's people in the centuries leading up to the dominance of the Roman Empire in the first century AD. This is highlighted, for example, in chapters 11 and 12. The anticipated pain of this future trauma is mixed with stubborn hope, sublimated into the prophetic oracles and apocalyptic visions splashing forth in the final chapters. These are oracles that also anticipate the coming of Jesus Christ, the Messianic King, and the fulfillment of the hope promised to the people of God. If Yahweh, whose promises always prevail, did not awaken the soul of Israel in Zechariah's time, then he would certainly do so at some moment in the future.

Zechariah, in his very heart and soul, was compelled to process a depressing shift in Israelite society. In the former classical era of David, Solomon, and their descendants, independent Israel had a stable separation of three powers: kings, priests, and prophets. At the beginning of the book, Zechariah hoped to restore this "trinity" by naming Zerubbabel (political) and Joshua (priestly) as the heirs of Moses and Aaron. However, the prophetic voice was no longer resonating with the people, and Zerubbabel was unable to assert any real political power in the shadow of the mighty Persian Empire. Relegated to the weaker role of "county commissioner," he faded from the scene.

Of the three pillars of Israelite culture, only the priestly one survived. The prophetic and royal branches evaporated before Zechariah's eyes. However, notwithstanding the contemporary discouragement, all eight visions granted to the prophet Zechariah (1:7–6:8) reinforce the hope provided in the divine revelation of God's redemptive program. The civil and religious roles played out by Zerubbabel and Joshua in Zechariah's day will be fulfilled in the crowning of the ultimate Messianic Priest-King.

Many scholars (Childs, LaSor, Baldwin, Klein, and most Jewish scholars) believe that the book of Zechariah is one cohesive unit. Others believe that some form of the last part of the book was added later. Given the heartrending, unified plot of the book, it makes little sense to divide it.

PURPOSE

In its final form, the book of Zechariah lays out the backstory of the failure of postexilic Israel to reclaim the glory of David, Solomon, and the original temple and reveals why that fumbled ambition had to be transposed into a new hope for a Messianic age to come. The promises of God and the faith heritage of Israel were simply too rich to abandon. The purpose of this book is much the same as that of Haggai, which was authored by Zechariah's contemporary.

Thus, Zechariah laid out a future hope for God's people throughout his prophecy. The eight night visions and accompanying revelations, along with the prophetic oracles in the second half of the book, reveal truly encouraging details of the hope that God clearly intended his discouraged people to understand and hold on to: God's intention to have his temple in Jerusalem rebuilt, in order to house his glorious return. His people will be fully restored to their homeland. They will be cleansed from all their sins and be granted a renewed prosperity. They will also ultimately enjoy a God-given peace, with their enemies destroyed by the hand of their Sovereign Lord. And in the end, the arrival of the Messianic, priestly Shepherd-King will terminate the succession of corrupt and wicked shepherd-rulers as he ushers in a kingdom of never-ending glory and righteousness.

Underlying Zechariah's message, as his name indicates, is the foundation of the divine plan of redemption. He wanted to remind the people of God that "YAHWEH remembers" his covenant promises. God had not forgotten his people then, and he has not forgotten us now.

AUTHOR AND AUDIENCE

Zechariah, like Ezekiel, was more of a priest who operated prophetically than the other way around. Hebrew names are more than just labels, and Zechariah's name means "YAHWEH remembers." There are over two dozen men in the Bible with that name.

Most likely, this Zechariah was born among the Israelite exiles during their captivity in Babylon. After the Persians destroyed Babylon, they set these exiles free, and Zechariah returned to Jerusalem with a wave of them, eager to lay eyes on the homeland that they had never seen. These returned exiles were his audience.

He came from a priestly family. His father, Berechiah, may have died when Zechariah was young, so it seems Zechariah was raised and adopted by his grandfather Iddo (Ezra 6:14; Zech. 1:1). Iddo was a priest (Neh. 12:1–4, 16), so Zechariah was born a priest with the heart of a prophet, much like Ezekiel and John the Baptist.

Zechariah and Haggai were contemporaries, with Haggai likely much older than the younger Zechariah. According to Haggai 1:1, Haggai's ministry began on the first day of the sixth month of the second year of Darius (520 BC), and Zechariah's prophetic ministry began roughly two months later in the same year (Zech. 1:1).

Zechariah dated his night visions (1:7–6:8) on the twenty-fourth day of the eleventh month of Darius' second year.

MAJOR THEMES

Yahweh as Commander of Angel Armies. Zechariah used the phrase "Yahweh, Commander of Angel Armies" (or "Yahweh Zebaoth"; Hb. *yahweh tseba'ot*) an astounding forty-seven times. This title was often translated "Lord of hosts" in older English usage, back when our word *hosts* was more commonly applied to military legions rather than hospitality directors. A *zaba* (or *tsaba'*) is an army of soldiers, and *zebaoth* (or *tseba'ot*) is the plural form. The extensive use of this title in the book of Zechariah underscores the predominant motif of the all-powerful Sovereign Lord of the universe as the heavenly commander of innumerable angelic warriors. Such an omnipotent force is irresistible and indestructible, and it emphasizes the reality that throughout history, the present, and the future, the enemies of God and his people will never be able to prevail against such an opponent.

The Day of Yahweh. Zechariah referred to the day of Yahweh over twenty times in his prophetic work. Most commonly, he referred to events that will happen "on that day," and these references bring out two contrasting emphases, one positive and one negative.

For the enemies of God and his people, such a day portends an ominous, catastrophic destruction, for then they will face the terrible wrath of the living God. However, for the people of God, the *ultimate* day of Yahweh will be one of unimaginable peace and joy, for in that day, God will be victorious over all his enemies and fulfill his plan of redemption and renewal for all eternity. But it must also be recognized that throughout the history of the Israelite people, they also suffered a day of Yahweh punishment for their sin—although such a judgment was temporary, never absolute. That terrible latter destiny is reserved for the unrepentant enemies of God.

And so, on that day, YAHWEH, Commander of Angel Armies, will execute justice, destroy wickedness, vindicate the faithful remnant, and set everything right. In New Testament terms, his kingdom is coming; his will shall be done on earth as it is in heaven. Heaven is literally and inevitably invading earth. And all of that is accomplished solely on the basis of the finished work of salvation in the person and work of Jesus Christ, God's Son, our Messianic King of kings. This theme of the day of YAHWEH is one that is consistently found throughout the Old Testament, incorporated particularly in the canonical Prophets, both Major and Minor.

Angelic Revelation. Throughout the Old Testament, certain concepts like angels, eschatology, and the afterlife gradually come into greater prominence and clarity over time. Revelatory angels—prominently though not exclusively found in Daniel and Zechariah—play a significant role in the increasingly frequent genre of prophetic-apocalyptic literature that began to emerge from the 500s BC onward. The book of Revelation is by far the best example of new covenant/New Testament biblical apocalyptic literature.

In Zechariah, there are two different kinds of angelic beings involved in communicating divine revelation to the prophet via the eight visions recounted in chapters 1–6. One is referred to simply as "the angel who was talking to me." Commentators generally refer to him as "the interpreting angel," for that is precisely his task: to explain to the prophet the meaning of the visions he is experiencing (1:9, 13–14, 19; 2:3; 4:1, 4, 11; 5:5, 10; 6:4–5). The other angel is a manifestation of God himself, designated here and elsewhere in the Old Testament as "the angel of YAHWEH." He is explicitly mentioned in 1:11–12; 3:1–3, 6. Elsewhere, the single term *angel* is likely to indicate this divine figure, as in 2:3; 3:4. Then the reference in 2:1 to "a man with a measuring line" is almost certainly to the angel of YAHWEH. This figure is uniformly understood throughout the Old Testament as a manifestation of God in human form, commonly referred to as a *theophany*. Because mortal eyes may never view the essential being of God himself, his visible presence to individuals chosen to receive divine revelation is most often, but not always, via the manifestation of such an angelic being.

God Communicating through Visions. It is evident in Scripture that God reveals himself and his ongoing redemptive plans to individuals in both dreams and visions. God gives dreams to those who are asleep, but visions occur while individuals are awake. In the case of Zechariah, the context suggests that he was most likely awake when he received these visions (see 4:1), apparently, all in one night.

Zechariah's visions have themes relating to both God's judgment on his people and his promise to redeem, renew, and restore them back in their homeland with a focus on the New Jerusalem and a dual priestly-royal leadership. There are eight visions:

- The horsemen (1:8–17)
- Four chariots (6:1–8)
- Causes of the exile
  - Four horns and four craftsmen (1:18–21)
  - The flying scroll (5:1–4)
  - The woman in a barrel (5:5–11)
- The New Jerusalem
  - The measuring man (2:1–13)
- Restoration of priestly-royal leadership
  - Clean clothes for the high priest (3:1–10)
  - The lampstand and two olive trees—Zerubbabel and Joshua (4:1–14)

The Prophet as "Custodian" of the Covenant. Underlying the message of the prophet Zechariah throughout the book is the foundational "scaffolding" of the divine covenant. Zechariah's language surrounding this phenomenon is proof of this. Most significant are the various references to the classic summary formulation of the covenant: "I will be your God, and you shall be my people" or variations on that wording (see Ex. 6:7; Lev. 26:12; Jer. 30:22, for example). Zechariah referenced this summary formula both explicitly (Zech. 8:8; 13:9) and implicitly (2:11; 10:6–7). In 9:11, he recorded the following words God revealed to him: "As for you, Zion, because of my covenant with you sealed with blood, I have set your captives free from the waterless pit of their prison." The context of this revelation makes it clear that it denotes the divine rationale for God delivering his people from exile in Babylon. Then, by way of contrast, Zechariah's sixth vision in 5:1–4 describes the application of the covenant curse to the people of God via the motif of a flying scroll. This scroll is a symbol of the covenant documents, and on each side is recorded the people's violations of the covenant statutes, which resulted in the Judean population being sent into exile in Babylon, along with the destruction of their homeland.

It is evident that Zechariah was keenly aware of the details of the covenant that God had made with his people so many years before, an awareness that other canonical prophets also clearly demonstrated. In short, Zechariah was well acquainted with these covenant statutes and what they entailed, including punishments (or curses) for violations and blessings for faithful observance of those laws. So when the prophet related both the judgments Yahweh handed down to his people and the blessings he had in store for them—as well as for the nations around them (see the discussion in the following theme)—we can be quite definite that it was the knowledge of what the divine covenant contained, what it meant for the postexilic community, and what it portended for the future that undergirded his prophetic work.

Thus the description of Zechariah as a "custodian" of the covenant is an apt one since it clearly indicates to his audience—both then and now—that God has never forgotten his people and that his covenant promises have always been front and center when it comes to the redemptive focus on his people.

Promises of Restoration and Renewal—Blessing for Israel and the Nations. The long line of Davidic royalty and the heroic prophets who boldly challenged the leaders with direct words from God was coming to an end. The priests, rabbinic sages, and apocalyptic visionaries were filling the vacuum. Zechariah personally embodied a bridge between these two eras. Zechariah spoke forth some of the last words of Old Testament prophecy ("I, YAHWEH, have this to say . . ."; e.g., 8:3, 6) and no doubt watched with keen interest and comfort for the fulfillment of the promise to renew and reforge the Davidic royal line by the merging of a priestly ruler (i.e., Joshua, the high priest) with that of a civil governor in the line of David (i.e., Zerubbabel). Zechariah's fourth and fifth visions in chapters 3 and 4 reveal this theme explicitly, and the oracle of 6:9–15 reinforces it. In other words, the line of King David would not be consummated by a traditional royal figure but by the emergence of the Messianic Priest-King, Jesus Christ—David's greatest son. The merging of the roles of Joshua and Zerubbabel prophetically anticipated this Messianic expectation. It is also worth mentioning at this point that the prophet Haggai, Zechariah's contemporary, reinforced the significant role Zerubbabel played in the redemptive plan of God when he likened the governor of the postexilic Judean community to the divine "signet ring" (Hag. 2:20–23), an indication that God had chosen Zerubbabel as a guarantee, or pledge, that someday the Messiah descended from David would certainly come.

And so, notwithstanding the significant disappointments at the time of Zechariah, God revealed to his servant, the prophet, promises of restoration and renewal that focused squarely on the covenant people of Israel as well as the surrounding nations; these promises are scattered throughout the prophecy. Casting aside the legacy of the old covenant era, Zechariah launched courageously toward the new covenant age with potent apocalyptic promises of a blessed hope and a victorious future. What do we do with deep disappointment in our lives? As people of faith, we would do well to imitate Zechariah, who picked up the pieces, trusted the promises of God, and painted a picture of a fresh future hope into which we can live.

Zechariah 2:1–13 and chapter 8 show God restoring Israel not only for her own benefit but also for the benefit of the other nations, to whom she would be a blessing. In other words, not only would the Israelite people be renewed in their covenant relationship with their Sovereign Lord, but people from many lands the world over would also be drawn to the worship of Yahweh and, by clear implication, be joined to the covenant people as gentile believers. This conclusion is made abundantly clear in 2:11 and 8:20–23 and was spectacularly fulfilled in the new covenant age of the Holy Spirit, after Jesus had ascended back to the heavenly realm to rejoin God his Father on the throne of the eternal kingdom. Such a blessing will continue as the gospel is proclaimed throughout the world until Jesus returns.

Seeing Jesus in the Book. Despite the disappointments and frustrations experienced by the prophet and the people to whom he was ministering, Zechariah gave powerful and encouraging Messianic images that anticipated the coming of Jesus into the world. These prophecies would have greatly encouraged Zechariah's 500s BC audience, providing they had ears to hear what God was saying. And in the first century AD, the first Christians—and all those generations that followed—would have seen in this book previews of the appearing of the Messiah. Zechariah records some of the most potent prophetic oracles and images related to the coming of Jesus, the Messianic Priest-King, in the canonical prophecies of the Old Testament and elsewhere. These are listed below:

- In 6:11–12, Joshua, the high priest, is about to be crowned as a priest-king, and in these verses, he is given the name of "the Branch," a Messianic title associated with the royal lineage of King David, as indicated in Isaiah 4:2; 11:1; Jeremiah 23:5; 33:15. The New Testament makes it clear that the fulfillment of the Messianic "Branch" is none other than Jesus Christ himself. John the apostle recorded in his vision of the heavenly Jerusalem the very words of the risen Christ to that effect in Revelation 22:16, and one of the elders surrounding the heavenly throne in Revelation 5:5 also testified to this identification.
- This title is also found in Zechariah 3:8–9, with the added feature of "the stone before Joshua," elsewhere referred to in the Old Testament as a "rock" or the "capstone" or "cornerstone" of the temple (Ps. 118:22; Isa. 8:14; 28:16; Dan. 2:34–35, 45). The prophet then mentioned in Zechariah 10:4 that from Judah will come the "cornerstone," which, in the context of this chapter, points to a victorious, divine Redeemer, who will conquer all the enemies of God's people. This symbol is an undeniable Messianic characteristic, as evidenced by the following New

Testament references that identify this "cornerstone" with the person of Jesus Christ: Matthew 21:42; Ephesians 2:19–22; 1 Peter 2:6–8.

- In Zechariah 9:9, the prophet described the arrival of the King in the city of Jerusalem, on the back of a donkey. The New Testament Gospel writers unequivocally identify this rider as Jesus, who entered Jerusalem on a donkey in the week before his crucifixion and death. Both Matthew (Matt. 21:5) and John (John 12:15) attest to this event on the first Palm Sunday as a direct fulfillment of the Zechariah prophecy.
- In Zechariah 11:12–13, Zechariah made reference to thirty pieces of silver being thrown to the potter inside the Jerusalem temple. The context in chapter 11 reveals Zechariah role-playing a shepherd-leader, commanded by Yahweh to pasture a flock marked for slaughter—that is, the rebellious nation of Judah. After revoking a covenant made with the rebellious "flock," Zechariah asked to be paid, and they gave him thirty pieces of silver. The Lord then commanded the prophet to throw the money to the potter in the temple.[a] This detail refers prophetically to the "blood money" that the Pharisees paid to Jesus' disciple Judas Iscariot for information leading to the arrest of Jesus in the garden of Gethsemane. See Matthew 26:14–15; 27:3–10.
- In Zechariah 12:10, there is a reference to the mournfully repentant inhabitants of Jerusalem, lamenting their murderous actions and gazing on "the Pierced One" (i.e., God himself). It is a repentant response that is triggered by an outpouring of the divine Spirit

---

a The allusion to the potter involves an incident in the life of the prophet Jeremiah, as recorded in Jeremiah 19:1–13. See Matthew 27:9–10.

of grace and supplication. This expression points, in prophetic anticipation, to the action of the Roman soldier in piercing Jesus' side with a spear as he hung dying on the cross while the crowd gazed at him. John 19:34–37 records this incident and quotes this prophecy, although the attitude of the watchful crowd in their hearts is not indicated in the gospel record. A spirit of sorrowful repentance, however—at least in some onlookers—may be implied by the citing of Zechariah 12:10.

- In 13:1, in association with the prophetic anticipation of the day of Yahweh, we read that "a flowing fountain" will be opened up "for the family of David and the people of Jerusalem—a fountain to wash away sin and impurity." The agent of that opening is undeniably Yahweh himself. Such a cleansing flow in the elimination of iniquity is an essential element in the prophetic outworking of the new covenant as indicated in Ezekiel 36:25. The supreme expression and fulfillment of the cleansing from sin is found in the shedding of Christ's blood on the cross, as recorded in Hebrews 9:14.
- In Zechariah 10:3 and 13:7 respectively, a contrast is drawn between Yahweh punishing the wicked, godless shepherd-leaders of Israel and then allowing his own righteous "shepherd" to be struck down, followed by the scattering of his people in judgment. In 13:8–9, mention is then made of one-third of the people being refined in that punishment, resulting in their profound spiritual renewal and transformation. This reveals God's mercy in the midst of judgment. However, the reference in 13:7 also anticipates the emergence of Jesus Christ as the "Good Shepherd," recorded in John 10:1–21, who was struck down at the instigation of the rebellious population in

Jerusalem. Jesus himself quoted Zechariah 13:7 in Matthew 26:31, with reference to the immediate consequences of Peter's denial (Matt. 26:69–74)—namely, the abandonment of Jesus by all of his band of disciples. However, God's redemptive grace ensured that a chosen worldwide "remnant"—past, present, and future—would be purged of their sin and redeemed by the atoning sacrifice of the Messianic Shepherd-King at Calvary.

- In Zechariah 14:4–5, we read about the victorious return of Israel's God to the Mount of Olives near Jerusalem after his all-conquering destruction of Israel's enemies. This is an event that is directly linked to a manifestation of the day of YAHWEH. Significantly, this text speaks of the legion of "holy ones" who will accompany their victorious Lord and God on his return. The accompanying host may include resurrected followers of YAHWEH as well as angels. This scenario anticipates the final return of Jesus Christ to earth with his "holy ones" at the end of the age, ushering in the final judgment. See Matthew 25:31; 1 Thessalonians 3:13; Jude (Judah) 14; Revelation 19:14.
- In Zechariah 14:8, there is another reference to a day of YAHWEH event: the phenomenon of "living waters" flowing out from Jerusalem to the Dead Sea (i.e., in the east) and the Mediterranean Sea (i.e., in the west). This is an allusion to the extended vision of an identical phenomenon witnessed by the prophet Ezekiel some fifty years prior to Zechariah's ministry (ca. 571 BC), recorded in Ezekiel 47:1–12 (and see Joel 3:18). These references to the flow of "living waters" are consummated in Revelation 22:1–2 where the river of the water of life flows from the throne of God and the Lamb down the middle of the street in the heavenly city of Jerusalem. What is also of special

significance here is that such a vision is a prophetic glimpse into the identification of Jesus as the essence of "living water" in John 4:10–14: the source of eternal life.

- And finally, in Zechariah 14:9, in another reference to the day of YAHWEH, we read that YAHWEH will be King over the entire earth. There is no doubt that this is another prophecy that points forward to the universal rule of the risen Lord Jesus Christ in the eternal kingdom of the new heavens and the new earth, a reign that comes to its supreme expression in the book of Revelation, especially in chapters 4, 5, 21, and 22.

For Zechariah (see chapters 7 and 8), the coming kingdom was *inevitable* (in terms of God's promise) but *conditional* (in terms of the people's spiritual readiness to experience such a restoration). Nonetheless, the context of these two chapters makes it clear that it is by God's gracious initiative and enabling alone that the people will be restored, redeemed, and renewed. In other words, this *conditionality* will also become an *inevitability*, as the people's initial unwillingness to practice justice, mercy, and compassion will be transformed—by implication—into faithful obedience to God and his covenant statutes. Chapter 8 reinforces this perspective when the Lord's promise to bless Jerusalem will result in the people's spiritual transformation, and the land will experience abundant joy, peace, and prosperity. These promises will find their ultimate fulfillment in the appearance of Jesus Christ, the Messiah.

ZECHARIAH

Affection and Union

Return to Yahweh

1 In October of the second year that Darius was emperor
of Persia,[a] Yahweh spoke to the prophet Zechariah
son of Berechiah,[b] son of Iddo, saying, 2"*I*, Yahweh, was
intensely angry with your ancestors. 3So give the people
this message: 'Yahweh, Commander of Angel Armies, says
to you: "Come back to me, and I will come back to you,"[c]
says Yahweh, Commander of Angel Armies.[d] 4Do not be
like your ancestors. Long ago my prophets warned them,
saying, "Turn your lives around completely and end your

---

a 1:1 The Hebrew text for "In October" is literally "In the eighth month"; this was the Hebrew month of October–November, 520 BC (Gregorian calendar). The Syriac adds "the first day," perhaps based on Jewish tradition.

b 1:1 There are verses that indicate Zechariah was the son of Iddo the seer (see 2 Chron. 12:15; Ezra 5:1; 6:14; Neh. 12:16); however, the Hebrew word for "son" can also mean "grandson." It is also possible that Berechiah was, indeed, Zechariah's father but died, leaving Zechariah to be raised by his grandfather. Iddo the priest is mentioned in Neh. 12:4 as one of exiles who returned to the land with Zerubbabel in 538 BC.

c 1:3 Or "Return to me, and I will return to you." This was a consistent message of God's prophets. See Isa. 31:6; Jer. 3:1, 22; Hos. 6:1; 7:10; Amos 4:6–11; Mal. 3:7.

d 1:3 This divine name (Hb. *yahweh tseba'ot*) is used by Zechariah forty-seven times. This name emphasizes God's power, majesty, and sovereignty over not only the nations of earth but also the angelic armies of heaven.

evil, wicked ways." But they refused to listen to me or obey me. [5]And where did they end up? And the prophets, did they live forever? [6]But my words and warnings, which I gave through my servants the prophets, proved to be true. *Your ancestors ignored them, and so they were punished.* As a result, they repented, saying, "YAHWEH, Commander of Angel Armies, has punished us as he warned he would do and as our sinful ways have deserved." ' "

The Eight Visions of Zechariah

[7]On February 15 (the month of Shvat), in the second year of Darius' reign,[a] YAHWEH spoke to the prophet Zechariah son of Berechiah, son of Iddo.

First Vision: The Horsemen

[8]That night I had a vision. Behold, I saw a man sitting on a reddish-brown horse in the shadows of a grove of myrtles.[b] And behind him I saw other horses—some brown, tan, and white *with riders upon them.* [9]There was *another* angel there who talked with me, and I asked him, "What do these represent, my lord?" And the angel[c] who was talking to me said, "Let me show you."

---

a 1:7 The Hebrew text for "February 15" is literally "On the twenty-fourth day of the eleventh month"; this was February 15, 519 BC (Gregorian calendar).

b 1:8 Isaiah referenced "myrtles" in connection to the Messianic age (Isa. 41:19; 55:13).

c 1:9 It is possible that the "man" on the horse was the same as "the angel who was talking to me." However, the text seems to imply (and most commentators agree) that this angel talking with Zechariah was an angel of interpretation sent to Zechariah to help the prophet interpret what he was seeing. This would mean that the horseman among the myrtle grove was a different angel, who is described in v. 12 as "YAHWEH's angel." Zechariah always referred to the "angel who talked with me" by the same words and mentioned this angel in several of his visions (see 1:19; 2:3; 4:1, 4–5; 5:5, 10; 6:4).

10 Then the man standing among the myrtles spoke up
and said, "These are YAHWEH's agents sent to patrol the
earth."[a]

11 Then the horsemen reported to the angel of YAHWEH
who stood among the myrtles, "We have been patrolling
the land,[b] and indeed, all is peacefully at rest."

12 YAHWEH's angel then spoke and said, "YAHWEH, Commander of Angel Armies, you have inflicted your anger
on Jerusalem and the cities of Judah for the past seventy years. How many more years will pass before you
once again show them that you love them?" 13 YAHWEH
then replied to the angel who was talking to me with kind
and comforting words. 14 So the angel told me to proclaim
these words of YAHWEH, Commander of Angel Armies:
"My heart burns with passion[c] for Jerusalem and Zion,
15 but I am deeply angry with the careless and complacent nations. I was only mildly angry *with my people*, but
the nations I used to punish them acted too severely.[d]
16 Therefore, I have returned to Jerusalem with mercy and
kindness.[e] I, YAHWEH, Commander of Angel Armies, have

---

a 1:10 Or "who are sent back and forth across the land."

b 1:11 Or "walking about the entire world." The Hebrew verb for "walking" is *halak*, used in Gen. 13:17 for Abraham walking over the land to possess it.

c 1:14 Or "jealousy." For the English reader, *jealousy* often carries a negative connotation. Here we see God's passion and caring love for Jerusalem and his people, but their waywardness has kept him from pouring out that love upon them.

d 1:15 Or "they [the nations] contributed to the disaster."

e 1:16 See Ezek. 43:1–5.

decreed to rebuild my house there.[a] *Surveyors* will stretch my measuring line over Jerusalem *to rebuild the city*."

17The angel also told me to proclaim, "I, YAHWEH, Commander of Angel Armies, decree that my cities will once more overflow with prosperity. I will comfort Zion once again and claim Jerusalem as my own."

Second Vision: Four Horns and Four Craftsmen

18Then I looked up and had a vision. Behold, *I saw* four
horns.[b] 19I asked the angel who was talking to me, "What do these represent?" And he answered, "These are the *four* horns that scattered Jerusalem, Judah, and Israel."

20Then YAHWEH opened my eyes to see four *conquering* craftsmen.[c] 21And I asked, "What are they coming to
do?" He replied, "They have come to terrify and hammer

---

a 1:16 The rebuilding of the Jerusalem temple reinforces the certainty of YAHWEH's intention to continue to pour out his mercy and compassion on his people now that they had been freed from their captivity in exile for some twenty years. The house of the Lord would, in fact, be completed within three years or so, in 516 BC. The same was true for the rebuilding of the city of Jerusalem, some eighty years in the future at the time of Nehemiah (ca. 444 BC).

b 1:18 Zechariah 2 in the Hebrew Bible begins with v. 18. Animal's horns are a consistent biblical symbol of strength and power (see Deut. 33:17; 1 Kings 22:11; Ps. 75:10; Ezek. 29:21; Mic. 4:13). They represent, in this context, four nations or, metaphorically, four principalities. The number four is a biblical number consistently representing the entire world (i.e., four compass directions; see Zech. 2:6; 6:5).

c 1:20 Or "blacksmiths," those who hammer out heated metal. See Isa. 54:16. This passage teaches us that for every evil on the earth, God has an answer, "craftsmen" who themselves become the solution. The four horns that scattered God's people are likely Assyria, Egypt, Babylonia, and Medo-Persia. The four conquering craftsmen are likely Egypt, Babylonia, Persia, and Greece. Whatever their precise identity may have been, the important point to note is that all the enemies of Judah will ultimately be destroyed.

out justice among the nations who lifted their horns to completely crush the land of Judah and scatter its inhabitants."

Third Vision: The Measuring Man

2 Then I looked up again and had another vision. Behold, I saw a man with a measuring line in his
hand.[a] 2I asked him, "Where are you going *with that*?"

"To measure Jerusalem," he replied, "to calculate her width and length."

3And behold, the angel who was talking with me left,
and another angel came out to meet him. 4He said to him,
"Run, and tell the surveyor[b] *to stop measuring*, for Jerusalem will be too full of people and animals to measure or
be enclosed by walls. 5So, I, YAHWEH, will be a protective
wall of fire surrounding her and a *radiant* glory within her."

Zechariah's Exhortation to the Exiles

6"Look out! Look out! Flee from Babylon,"[c] declares YAHWEH, "for like the four winds of heaven I have scattered you in every direction," declares YAHWEH. 7"Escape,[d]
Zion, you who live within the fair city of Babylon!"

---

a 2:1 Compare Ezek. 40:3.
b 2:4 Or "young man."
c 2:6 Or "from the land of the north."
d 2:7 Or "break out."

8For Yahweh, Commander of Angel Armies, sent me
after glory.[a] And he warns the nations who plundered
you: "Whoever touches you, *my precious ones*, touches the
apple of my eye.[b] 9Now behold, I will raise my fist against
them to crush them, and those whom they enslaved will
plunder them. Then you will know that Yahweh, Commander of Angel Armies, has sent me."

10I, Yahweh, declare to you: "It's time to sing out and
rejoice, my daughter Zion, for now I am coming to live
among you."[c]

11At that time, people from many nations will be converted to Yahweh and become his people, and he will
live among them. Then you will know that Yahweh, Commander of Angel Armies, has sent me to you.

12The people of Judah will become Yahweh's special
people, his inheritance[d] in the holy land,[e] and he will again

---

a 2:8 Scholars are divided over the exact meaning of the words "after glory." It is possible that *glory* is just another way of referring to God himself. Some believe this glory refers to the vision of vv. 1–5 (i.e., "after the vision of glory he sent me"). Others take the words to mean "he sent me with his glory" or "he sent me in the wake of his glory." Still others believe this means "with insistence he sent me." Some believe it should be translated "after he has honored me and sent me." Some Jewish scholars change two letters of the text and translate it as "he whose glory has sent me" or "he sent me on a glorious mission."

b 2:8 See Deut. 32:10; Ps. 17:8. The Hebrew phrase *'ishon 'ayin* refers to the pupil or dark part of the eye. However, etymologists see *'ishon* as a diminutive form of "man" (*'ish*), which could then be translated "the Little Man of the Eye." Or using anthropomorphistic language, when God looks at his people, they become the reflection of his "eye."

c 2:10 Or "in the center of you." See v. 11.

d 2:12 See Eph. 1:18.

e 2:12 This is the only time in the Old Testament where the actual designation "holy land" (*'admat haqqodesh*) is found, although the notion of Israel and Judah as a holy land, or nation belonging to God, is a common theme.

choose Jerusalem. 13Let everyone be silent before YAHWEH, for now he is stirring from his holy dwelling place.

Fourth Vision: Clean Clothes for the High Priest

3 1-3Then I was shown another vision.[a] I saw Joshua the high priest standing before the angel of YAHWEH dressed in filthy[b] clothes. On Joshua's right was the accuser,[c] standing there ready to prosecute him. The angel of YAHWEH[d] said to Satan, "YAHWEH rebukes you, Satan! *Yes*, YAHWEH rebukes you, for he has chosen Jerusalem. And he has rescued Joshua, like a stick snatched out of the fire."[e]

---

a 3:1–3 Although the text does not state who revealed this vision to Zechariah, according to some manuscripts of both the ancient Greek and Latin versions, it was YAHWEH. The prophet received a vision of what was happening in the heavenly court.

b 3:1–3 The Hebrew word *tso'im* is frequently used for excrement. See Isa. 4:4.

c 3:1–3 Literally "the satan." *Satan* means "the accuser." Satan traffics in accusation (see 1 Chron. 21:1; Job 1–2; Rev. 12:10). Regarding him being on Joshua's "right," see Ps. 109:6–7. Note that the accuser is silenced even before he can bring his accusation.

d 3:1–3 Or "YAHWEH." There is considerable debate over who is speaking, YAHWEH himself or "the angel of YAHWEH."

e 3:1–3 See Amos 4:11. Joshua became a representative of the exiles who had returned to Jerusalem (see Ezra 2:1–2). They are likened to a half-burnt log that was rescued from the fire of their captivity. Joshua coming back as the high priest to Jerusalem after years of Babylonian captivity was a miracle. According to the Talmud, this statement of Joshua being like a stick snatched out of the fire literally happened. In Jer. 29:21–23, it was prophesied that Nebuchadnezzar would have two false, adulterous prophets thrown into the fire. In the account of this prophecy's fulfillment given by the Talmud, the false prophets pleaded to have one more join them, imitating Daniel's three friends who were spared in the fire. So Joshua the high priest was chosen to join them in the flames, with the hopes that this would guarantee their deliverance. However, the two false prophets were roasted alive while Joshua was miraculously spared, like a stick snatched out of the fire. See Sanhedrin 93a.

4Then the angel said to those *heavenly council members* who were standing before him,[a] "Remove Joshua's filthy clothes." Then he said to Joshua, "Behold, I have taken your guilt away, and I will clothe you with splendid robes."[b] 5And I spoke up and requested, "Let them also put a clean turban on his head." So they dressed him in clean clothes and put on his head a clean turban while the angel of Yahweh stood nearby.

6So the angel of Yahweh solemnly assured Joshua with these words: 7"Yahweh, Commander of Angel Armies, declares to you, 'If you walk in my ways and live in obedience to me, you will preside over my temple and keep watch over my courts. And I will let you come and go in the same way as *your fellow council members* standing here.' "

The Coming of the Branch

8" 'So listen, high priest Joshua, you and your fellow priests seated here are *beautiful* symbols[c] *of what is to come*. Behold, I will reveal my servant, the Branch![d] 9And behold, I have laid a stone before Joshua, a *precious*,

---

a 3:4 That is, attendants assembled in the courtroom of heaven.

b 3:4 Or "festive robes."

c 3:8 Or "signs" or "wonders." See Isa. 8:18.

d 3:8 This is a Messianic term for Christ, who fulfills the prophecies concerning the Branch. Indeed, he told his disciples that he is the Vine (Branch). See Isa. 4:2; 11:1; Jer. 23:5; 33:15; John 15:1–8. The Septuagint reads "Rising Sun" in place of "Branch" (see Luke 1:78).

unique stone[a] with seven eyes.[b] And I will engrave a *spe-*
cial inscription on it,'[c] says Yahweh, Commander of Angel
Armies.
" 'And in a single day, I will remove the sin *of the people*
of this land. 10And at that time, everyone will invite his
friends to come *and have fellowship* under their own vine
and their own fig tree.[d] I, Yahweh, have spoken.' "

---

a 3:9 We are living stones made into a temple. See 1 Peter 2:5.

b 3:9 See Zech. 4:10; Rev. 5:6. A stone with seven eyes would be a living stone. In the Bible, the number seven means completion intensified. Not only is this stone living, but its life is also intensified sevenfold. In one day, our living Stone removed sin (see John 1:29). This stone is the Lamb of God. Another verse that proves that this stone is the Lamb of God is Rev. 5:6. This verse says, "Then I saw a young Lamb standing before the throne. . . . He had . . . seven eyes, which are the seven Spirits of God." The Lamb with seven eyes and the Stone with seven eyes are the same person. The Lamb is Christ, and the Stone is Christ. Christ is our living, redeeming Stone with seven eyes, who has made us living stones (see 1 Peter 2:4–5). Interestingly, the Hebrew word for "eyes" (*'ayin*) has a homonym that can be translated "fountains"—a stone with seven fountains.

c 3:9 We are not given the words of the inscription. Perhaps, like the stones of the breastplate of the high priest, the names of the twelve tribes were engraved (see Ex. 28:9–11). Some scholars suggest that it was the name of the Messiah inscribed upon the stone. Still others believe it may have been the motto "Holy to Yahweh," which was engraved on the gold plate attached to Aaron's turban (see Ex. 28:36; 39:30; Zech. 14:20). The words "Holy to Yahweh" are seven Hebrew letters, which fits the context of seven eyes. With a slight emendation of the text, the words "I . . . will engrave" are translated in the Septuagint as "I will reveal its meaning to you."

d 3:10 The vine and the fig tree were frequently used as symbols of the peace, prosperity, and security that the Messiah would bring. See 1 Kings 4:25; 2 Kings 18:31; Mic. 4:4.

Fifth Vision: The Lampstand and Two Olive Trees

4 Then the angel who had been explaining *the visions* came back and roused me as someone awakened from sleep. 2And he asked me, "What do you see?"

As I focused my eyes, I replied, "I see a solid gold lampstand[a] with a bowl *for the oil* on top. It has seven lamps, and each lamp has a golden spout for the wicks.[b] 3And I also see two olive trees *overshadowing* the lampstand, one on the right and one on the left." 4So I asked the angel who was talking to me, "My lord, what do these things represent?"

5The angel answered, "Do you not know what they are?"

"No, my lord," I said.[c]

God's Message to Zerubbabel

6Here is the message of YAHWEH to Zerubbabel:[d] "*You will not succeed* by *military* might nor by your own strength but by my Spirit,"[e] says YAHWEH, Commander of Angel

---

a 4:2 In the New Testament, a lampstand is a picture of the church (see Rev. 1:20) that gives light to a city and influences that city for God. When Jesus spoke of removing a church's lampstand from its place (see Rev. 2:5), he referred to removing its influence in a city.

b 4:2 Or "seven pipes [lit. "lips"], yea, seven to the lamps." The exact meaning of this verse is uncertain with many varied opinions among scholars.

c 4:5 The prophet asked the angel of interpretation a question in vv. 4–5, but the angel didn't begin to answer the question until v. 10b. Many commentators are agreed that vv. 6–10a should be read after vv. 10b–14. Some modern translations incorporate this recommended change of order.

d 4:6 Zerubbabel was the "prince" or governor of Judah and grandson of Jehoiachin, the penultimate king of Judah, prior to the Babylonian exile. He was the last of the Davidic royal lineage entrusted with political authority by the governing powers in Persia. His work and ministry are extensively treated in the books of Ezra and Haggai.

e 4:6 The Hebrew text is short and concise without using any verbs.

Armies. 7"And what are you, O mighty mountain?[a] Before
you, Zerubbabel, this mountain *of obstacles* will crumble.[b]
Then he will set the capstone in place to shouts of 'Grace
and beauty be upon it!' "[c]

8Then another message from YAHWEH came to me:
9"With his own hands, Zerubbabel has laid the foundation of this temple,[d] and with his own hands he will finish it.[e] Then you will know that YAHWEH, Commander of Angel Armies, has sent me to you.

10"Those who despise the day of small beginnings will rejoice when they see Zerubbabel holding the plumb line[f] in his hands.

"The seven *lamps* represent the seven eyes of YAHWEH that keep a close watch over everything on earth."[g]

11Then I asked the angel *two questions*: "What about
these two olive trees on each side of the lampstand?
12And what are the two branches from which golden oil[h]
flows through the two golden pipes?"

---

a 4:7 Compare to Isa. 40:4. This rhetorical question is symbolic in meaning. The mighty mountain represents the obstacles in front of Zerubbabel, including the rubble of the temple site, political problems in establishing his leadership, and rival officials.

b 4:7 Or "become a smooth plain."

c 4:7 The Hebrew text here, *chen chen lah*, amounts to a repeated shout of a term that denotes divine favor or grace as well as beauty.

d 4:9 The foundations of the temple, under the supervision of Zerubbabel, were laid ca. 537–536 BC (see Ezra 3:8–11).

e 4:9 The temple was then completed, again under Zerubbabel's supervision, in 516 BC (see Ezra 6:14–16).

f 4:10 There is a play on words in the Hebrew that is lost in translation. The Hebrew word for "plumb line" can also be translated "chosen stone." See 3:9.

g 4:10 See 2 Chron. 16:9; Prov. 15:3.

h 4:12 The Hebrew word for "oil" is the same as the Hebrew word for "gold." This is likely a metonymy for the color of the oil.

13He replied, "Don't you know what these are?"
"No, my lord," I answered.
14So he explained, "These branches are the two sons of oil[a] who serve the Lord of all the earth."

Sixth Vision: The Flying Scroll

5 Then I had another vision. I looked up and saw a flying scroll. 2*The angel* asked me, "What do you see?" I replied, "I see a flying scroll. It looks about thirty-five feet long and seventeen feet wide."[b] 3Then he explained to me its meaning:

---

a 4:14 The two "sons of oil" point to Joshua (the priest, holding spiritual authority) and Zerubbabel (the governor, holding civil authority). Both kings and priests were anointed with oil as a symbol that they were being set apart by the Holy Spirit to fulfill God's purposes. They represent the joining of the priestly and kingly anointing. Symbolically, the sons of oil can represent the Word (truth) and the Spirit (power). See Rev. 11:4. In a sense, every believer today should be a "son of oil," filled, refreshed, and full of life (see Ps. 92:10). Jesus taught a parable of the wise and foolish virgins (see Matt. 25:1–13), in which the wise virgins had fresh oil to supply their lamps when the bridegroom arrived so they would be ready to go meet him. They were the daughters of oil.

b 5:2 Or "twenty cubits long and ten cubits wide" (about ten meters long and five meters wide). It is difficult to be precise in the length of a cubit. Generally, a standard cubit is believed to be about 17.5 inches or 0.44 meters. A long cubit was a cubit plus a handbreadth (3.5 inches or 90 millimeters); in total about 21 inches or 0.53 meters. Unless otherwise noted, conversions from cubits to modern units in this translation will be calculated using the long cubit measurement. The measurements of the scroll are identical to the measurements of the porch of Solomon's Temple (see 1 Kings 6:3).

"This *scroll* contains God's curse *against evildoers* sweeping over the whole land. On one side of the scroll, it says that the Lord will banish[a] every thief. On the other side, it says that he will banish everyone who lies using his name.[b] 4Yahweh, Commander of Angel Armies, declares, 'I will release this curse, and it will enter the house of the thief and of anyone who lies using my name. The curse will remain in his house until it consumes it—walls, beams, and all.' "

Seventh Vision: The Woman in a Barrel

5Then the angel who was talking to me appeared and said, "Look at what is coming." 6I asked, "What is it?" He replied, "It is a barrel, and it is carrying the guilt[c] of all the people of the land of Judah."

7As I looked, the angel removed the *heavy* lid made of lead from the barrel, and a woman was seated inside. 8The angel said, "This is Lady Wickedness."[d] And he shoved her back into the barrel and clamped the lead lid over her.

---

a 5:3 The Hebrew verb found here (*naqah*) in the Niphal form may carry the underlying sense of "purge" or "empty," and in this context, "banish" is an appropriate reading. The same translation is employed in the next sentence.

b 5:3 Or "How long the thief has gone unpunished! How long the perjurer has gone unpunished!" Ezekiel also had a vision of a scroll written on both sides (see Ezek. 2:10). To steal and to speak falsely in God's name are sins against man and God. They represent some major aspects of the Ten Commandments and, collectively, the whole law.

c 5:6 Although the Hebrew text reads "their eye," most modern translations follow the Greek and Syriac texts, which have "their iniquity" or "their guilt." Apparently, these ancient translations are based on a Hebrew text that differs by only one letter from the traditional text.

d 5:8 Or literally "the Great Disturbance." In the context, Lady Wickedness is associated with idolatry.

9I looked up and *suddenly* two women appeared, soaring swiftly in the sky with outstretched wings like those
of a stork. They lifted the barrel high in the sky and flew
away with it. 10So I asked the angel who was talking to
me, "Where are they taking the barrel?"
11He replied, "To *the wicked land of* Babylon,[a] where
they will build a temple and make a pedestal for it. They
will place it there and worship it."[b]

Eighth Vision: Four Chariots

6 Then I looked once more and had another vision. I
saw four chariots[c] coming out between two mountains
of bronze.[d] 2The first chariot was pulled by reddish-brown
horses, the second by black horses, 3the third by white
horses, and the fourth by dappled horses—all of them
mighty. 4I asked the angel who was talking to me, "What
do these represent, my lord?"

---

a 5:11 Or "Shinar," an ancient, poetical name for Babylonia.

b 5:11 See Rev. 17–18.

c 6:1 These four (the number of completion) chariots signify the four winds (see vv. 4–8) from the four corners of the earth (see Rev. 7:1–3). These four chariot-winds implement God's administration worldwide. God uses them to carry out his judgment not only on people but also on nations, governments, and kingdoms.

d 6:1 The two mountains likely represent the gateway of heaven. There were two bronze pillars on either side of the entrance to the temple (see 1 Kings 7:13–22). To access God's presence, one had to pass through the gateway with pillars of bronze on each side. These pillars are now mountains, signifying access in and out of God's heavenly dwelling. Bronze or brass are biblical symbols of judgment. The Hebrew verb for "coming out/going out" in its participial form is the word for "sunrise," thus the shining color bronze on the mountains. You can find God coming from between two mountains: Sinai and Zion. Additionally, some of the imagery of these verses points us to Ezekiel's vision of the four living creatures transporting the chariot of God (see Ezek. 1).

5The angel explained, “These are the four winds of
heaven. They are being dispatched after standing before
the Lord of all the earth. 6The black horses are leaving
for the land of the north,[a] the white ones for the west, and
the dappled for the land of the south.”[b] 7The strong horses
came out eager to patrol the world. He said, “Go and patrol
the earth,” and off they went. 8Then he called to me and
said, “Watch, the ones going to the land of the north are
going to make my Spirit descend upon that region.”[c]

Joshua, a King-Priest

9Then another message from YAHWEH came to me: 10“Go at
once to the home of Josiah the son of Zephaniah. There
you will receive *gifts* from Heldai, Tobijah, and Jedaiah,
who have just arrived among the exiles in Babylon.
11Accept their gifts of gold and silver and make a crown
to place on the head of the high priest Joshua son of
Jehozadak.[d] 12And say this to him, ‘This is what YAHWEH,

---

a 6:6 The word for “north” (Hb. *tsapon*) was often associated with darkness, and it was from the north that Judah’s enemies would attack.

b 6:6 The chariot with horses signifies the quick movement of God’s judgment. From our point of view, God’s judgment may be slow in coming. However, according to God’s view, his judgment comes swiftly with a quick movement. This passage identifies the horses by only three colors and going in three directions. The reddish-brown horses and the direction of the east are deliberately absent.

c 6:8 Or “give my Spirit rest in the land of the north.”

d 6:11 The crowning of a high priest, representing him becoming a king, had never been done before. Priests had their duties, and kings had their offices, but Joshua (typifying Christ in his priesthood) received the privilege of holding the two offices, the priesthood and the kingship, in peace on his throne (see vv. 9–13). Prior to the time of Zechariah, no one had held both offices, for the priesthood was of the tribe of Levi and of the family of Aaron, and the kingship was of the tribe of Judah and of the family of David. So Jesus (our Joshua) is crowned as King of Eternity and a High Priest after the order of Melchizedek.

Commander of Angel Armies, says: "Behold the man
whose name is the Branch![a] He will branch out and flourish from his place,[b] and he will build Yahweh's sanctuary.
13 Yes, he will build Yahweh's sanctuary and will be clothed
with majesty. He will sit on his throne and rule. He will be
a priest ruling on his throne. These two *offices* will flow
together with perfect harmony. 14 Joshua's crown will be
placed in my temple as a memorial to *the donors* Heldai,
Tobijah, Jedaiah, and *in recognition of* the generosity of
Josiah the son of Zephaniah. 15 And those in distant lands
will come to assist the building of Yahweh's sanctuary."

" 'When this happens, you will know for certain that Yahweh, Commander of Angel Armies, has sent me to you. This will happen if you faithfully obey the voice of Yahweh your God.' "

---

a 6:12 See Matt. 2:23, where this verse is quoted, fulfilling the prophecy that Jesus would be raised in "Branchtown" (Nazareth). See also Zech. 3:8. The Hebrew Scriptures give us a wonderful truth about the Branch (Sprout) of the Lord that would come and establish righteousness. The Hebrew word for "branch" or "sprout" is *netser*, the root word for *Nazareth* and *Nazarene*. The teaching of the Branch of the Lord is a concept taught throughout the Bible, from the Tree of Life to the seven branches of the lampstand to Jesus the Vine calling us his branches. Jesus is a scion, a branch that can be transplanted and grafted into a human life. Another variant form of this amazing word *netser* can be translated "keeper," "watchman," "one who keeps secrets," "guardian," or "one who keeps watch." All these words are true of Jesus, the Branch, who was raised in the village of the Branch (Nazareth). Additionally, the Aramaic word for *Nazareth* means "heir of a powerful family [scion]." See Isa. 11:1; 60:21; Dan. 11:7. See also Isa. 4:2; Jer. 23:5. Here in Zech. 6:12, the Hebrew is *tsemach*, a synonym for *branch*.

b 6:12 Or "the shoot will shoot up from beneath." Jesus branched out with heavenly life from his manger in Bethlehem to now dwell in us. His place is now within us, Yahweh's sanctuary. Jesus branches out through us to reveal his glory, his works, and his love. He is the true Vine, and we are his fruitful branches (see John 15; Gal. 5:22–23).

A Question about Fasting

7 In the fourth year of Emperor Darius, on the seventh
of December,[a] YAHWEH spoke again to Zechariah. 2Now
the people of Bethel had sent Sharezer and Regem-Melech
with a delegation *to Jerusalem* to pray for the favor of
YAHWEH. 3So they went to the prophets and priests who
were at the Temple of YAHWEH and asked them: "For many
years, each July[b] we have mourned and fasted.[c] Should
we continue to do this?"

Insincere Fasting Is Wrong

4Then YAHWEH spoke this message to me: 5"Ask all the
priests and the people of the land: 'For nearly seventy
years, you have been fasting and mourning in the fifth
and seventh months. Have you truly been doing this to
honor me? 6And when you ate and drank, were you not
doing it for your own pleasure? 7Did not YAHWEH speak
these things to you through the prophets in the past? *Have
you forgotten what he told you* when Jerusalem and the

---

a 7:1 Or "on the fourth day of Kislev, the ninth month," which in modern terms was December 7, 518 BC, almost two years after the eight visions of Zechariah in chapters 1–6.

b 7:3 Or "the fifth month." The Babylonians had destroyed Solomon's Temple on the seventh day of the fifth month (June–July) in 586 BC. See 2 Kings 25:8. The Jews mourned its destruction each year afterward by observing a fast in the month of July (ninth of Av). Now with the rebuilding of the temple underway, fasting seemed unnecessary. So the delegation from Bethel put this question to the spiritual leaders in Jerusalem. The Lord did not supply their answer until Zech. 8:18–19.

c 7:3 The twin practices of mourning and fasting were very frequently combined throughout the era of the law in Israel. The Hebrew verb for "fasting" is *nazar* and means literally "to consecrate [oneself]." In this context, the means of such a consecration is by fasting.

surrounding towns were prosperous and secure and when the southland and western foothills were inhabited?' "

The Reasons for Their Exile

8YAHWEH spoke again to Zechariah, saying, 9"Here is the message of YAHWEH, Commander of Angel Armies:

"Apply the law fairly.[a]

"Demonstrate tender love[b] and compassion toward all.

10"Never oppress the widow and the fatherless, the foreigner and the poor.

"And do not secretly plot to harm someone."[c]

11But they would not listen; they turned their backs on him, and they stopped up their ears rather than stopping to hear. 12Their hearts became as hard as a rock. They refused to listen to the teaching of YAHWEH, Commander of Angel Armies. And they would not hear the words he spoke by his Spirit through the earlier prophets. So YAHWEH, Commander of Angel Armies, became very angry.

13YAHWEH, Commander of Angel Armies, says, "Even when I called for them, they would not listen. Therefore, I would not listen when they prayed to me *for help*. 14Like a whirlwind, I swept them away to live in distant lands as foreigners." After they were scattered, the country was left so desolate that it became impassable. What once was a land of delights they turned into a desert of desolation.

---

a 7:9 See Isa. 1:17; Jer. 21:12; 22:3; Amos 5:14–15, 24.

b 7:9 Or "loyal [covenant] love." The Hebrew word *chesed* is connected to a love based on covenant relationships. Since the Jews had a covenant relationship with God's loyal love, they were expected to demonstrate this virtue in their attitudes toward each other.

c 7:10 See Mic. 2:1.

A Promise of Restoration

8 YAHWEH, Commander of Angel Armies,[a] spoke to me, saying, [2]"I, YAHWEH, Commander of Angel Armies, say to you: My heart burns with passion[b] for Zion, and my jealousy for her makes me red-hot with anger *toward her enemies.*

[3]"I, YAHWEH, have this to say: I will return to Jerusalem and live there on Mount Zion.[c] Then Jerusalem will be known as my faithful city[d] and Zion as my holy mountain, the mountain of YAHWEH, Commander of Angel Armies.

[4]"I, YAHWEH, Commander of Angel Armies, say to you: Men and women will once again sit in the parks and squares of Jerusalem, each with a staff *to lean on* because of their great age.
[5]And the parks and squares of the city will bustle with boys and girls playing outside.

[6]"I, YAHWEH, Commander of Angel Armies, have this to say: If this seems too marvelous for the remnant of my people to believe today, remember this—is there anything too marvelous for me?[e] For I, YAHWEH, Commander of Angel Armies, have spoken.

[7]"Here is what I, YAHWEH, Commander of Angel Armies, say to you: Behold, I will rescue my people from the

---

a 8:1 Zechariah uses this divine name, *yahweh tseba'ot*, forty-seven times, seventeen times in this chapter alone. This name emphasizes God's power, majesty, and sovereignty over not only the nations of earth but also the angelic armies of heaven.

b 8:2 Or "jealousy." For the English reader, *jealousy* often carries a negative connotation. Here we see God's passion and caring love for Jerusalem and his people, but their waywardness has kept him from pouring his love out upon them.

c 8:3 Or "I have returned to Jerusalem and live in Zion."

d 8:3 That is, "the city filled with faithful people," or "the city of truth." See Isa. 1:21, 26.

e 8:6 Or "It may seem marvelous to the remnant of this people in that day, but will it not seem marvelous to me?" See Gen. 18:14; Jer. 32:17, 27.

countries of the east and the west.[a] 8I will bring them back to live in the heart of Jerusalem, and they will be my *beloved* people, and I will be their faithful God.[b]

9"This is what I, YAHWEH, Commander of Angel Armies, have to say: *Be encouraged*, you who now hear these words spoken by the prophets who were there when the foundation was laid for the house of YAHWEH, Commander of Angel Armies. May your hearts be brave[c] so that the temple may be built. 10For up till now, there was no money to hire men or animals; neither has there been security for people to come and go because I had turned them against each other. 11But now, I, YAHWEH, Commander of Angel Armies, will not treat the remnant of this people as I have in the past. 12For now they will plant in peace. Fresh dew will fall from the sky, and the soil will be fertile. Their vineyards will be lush and fruitful. I will grant the remnant of my people all these things. 13Judah and Jerusalem, your names have been used as curses among all the nations, but now you will become the symbol of a blessing. *Yes*, I will save you to be a blessing, so do not be afraid. Let your hearts be brave!

14"For I, YAHWEH, Commander of Angel Armies, say to you: Just as I determined to bring calamity when your ancestors made me angry and I showed no pity, 15so now I have determined to treat Judah and Jerusalem well and make them prosperous. So do not be afraid!

---

a 8:7 Babylonia and Persia were in the east with Egypt and Assyria in the west. However, *east* and *west* may stand for nations in every direction (see Pss. 50:1; 113:3; Isa. 59:19; Mal. 1:11).

b 8:8 This verse implies the restoration of the covenant between YAHWEH and Israel. See Lev. 26:12; Jer. 7:23; 11:4; 24:7; Ezek. 11:20; 36:28; 37:23, 27.

c 8:9 Or "your hands be strengthened," likely a figure of speech. See v. 13.

[16]"Here is what you must do: Speak the truth to one
another. Pursue justice in your courts, and hand down
verdicts that are sound. [17]Have no evil scheme in your
hearts against one another. Do not take delight in committing perjury, for these are things that I hate, declares
Yahweh."

The Answer to the Question on Fasting

[18]Then Yahweh, Commander of Angel Armies, spoke these
words to me: [19]"I, Yahweh, Commander of Angel Armies,
say this to you: Instead of having days of fasting in the
fourth, fifth, seventh, and tenth months,[a] the people of
Judah are to have cheerful, joy-filled festivals. Simply live
together peacefully and love truth."

A Prospect of Salvation

[20]Yahweh, Commander of Angel Armies, says this, "In the
future, people from many nations and cities will come
streaming to Jerusalem. [21]Citizens of one city will say to
the people of another city: 'We must certainly go and worship Yahweh, Commander of Angel Armies, and seek his
blessing. I am determined to go.' " [22]Yes, many peoples
and many nations will worship Yahweh, Commander of
Angel Armies, in Jerusalem and seek his blessing.

[23]Yahweh, Commander of Angel Armies, says this, "In
that day, there will be ten men who take hold of the robe
of a Jew. They will come from all nations, speaking every
language, and will say: 'We have heard that God is with
you! We want to go with you.' "

---

a 8:19 That is, early summer, midsummer, autumn, and winter. Each of these fast days lamented catastrophic events surrounding the destruction of Jerusalem and the invasion of the land of Judah by Nebuchadnezzar and the Babylonian armies (see Jer. 52:6–7, fourth month; 2 Kings 25:8–10, fifth month; Jer. 41:1–3, seventh month; Jer. 39:1, tenth month).

Prophecies concerning the Nations

9 A prophecy: The weighty message of Yahweh pertains to the region of Hadrach,[a] and it will come to rest upon Damascus.[b]

"Yahweh keeps an eye on every person[c]
and on all the tribes of Israel
2 and even on Hamath, which borders Damascus,
and on Tyre and Sidon with all their great wisdom.
3 The people of Tyre have built for themselves a
fortress.
They have swept up piles of silver like dust
and gathered mounds of gold like the dirt of the
streets.
4 Behold! The Lord will take away all she has,[d]
burn her city to the ground,
and sink her warships into the sea.[e]
5 Ashkelon will see it and be afraid;
Gaza will see it and writhe in agony.
Ekron will witness the loss of her hopes;
the king of Gaza will perish,
and Ashkelon will be deserted.

---

a 9:1 This is the only reference in the Bible (a hapax legomenon) to the land of Hadrach. Although there are many opinions concerning the location of the land of Hadrach, it is believed to be Aram (Syria), the region around the city of Damascus, north of Israel.

b 9:1 Literally "Damascus its resting place." However, there is a masculine singular suffix on "resting place," which points to the antecedent of the masculine "message [word]." The words for "region" and "Hadrach" are both Hebrew feminine words.

c 9:1 Or literally "To Yahweh the eye of Adam [mankind]"—that is, "All people will look to Yahweh."

d 9:4 Or "the Lord is going to take possession of her" (LXX, Vulgate).

e 9:4 Or "he will hurl down her fortress into the sea."

6 Foreigners[a] will live in Ashdod.
Yes, I will destroy the pride of the Philistine people.
7 I will stop them from eating meat with its blood
and take the forbidden food from between their teeth.
But their remnant, too, will become a part of the
people of God,[b]
like a clan in Judah.
And the people of Ekron will also become *a part of*
God's people
as did the Jebusites.[c]
8 I will stand guard before my temple
to defend it from all who march against it.
No oppressor will overrun them ever again,
for now, I am constantly on the alert."[d]

The King of Zion

9 "My daughter Zion, let your heart and soul rejoice!
Rejoice, my daughter Jerusalem, and shout your
cheerful praises!
Look! Your King comes to you.

---

a 9:6 That is, a mixed population due to the colonization of the land.

b 9:7 God will give his unexpected and undeserved grace to gentiles and will include them as part of his people. This has happened through the blood of Jesus Christ, who has broken down every dividing wall between the races and ethnicities. See Eph. 2:11–19.

c 9:7 The Philistine city of Ekron is likely a metonymy for the Philistines in general. The Jebusites once held as their capital the city of Jerusalem, called Jebus before it was captured by David (see 2 Sam. 5:6–7; 1 Chron. 11:4–6). The Jebusites were not annihilated, but a remnant survived and was absorbed into the community of the people of God (see Josh. 15:63; Judg. 1:21; 1 Kings 9:20–21). Even the ancient enemies of Israel, the Philistines, will be granted grace to mingle with God's people and become part of their communities. Mercy triumphs over judgment.

d 9:8 See Deut. 11:12.

He is righteous and fully qualified to save you.[a]
Yet he comes to you so humbly, riding on a donkey;
sitting meekly on a colt, a young foal of a donkey.[b]
10 I, *the Lord*, will banish
war chariots and horses from Israel[c] and Jerusalem.
I will break the bows used in war.
Your king will proclaim peace and well-being to the nations.[d]
His dominion will stretch from sea to sea,[e]
from the river to the ends of the earth.
11 As for you, *Zion*, because of my covenant with you sealed with blood,
I have set your captives free
from the waterless pit of their prison."[f]

Prisoners of Hope

12 "Come running back home to your fortress,[g]
you hope-filled prisoners!
This very day, I vow

---

a 9:9 Or "he is righteous [fulfilled all the qualifications] and victorious [able to save]." See Isa. 32:1; 46:13; 51:5; Jer. 23:5.

b 9:9 Rejecting the pomp and fanfare of most kings riding on a war horse (see Jer. 17:25; 22:4), King Jesus the Messiah fulfilled this prophecy by riding into Jerusalem on the back of a donkey, the traditional mount of princes (see Gen. 49:11; Judg. 5:10; 10:4; 12:14; Matt. 21:5; Mark 11:1–10; John 12:14–16).

c 9:10 Or "Ephraim," a metonymy for the entire Northern Kingdom of Israel.

d 9:10 See Isa. 2:4; Mic. 4:3–4.

e 9:10 See Ps. 72:8.

f 9:11 See Gen. 37:24.

g 9:12 The Hebrew word for "fortress" is a hapax legomenon, and its meaning is uncertain. Others translate it "stronghold," "citadel," or "place of safety." For the believer today, our fortress is the heart of God, where we are sheltered in his goodness and mercy.

I will restore to you double *blessing for your trouble.*[a]
13 *My people will be my weapons*,
for I have bent Judah as my bow
and made Ephraim my arrow.
I will awaken and stir up your sons, Zion,
against the sons of Greece.
I will use you like a warrior's sword."
14 Then YAHWEH will appear above them,
and his arrow will flash like lightning.[b]
The Lord YAHWEH will sound the shofar
and advance in the great storm of his power.
15 And YAHWEH, Commander of Angel Armies, will be their shield.
Their slinging stones shall conquer and subdue *the enemy*,
spilling their blood like wine from an overfilled bowl,
like the blood that stains the corners of the altar.
16 On that day, YAHWEH their God
will rescue them and make a way.
For they are like a beloved flock of sheep to him,
yes, precious like the gemstones of a diadem
that will sparkle throughout[c] his land.
17 How beautiful and splendid they will be!
Young men will flourish by eating the grain,
and the maidens by drinking the new wine.[d]

---

a 9:12 See Isa. 40:2; 61:7; Hos. 2:15.

b 9:14 See Ps. 18:14; Hab. 3:4, 11.

c 9:16 Or "be lifted up over" or "be raised up over."

d 9:17 Grain and new wine can also be taken as metaphors. Grain is a picture of resurrection life that springs up from the ground. Joshua's generation was given a new diet of eating the grain of the promised land (see Josh. 5:11–12). New wine is a consistent emblem of the new life of the Spirit that empowers us (see Matt. 9:17; Luke 5:37–38). Resurrection life and the empowerment of the Spirit become the source of our victorious life in Christ.

Yahweh Cares for His People

10 Ask Yahweh for rain
in the season of the latter rain.
For Yahweh is the Thunderstorm-Maker.
He will give them the outpouring of rain,
causing the grain of the field to flourish.
2 The household gods[a] babble nonsense,
the fortune tellers see false visions,
dreamers peddle delusions and give comfort in vain.
Therefore, the people have strayed like scattered,
suffering, lost sheep
because they have no shepherd.

3 "I am enraged at the so-called shepherds,
and I will vent my anger and punish the proud
leaders.[b]
I, Yahweh, Commander of Angel Armies,
care deeply for my flock, the people of Judah.
I will transform them *from a shepherdless flock of
sheep*
into *brave* battle horses of splendor.
4 Out of them will emerge the cornerstone[c] and the tent
peg.[d]
From them will emerge battle bows
and warrior captains.

---

a 10:2 Or "teraphim," a term used for family gods passed down through generations, usually figurines in human form. God was saying, "Don't ask idols to help you; it will be in vain. I am the one who will provide the rain, crops, and all that you need."

b 10:3 Or literally "he-goats," a metaphor for domineering, oppressive leaders. See Isa. 14:9; Ezek. 34:17.

c 10:4 This can be viewed as a Messianic prophecy of Christ, our Chief Cornerstone. See Ps. 118:22; Isa. 28:16; Mark 12:10; Acts 4:11; 1 Peter 2:5–8.

d 10:4 See Judg. 4:21–22; 5:26; Isa. 22:23–24.

Together 5they will be like warriors
trampling *the foe* in battle like mud in the streets.
They will fight because YAHWEH fights with them;
they will defeat and humiliate the horsemen.

6"I will make the people of Judah mighty
and the descendants of Joseph victorious.
And I will bring them back home
because I have compassion on them.
They will be as though I had never rejected them,
for I am YAHWEH their God, and I will answer their prayers.
7The people of Israel[a] will be like warriors.
Their hearts will be cheered as though by wine.
Their children will see this and be full of joy,
and their hearts will celebrate and rejoice in YAHWEH.

8"I will whistle to call them home *as a shepherd gathers his sheep*,
for I have redeemed them.
And they will be as numerous as ever before.
9Though I sowed my people as seed among the nations,
they will remember me in those faraway lands.
They will all return and rear their children.
10For I will bring them home from Egypt
and gather them back from Assyria;
I will lead them back into the land of Gilead and Lebanon,
yet even there they will not have enough space.

---

a 10:7 Or "Ephraim," a metonymy for the Northern Kingdom of Israel.

11 "I[a] will cross the turbulent sea of trouble
and calm its waves.[b]
All the depths of the Nile will dry up.
I will humble arrogant Assyria
and dismantle the power[c] of Egypt.
12 I will make my people mighty in me,
and they will walk[d] in my name.
I, YAHWEH, declare it."

God Will Overthrow Mighty Empires

11 Open your borders,[e] Lebanon.
Let fire consume your cedar trees.
2 Cry in sorrow, cypress,
for the towering cedar trees have toppled—
the high and mighty ones are destroyed.
Wail, oaks of Bashan,[f]
for the thick forest has been felled.
3 *Listen!* It's the sound of the wailing of shepherds.
Their glory is gone, their rich pastures destroyed.
Listen! It's the sound of the young lions roaring.
The thickets of the Jordan have been ravaged.

---

a 10:11 That is, the Lord. The Hebrew is "He," and the Greek is "They [the people of Israel]."

b 10:11 Or "strike down its waves." Jesus calmed the troubled sea (see Matt. 8:23–27; Mark 4:35–41).

c 10:11 Or "scepter," a metaphor for the power and dominion of Egypt.

d 10:12 Or "glory [boast]" (LXX).

e 11:1 Or "your doors."

f 11:2 The "cypress," "towering cedar trees," and the "oaks" are all metaphors for the pride and arrogance of the leaders of the empires that failed to come to Israel's aid. Zechariah was dealing with three of the key borderlands of Israel: the northwest (Lebanon/Phoenicia), the northeast (Bashan/southern Syria), and east (Transjordan). Israel's neighbors showed little solidarity with her as the Assyrians and then the Babylonians came in and ravaged the land.

The Two Staffs

4This is what my God, YAHWEH, says: "Shepherd *the inhabitants of this land, for they are like* a flock doomed for slaughter. 5–6Those who buy them slaughter them without remorse. And the merchants who sell them say, 'Blessed be YAHWEH, I have become rich!' Even the hirelings—their own shepherds—show no pity for the sheep. I will no longer show mercy to the inhabitants of the land," declares YAHWEH. "Instead, I will cause each one to fall into the clutches of his neighbor and into the clutches of his king. They will devastate the land, and I will not rescue anyone from their power."

7So I[a] became a shepherd for the sheep doomed for slaughter, especially for those sheep who had been trafficked. I took two staffs *in my hand*; one I named "Affection,"[b] and the other I named "Union,"[c] and I cared for the sheep myself.[d] 8So I removed three shepherds in one month, for I ran out of patience[e] *with the sheep-traffickers*, and they hated me. 9And I told them, "I am not

---

a 11:7 That is, the prophet himself, Zechariah, became a "stand-in" shepherd.

b 11:7 Or "Pleasantness" (NET), "Favor" (NIV), "Beauty" (KJV), or "Mercy" (CEV).

c 11:7 This participial Hebrew verb form *chobelim* derives from the verb *chabal* with the sense of "to bind [someone] by a pledge." So in this context, this symbolic name for the second shepherd's staff may denote the "union" of brotherhood.

d 11:7 How grateful we can be that our mighty God holds these two staffs: Affection and Union. They become the great powers to shape our lives, to protect us, to care for us, and to instruct us. We need God's affection (grace), and we need to realize our union with Christ to access the fullness of God. The Hebrew word translated "affection" (*noʿam*) can also be translated "pleasant." How pleasant it is when we dwell in union with Christ and unity with one another! See Ps. 133.

e 11:8 This is a Hebrew idiom, "my soul was short."

going to be your shepherd anymore. Those doomed to die can die; those doomed for destruction can perish; and the rest can devour one another."
10Then I took my staff, "Affection," and broke it in half to revoke the covenant that I had made with the whole nation *of Israel.*

11So it was annulled on that day, and the sheep-traffickers, who were watching me, realized that YAHWEH was speaking through me.
12Then I said to them, "If it seems right to you, give me my wages; if not, never mind." So they weighed out my wages: thirty shekels of silver.[a]

13YAHWEH said to me, "Now, hand your silver over to the treasury,[b] these thirty pieces of silver—this wonderful sum at which they valued me." So I took the thirty shekels of silver and handed them over to the treasury in the house of YAHWEH.[c]

---

a 11:12 Thirty shekels of silver was the amount of compensation an ox owner paid to a slave's master if the owner's ox injured the slave (see Ex. 21:32). In effect, this was a statement of devaluing Zechariah and his ministry, and it was ultimately an insult to the Lord, who spoke through Zechariah. Judas betrayed (sold) Jesus for thirty pieces of silver. Zechariah was told to throw his silver to the treasury (or "potter"; see the following footnote). Judas' silver was used to buy a field from a potter (see Matt. 27:6–10). It seems that the three "shepherds" that God removed were the elders, the chief priests, and the scribes (see Matt. 16:21) who had "trafficked" his sheep. Today, he is raising up shepherds who have his heart (see Jer. 3:15) and who will use his staffs of grace and union to help and guide his flock.

b 11:13 As translated from an emendation of one letter of the Masoretic Text. The unamended Hebrew word is "smelter [silversmith]" or "potter."

c 11:13 Or "I cast them into the treasury in the house of the Lord."

[14]Then I broke in half my second staff, "Union," to symbolize the breaking of brotherly bonds between Judah
and Israel.[a]

[15]Next, YAHWEH said to me, "Once again, act the part of
a worthless shepherd and take with you the shepherd's
gear. [16]For behold, I am now raising up a shepherd in
the land who will not care about the lost, who will not go
in search of the stray, who will not heal the injured, who
will not feed the healthy sheep, but instead, he will eat the
meat of the fattest sheep and even tear off their hooves.[b]

[17]"Doom is ahead for the worthless shepherd[c]
who deserts his flock!
May the sword strike his arm
and *gouge* his right eye![d]
May his arm shrivel completely
and his right eye be totally blind!"

---

a 11:14 This breaking of the brotherly ties of Israel and Judah points to the Samaritan schism. Josephus wrote that it was in about the year 328 BC that the Samaritans built their rival temple on Mount Gerizim. The breaking of "Union" would symbolize the outbreak of foreign oppression (see v. 10) and the resulting schism between Israel and Judah.

b 11:16 Most Jewish commentators view this "shepherd" as the cruel and heartless Herod.

c 11:17 Or "the shepherd of nothingness."

d 11:17 The "arm" is a consistent biblical symbol of strength (see Ex. 6:6; Isa. 51:9; Ezek. 30:21). A warrior would hold his shield in his left hand and would peer around the side of his shield with his right eye. A man blinded in his right eye was worthless in battle and unable to stand and fight.

Yahweh Rescues Jerusalem

12 A prophecy. A message of Yahweh to Israel.
"I, Yahweh, the Heaven-Unfolder, the Earth-Foundation-Layer, and the Spirit-Shaper of every human spirit, announce to you:

2"Behold! I am about to make Jerusalem an *intoxicating* cup *filled with the wine of my wrath*. Any nation around her who dares to drink from it will stagger and fall. And a siege will be laid against Judah and Jerusalem.

3"In that day, when all the nations join forces against her, I will make Jerusalem like a heavy stone. All who lift it will severely injure themselves.

4"In that day, I will confuse every horse with panic and their riders with madness," says Yahweh. "*Yes*, I will strike the horses of the enemies with blindness, but I will watch
over the people of Judah. 5Then the leaders of Judah will say to themselves, 'The people of Jerusalem are strong[a] because Yahweh, Commander of Angel Armies, is their God.'

6"In that day, I will make Judah's leaders like a blazing pot in a pile of dry brush, like a flaming torch in straw. They will destroy in all directions the surrounding nations. The people of Jerusalem will continue to live safely in
their own city. 7I, Yahweh, will save the tents of Judah first so that the descendants of David and the people of Jerusalem do not receive more honor than the rest of Judah.

8"In that day, my *wraparound* presence will protect the people of Jerusalem. And in that day *I will transform* the weakest[b] among them to become as mighty as David, and

---

a 12:5 Or "The people of Jerusalem are my strength."
b 12:8 Or "the most frail" or "the one who [repeatedly] stumbles."

the dynasty of David will be like God, like the angel of Yahweh going before them."[a]

The People Mourn

9"I am determined in that day to destroy all the nations who attack Jerusalem. 10But I will pour out over the rulers and people of Jerusalem the Spirit of Grace and the *Spirit of* Prayer.[b] And they will gaze upon me, the Pierced One.[c] They will mourn for the one they pierced as though for an only child and weep bitterly for him as people weep for a firstborn child. 11In that day,[d] the mourning in Jerusalem will be as great as the mourning for Hadad Rimmon in the Plain of Megiddo.[e] 12And the people of the land will mourn each clan by itself and their women[f] by themselves:

---

a 12:8 If the weakest will have the mighty strength of the famous King David, those who are of David's descendants and have his character will have superhuman strength, the strength of God. See Ex. 4:16; see also Ex. 14:19; 23:20; 32:34.

b 12:10 Or "the Spirit of Favor [acceptance] and the Spirit of Mercy [compassion]." The word translated "prayer" is *tachanunim*, which denotes pleas for favor or mercy, or "supplications." By implication, it is the Spirit of Intercession that God always pours out prior to, and as a part of, revival.

c 12:10 See John 19:37; Rev. 1:7.

d 12:11 This is the seventh and final occurrence of the discourse marker "In that day" found in this chapter.

e 12:11 Hadad Rimmon is mentioned only here in the Bible. Hadad Rimmon may be the name of a West Semitic storm god (Tammuz; see Ezek. 8:14) since the etymology of *Rimmon* points to the connotation of "thunderer." Others view it as a toponym for a high place (shrine) or village (see 2 Kings 5:18); however, archaeologists have not found a place with that name near the Plain of Megiddo. The Plain of Megiddo, also known as the Valley of Jezreel, is a large agricultural area in the north of Israel (see Judg. 6:33; Hos. 1:5).

f 12:12 Or "wives" and likewise in the following verses.

The clan of David's family and their women,
the clan of Nathan's family and their women,[a]
13 the clan of Levi's family and their women,
the clan of Shimei's family and their women,[b]
14 and all the rest of the clans and their women."

A Cleansing Fountain

13 "In that day, *I* will tear open a flowing fountain[c] for
the family of David and the people of Jerusalem—a
fountain to wash away sin and impurity."

Idolatry Removed from God's People

2 "I, Yahweh, Commander of Angel Armies, declare: In that
day, I will eliminate idolatry from the land, and no one
will remember the names of idols anymore.[d] I will also rid
the land of *false* prophets and unclean spirits.[e]
3 Therefore,
if anyone continues prophesying *falsely*, his parents who
gave him life will say to him, 'You must forfeit your life
since you speak lies in Yahweh's name.' And even while

---

a 12:12 That is, Nathan the son of David (see 2 Sam. 5:14; 1 Chron. 3:5; 14:4; Luke 3:23–38).

b 12:13 Shimei was likely the grandson of Levi and son of Gershon (see Num. 3:17–18; 1 Chron. 6:16–17).

c 13:1 Or "a spring." See Isa. 12:3; Ezek. 36:25; 47:1. This fountain will cleanse the leaders and people both morally and ritually. Although difficult to express in English, the verb "open" is not a simple verb form but a form of the verb "to be" plus a participle. This Hebrew verb construction implies that it is not a single act of opening a fountain but rather a continuous state in which, after the fountain is opened, it remains so constantly. Thus, a forever flowing fountain of grace and cleansing is available for us today. Your sin will not close that fountain once grace has opened it.

d 13:2 See Hos. 2:17.

e 13:2 If the Hebrew clause is considered to be a hendiadys, it could be translated, "the false prophets moved by an unclean spirit."

he is prophesying, his parents who gave him life will
pierce him through.[a]
4"In that day, every *false* prophet will be ashamed to
prophesy and share their so-called visions. No longer will
false prophets wear the coarse robe[b] to deceive people
into thinking they are genuine prophets. 5Instead, they
will admit, 'I am not a prophet. I have been living off the
land[c] as a farmer ever since my youth.' 6And if anyone
asks him, 'What are those scars on your back?'[d] he will
reply, 'I was wounded in the house of my dear friends.' "

The Shepherd and His Sheep

7"Awake my sword! Strike my shepherd!
Strike the man who stands close to me,"
declares YAHWEH, Commander of Angel Armies.
"If you strike the shepherd, the sheep will scatter.[e]
I will even set myself against the young ones.[f]

8"So it will be, throughout the land,"
declares YAHWEH, Commander of Angel Armies.

---

a 13:3 In this context, the false prophets are those who turn God's people to idolatry and who operate under the influence of a demonic (unclean) spirit. See Deut. 13:6–10. The verb for "pierce" is a form of the same Hebrew verb as that used in Zech. 12:10. The implication is that the "Pierced One" of 12:10 was, in fact, a true prophet who had wrongly been killed because he was considered to be a false prophet.

b 13:4 This coarse robe was apparently the garment typically worn by prophets of God. See 1 Kings 19:19; 2 Kings 1:8; 2:12–13; Matt. 3:4.

c 13:5 Or "I was bought as a slave."

d 13:6 Or "between your hands."

e 13:7 Jesus applied this prophecy to himself. See Matt. 26:31; Mark 14:27.

f 13:7 "Young ones" may refer to the scattered flock, but more likely, it refers to young shepherd boys.

"Two-thirds[a] of the people will be struck down,
and the other third will remain.
9I will cause the remaining third to pass through the
fire,
to refine them as silver is refined.
And I will test them as gold is tested.[b]
They will call on my name,
and I will answer them;
I will say to them, 'You are my people,'
and they will say, 'YAHWEH is our God!' "

The Final Battle and the Coming of YAHWEH

14 Behold, YAHWEH, will have his day! And *Jerusalem*,
when that day comes, your plunder will be divided
in your midst. 2For I will gather all the nations to Jerusalem for battle.[c] The city will be captured, the houses
ransacked, and the women raped. Half the people will
go into exile, but the rest will be allowed to remain in the
city.[d] 3Then YAHWEH will intervene and fight against those
nations as when he fights on a day of battle. 4On that day,
his feet will stand on the Mount of Olives, east of Jerusalem. Then the Mount of Olives will be divided down
the middle, forming a wide valley that runs from east to
west. So half the Mount will move backward to the north
and the other half to the south. 5When this happens, you
will escape by way of my newly formed valley, which will

---

a 13:8 The phrase "two-thirds" is literally "mouth of two," an idiom for "two parts [two-thirds]" or "a double portion." See Deut. 21:17; 2 Kings 2:9; Ezek. 5:1–4, 12.

b 13:9 God will use the "fire" of testing to purify our lives and make us holy. See Ps. 66:10; Prov. 17:3; Isa. 1:25; 48:10; Jer. 9:7; Ezek. 22:17–22; Mal. 3:3; 1 Peter 1:7.

c 14:2 See Ezek. 38.

d 14:2 Or literally "will not be cut off from the city."

extend as far as Azal.[a] You will flee as your ancestors fled from the earthquake in the days of Uzziah king of Judah.[b] And Yahweh your God will come and all the holy ones with him.[c]

6On that day, there will be no light, neither cold nor frost.[d] 7It will be a unique day, a day known only to Yahweh.[e] There will be no more day and night, and even at evening, it will remain light.

8On that day, living waters will flow from Jerusalem, half toward the Dead Sea, half toward the Mediterranean Sea.[f] And they will flow in the summer and winter. 9Then King Yahweh will rule over the whole world. When that day comes, Yahweh will be the one and only God, and everyone will acknowledge him by one single name.[g] 10The entire land of Judah will be transformed into a fertile plain, from Geba *in the north* to Rimmon south of Jerusalem. But Jerusalem will remain standing high above the plain from the Benjamin Gate to the site of the first gate, to the Corner Gate, and from the Tower of Hananel to the king's winepresses. 11People will live there *securely*,

---

a 14:5 Azal or "Azel" may be the place referenced in Mic. 1:11, "Beth Ezel."

b 14:5 King Uzziah reigned from 792 BC to 740 BC. This massive earthquake is mentioned by the Jewish historian Flavius Josephus, in Amos 1:1, and possibly in Isa. 6:4.

c 14:5 Or "Then the Lord my God will come and all his holy ones with me" (Hebrew). See Jude (Judah) 14.

d 14:6 As translated from the Septuagint, Syriac, Vulgate, and Targum. The Hebrew is uncertain.

e 14:7 See Matt. 24:36. For Zechariah, the promises of God were inevitable—they would be fulfilled. What is conditional is the timing. The promises will be fulfilled when we are ready to receive them. God is like a pilot who wants to "land" his promises. We just have to clear the runway so he can land them.

f 14:8 Or "the eastern sea . . . the western sea."

g 14:9 That is, the holy name of Yahweh. See Deut. 6:4–5; Mal. 1:11.

for the city will never again be doomed to destruction.
Jerusalem will be safe to live in.

[12]And YAHWEH will bring a devastating plague upon all
the nations who have fought against Jerusalem. Their
flesh will rot while they stand on their feet. Their eyes
will rot in their sockets, and their tongues will rot in their
mouths. [13]And on that day, YAHWEH will cause their hearts
to panic. Each one will seize his neighbor and strike him.
Fighting will break out one against another [14]until even
the people of Judah will fight against[a] the people of Jerusalem. The people of Jerusalem will gather all the riches
of the surrounding nations: vast amounts of gold, silver,
and clothing. [15]And a similar plague will afflict the horses,
mules, camels, donkeys, and all the other animals in the
camp of their enemies.

[16]Afterward, the survivors of all the nations that have
attacked the city will return to Jerusalem each year to worship the King *of the world*, YAHWEH, Commander of Angel
Armies, and to celebrate the Feast of Tabernacles.[b] [17]And
if any of the people groups of the world do not go up to
Jerusalem to worship the King *of the world*, YAHWEH, Commander of Angel Armies, no rain will fall upon their land.
[18]And if the Egyptian people do not make this pilgrimage,

---

a 14:14 Or "in [at] Jerusalem."

b 14:16 See Lev. 23:33–36. That is, Sukkot, a major theme for the rest of the book of Zechariah. The seven days of rejoicing commemorates the seven days of instruction Moses gave to Aaron and his sons before the people waited on the Shekinah to descend on the new dwelling place (or "tabernacle"; Hb. *mishkan*). It was days of dancing (circles) and (required) joy. Especially for the leaders of the people who were always concerned with their dignity (priests, princes, etc.), they, too, were required to dance and rejoice with abandon. They once danced around the golden calf, and now they were to dance with holy abandon in the joyful worship of God.

then YAHWEH will[a] send the same plague he sent the other
nations that did not celebrate the Feast of Tabernacles.
19This will be the punishment for Egypt and the punishment for all the nations that fail to come up to keep the
Feast of Tabernacles.

20When that day comes, the very bells on the horses
will have inscribed on them, "Holy to YAHWEH."[b] Even the
cooking pots of the house of YAHWEH will be as sacred as
the *sprinkling* bowls set before the altar. 21*Yes*, every cooking pot in Jerusalem and in Judah will be holy to YAHWEH,
Commander of Angel Armies, and acceptable to use for
anyone who comes to offer a sacrifice. And at that time
there will be no merchant[c] in the house of YAHWEH, who
commands the armies of heaven.

---

a 14:18 Although the Hebrew is "will not send the plague," the context supports the reading of the Greek, which is followed here by nearly every modern translation.

b 14:20 This same inscription, "Holy to YAHWEH," was also on the gold plate attached to the turban of the high priest (Ex. 28:36; 39:30). The sense of this passage is to teach that even the mundane, natural things can be holy to God when believers dedicate them and set them apart for heaven's purposes. The difference between secular and sacred is meant to disappear. For the believer today, all of life is set apart for God (see Rom. 12:1–2).

c 14:21 Or "Canaanite."

THE BOOK OF

MALACHI

The Messenger of YAH

BroadStreet
PUBLISHING

MALACHI

Introduction

AT A GLANCE

Author: Malachi delivered these prophecies, although they may have been published by others

Audience: The Kingdom of Judah (Persian province of Yehud)

Date: A definitive date is not possible here. The likely period of Malachi's ministry and the recording of his prophecy lies between the building of the Second Temple and the period of the Ezra-Nehemiah reforms—that is, between 515 BC and 430 BC. Given the similarity between Malachi's concerns and those of Nehemiah, the latter end of the range is the more likely date.

Type of Literature: Prophecy

Major Themes: Doubting God's love; contempt for the law; corrupt worship; false teaching; violation of the marriage covenant; injustice and oppression; profaning God's name; the day of Yahweh; seeing Jesus in the book

Outline:

I. Superscription: author and setting — 1:1

II. Doubting God's love — 1:2–5

III. Dishonoring God's name — 1:6–2:9

  a. The people dishonor God by bringing him defiled, blemished sacrifices — 1:6–14

  b. The priests violate God's covenant through false teaching and a profane lifestyle — 2:1–9

IV. Disobeying God's covenant — 2:10–16
  a. Judah's culpable ignorance of their guilt in violating the divine covenant — 2:10
  b. First illustration: marrying idol-worshiping pagan women — 2:11–12
  c. Second illustration: divorce arising from violations of the marriage covenant — 2:13–16

V. Defaming God — 2:17

VI. Defining the day of God's coming — 3:1–5
  a. God will send his messenger to the temple to prepare the way — 3:1
  b. God will appear like a refining fire among the Levites, purifying worship — 3:2–4
  c. That day will result in judgment on Judah for their civil, spiritual, and economic transgressions — 3:5

VII. Defrauding God — 3:6–12
  a. The people rob God by refusing to bring all their tithes and offerings to the temple — 3:6–9
  b. God promises to renew the people's material prosperity if they stop defrauding him — 3:10–12

VIII. Discerning the wicked and the righteous — 3:13–18
  a. The wicked reveal themselves as such by declaring that serving God is futile — 3:13–15
  b. The righteous reveal themselves as such by devoutly fearing YAHWEH — 3:16–18

IX. Dual destinies on the day of YAHWEH — 4:1–6
  a. The day of YAHWEH will result in the fiery destruction of the wicked — 4:1
  b. The day of YAHWEH will result in healing and salvation for the righteous — 4:2–3

c. God promises to send "Elijah" the prophet[a] as a forerunner to prepare the people for his coming — 4:4–6

ABOUT THE BOOK OF MALACHI

The sun was about to go down on one of the world's greatest spiritual/literary traditions, Israelite prophecy. Nothing quite like it exists in any of humankind's written history, and its last embers, which had once reached wildfire levels with Jeremiah and Amos, were growing cold and dark. Prophecy, far from mere "fortune telling," was a mighty counterweight to the priestly and royal-military powers of the day. The prophets literally spoke for God and could shake any city or nation to its very foundations.

As the prophetic era was eclipsing, the season of scholars, sages, and rabbis emerged to replace the prophets. Footnoters and commentators diluted and obscured the passion of the prophets who spoke the words of Yahweh. A culture of scholastic legalism started taking shape as the prophets went silent for centuries. Malachi was the last in the classical prophetic line, and he tied a bow on the Torah (Moses) and the prophets (Elijah) in Malachi 4:4–5. It is no accident that Jesus met with these two pillars of the Hebrew Bible at his transfiguration.

Malachi was also the last book of the Bible written from start to finish in the earthy and potent Hebrew language. The children of Israel were adopting the languages of their conquerors, Aramaic and eventually Greek. Hebrew, the magnificent and emotionally soaring tongue of King David and the Psalms, was about to go nearly extinct. It was limited mostly to use in synagogues only to be

---

a This "Elijah" is revealed in the Gospels as John the Baptist, who prepared the way for the public ministry of Jesus Christ (Matt. 11:13–14; 17:11–13; Mark 9:12–13; Luke 1:17).

reawakened as the national language of the modern state of Israel over two millennia later.

The book of Malachi is shaped by a series of dialogues, or disputes, between the prophet and those he was addressing. It is not clear whether these dialogues took place or whether they are just a common literary device known as prosopopoeia, used to give a framework to the book. Prosopopoeia is "a figure of speech in which an imaginary or absent person is represented as speaking or acting."[a] In Malachi, these "dialogues" begin in 1:2, with God affirming his love for his people: "I have always loved you." Then the nation of Judah challenged that declaration by asking: "How have you shown us your love?" This is then followed by a detailed divine response. The remaining "dialogues" all begin with God leveling charges of covenant violations against his people, followed by the people questioning those accusations, asking if they've really done such things (1:6–7; 2:17; 3:8; 3:13). And each of these is followed by God's detailed response. Although we do not know for certain whether the responses of God's people in these various contexts were actual or imagined, we must not underplay the reality of their sinful mindset. The disputations read like an FAQ table, listing the main controversies of Malachi's day.

Much like the sages and teachers who would replace Malachi and the prophets, Malachi taught in catechetical style. The root word of *catechesis* is "echo," and it's a method that Martin Luther (AD 1500s) used in his *Small Catechism*. Question and answer. Echo and repeat.

Malachi 3:4–4:6 forms the basis for the modern Jewish liturgy of *Shabbat Ha-Gadol* (Big Sabbath) right before

---

a *Merriam-Webster*, s.v. "prosopopoeia," accessed June 2, 2023, www.merriam-webster.com.

the Passover, perhaps because of its reference to Elijah, whose empty chair at the Seder meal evokes hope for a blessed future. Note that Jewish Bibles and some modern Christian Bibles number verses in Malachi differently from most English-language Bibles. It's the same content but with different numerical designations.

Malachi seems to fit, in terms of a timeline, between the reforms of Josiah and the reforms of Ezra and Nehemiah. It is likely that he was very familiar with the same issues as Nehemiah, and perhaps Malachi's fiery prophecies served to reinforce the concerns of the rebuilder of the city of Jerusalem.

With a dramatic flair, Malachi, in the classic prophetic tradition, brought deep conviction to his rebuke. This book is a literary masterpiece meant to stir the hearts of God's people and evoke a response.

PURPOSE

The priceless repository of the canonical prophetic writings of Holy Scripture was forged in countless seasons of great pressure and daunting challenges. Malachi faced these threats with defiance and faith. His general overarching purpose was twofold: First, he determined to record the dire threats to the spiritual vitality of the people of Judah and Jerusalem, warning them that if they refused to mend their ways, catastrophic divine judgment would follow. Second, at the same time as he was issuing these warnings, Malachi also had a clear intention to offer to the postexilic community of God's people the hope of a blessed future in which God would purify and refine them, renewing and restoring them to a rightly ordered and God-honoring system of worship. They would then subsequently live their lives in an attitude of reverential awe toward their Lord, honoring his name in everything they did. They would also be transformed into a people renowned for their obedience to the divine law. The vehicle that would encapsulate this twofold purpose was the coming day of YAHWEH.

Several generations had passed since the Israelite exiles started returning from captivity in Mesopotamia (Babylon and Persia). The mighty kingdom of David and Solomon, with its gleaming temple, had not yet been fully restored as they had hoped. Governors reporting to Persia were in charge. Religious and spiritual life was at a low ebb. The priests were discouraged and corrupt. Israel had been reduced to a struggling little nation, desperately trying to rebuild. People were neglecting their tithes, which were to provide resources for God's house. "It's not like it used to be, that's for sure," was the going sentiment of Malachi's times. The hope for a renewed Davidic kingdom had not come to pass, and the newly rebuilt Second Temple in Jerusalem was a shadow of what Solomon's First Temple had been.

The cultural and spiritual application of the message and purpose of Malachi—given to the postexilic Israelites in the 400s BC—cannot be simplistically and literally equated with contemporary twenty-first century AD new covenant experiences. However, the underlying spiritual principles articulated by Malachi are timeless.

In many ways, the way the people of God felt then is much like how many of us feel about the current condition of church life in Western Europe and North America. Especially since the COVID-19 pandemic, many of our worship buildings are no longer filled on Sundays, and we may be discouraged when we see old photos of huge post-WWII youth groups and thousands getting baptized in the Jesus Movement of the 1960s and '70s. Not a few modern churches and key leaders have been rocked by scandals. Churches are hurting for money as the faithful, generous, older believers go to receive their reward.

Many Christians are more passionate about partisan political issues than biblical issues and have lost any sense of urgency for reaching the lost. It's not like it used to be, that's for sure. Like the ancient Israelites in Malachi's day, a significant number of new covenant believers have lost sight of the importance of living lives that are consistent with divinely revealed moral, cultural, and spiritual values. The parallels are stark. Skepticism and indifference prevailed in Malachi's time, and both are very present in our culture today. Thus, reading Malachi seems strangely relevant to us.

Malachi covered an amazing number of big-ticket social issues in a very short book. He was the polar opposite of a one-theme prophet. He went after the whole laundry list of problems in Jerusalem and the surrounding countryside and did not hesitate to use language that pierces the heart.

Malachi intended for his blaring claxon to sound the alarm and wake us up, straighten us out, and fill us with the ultimate hope and promise of God's future. This is the life message of the Israelite prophetic tradition. Israelite prophecy was a relay race stretching back to the earliest times, and Malachi took the baton to run the anchor leg.

AUTHOR AND AUDIENCE

Malachi was the last of the Old Testament prophets but wrote nothing about himself. He gave us nothing about his ancestry, his call, or his personal life. But such is the way of a messenger. It is the message, not the messenger, that we are supposed to remember. In fact, the name *Malachi* means "my messenger" (3:1; or "my angel," as the word for "angel" also means "messenger"). This possible "pen name" has caused some scholars to believe that he was writing as an anonymous prophet or, according to some Talmud and Targum writings, that the author of

Malachi was Ezra, the scribe.[a] Christian scholars are split on what the label *Malachi* means (much as they are with Luke's *Theophilus*, which could either be a proper name or a reference to an unnamed "lover of God" as the Greek word literally denotes). However, even the most critical contemporary Jewish commentators tend to assume that Malachi was the prophet's given name.

Unlike most prophets, who spread their displeasure around to all the nations of the region, Malachi reserved his ammunition for Israel and was not afraid to use it. Israel was no longer an independent nation with its own king. The nation was now known as Yehud, a province of the Persian Empire ruled by a governor. Estimates of the population are shockingly low, with a few thousand living in Yehud's capital city of Jerusalem and perhaps twenty thousand in the surrounding countryside.

The temple had been rebuilt, but it didn't impress anyone. People had stopped providing offerings for the work of the temple, and the priests, under financial stress, resorted to corruption and apathy. The prevailing thought among the priests was, "You pretend to pay us, and we will pretend to work." Secular thinking was taking root: "If God were real, things would be better." This led to a weakening of holy fear and respect for God, and people started offering their lame animals and discard produce for sacrifice at the temple, much like the stuff we would donate to a thrift shop or just toss in a dumpster.

This was the world in which Malachi lived, and such was the malaise that he felt led by God to confront. The most challenging assertion of the local people at the time

---

a For a masterful overview of the authorship of Malachi and varying views, see Joyce Baldwin, *Haggai, Zechariah, Malachi: An Introduction and Commentary*, Tyndale Old Testament Commentaries (Westmont, IL: InterVarsity Press, 1981), 225–28.

was that God did not love them. And that's where Malachi opened his book.

MAJOR THEMES

Doubting God's Love. The book of Malachi opens with this theme, and in one sense, Judah's doubting of God's love may be said to pervade the entire prophecy. God began by declaring that he had loved his people. But then, in the first of several exchanges that are either real or imagined,[a] the postexilic remnant community of Judah questioned that declaration by asking, "How have you shown us your love?" (1:2). The clear implication is that they genuinely doubted that God's love for them was real. This had, and will have, disastrous consequences—potential and actual—for their ongoing relationship with Yahweh. These consequences will be further examined in the discussion of the themes that follow.

Contempt for the Law. This is a pillar of the book that has several subthemes, all of which are of equal significance and discussed over the next four Major Themes. In reality, the sinful behaviors of corrupt worship, false teaching, violation of the marriage covenant, and injustice and oppression are the outward workings of an inner utter contempt for the law of God that banned such actions and attitudes. Each of these five behaviors shatters a key element of the law. It may be argued that such contempt was at least in part triggered by a sense of disillusionment and disappointment in the hearts and minds of the remnant community. After returning from captivity perhaps as much as one hundred years prior to the prophetic ministry of Malachi, the elation of that release had all but worn off, as the promised revival of the kingdom of

---

a See the discussion about the dialogue format in About the Book of Malachi.

Israel and Judah had not yet materialized. Furthermore, the size of their territory and population was miniscule compared to the nation's former glory days. The people had lost heart and were genuinely wondering if God had abandoned them. Such disappointment does not excuse their contempt for the law, although it may help to explain it. In essence, the Judean community had dropped their bundle and lost all interest in maintaining obedience to God's covenant statutes. Such a stance would draw down dire warnings and judgment from God via his servant-prophet Malachi.

Corrupt Worship. The first indication of the community's contempt for the law centered on its corrupted worship, which expressed itself in three areas. The first of these was the people's presentation of defiled offerings (1:6–14)—food that had been desecrated by priests who had physical defects or disease. Consequently, they were ceremonially unclean and therefore prohibited from accepting food and offering it to YAHWEH at the altar (Lev. 21:8, 21). Their corrupt worship also included the offering of diseased animals, which was also forbidden under the law (see Deut. 15:21). Such violations reflected a couldn't-care-less attitude, and that indifference revealed, at its heart, contempt for the worship of YAHWEH.

The second expression of the people's contempt for the practice of God-honoring worship was their withholding of tithes, a mandatory, nonnegotiable element of Israelite law. Failing to tithe was tantamount to robbing God (Mal. 3:7–9), who had designed the tithe to provide tangible, material support for the priests and Levites who served him in the temple. Again, this behavior illustrates the people's utter disregard for the sacred worship of YAHWEH.

The final expression of the nation's contempt for divinely mandated worship is found in the brief mention of sorcery in 3:5. Participating in sorcery would certainly bring God's punishment. Sorcery was, and still is, forbidden because it is an illegitimate, demonic attempt to open a door, totally independent of God, to the spirit world and access secret knowledge and skills. YAHWEH alone is the sole, legitimate source of spiritual knowledge, and any attempt to bypass him in this way is an act of blasphemy. Once again, the Israelite people demonstrated their contemptible disregard for the God-ordained sanctity of worship by participating in a practice that attempted to sideline God, and they did this without any trace of godly fear, that awesome reverence that is his due whenever his people step into his presence to worship him.

False Teaching. We see the second example of the people's contempt for God's law in the behavior of the priesthood. Responsibility for instructing the Israelite people accurately and appropriately in the full dictates of the law lay wholly with the priests and Levites. They are referred to in Malachi, in an ideal sense, as the messengers of YAHWEH, who rules over all (2:7). However, in 2:1–9, God condemned the priests for totally failing to carry out the solemn responsibility of teaching the people the sacred laws and statutes of the covenant. Instead of building the people up in their faith and knowledge of YAHWEH, the priests turned their backs on these truths and perpetrated false teaching—their own ideas, in effect—and caused many to stumble in their relationship with God. The root cause of this contemptible violation of the Levitical covenant was their callous indifference to the sanctity of God's law. It simply did not matter to them.

Violation of the Marriage Covenant. The third illustration of the people's contempt for the law lay in their toleration and wholesale acceptance of marriage with idol-worshiping pagan women. Malachi rightly voiced

God's scathing disapproval of this blatant disregard for the sacred institution of the marriage covenant.

To begin with, Deuteronomy 24:1–4 gives a lot of latitude for divorce, allowing a man to issue a certificate of divorce to his wife after he had found something indecent about her. However, there is a caveat to this latitude, which Jesus made clear during his teaching ministry. Malachi also took a much more restrictive view to the Deuteronomic statute and urged men to stay with the wives of their youth. Theologians and Bible scholars have speculated that the men of Jerusalem were marrying young to Jewish women but that as the men grew older, they were then adding to their harem women from other cultures with other gods, often discarding their first wives in the process. This is exactly what got King Solomon into trouble. For this tiny, rebuilding nation to survive, the men of Israel would have to avoid such marriages and the resulting assimilation of the Jews into the much larger surrounding empires and kingdoms.

Without stricter rules, the Jews would dissolve into the whirlpool of ancient Near Eastern nations, and their heritage and the revelations God made through them would be lost. Thus, the covenant with YAHWEH, the superordinate principle that defined the people of Israel, had to be cleansed from outside influences, renewed, and reformed on a regular basis. Malachi found himself in a low ebb between the earlier covenant reforms of Josiah and those of Ezra and Nehemiah. He had an uphill struggle in front of him to convince the people that their decision—whether or not to be faithful to the covenant—meant life or death for their national identity. Because of Malachi and others, Second Temple Judaism not only survived but flourished.

All three Synoptic Gospels include Jesus' teaching on marriage and divorce: In Matthew 5:31–32, Jesus cited the Mosaic teaching on the subject but then added his own authoritative "codicil" to replace that provision by stating that the only grounds for divorce were marital unfaithfulness. Then in Matthew 19:7–9, Jesus explained that Moses had allowed for divorce as a concession to the people's hardness of heart, and then he added that God originally designed marriage as a lifelong covenant bond between a man and a woman and that only marital infidelity could break that bond while both husband and wife were alive. There is no doubt that Jesus would have upheld Malachi's passionate defense of the sanctity of the marriage covenant, a position made abundantly clear in Malachi 2:13–16. The people's obvious abandonment of this covenant bond through their unquestioning acceptance of marriage with pagan women is yet another reflection of their contempt for God's sacred law.

Injustice and Oppression. The fourth illustration of the people's contempt for God's law is the brief but powerful indictment in 3:5. Here the prophet condemned the people for their flagrant spiritual, moral, social, and economic abuses. In particular, the latter two offenses relate to defrauding workers of their wages, oppressing widows and orphans, and denying justice to vulnerable aliens (or immigrants) who were sheltering in their land. These offenses demonstrate the people's brutality, lack of compassion, and disregard for justice and righteousness. Maintaining the two latter virtues, justice and righteousness, and shunning oppression of any kind were central elements in the ethos of the law. The postexilic community's rank dismissal of these statutes yet again highlights their unmitigated contempt for the law of God.

Profaning God's Name. The sinful action of profaning God stems from the same place as contempt for the divine law. To profane someone is to treat that person as if they are not worthy of respect. The remnant community of Judah and Jerusalem had reached the point where they no longer had respect for God or his character. In this context, the people of God no longer regarded him as holy or righteous and therefore attributed to him actions and attitudes characteristic of fallible human beings.

In 2:17, God accused the people of wearying him with their words, including their claim that those who were evil were seen as good in the eyes of God and alleging that God had no interest in maintaining justice. Similarly, in 3:13–15, the people claimed that serving God was a waste of time, that evildoers prospered, and that those who challenged God with their wrongdoing escaped punishment. In short, the action of profaning God attempted to strip him of his deity and his moral perfections and treated his holy name with contempt.

The Day of Yahweh. The Hebrew word *yom*, which we translate as "day," is richly symbolic and complex when associated with the person of Yahweh and not just a twenty-four-hour chronometer measurement. The prophets make frequent use of the phrase *the day of Yahweh* (or *the day of the Lord*), and it always reflects a manifestation of divine judgment and blessing. It is a prophetic motif with many levels of fulfillment throughout the prophetic canon of Scripture. This warning announces bad news for the bad people, when the cosmic checkbook will be balanced and justice will be done. On the other hand, such a day is *good news* for the faithful remnant, for they shall inherit all the promises of God.

One can misapply the message of the "day of Yahweh" by overspeculating about the exact time this will occur. Even Jesus warned against this. However, what we *can* confidently affirm is that the day of Yahweh came to its first climactic fulfillment in the earthly ministry of Jesus the Messiah. The final words of Malachi's prophecy (4:1–6) anticipated this fulfillment when God announced via his prophet that he would send "the prophet Elijah" to prepare the way for his coming. The second, and absolute, fulfillment of this day is still to come: the consummation of divine judgment in the manifestation of the new heavens and the new earth at the end of time, when Jesus returns. Meanwhile, the whole idea is that we live our lives *today*, trusting that God's justice will be done and that he will keep his promises to his faithful followers. In Malachi's time, this trust was eroding, and the survival of what was left of Israel was hanging in the balance because of it.

Seeing Jesus in the Book. The key to understanding where the prophetic anticipation of the coming of Jesus the Messiah lies in the book of Malachi is in the motif of the day of Yahweh. This has already been mentioned in the preceding discussion of that theme. The complexity of this motif has also been noted. There is no doubt that the day of Yahweh reached a climactic fulfillment in the death and resurrection of Jesus Christ. His death on the cross signaled the final doom of Satan and his followers, when sin and death were destroyed in principle. In addition, Jesus' atoning sacrifice, along with his resurrection from the dead, accomplished the total forgiveness of sin and the eternal salvation of all those who put their faith and trust in him as their Savior and Lord. And there is still the consummate climax of the day of Yahweh to come, the ushering in of the eternal kingdom of heaven with God on the throne, the risen Lamb of God beside him, and all wrongs righted.

All this is implicit not only in the final chapter of Malachi's prophecy (4:1–6) but also in those passages that speak of the coming renewal and restoration of the people of God, after they have been purified and refined through God's fiery judgment (see 1:11; 3:1–4, 10–12, 16–18).

MALACHI

The Messenger of Yah

Doubting God's Love

1 This is *divine revelation*—the message[a] Yahweh gave to
Israel through Malachi.
2"I, Yahweh, say to you: I have *always* loved you.
"But you ask, 'How have you shown us your love?'
"I, Yahweh, say to you: Were not Esau and Jacob twins?
Yet I have loved Jacob *and his descendants* 3more than
Esau *and his descendants*, whom I rejected.[b] And I have
turned the hill country of Esau into a barren wasteland
and left his land to the desert jackals.
4"The people of Edom vow, 'Though we have been shattered, we will rebuild the ruins.'
"But this is what I, Yahweh, Commander of Angel Armies, say: You may build, but I will demolish it again. People will call you 'The Wicked Land' and 'The People under the Perpetual Anger of Yahweh.'

---

a 1:1 Or "burden." The Hebrew implies a courier carrying a message that he is obligated to bring to God's people.

b 1:3 Or "I have accepted Jacob [Israelites] and hated [rejected] Esau [Edomites]." Both of Isaac's sons had an equal opportunity to lay claim to the covenant of God, which was their birthright. But Esau abandoned his claim to the birthright, and Jacob schemed to steal it from the firstborn, Esau (see Gen. 25:29–34). Although the Hebrew is simply, "I have loved Jacob and hated [rejected] Esau," *Jacob* and *Esau* are to be viewed as metonyms, representing the Israelites and the Edomites (descendants of Esau). See Deut. 4:37; 7:7–8; 10:15; Rom. 9:10–13.

[5]"*Israel*, you will witness this with your own eyes and
say, 'The greatness of YAHWEH extends even beyond our
own borders.' "[a]

Blemished Sacrifices

[6]"I, YAHWEH, Commander of Angel Armies, say to you
priests, 'Sons honor their fathers, and servants *respect*
their masters. Yet if I am your father,[b] why don't you
honor me? If I am your master, why don't you respect
me? You have despised my *glorious* name.'

"But you ask, 'How have we despised your name?'

[7]"You place defiled food on my *sacred* altar.

"Still you ask, 'How have we defiled you?'

"By treating YAHWEH's table as though it deserves no
respect.[c] [8]Is it not wrong to offer your blind, lame, and
sick animals as sacrifices to me?[d] Try offering them to
your governor! Would he be pleased with you? Would
he show you favor?" asks YAHWEH, Commander of Angel
Armies.

[9]"Now try flattering[e] me with inappropriate sacrifices
that I may be gracious to you. When you offer me such

---

a 1:5 Or "You who are beyond the borders of Israel will say: YAHWEH is great!"

b 1:6 See Deut. 32:6; Isa. 63:16; 64:8; Jer. 3:4; 31:9; Matt. 6:8–9. This verse presents some of the strongest Father imagery for God before the birth of Christ.

c 1:7 Although it is possible that Malachi was referring to the table of the sacred bread (or the table of fellowship) in the Holy Place, it is more likely in this context that the "table" is the bronze altar where sacrifices were offered.

d 1:8 See Lev. 22:18–25; Deut. 15:19–21. It was the duty of the priests to ensure that offerings to God did not include unacceptable animals.

e 1:9 Or "stroke the face of God" or "seek the face of God." This can be seen as God being sarcastic because the triliteral verbal root (Hb. [c]*hlh*, which means "flattering") is the same as the word used to describe the sick animals in the previous verse.

sacrifices, do you expect me to show you favor?"[a] asks
YAHWEH, Commander of Angel Armies.
10"It would be far better *to halt temple worship altogether*
and one of you shut the temple gates so that you would
not keep lighting worthless[b] fires on my altar. I am not
pleased with you, and I will not accept any offering from
your hands," says YAHWEH, Commander of Angel Armies.
11"From one end of the world to the other,[c] my name
will be great among the nations. In every place, incense
and a pure offering will be offered to my name.[d] All over
the world my name will receive honor," says YAHWEH,
Commander of Angel Armies.
12"But your actions dishonor me. You profane my *name*
by being bored with the Lord's table and considering it
to be common. You say that what you offer me has no
worth.[e] 13You also say, 'We're fed up with all this!' And you
turn up your nose in disgust," says YAHWEH, Commander
of Angel Armies.

"You offer me injured,[f] crippled, or diseased animals, but I won't accept your sacrifices. This is YAHWEH speaking to you.

---

a 1:9 Or "to lift up your faces?"

b 1:10 There is a subtle wordplay that is lost in translation between the Hebrew word *chinnam* (meaning "worthless" or "in vain") and the root [*c*]*hnn* translated "be gracious" in v. 9.

c 1:11 Or "from the rising of the sun to the setting of the sun"—that is, from east to west.

d 1:11 For possible alternate meanings of this verse and the problems associated with each, see Howard A. Hatton and David J. Clark, *A Handbook on the Book of Malachi* (New York: United Bible Societies, 2002), 389–90.

e 1:12 Or literally "You poke holes in it [my honor?] in saying [whispering?] that the master's table is contaminated and that the food you place on it is worthless." This is almost like spreading doubt in God through gossiping.

f 1:13 Or "stolen animals" (LXX, Vulgate).

[14]"A curse rests on the cheat who has a perfect male offering in his flock and vows to give it[a] but then sacrifices a puny, imperfect animal to me. For I am a great King," says YAHWEH, Commander of Angel Armies, "and my name is to be formidable[b] among the nations."

Unfaithful Priests

2 "And now, this is my warning for you priests: [2]I, YAHWEH, Commander of Angel Armies, am speaking to you. If you do not listen and *fervently* devote your heart to honor my name, then I will send the curse[c] upon you and convert your blessings into curses. Yes, I have already done so since you have not dedicated your heart to honor me.

[3]"Behold! I will rebuke your descendants. I will smear feces on your faces—the dung from your festival sacrifices—and you *priests* will be tossed away with the animal waste. [4]And then you will know that I, YAHWEH, Commander of Angel Armies, have sent you this commandment so that my covenant with Levi may endure. [5]My covenant with his tribe was a covenant to give them a full, peaceful life. All this I gave to him so that he would revere me, and indeed, he honored me and stood in awe of my name. [6]He gave *the people* solid instruction and spoke nothing false.[d] He walked with me in peace and integrity and turned many from evil.

[7]"Listen, you priests, *descendants of Levi.* Your lips should be a gateway to sacred truths when people come to you for instruction because you are the messengers of

---

a 1:14 See Lev. 22:17–25.

b 1:14 Or "reverenced" or "feared."

c 2:2 For the curse, see 3:9.

d 2:6 Or "True instruction was in his mouth, and nothing false was found on his lips."

YAHWEH, who rules over all. [8–9] But you have turned from *my* path, and your teachings have caused many to stumble. You have corrupted the covenant with Levi. So I have caused you to be despised and humiliated before all the people. For you have not followed my ways but have shown partiality in matters of the law.[a] This is YAHWEH, Commander of Angel Armies, speaking to you."

Malachi Rebukes Unfaithful Israel

[10]Have we not all one Father, the one God who created us? So why do we cheat one another and violate the covenant that God made with our ancestors?

[11]The people of Judah have been unfaithful. A horrible atrocity has been committed throughout the land and even in Jerusalem. They have married foreign women who worship their strange gods[b] and in this way have defiled YAHWEH's temple, which he loves. [12]May YAHWEH punish the one who has done such a despicable thing, whoever he may be,[c] even though he brings offerings to the Lord Almighty. May *YAHWEH* banish his entire family from the community of Israel![d]

[13]Another thing you do: You drown YAHWEH's altar with tears. You weep and wail because he no longer values

---

a 2:8–9 Or "lifting up faces in the law," a Hebrew idiom for showing partiality to the rich and depriving the poor of justice (see Mic. 3:11). However, an alternate interpretation could be, "You have failed to bring people blessing [lifting up faces] by your teaching."

b 2:11 See Deut. 7:3–6. It is possible that married men were taking second wives who were gentiles.

c 2:12 There are two Hebrew words in the text that pose a real difficulty for understanding. They are *ʿer weʿoneh*, connected with those whom God condemns for idolatrous marriages with gentile women. The literal reading is "one who is awake and one who answers," which is possibly a figure of speech for anyone who is alive or "whoever he may be."

d 2:12 Or "May YAHWEH cut him off from the tents of Jacob."

your offerings or accepts with pleasure what you bring
him.

14"Why not?" you ask.

It is because you promised before YAHWEH to be faithful to the wife you chose in your youth. She is your partner, and you are bound to her by covenant, yet you have
betrayed her. 15Has God not made them one with a shared
Spirit in their union?[a] And what does he desire but godly children from your union? So guard your spirit and do not be disloyal to the wife of your youth.

16"I, YAHWEH, the God of Israel, say to you: 'He who does not love his wife but hates her and divorces her[b]

---

a 2:15 Or literally "And not one has made and a residue of spirit to him." Some possible translations include "Didn't the one [God] make us and preserve our [life] breath?" or "Didn't the one [God] make her, both flesh and spirit?" or "No one with even a [small] portion of the Spirit in him will do this." Some Jewish scholars (such as Cashdan) see a reference here to Abraham as "the one" who did not divorce his wife Sarah even when she was apparently too old to bear children. With this understanding, this verse could be translated, "But you say, 'Didn't our one ancestor Abraham do this? Surely there was a spirit of loyalty in him?' " However, most Christian scholars interpret this as God making Adam and Eve "one flesh" (Gen. 2:24). Because the Hebrew is uncertain and, in a measure, unintelligible, there are many varying viewpoints as to its meaning. For an extensive review of these interpretations, see Pieter Verhoef, *The Books of Haggai and Malachi* (Grand Rapids, MI: William B. Eerdmans Publishing, 1987), 275–77.

b 2:16 As translated from the Septuagint, Latin Vulgate, Luther, Dead Sea Scroll 4QXII[a]. Most translations change the vowels of the traditional Hebrew "he [one] hates" to make it read "I hate [divorce]." In spite of textual variation, the sense of God's hatred of divorce is clear throughout the Bible. See Deut. 24:1–4; Matt. 5:31–32; 19:4–9. Clearly, God is the enemy of divorce because it hurts the people he loves.

overwhelms her with cruelty.[a] So guard your spirit and do not abandon her.' This is YAHWEH, Commander of Angel Armies, speaking to you."

Calling Evil Good

17You weary YAHWEH with your words.
Yet you ask, "How have we wearied him?"
By saying, "Evildoers are good in the eyes of YAHWEH, and he is pleased with them."
And you ask, "Where is the God of justice?"

The Messenger of YAHWEH

3 "Behold! I am sending my messenger, who will prepare the way before me.[b] Then suddenly, the Lord whom you long for will enter his temple. The messenger

---

a 2:16 Or "covers his garment with violence." Some see the word *garment* as a symbol for the wife because spreading a garment over a woman was symbolic of a marriage proposal (see Ruth 3:9; Ezek. 16:8). See also Deut. 24:1–4. An alternate translation of the first sentence of v. 16 could be "YAHWEH, God of Israel, says, 'Let anyone who hates his wife divorce her.' Yet such a person covers himself with violence [acts like a robber]."

b 3:1 The Hebrew word for "my messenger" is *mal'aki*, which is the prophet's name, Malachi. This messenger is identified as Elijah in 4:5, and the prophecy was fulfilled in the person of John the Baptist. See Isa. 40:3; 57:14; 62:10; Matt. 11:10; Mark 1:2; Luke 7:27.

of the covenant,[a] your soul's delight, will certainly come,"
says YAHWEH, Commander of Angel Armies. 2But who can
endure the day of his coming?[b] Who will not fall down
in worship when the Lord is unveiled?[c] *For he will carry*

---

a 3:1 There are three persons mentioned in this verse: "my messenger . . . the Lord . . . the messenger of the covenant." John the Baptist is the one mentioned first ("my messenger"; see preceding footnote). It is likely that "the Lord" and "the messenger of the covenant" are the same person. The chiastic structure likewise strengthens the view that they are identical. This then leaves us with: "Behold! I [YAHWEH] am sending my messenger [John the Baptist], who [John] will prepare the way before me. Then suddenly, the Lord [Jesus] whom you long for will enter his temple [both the temple in Jerusalem and the temple of the body of Christ]. The messenger of the covenant [Jesus], your soul's delight, will certainly come." Chapter 3 of Malachi opens with one of the greatest prophecies of hope in all the Old Testament. The Lord, the messenger of the covenant, is coming to purify hearts and to establish a new covenant. This is the only place in the Bible that the phrase *messenger of the covenant* is found. It probably means "the one who brings a message about the covenant" or "the messenger whom the covenant speaks about." See Deut. 18:15, 18.

b 3:2 Although the Hebrew word *bo'* is usually translated "coming," it can also mean "to fall upon" or even "to attack." Who can abide the day of his falling upon us?

c 3:2 Or "who will remain standing when he is unveiled." See Judg. 13:20; 1 Kings 18:39; Ezek. 1:28; Dan. 10:9; Luke 5:8; Phil. 2:10; Rev. 1:17; 22:8.

out a purifying process. He will be like a refiner's fire or a launderer's bleach.[a] 3He will be as a *silversmith* who sits refining and purifying silver.[b] He will purify the Levites, refining his *priests* until they are like *pure* gold and *fine* silver. Then I, YAHWEH, will have those who bring me offerings in righteousness. 4And the offerings of Judah and Jerusalem will be pleasing to me, as in former times and years past.

5"So I will come near to you and put you on trial. I will be quick to testify against sorcerers, adulterers, and those who lie under oath, against those who cheat workers of their wages, who oppress the widows and orphans and ignore the immigrants[c] but who do not live in awe of me. This is YAHWEH, Commander of Angel Armies, speaking to

---

a 3:2 This purifying process is described by means of two similes, likening the messenger to a refiner's fire and a launderer's bleach. The image of a refiner's fire is taken from the process of the melting and heating of metal in a furnace to purify or refine it. As the metal is melted, the impurities either burn away or come to the surface, where they can be skimmed off (see Ps. 66:10; Isa. 1:25; 48:10; Ezek. 22:17–22; Zech. 13:9). The second image compares the messenger with launderer's bleach. The Hebrew word *borit* refers to a powerful chemical agent with a strong cleansing effect that is similar to lye. It is thus best described not as soap but rather as a much harsher cleanser, such as bleach or lye. There is a deliberate wordplay with the word for "covenant" (Hb. *berit*) and the word for "launderer's bleach" (Hb. *borit*) that is lost in translation. This *borit* is an alkaline liquid containing potassium hydroxide that was gathered by percolating water through wood ash. Washing cloth in this cleaner was an effective way of removing greasy and oily stains. Jesus has come to set this purifying fire in our hearts and to cleanse us of the deepest stain of sin and shame.

b 3:3 See Ps. 12:6; Isa. 1:25; 48:10.

c 3:5 Or "turn away the foreigners."

you. 6Truly, I, Yahweh, have not changed. And you, children of Jacob, you haven't changed either."[a]

A Call to Repentance

7"Ever since the time of your ancestors, you have turned away from my laws and evaded them. Return to me, and I will return to you," says Yahweh, Commander of Angel Armies.

"But you ask, 'How do we need to return?'

8"Is it right for people to rob God? Yet you rob me.[b]

"But you ask, 'How could we *possibly* rob you?'

"You withhold your tithes and offerings. 9You are under a curse—the whole lot of you are guilty of robbing me. 10Bring the full amount of your tithes into the *temple* treasury[c] so that there may be ample provisions in my house. Test me and see if I, Yahweh, Commander of Angel Armies, will fling open the floodgates of heaven for you and pour down upon you an overflowing blessing that you will not

---

a 3:6 This final clause is based on variant readings found in the Septuagint and the Peshitta (Syriac) traditions of the Old Testament: "And you, children of Jacob, have not changed either." There is more than a hint of sarcasm here, for God was saying that his people hadn't changed a bit. True to the character of Jacob, who cheated (robbed) his brother, the people's hearts remained unchanged over the years, and they were cheating (robbing) God like Jacob did to Esau. The Masoretic Text reads "have not ceased to be [destroyed]."

b 3:8 The Septuagint is perhaps based on a slightly different Hebrew order of consonants for the word *rob*. The triliteral root, *ʿqb*, has the same three consonants but in a different order. The meaning of this root is "to deceive," and it is the root from which the name Jacob (Hb. *yaʿaqob*) is formed. If this theory is true, this is a clever pun on the name of Jacob.

c 3:10 Or "the storehouse," a reference to a certain part of the temple area. See 1 Kings 7:51; 2 Chron. 31:11; Neh. 10:38–39; 13:4–12.

be able to contain. 11I will defeat the devourer[a] so that it will not destroy the fruits of your fields, and your vines will be full of grapes," says YAHWEH, Commander of Angel Armies. 12"Then all the nations will call you blessed, for you will be a land in which God takes delight. I, YAHWEH, Commander of Angel Armies, promise you this."

God Rewards the Faithful

13"Your harsh, rebellious words are in defiance of me,"[b] says YAHWEH.

"But you ask, 'What words are you talking about?'

14"You have said, 'It's no use serving God. What do we gain by keeping his requirements and observing these mourning ceremonies before YAHWEH? 15But now, we will call proud people blessed. Even evildoers prosper, and those who provoke God escape *punishment*.' "

16Then those who lived in awe of YAHWEH began discussing these things, and YAHWEH noticed and listened. A scroll of remembrance was written in the presence of YAHWEH. It included the names of those who lived in awe of YAHWEH and honored his name.

17"They will be mine," says YAHWEH, Commander of Angel Armies. "And on the day when I make up my treasured possession, I will show them mercy, just as a compassionate father is gentle with his faithful son. 18And you will once again see that I make a distinction between the righteous and the wicked, between those who serve me and those who do not."

---

a 3:11 As with many portions of Scripture, this verse has multiple meanings. The "devourer" was the term used for the massive swarms of locusts that would devour the crops. Yet the devourer could also be a term for the devil, who seeks to devour believers (see 1 Peter 5:8) and to destroy our spiritual harvest.

b 3:13 Or "Your words have prevailed against me." See Ezek. 35:13.

The Sun of Righteousness

4 [a]"You see, there is a day coming, raging like a fiery
furnace. On that day, all the proud and wicked people
will burn up like straw thrown into a furnace. Neither
stalks nor roots will remain. I, YAHWEH, Commander of
Angel Armies, declare it.[b]

2"But for you who stand in awe at the sound of my
name, *a new dawn is coming*. For the sun of righteousness will rise with healing radiating from its wings.[c] And
you will be free and leap for joy like calves released from
the stall. 3In the day that I, YAHWEH, Commander of Angel
Armies, am preparing, you will overcome and trample
down the wicked like they were ashes under your feet."

The Return of Elijah

4"Remember the law of my servant Moses, the commands
and instructions I gave him at Mount Sinai[d] for all Israel
to obey.

---

a 4:1 The Hebrew Bible has the verses in this chapter numbered 3:19–24.

b 4:1 See Isa. 10:16; 30:27; Jer. 21:14; Zeph. 1:18; 3:8.

c 4:2 See 2 Sam. 23:4; Ps. 84:11; Isa. 30:26; Matt. 17:2; Luke 1:76–79; John 1:4–5; Heb. 1:3; Rev. 1:16. We see the dawning of the new day in the shining light of Christ, our "sun of righteousness," who brings healing, salvation, wholeness, and blessing to the people of earth. The rays of his love and power will radiate healing for troubled minds, broken hearts, and wounded souls. There will be no more gloom. See also Isa. 9:1–2.

d 4:4 Or "Horeb," the common name in the Torah for the mountain usually called Sinai.

5“Keep watching, for I am sending you the prophet Elijah before that great and fearful day of Yahweh arrives.[a]
6He will return the fathers’ hearts to their children and the
children’s hearts to their fathers so that I can come *and
bless* and not strike the land with a curse.”[b]

---

a 4:5 See Matt. 11:9–14; 17:12; Mark 9:10–13; Luke 1:16–17. Jesus confirmed that the “Elijah” who was coming was John the Baptist. Although Elijah never died, John was not Elijah reincarnated. John’s ministry would be like that of Elijah. John the Baptist dressed like Elijah (see 2 Kings 1:8; Matt. 3:4), John preached a message of repentance in the wilderness like Elijah (see Matt. 3:1), and both John and Elijah had high-profile political enemies (see 1 Kings 18:16–17; Matt. 14:3). To this day, Jews celebrating Passover Seders will place an empty chair at the table just in case Elijah returns to announce the Messiah’s coming. The day of Yahweh will be “great” for the believers and “fearful” for the lost.

b 4:6 The Old Testament ends with “a curse.” For this reason, when Jews read this passage aloud, they repeat v. 5 after reading v. 6 so that they won’t end on a note of doom. The Hebrew term translated “curse” is *cherem*, which has the formal meaning of a “ban.” It is used in the Old Testament to denote a divine “devoting to destruction” (or “annihilation”), a judgment handed down, for example, to the original gentile nations of the land of Canaan (see Deut. 7). Recognizing the terrible nature of this divine judgment makes the final short chapter of Malachi an even stronger testimony to the wonderful mercy and love of our God in sending his Son to die on our behalf so that we will never have to suffer such a terrifying judgment.

YOUR PERSONAL INVITATION TO FOLLOW JESUS

We can all find ourselves in dark places needing some light—light that brings direction, healing, vision, warmth, and hope. Jesus said, "I am light to the world, and those who embrace me will experience life-giving light, and they will never walk in darkness" (John 8:12). Without the light and love of Jesus, this world is truly a dark place and we are lost forever.

Love unlocks mysteries. As we love Jesus, our hearts are unlocked to see more of his beauty and glory. When we stop defining ourselves by our failures and start seeing ourselves as the ones whom Jesus loves, our hearts begin to open to the breathtaking discovery of the wonder of Jesus Christ.

All that is recorded in the Scriptures is there so that you will fully believe that Jesus is the Son of God and that through your faith in him you will experience eternal life by the power of his name (see John 20:31).

If you want this light and love in your life, say a prayer like this—whether for the first time or to express again your passionate desire to follow Jesus:

> Jesus, you are the Light of the World. I want to follow you passionately and wholeheartedly. But my sins have separated me from you. Thank you for your love for me. Thank you for paying the price for my sins. I trust your finished work on the cross for my rescue. I turn away from the thoughts and

deeds that have separated me from you. Forgive me and awaken me to love you with all my heart, mind, soul, and strength. I believe God raised you from the dead, and I want that new life to flow through me each day and for eternity. God, I give you my life. Fill me with your Spirit so that my life will honor you and I can fulfill your purpose for me. Amen.

You can be assured that what Jesus said about those who choose to follow him is true: "If you embrace my message and believe in the One who sent me, you will never face condemnation. In me, you have already passed from the realm of death into eternal life!" (John 5:24). But there's more! Not only are you declared "not guilty" by God because of Jesus, you are also considered his most intimate friend (see John 15:15).

As you grow in your relationship with Jesus, continue to read the Bible, communicate with God through prayer, spend time with others who follow Jesus, and live out your faith daily and passionately. God bless you!

ABOUT THE TRANSLATOR

Brian Simmons is known as a passionate lover of God. After a dramatic conversion to Christ, Brian knew that God was calling him to go to the unreached people of the world and present the gospel of God's grace to all who would listen. With his wife, Candice, and their three children, he spent nearly eight years in the tropical rain forest of the Darien Province of Panama as a church planter, translator, and consultant. Having been trained in linguistics and Bible translation principles, Brian assisted in the Paya-Kuna New Testament translation project, and after their ministry in the jungle, Brian was instrumental in planting a thriving church in New England (US). He is the lead translator for The Passion Translation Project and travels full time as a speaker and Bible teacher. Brian and Candice have been married since 1971 and have three children as well as precious grandchildren and great-grandchildren.

Follow The Passion Translation at:

Facebook.com/passiontranslation
Twitter.com/tPtBible
Instagram.com/passiontranslation

For more information about the translation project please visit:

ThePassionTranslation.com